THE MACNEILS

OF

NAGASAKI

By Jack Seward

The Annals of the Macneil Clan in Japan

Volume I

Yugen Press

First published in 1994 by
YUGEN PRESS
10507 Brinwood Drive
Houston, Texas 77043

Distributed by Charles E. Tuttle Company, Inc.

ISBN 0-8048-3024-X

Printed in the United States of America

10507 Brinwood Drive
Houston, TX 77043
U.S.A.

For Jeannie

in

Appreciation of

Her Love and Support

The Author

For 50 years, Jack Seward has been a Japan area-and-language specialist: living in Japan or teaching its culture and language in the United States. He is the author of more than 30 books.

In 1986, for Seward's efforts to deepen understanding and friendship between Japan and America, the emperor of Japan awarded him the Order of the Sacred Treasure. The author lives with his wife, the former Aiko Morimoto. They have two sons, Bill and John.

Author's Note

THE MACNEILS OF NAGASAKI takes place during the chaotic Bakumatsu Era (1853-1868) in Japan.

Where fact leaves off and fiction takes over in the novel is hard to define precisely. The Bakumatsu Era was a tumultuous time when Japan, prompted by internal dissidence and prodded by foreign intrusions, was shedding its cloak of seclusion and beginning reluctantly to experience the rapid changes of this "strange new age." Although a recounting of history is not the primary purpose of the story, nonetheless it may illuminate for some readers a time that did much to shape the national character of modern-day Japan.

Most of the major events in *Nagasaki* actually took place, just as the named historical personages trod this stage. However, the author has taken a few liberties with dates, squeezing fifteen years into eleven. And certainly, the words and no few of the acts of the real people in this book are more the product of his imagination than can be proved by extant records.

The main character—Neil Macneil—illustrates this blend of history and fiction. Two men from the real past inspired his birth in the author's mind. One was the strange but wondrous Ranald MacDonald, son of a Scot trader and a Chinook Indian princess, who was born and raised in the Oregon Territory. Having seen several Japanese sailors whose storm-damaged ships had drifted to the Northwest coast of the North American continent, this restless, inquisitive adventurer convinced himself that the Japanese were closely akin to his mother's people. He determined to see the Japanese in their home islands, and so in 1848 he smuggled himself into Japan off a whaler.

Almost at once he was captured, but the Japanese were quick to realize this half-native American, half-Scot was quite different from the rowdy, nearly illiterate whalers who had landed from time to time on the forbidden coasts of Nippon. For one thing, MacDonald's captors were impressed to discover that the young American's seabag was crammed with books, not bottles of rum.

After marching the Oregonian south a thousand miles or more from the north of Honshu to Nagasaki, they confined him, although under rather loose restrictions, until a passing foreign vessel could make port and take him away. During those months of restraint a group of intelligent, far-sighted samurais visited the young adventurer almost daily to study English. Most of these warriors later became influential in Japan's international affairs.

Thereafter, Ranald MacDonald disappeared from the pages of Japan's history, but it has been said that his influence on Japan's encounters with the West was so strong every "subsequent diplomatic treaty" was filtered through a Japanese mind trained by MacDonald. (He died in Canada in 1894, after a lifetime of high adventure.)

The other "foster parent" of our hero Neil Macneil was Thomas Glover, another young Scot who a decade after MacDonald entered Japan legally when the port of Nagasaki was opened to trade with the U.S., Great Britain, and other Western powers.

The remarkable Glover built a commercial empire based on arms, ships, railways, coal mines, and trade goods; married a Japanese woman; helped restore the emperor to his throne, and invested heavily in Japan's future. Maintained by the City of Nagasaki, Glover's home is today a tourist attraction that overlooks the still waters of this lovely port. The house is reputed, although falsely, to be the site of the events in the Madame Butterfly tale.

While these two men—Ranald MacDonald and Thomas Glover—guided the author to his creation of Neil Macneil, what Macneil does in this story has only a limited connection with the actual lives of his models.

In matters of language, the author has given Japanese names with their surnames last, as in English. Japanese words familiar to Western readers have been treated as English words of foreign derivation and as such have not been italicized. Although it will sound strange to persons competent in Japanese, these words may have singular and plural forms: shoguns, samurais, geishas, *inter alia*. Less familiar Japanese words, for instance, are shown in italics and may be singular or plural: i.e., six *norimono*, three *torii*.

In a few instances, the author has elected for the sake of clarity to use redundant phrases: "*dotera* robes" and "*kanzashi* hairpins."

Jack Seward
Tokyo, Japan

THE ANNALS OF THE MACNEIL CLAN IN JAPAN will comprise three and possibly four volumes. The second, THE MACNEILS OF YOKOHAMA, has been completed and is set in the 1870s. The projected third volume will be THE MACNEILS OF TOKYO. If there is a fourth, its geographical center may well be Kyoto.

These historical romances are played against a backdrop of Japan's emergence onto the international stage, from 1853 to the present. The Macneil clan will provide leading actors in each volume.

Introduction

Since 1636, peace and stability had prevailed in Japan. The Tokugawa clan had ruled the island empire with an iron fist.

This was the *sakoku jidai* of Japan—the "closed-country period." Under pain of death, no Japanese was permitted to emigrate or travel aboard. Nor were any except a handful of Dutchmen and Chinese in Nagasaki allowed to enter the country. Even curiosity about the outside world was harshly discouraged.

Yet before the Tokugawas took up the reins of power, European traders and missionaries had entered Japan freely. The religion of the missionaries—Catholicism—was prospering, in some areas threatening the ascendancy of native Buddhist sects.

Fearful the European priests and traders would be followed by soldiery—as had happened in the Philippines, the shogun expelled most Europeans and slammed the gates of Japan. The gates remained shut for two and a half centuries.

Then, during the first half of the nineteenth century, winds of change began to buffet the castles and flimsy thatched houses of the feudal empire. Americans had already tasted the handsome profits to be made in whaling; an investment in one whaler could be doubled or tripled in a single voyage. In 1820, 120 American whaling ships were working the Pacific. By 1846, the Yankee whaling fleet had increased to 736 vessels, most harvesting the Japan Grounds, where whales were plentiful.

It was inevitable the whalers would attempt to approach the coast of Japan for repairs or provisions. Whenever they tried, most were driven away, but a few succeeded—with mixed consequences. Landing in 1824 on the east coast of the southern island of Kyushu, one American whaling crew pillaged three villages.

Thereafter, the whalers' reception was even chillier. Some sailors were jailed, others never heard of again.

The New England owners of the whaling fleets pressed the American government to force Japan to open its ports. Eager for trade, European nations also watched for opportunities to share in the bounty.

In Japan, influential men with inquisitive minds had begun to wonder what lay beyond the surrounding oceans—and why they could not leave to see for themselves. Without any wars to fight for more than two centuries, the samurais were becoming an idle and potentially disruptive class, all too ready for bloody adventure and opportunities for fame and advancement. Peasant discontent was apparent in the increasing incidence of rice riots. Through habit and complacency, the governing Tokugawas were no longer the virile, vigorous clan they had been.

By the 1850s, those buffeting winds of change reached typhoon strength.

BONNO NO INU WA OEDOMO SARAZU.

No matter how often they are driven away,

the hounds of passion always return.

—*Japanese proverb*

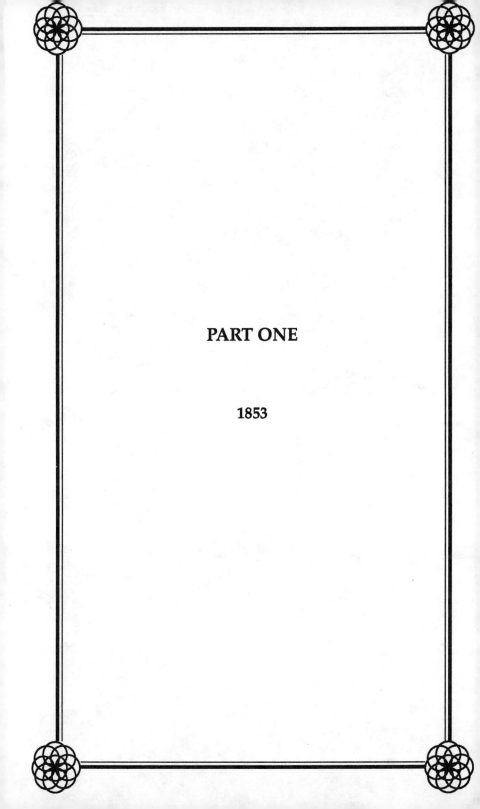

PART ONE

1853

CHAPTER I

Northern Japan

Steadily, the sound grew louder.

It came from behind Macneil—along the mountain trail. The throbbing crescendo of pounding hooves enveloped him.

Desperately, he plunged through the dense underbrush into the darker shadows of the forest of towering pines.

Like demons from a nightmare, three mounted men appeared, their galloping horses lathered and blowing hard. Each warrior wore a hideous scowling mask of iron and lacquer with lion-like whiskers. Behind their helmets long horsetail streamers floated in their wake. Vivid colors decorated the breastplates of their armor and each carried a lance and two swords—one long, the other short.

Intent on their pursuit, the masked horsemen swept past Macneil's hiding place. His heart swelled with pity for their quarry.

Then, with dismay, he wondered if he could be the one they sought. Since landing he had seen no one, but he might have been seen and reported to the nearest magistrate. No Westerner had come ashore in this part of Japan in many years, if ever, so the mere sight of him would surely arouse attention.

In the early evening of the day before, he had lowered his kayak over the side of the whaler *Phoenician* and rowed to the nearby shore. The beach being deserted, he had slept on the sand until awakened that morning by the harsh cries of a curious fish-hawk, the same species he had often seen near his home in the Oregon Territory.

He had leapt to his feet and stared wild-eyed around him, but had seen no human signs. Swallowing two handfuls of the hardtack and fatty whale meat brought from the *Phoenician* galley, he had shouldered a sailor's bag with his name "Neil Macneil" stitched on its flap and started clambering up the steep slope into the pine-covered mountains of northern Honshu, the main Japanese island.

The bag held the young man's kilt, bagpipe, Navy Colt revolver, ammunition, telescope, canteen, sketch pads and pencils, dictionaries, and other odds and ends—what the mountain men of the American West had called their "possibles." He would have left the kilt on the whaler had not the Japanese sailor told him that one day dressing up in such an outlandish outfit might save his life.

Following the instructions of that same sailor aboard *Phoenician,* Neil Macneil turned south on the first mountain trail he crossed and struck out toward the town of Morioka. The daimyo there, he had been told, did not despise Christians as did many other lords of the 265 fiefs making up this tightly-sealed, forbidden empire in these 1850's.

Although the Morioka lord might not welcome Macneil to his fiefdom with banquets and dancing girls, the American's informant aboard *Phoenician* thought at least the daimyo would not "shorten him by a head." That was the fate he could expect from many of the other lords and, no doubt, from those fierce warriors who had just galloped past, flying their white *mujōki*— their "banners of heartlessness."

Macneil waited half an hour, then struggled up through the thick underbrush to the hill above the ridge. Lying prone, he took his spyglass from the seabag slung over his shoulder. Blinking several times to clear his vision, he looked through the smaller end.

At first, he could hardly believe what he saw. With his sailor's kerchief, he wiped both ends of the glass, then peered again.

Three large crosses of peeled pine logs rose from the valley floor. Men in loincloths were nailed to them. Around two campfires near the crosses squatted ten samurais who had laid aside their helmets and armor and were eating with chopsticks from bowls. Off to one side stood their hobbled horses, shod with straw sandals. Three of the mounts were still lathered, so Macneil knew they were the animals that had galloped past him.

Menservants bustled about attending to their masters' needs. Now and again, a warrior set aside his bowl, stood up, and carrying a lance or sword strolled casually over to a victim and pierced his flesh. The act must have amused the samurai's comrades, because they laughed and jeered.

The crucified men seemed near death. Two barely flinched when jabbed. The third—closest to Macneil—appeared stronger than the others. For a moment or so, he raised himself so his body weight was borne by the spike through his crossed feet. Then his body sagged, his knees bowed, and he hung limp again. Laboring mightily, his lungs swelled in attempts to supply his body with oxygen.

Macneil felt overwhelmed by sympathy for the sufferers, longing to release them or somehow to ease their suffering. But he could think of no way to do so. Had there been only two or three warriors, he might have charged them, firing his .36-caliber Navy Colt revolver, but to attack ten well-armed men was beyond consideration.

Macneil also realized he had a more pressing duty. Losing his life or freedom in this rocky valley in northern Japan would erase all hope for his loved ones' rescue. Realizing that, he reluctantly slid down through the brush toward the trail, but as he came to the last barrier of undergrowth, he stopped and crouched out of sight again.

Coming up the path was a slight form with its head mostly concealed beneath a dark hood. The figure—a man? a boy?—flitted from spot to spot like a bird making its way erratically among tree branches.

When not turning his head slowly from side to side, the hooded figure studied the path before him. Clearly, he was following a trail.

His jacket and pantaloons were reddish-black, as was the band of cloth around his waist. The hood covering most of his face and head was tied at his throat. His footwear resembled canvas on top, buttoned or clasped at the heel, with a split toe. He was carrying a long bow and a quiver of arrows.

Reaching the top of the ridge, the figure bounded atop a large rock almost as tall as Macneil, who stood six feet and one inch. This effortless leap amazed the American. From that vantage, Macneil knew, the stranger could see the crosses and samurais on the floor of the valley.

The hooded figure paused on the rock only for a moment before dropping silently to the ground on the other side.

Still concealed, Macneil inched over to the boulder beyond which the youth had disappeared. Peering around it, the American stared down the sinuous path leading to the valley floor. Now the youth was behind another boulder, thirty yards farther down and about forty yards from the crosses.

The trim figure eased the bow from his shoulder and chose three arrows from the quiver, making sure each shaft was perfectly straight. Then the archer lowered his head, apparently in prayer, and made the sign of the Christian cross.

With speed and sureness that would have shamed a champion archer, the youth loosed the three arrows from the right side of his bow. The third was in flight before the first reached its target.

CHAPTER 2

Macneil's eyes followed the flight of the shafts. He wondered if all three would find victims and if a samurai or servant would be the first target, but none of the arrows struck them or their mounts. Instead, each buried its sharp steel point in the chest of a crucified man.

Unable to tear his eyes away, Macneil stared transfixed as the feeble tremors of the dying men ended. No one in the camp seemed yet to be aware of the deaths. A few minutes passed, then a samurai arose to take his turn as tormentor. As soon as he saw he had been cheated of his sport, he stopped short and roared.

Macneil looked around and saw that the archer had disappeared. Scanning the valley, he saw the lad in the middle distance, racing along another path leading toward the upper end of the valley. He was well out of sight of the men in camp.

Grabbing their helmets, but leaving behind their armor, all ten samurais vaulted into their saddles and charged up the path in the only direction from which the arrows could have come. The riders yelled, brandishing their swords and spears, and roiling the dust in thick clouds behind them.

At the top of the ridge, the ten warriors split into two groups. One dashed along the path from which the archer and Macneil had come, while the other sped over the trail by which the executioner had fled.

It was logical, he thought, that the ten riders would separate into even smaller groups as they discovered other possible avenues of flight.

Once quiet had settled again over the valley and its surrounding ridge, Macneil slipped back onto the trail he had been following. He considered three options: he could go back the way he had come, cross the floor of the valley past the crosses, or take the archer's escape trail. That trail seemed to follow the top of the ridge and lead toward the upper or western end of the rock-strewn valley. Retreating was pointless, and crossing the valley floor would put him in plain sight for too long, so he decided to make his way—with extreme caution—along the archer's route.

In mid-afternoon, Macneil passed through a glade near the top of the ridge where pine trees pressed close to the trail. He was more relaxed, surer now that he had removed himself from any danger of discovery. The glade was a pleasant, shady place in which to catch his breath, so he left the trail and hid behind the nearest trees. Hardly had he sprawled on his back in the soft grass, when he heard the muffled, thudding sounds of horses' hooves in the dust of the path. When the hoof-beats became less audible, the American thought the animals must now be crossing the luxuriant grass of the glade.

Peeking out cautiously, Macneil recognized two of the mounted warriors. They were leading the archer with a rope around his neck. The samurais reined in their steeds, but as they did, their hooded captive slipped his hands from their rope bonds, tore the noose off his neck, and dashed back along the path. Stunned momentarily, the samurais sat gaping and motionless.

Macneil was sure the archer would escape when at the western entrance to the glade, a third mounted samurai suddenly appeared. Swinging a cudgel, he struck the archer a sharp blow on the side of his head. The youth crumpled senseless onto the grass, and the samurai leapt from his horse with a shrill cry of triumph. By his mount's jet-black color, Macneil knew the man to be the leader of the samurais—the man who had led the posse from the camp in pursuit of the archer.

Dragging the hooded, unconscious body to the center of the glade, the leader began to yell at his two companions, as if berating them for letting their prisoner escape. At the chief's command, the guards carried the motionless figure to a tree and bound it to the trunk with ropes.

After hobbling their horses, all three samurais removed the bridle bits so the animals could graze. For a few minutes, the hunters huddled and spoke in low voices. Then they removed their helmets, set aside their weapons, and stretched out to rest.

Unnoticed by the warriors, the archer had recovered consciousness. Although there was no motion in his body, his eyes had flickered open.

At last, the leader rose and stretched. "*Yoshi, yatchaō,*" he grunted. The American understood those words to mean, "All right, I'll do it."

Strutting over to the bound archer, the rider of the jet-black horse grated out words Macneil did not understand. In response, the archer spat in the samurai's face.

"*Chikusho!*" the warrior cursed. At his command, his two companions slashed the rope binding the archer's hands and dragged him to the center of the glade. There they hurled him to the ground face up and began to tie his hands and feet to stakes the leader had pounded into the soft earth with the blunt end of a hatchet. Before they finished, the archer again slipped from their grasp, only to be subdued by a blow to the head—this time from the flat side of the hatchet.

Agitated and frustrated, Macneil struggled to resist taking any action. Only by calling up a vision of Anne's face was he able to fight back the mounting compulsion to rescue the youth.

Drawing his short sword, the rider of the black horse sliced open the prisoner's clothing from knee to chin and nudged the garment open with the sword. Dismayed, Macneil saw that the prisoner was a girl.

The samurai leader kicked off his pantaloons, his intent as apparent as his erect phallus.

Shaking his head to clear his vision of Anne, Macneil slithered on his belly through the grass to the edge of the glade. He drew and quietly cocked his Colt. The samurai leader was kneeling between his captive's spread thighs, only a dozen yards from Macneil, when he held his breath, took careful aim, and fired.

The .36-caliber ball slammed into the samurai's rib cage, piercing his heart. He fell over, then moved no more.

The other two samurais, who had laid aside their weaponry, yelped and spun about, spotting at once the powder smoke from Macneil's shot.

Neither lacked courage; Macneil had to give them that. They snatched up their weapons and charged him even as he was aiming his second shot. The thought crossed Macneil's mind that without armor, helmets, and masks, the dreaded samurais were only short, insignificant men with sunken chests and very little muscle.

Macneil's second ball caught the warrior on his right solidly in the solar plexus. Even though the Navy Colt was classed as a light-calibered weapon, at point-blank range its ball had sufficient force to stop that attacker dead in his tracks.

Then the third samurai was upon Macneil. From his throat erupted a victorious battle cry. His flashing sword whispered in the air like the wings of a great bird in flight.

CHAPTER 3

The surviving samurai swung his blade a second too late. Macneil snapped off his third shot without aiming, but the ball caught the warrior in the groin, where it made a wound from which a man might linger in agony for hours.

The interval from Macneil's first shot till the last could not have been more than twenty seconds. There had been no time for hesitation or doubts on his part. Frightened and angry, he had done the only thing it seemed he could.

Reaction set in, and Macneil trembled as if with the ague. Several times back home in Oregon, he had fired at marauding Indians, but he had not been sure what harm, if any, his shots caused. This was different. Here he had killed or fatally wounded three men in less than half a minute. His heart pounded; his mouth was dust dry. Crawling back to his sailor's bag, Macneil found his canteen and gulped half of it. Then he collapsed face down on the earth and waited to catch his breath.

A moan from the third samurai brought Macneil slowly to his feet. He had to make sure the wounded Japanese was incapable of attacking again. The warrior looked up at the American with deep puzzlement in his eyes. Macneil was likely the first Westerner he had ever seen. Macneil decided the man was too near death to waste another precious cartridge on.

The other two were stone dead. A fly was already strolling across the open right eyeball of the would-be rapist.

Macneil knelt beside the girl. She too stared at him in puzzlement. He pulled her ripped garments together and cut the thongs binding her hands and feet to the four stakes.

"*O-namae wa?*" He asked her name.

"*Ai,*" she said, pronouncing it as "*Ah'-ee.*"

"*Ai?*" he repeated.

"*Ai,*" she said again.

Eyeing him cautiously, she sprang to her feet and went over
to the fallen samurais.

In the leader's face, she spat for a second time, then kicked
the next man in the throat. Satisfied they were dead, she approached the third, who was still writhing feebly and groaning.
When Ai saw where her rescuer had shot him, she nodded as if
in approval, then drew from within her reddish-black jacket,
which appeared to contain many inner pockets, a knife with a
six-inch blade.

Kneeling beside the samurai, she took his topknot in her left
hand, pulled on it to expose his throat, and slit the throat neatly.
Air escaped with a hiss amid a shower of arterial blood.

Macneil had never witnessed such a deliberate killing. In
profound amazement, he stood still, staring at her. Where her
outfit had been slashed open, he had a generous view of her
female parts.

When Ai became aware of Macneil's gaze, she nonchalantly
removed her torn clothing to stand before him as naked as the
moment of her birth. With limpid, untroubled eyes, she returned
his look with one equally candid, as if considering whether she
should let him come to her bed that night. Their eyes locked,
Macneil looked away first, even as he felt a surge of blood in his
loins. *Damn, it's that cursed—and blessed—lustiness of the Macneil
clan*, he thought. *My father warned me about it often enough. He said
passion—unbridled lust—had undone more than a few Macneils.*

Finding a miniature sewing kit in another jacket pocket, Ai
sat cross-legged on the grass to stitch together the pieces of her
outfit. The leaves must have tickled her *imbu*—the word William
Amanuma had taught Neil for the female sex organ—for she
plucked and tossed aside three offending tufts with a half smile,
half grimace.

Macneil guessed Ai's age at fifteen. Her hair was cut short
and was straight and black—no curls, ringlets or falling locks.
Her large black eyes were slightly slanted at their outer ends, but
without the common Mongolian fold in their inner corners.

Ai's face was oval with even features, a fairly high nose,
and clear, fine-textured skin. Her casual throat cutting and her
carefree nudity so dominated Macneil's thoughts that he was
slow in making further judgment about her overall feminine
attractiveness.

Her beauty was not so overwhelming as his fiancee Anne's,
which had stunned him into silence at first sight. While not
Anne's equal, Ai was quite pretty, Neil decided. Her body was
superb. Her breasts, not quite mature, were high, firm, and
tipped with delicate nipples. The muscles in her legs and arms

were not obtrusive, but her hands, scarred and callused, would have caused a fashionable lady in London or Washington to go into tearful and prolonged seclusion. Her hands clearly were not meant for piano playing or wearing white kid gloves or for coquettish twining around other fingers in the dark. Yet callused though her fingers were, they were capable of handling a needle and thread with skill, and Ai was back on her feet and stepping into her mended pantaloons while Neil still stared at her.

Turning, she looked him over.

"*Koitsu-ra no itai wo umi ni nagekomu kara tetsudatte okure,*" she said in a carefully modulated tone. Macneil had asked in Japanese what her name was, so she must have concluded he spoke her language well enough to understand that sentence.

Macneil looked at her blankly.

She repeated herself.

He maintained his blank gaze.

Exasperated, she began again, more slowly, pointing first to the fallen warriors, then to their horses, and finally toward the seacoast.

Now Macneil understood. Nodding, he helped her tie the three bodies onto the horses. Ai collected their gear, putting what she wanted to keep in a sack tied to a saddle and throwing the rest away in the brush.

When evidence of the recent struggle had been reduced to a few patches of crushed grass and earth wet with blood, Ai tied the jet-black horse to the saddle of the one she would ride, took off all their hobbles, and signed for Macneil to mount the third animal and follow her. She got aboard her horse from the right side, as the samurais had.

The path to the seacoast was faint and less used than the one Macneil had been following. Even so, Ai often rode ahead to make sure they would not encounter other travelers without warning.

When the sun was directly overhead, she halted their caravan to take fresh straw sandals from the sacks tied to the saddles and put them on the hooves of the horses to replace the worn ones. Macneil got out part of his store of weevil-infested hardtack. He offered a share to Ai but she preferred to eat the rice balls and dried fish strips taken from the dead men. The samurais had carried hollow gourds with wood stoppers as canteens, and Ai had also confiscated these. One held a clear liquid Macneil knew was not water. He handed it to Ai to smell.

"*Sake da.*"

Knowing the word for rice-wine, he put the gourd aside. At a time like this, he needed his wits about him.

Resting a little way off the trail after their meal, they tried again to communicate with each other.

"*O-namae wa?*" she asked Macneil, using the words he had spoken to her.

He told her it was Neil Macneil, pronouncing his first name as William Amanuma had always said it—"*Niru.*"

"*O-uchi wa doko desu ka?*" He asked her where her home was.

She gestured vaguely off to the south.

"*Doko kara kita no?*" Where was he from, she asked.

"*Amerika kara.*"

Her eyes widened. "*Do yatte kita no?*" How did you get here?

"On a whaling vessel called *Phoenician*," he said in faltering Japanese.

"*Do shite Nihon ni kita no?*" She asked why he had come to Japan.

The American got out the letter that William Amanuma, the Japanese sailor aboard *Phoenician*, had written in his native language at Neil's request. Translated, it read,

> This will introduce Neil Macneil from Fort George in the Oregon Territory in the United States. His father, sister and fiancee were aboard a Hong Kong-bound ship, *Eliza Grayson*, when it was struck by a typhoon near Hachinohe on Honshu. His sister Margaret Macneil and his fiancee Anne Macneil (also his cousin) were put into one lifeboat and his father Nairn Macneil into another.
>
> It is not known if any or all of them reached the shore safely.
>
> Having no contrary evidence, Neil Macneil hopes they did. Even though such entry is forbidden by the shogun's laws, he plans to land in Japan near where *Eliza Grayson* encountered the storm to begin his search for them. Please extend your help to this young American. He has been most kind to me.
>
> *Tokutaro Amanuma*

After reading it, Ai asked in Japanese, "A man named Tokutaro Amanuma wrote this?"

"Yes, but we Americans called him William."

"And he is the one who taught you Japanese?"

"With his help, I studied two or three hours every day during the months we were aboard the whaler."

"Why did he not come with you?"

"We planned that he would, but he was injured by a whale two days before I left *Phoenician.*"

Now Macneil had to satisfy his own curiosity. Not knowing the right words, he first pointed toward the crucifixion scene and made a cross with two straight twigs. Then, he touched her arrows and bow and, going through the motions of shooting three arrows in the air, he asked why: "*Do shite?*"

"*Hitori wa uchi no ani datta.*"

He understood her to say one of the crucified men had been her older brother. Again, he used pantomime to suggest a man on the cross and a samurai stabbing at him with a sword. "*Do shite?*" He asked why again.

"*Uchi wa kakure-Kirishitan da.*"

Those words did not come across at all. *Uchi* meant "our home" or "family," Macneil knew, and *Kirishitan* was obviously from the English "Christian," but *kakure* was not among the words in his limited vocabulary.

Digging out his Japanese-Dutch dictionary, he found the verb *kakureru.* The Dutch equivalent meant nothing to him, but remembering its spelling, he looked for the word in his Dutch-English dictionary. It meant "to hide."

A hiding Christian? A hidden Christian? That had to be it. William Amanuma had told him many Japanese were converted to Christianity between 1549 and 1638, during the so-called "Christian century" in Japan. St. Francis Xavier reached the islands in 1549, after which Catholicism flourished until 1638 when the final edict expelling Christians was issued, right after the Shimabara Rebellion.

During this Christian century, Roman Catholic missionaries poured into the island empire, converting as many as 200,000 Japanese. Prominent among the converts were numerous powerful daimyos, curious court nobles, and cultivated ladies of high rank, as well as ambitious generals and battle-hardened samurais. So charmed were certain daimyos by the exotic religion that they not only took devotional vows themselves but also commanded everyone in their fiefs to convert. Favoring the spread of Catholicism was the belief that accepting this religion would bring commercial profit through dealings with the merchants who followed hard on the priests' heels.

Toward the end of the Christian century, the shogun began to fear that after the priests and merchants would come soldiers to subjugate the natives, as he had learned was happening in the Philippines. While he was considering whether he should expel the priests, he chanced upon a certain Christian girl who appealed to him. When he asked her to become a concubine in his castle, the deeply religious girl rejected his proposal with outrage.

So the shogun decided *Mono ni wa hodo ga aru*—that enough was enough. If Christianity bred converts so impudent and insensitive as to refuse the opportunity to share his *futon*, the shogun had no recourse but to outlaw what he now liked to call the *Jashumon*—the "evil Christian creed."

Thereafter, anyone even suspected of being a Christian was forced to perform the rite of *fumi-e*—literally, "treading on a picture," the picture being an image of Christ. Those who committed this sacrilege only to save their lives would often, on returning home, wash their feet and drink the water—or burn the straw sandals they had worn, mix the ashes with water, and swallow that mixture. Those refusing to step on Christ's sacred image were banished or executed. Fear of having to make such a hard choice motivated many to become "hidden Christians," who practiced their religion in secret, often in hidden mountain valleys.

If Macneil understood Ai correctly, her brother—and probably her whole family—were among these "hidden Christians." Her brother and the two who died with him had been accused and exposed. Whoever ordered their execution must have known how Christ died and specified crucifixion as a perverted honor.

Kneeling, Ai bowed her head and started to pray. Her fingers worked at her neck as if counting the beads of a rosary. The prayer over, she made a cross from two twigs and kissed it. Macneil supposed she did not dare carry a cross or a rosary on her person.

For an hour, Ai and Neil talked, their hit-and-miss communication often more miss than hit. She told him she was twenty years old, but that meant nineteen, since the Japanese way of counting age was different.

"Are all Americans like you?" she asked.

"What do you mean?"

"Tall, blue eyes, yellow hair?"

"We come in all sizes shapes, and colors."

"I've seen a few Hollanders living on Dejima island in Nagasaki harbor. They weren't like you."

"How were they different?"

"They had beards and big noses. Two of them were fat—and smelled bad."

Ai glanced up at the sun, which was slanting west. Jumping to her feet, she motioned for Macneil to follow her.

By late afternoon, they stood on a cliff overlooking a sheer drop to the sea. With Macneil's help, Ai tossed the three bodies into the pounding surf with the same indifference she had shown when slitting the third samurai's throat.

"*Chikusho!*" she cursed, spitting after them.

Mounting their horses—with the third animal trailing on a lead rope—they rode on till they reached a broader forest path, then started south at a smart pace.

"*Doko e ikimasu ka?*" Macneil asked Ai where they were going.

"*Morioka e.*"

"*Morioka de nani wo suru ka?*" he asked, wanting to know what they would do in the town of Morioka.

"*Sagasu nda,*" she said. They would search.

Filled with gratitude and hope, he struggled to compose a sentence in his mind, then kicked his horse to catch up with Ai, who sat on her horse as if molded to it.

"*Do shite watakushi wo tetsudatte kuremasu ka?*" Macneil asked why she had decided to help him in his search.

"*Datte, inochi no onjin desu mono.*"

He didn't understand her then but puzzled it out later with aid from his two dictionaries.

She would help find his family because she owed him her life.

CHAPTER 4

En route to Morioka

Next day, they made slow progress on their way to the castle town of Morioka, from which Lord Nobuoki Nambu ruled his part of the fief called Mutsu. In William Amanuma's estimation, Neil Macneil's lost relatives had probably come ashore somewhere between Morioka and Hachinohe to the north. The Japanese sailor had said that Lord Nambu was one of the few daimyos who had the reputation of being more tolerant of Christians, both native and foreign, than most of the rulers of the other 264 fiefs.

Frequently, Ai left Macneil holding the three horses to run ahead to a rise in the ground where she could see what lay beyond and, if possible, behind. They had been following roundabout, seldom-used paths, which slowed their progress, frustrating Macneil when he thought about Anne, Margaret and his father Nairn. Even now, they might be suffering as captives in the castle town toward which Ai was leading him.

If their progress along those dim trails through the tall pines was slow, his progress with the Japanese language was speedier. Already he realized it was not a tongue to be acquired with ease. Still, the many hours of tutoring by William Amanuma aboard the whaler were paying off, like seeds planted in early spring whose shoots now began to crack the earth as the sun brought on the warmth of summer. In this case, his sun was the mysterious, wonderfully competent Ai Koga.

In the evenings, Ai and Macneil sat opposite each other in the falling dusk of summer and talked about every subject under the moon—except Ai herself—while he added words to his vocabulary and learned new ways to use the words he already knew.

Ai had hundreds of questions. Although at first his replies were slow and crippled, the more fluent Macneil became, the more she wanted to know.

Ai's first avalanche of questions was about Macneil's family back in the Oregon Territory. He decided to tell her the whole story, composing it after much consultation with his dictionaries. That was easier than trying to paint the picture one small stroke at a time.

"Now, I want you to be quiet and listen," Macneil began.

"May I interrupt if I don't understand your meaning?"

That seemed reasonable, so he agreed. "The Macneils are a clan who live on the Isle of Barra in Scotland," he began. "My father Nairn came to America and later made his way, with my mother and sister Margaret, to Fort George in the Oregon Territory. There, he founded a trading post and started to do business with the Nootka Indians and the new settlers coming from back East. I was born there, and my mother died not long after of a fever. Margaret then became more a mother to me than a sister."

Ai nodded to show that she understood.

"My father Nairn had an older brother named Neville who had been sent by his trading company in Glasgow first to India and then to Hong Kong to open new offices. Neville's wife refused to go with him to Asia, so he left her and his baby daughter Anne behind in Scotland. He hoped his wife would one day change her mind and join him, but she never did."

Black eyes alive with interest, Ai edged closer.

"Neville prospered in Hong Kong until a fire destroyed the uninsured opium warehouse of his company. His employers then closed down their commercial activities in the Far East, leaving Neville free to go into business for himself as Macneil Ltd.

"When Uncle Neville's wife died in Scotland, it was decided that Anne, then fifteen, would go to Hong Kong to live with her father. Neville sent her money for the passage and told her to travel by way of San Francisco and Fort George to try to persuade my father to join Neville in Hong Kong. Neville needed my father's help in his growing business. After much discussion during the several months she spent with us, Anne convinced my father to do this. And during that time, Anne and I fell in love with each other, even though we were first cousins."

Ai looked shocked but didn't speak.

"My father and sister, together with Anne," Neil continued, "left Fort George for San Francisco to board a vessel for Hong Kong. I stayed behind in Oregon to sell the trading post. After the sale, I too was to leave for Hong Kong."

Ai nodded her understanding. "And their ship sank in a

typhoon near here?"

Neil Macneil was chilled by the memory. "Captain Jared Winslow of *Eliza* was certain his damaged ship would sink, so he ordered two lifeboats lowered to take the Macneils and two crew members to shore. Winslow saw the sailors in the lifeboat carrying Anne and Margaret swept overboard by high waves, and the last he saw of that lifeboat, the girls were trying to row it themselves."

Having to grope for ways to express his meaning, Macneil had grown tired of the effort and wanted to wind up his account quickly.

"Though badly damaged and without masts, *Eliza* didn't sink, but drifted helplessly south until sighted by a Manila-bound trading ship. From there, Captain Winslow sent word back to me in Oregon. When I heard, I sold the trading post at a loss to the next bidder, and went to San Francisco to look for passage to Japan. After two weeks, I found a whaler called *Phoenician*, whose captain agreed to carry me and my gear to a point close to the shore of Honshu on his way to the north Pacific whaling grounds. Of course, I had to pay him a fare. I even agreed to work as an extra deck hand when the ship had a whale alongside. The captain got the better of me there, and I would have waited for another ship if there had not been a Japanese seaman aboard *Phoenician*."

"Tokutaro Amanuma?"

"Yes. William. Captain Hiram Stillwell had rescued him from a derelict fishing boat two years earlier. Amanuma had stayed aboard to work as an able-body on the whaler even though Stillwell could have put him ashore in Japan."

"So why did this Amanuma not want to come home?"

"He was afraid."

"Of what?"

"Of the shogun's death penalty for those who leave Japan."

"But you said he was going to land with you."

"Homesickness got the best of him. He thought he could start me out on my search for my family, then sneak back to his fishing village. It was such a tiny, isolated place that he might never have been missed by the authorities."

"So after Amanuma-*san* was injured by a whale, you decided to come ashore alone?" Ai asked. "That was stupid."

"What choice did I have? I couldn't just let my family rot in a Japanese jail for the rest of their lives, could I?"

"Why do you think they're in a jail?"

"Surely you don't believe they are living in contented luxury in some daimyo's mansion, do you?" Macneil had puzzled for three minutes over the words "contented luxury" and "mansion." He was pleased when Ai understood.

"How did you get ashore from the whaler, and then how did you get here?"

"I left the whaler in a..." Macneil started to say canoe but having no idea what such a word would be, he settled for small boat. "I slept one night on the beach—it was deserted—and the next morning I climbed into the hills and found a trail. The whaler captain had a map that didn't show much to the north, but to the south it showed Morioka and the castle of Lord Nambu."

"Tell me more about your fiancee. What does she look like?"

Macneil doubted he could do Anne justice in English, much less in Japanese. He managed, however, to get across that her hair was the color of gold. He wanted to say Florentine gold but did not know how. It was long and gathered in a chignon in back. Her forehead was high, her eyes brownish-green, her lips full and mobile. Her skin? Ah— He struggled to find the words in Japanese for its fine texture and creamy surface.

Sourly, Ai grumbled, "You make her sound perfect."

"Oh, no. Not perfect. Her teeth are a little uneven, and she has an inch-long scar on the right side of her neck. Her ears," he pointed to a lobe, "are larger than most, and when she's angry, or excited, she doesn't speak clearly." Those small imperfections pleased Macneil. What man could risk marriage with a perfect angel descended from Heaven? She would be spirited away while still a bride.

As he told Ai about Anne, he got out his sketch pad and drew his fiancee writing at a table.

Ai, delighted, leaned against him and watched him sketch. When he had finished, Ai asked, "What's she doing?"

"Writing poetry or making entries in her diary." The word "diary" sent Neil to his dictionaries again.

"Did she always show you what she had written?"

"Any time I wanted to look at it."

"What did she write about?"

"I don't know."

"Why not?"

"I couldn't read what she had written."

A small smile of satisfaction flitted around Ai's lips. "I see. I suppose her handwriting was such an uneducated messy scrawl that..."

"No, indeed. I couldn't read what she wrote because it was in shorthand."

He had to say "shorthand" in English, certain there would be no Japanese equivalent.

"Shorthand? What's that?"

"An easier, quicker way to write. It was invented a few years ago by an Englishman named Isaac Pitman." On the margin of his sketch of Anne, Neil scribbled a line of slashes, whirls, circles, and curves. He knew the symbols were mere gibberish in shorthand, but they gave Ai a general idea of what he meant. "Anne learned it so she could work as her father's secretary when she got to Hong Kong."

As fascinated as Ai seemed to be by everything Western, she drew the line at his bagpipe. When he played it for her, she covered her ears and started up in alarm.

"In Nagasaki one time, I watched a Chinese family beat a puppy to death with sticks," she said. "It sounded very much like this barbaric instrument of yours."

"Why on earth should anyone want to beat a puppy to death with sticks?" he asked. Her criticism did not sit well with him.

"To make its meat tender, of course."

For every ten questions Ai asked Macneil, he managed to ask one of his own. First, he wanted to know about the daimyos of Japan.

"You already know much, Neil-*san*," she said. "There are 265 fiefs—like small kingdoms—in Japan. Each has a daimyo in charge. There are two kinds of daimyos: the *fudai* and the *tozama*. The *fudai* support the Tokugawa shogun, and the *tozama* oppose him. The *tozama* have never been fully trusted, though some are very rich and powerful. The shogun has placed *fudai* daimyos between *tozama* daimyos to prevent the *tozama* from uniting against him."

"And the emperor?"

"The imperial court is in Kyoto. The emperor has little to do with running the country."

And so it went. Ai was tireless in correcting Neil's pronunciation and equally tireless in repeating the many sentences and phrases he did not understand.

On the morning of the eighth day after his landing, Ai led Neil off the trail into the depths of the forest. Dismounting, she began unloading the three horses.

Neil asked her what she was going to do.

"*Kono uma wo koroshimasu*," she said. She was going to kill the horses.

Macneil was overcome with dismay. What had those animals done to deserve such a fate?

"*Iya da wa!*" he blurted.

For the first time since he had met her, Ai really laughed. For a girl who seldom even smiled, her wild laughter was shocking. She had to lean against a tree to keep from falling.

"*Do shimashita ka?*" Neil asked what was wrong.

"You fool! You talk like a woman," she said between shouts of merriment.

He told her that if that was true, he could not help it, having learned the words from her. "How should I have told you not to kill them?"

She told him the correct masculine words and word endings, which he repeated over and over, and she said that from then on she was going to speak to him as one man would speak to another, to teach him masculine forms of speech. If he went on speaking like a female, he would be a laughingstock among Japanese wherever he went.

Neil still didn't want her to kill the horses, so they argued at length.

Neil held that killing the horses was an unnecessary cruelty. They could simply be set free in the forest instead, and the animals could graze and fend for themselves until eventually someone who needed horses found them.

Ai argued that few people below samurai rank ever owned or rode horses. When these mounts were found, they would surely be taken to a magistrate. If that official had already received a report about the archer who had slain the crucified men, killed the samurais, and taken the horses, he might turn the steeds over to comrades of the three dead warriors. This would furnish a clue as to the direction in which Ai had escaped.

Granting she might be right, it still went against his grain to kill animals that had helped them so much while doing them no harm.

Eventually, he had his way. *Probably,* he thought, *I can thank her indebtness to me for saving her life or male superiority in Japanese society for this small victory,* although little else that he had seen about this girl suggested a female subservient to men.

Still debating the wisdom of doing so, they led the horses deeper into the forest and set them free. Ai and Neil looked through the sacks that had been tied to the saddles, keeping the food and whatever else they could use and carry, including two long swords and a short one. Neil asked Ai why the short blade was grooved in the middle along its length.

"When you plunge a blade into someone, the wet flesh clings and forms a suction. The groove breaks that suction and makes it much easier to pull out the blade."

Neil decided not to ask her how she had learned that.

He added the swords and Navy Colt to his sack of "possibles," which already held his spyglass, canteen, and kilt.

Although he would have left the kilt on the whaler had not the Japanese sailor advised him to carry it, not for an instant had Neil thought of parting with his bagpipe. *How aptly,* he thought, *has it been called the soul of a Scot.*

"I must do something to make you look more like a Japanese," Ai said as she rummaged through the samurais' sacks. She found a dead man's pantaloons that she was able to alter so they would fit him in the waist.

Straw sandals and his own tattered shirt and sailor's jacket completed his outfit, the overall effect of which caused Ai to shake with laughter for the second time. Humor gave her face an impish quality not at all displeasing.

She bedded down that night on pine needles at her customary ten or so yards from Neil, after grumbling she was still not satisfied with his appearance.

Next morning, Ai was scouting ahead and Macneil was waiting beside the path for her return, when a bent old woodcutter approached. A massive load of kindling was strapped to his back on a ladder-like carrying device. Too late, Macneil scrambled for the protection of the brush beside the trail. The woodcutter had seen the American, and his features wore an expression so startled that it was comic.

Dropping his kindling, he spun and dashed away in the direction from which he had come, his old bowed legs making him look like a clumsy two-legged crab running desperately for the sea.

When Ai returned and heard what had happened, she snatched up her sack and signed for Macneil to follow her.

They ran for hours, resting one minute in every ten. He had thought that his outdoor life back home in Oregon—often he had won footraces against even Indians—had kept him in top condition, but now he was like a sack of mush with legs of straw compared to Ai. *I'll bet she could run all day without stopping to rest,* he thought sourly. Whenever he gasped that he had to stop, she would cast a look of utter contempt at him, then pull and push him onward for two or three minutes more before relenting and letting him catch his breath.

At dusk, his calf and thigh muscles would cramp after running even a short distance. When Ai's massaging brought them only brief relief, she finally said it was time to eat and sleep, leading him deeper into the surrounding forest than usual. Leaving Neil to collapse on the ground, she disappeared.

Ai was gone so long Macneil began to wonder if she had

deserted him. But at midnight, she appeared suddenly and sat beside him. He had not heard her approach. She brought out a double handful of rice from one of her pockets and shared it with Macneil. Then she had handed him something else.

"Eat this."

In the darkness, whatever it was she gave him was damp and cold and fine-textured. He took one bite. It had substance but little taste.

"What is it?" he asked, about to take another bite.

"Chicken."

So it was, only the fowl was fresh-killed and uncooked.

Macneil almost gagged, then remembered the first bite had not been actually repellent. He forced down the raw fowl's leg and thigh and soon felt stronger for it.

"Tomorrow, you stay here all day," Ai said.

"Where are you going?"

"I must find clothes to change your ridiculous appearance."

After eating the chicken, which Macneil imagined in the darkness to be bloody, Ai asked him to pour a cupful of water from his canteen over her callused hands so she could clean them.

He had noticed her continually washing herself. Every stream presented an opportunity for a quick bath for her—what she called a *"karasu no gyosui"* or a crow's bath—a lick and a promise with a lot of splashing about. *Is she always so unconcerned about her nudity in front of men?* Macneil wondered.

After washing her own hands, Ai held out her canteen to offer him the same service. When he did not do as thorough a job as she wanted, she finished the task for him. In the darkness of the woods, the touch of her hands caused a rush of hot blood to his loins, and an uncomfortable swelling of flesh. He reached for Ai, but she shoved him away and retreated to her own bedding ground off somewhere in the darkness.

Macneil reflected on the contrasts embodied in this nine-teen-year-old girl: she was capable of utter ruthlessness, a man's equal in the strenuous uses to which she could put her body, and shameless about the exposure of her nudity. Yet she was no rural trollop to welcome a toss in the hay whenever it was offered.

What, he wondered again and again, was she? Where did she come from? How did she earn a living? Who were her family, aside from the brother who died on the cross? Where would she go after Morioka?

What would he do if they found his relatives in Morioka? Macneil had no gold to buy their release, if they were in prison there. Would his pleas for justice from Lord Nobuoki Nambu fall on receptive ears? Would he ever reach those ears?

If, with Ai's help, Macneil could rescue or ransom them, could he and his relatives go on living in these wooded mountains until the first of October, when Captain Hiram Stillwell had promised to lay *Phoenician* off the coast for two days, on lookout for two bonfires burning side by side on a secluded beach? If Stillwell sighted them, would he send a boat to pick them up, as agreed?

Had Macneil undertaken an impossible and foolish task that meant his own doom without any chance to save Anne, Nairn and Margaret?

Yet what choice had he? Could he have carried on his father's business year after year at the trading post in Oregon, waiting with growing hopelessness for news that never came? Or, had he gone to Hong Kong to join his uncle, Anne's father, could he have found a way to open the closed doors of Japan just wide enough to let escape three innocent human beings whose only sin had been to be shipwrecked off the coast of a nation that hated intruders?

William Amanuma had heard rumors about foreign sailors being executed immediately after landing in Japan. Their fate, he said, depended on the whim of the local daimyo.

Macneil could only pray that his family, if alive, were being held by one of the more humane daimyos.

CHAPTER 5

Morioka and vicinity

The two hands of Macneil's Waltham hunter pointed at six-thirty when he shook himself awake the following morning and got stiffly to his feet.

Where was Ai? He found her pine needle bed and sack of belongings beneath a clump of bushes, but there was no sign of her. Where would she have gone at this hour?

Since there was nothing to do but wait until she reappeared, Macneil turned his mind to the samurais whose bodies they had thrown into the sea. The warriors would be missed and Lord Michinobu Nambu, whose vassals Ai said they were, would surely have men out looking for them.

Would the searchers scour this deep into the territory of Lord Michinobu's hostile cousin? Ai had said there were sure to be guards and travel control points on the main roads, but she and Macneil, sticking to mountain paths, had seen none. Michinobu's search parties might have avoided them, too.

Macneil's sixth sense told of danger. The alarms sounding in his mind set his pulse racing. Anxiety gripped him.

With water, he washed down the last of the hardtack, which Ai said tasted like *ogakuzu* or sawdust, and forced his burning, cramping leg muscles into a crippled walk. He stumbled up the path toward a crest a hundred yards south.

At the crest, he sat down on a rock to rub his sore legs. Before him stretched a fertile valley, in the center of which stood a castle town that must be Morioka. So far, he had traveled through forests and over mountains and down narrow valleys like the one where Ai's brother and his two companions had been crucified. But this place was different, the valley so broad Macneil could not see across it. It was perfectly flat, with no geological interruptions, and intensely cultivated. Wet rice paddies occupied eighty percent of the land, interspersed with vegetable patches, bamboo groves and fields of cotton.

The valley was a marvel of agricultural efficiency. There were numerous thatched farmhouses, each with a row of trees to protect it and its two or three small paddies from the prevailing wind.

Every paddy was flooded within its dikes, with vivid green rice shoots reflected in the shimmering paddy water. The paddies were crowded with men and women knee-deep in the water, legs spread wide, backs bent double. All wore broad straw hats with crowns like shallow cones. They groped in the mud to plant the rice shoots that would produce the grain which was more important than anything else to their race's survival.

Others carried to the vegetable patches buckets they filled from pits in the ground. When they had carefully ladled out the contents of the buckets on the ground around the cabbages, peas, beans, onions and cucumbers, they returned for refills.

From the crest where Macneil sat, the path ran steeply down the slope to the bottom of the valley, where it became a road winding through the rice fields for about two miles to the edge of Morioka, a town dominated by the castle Ai had called the White Phoenix. Its white walls and copper roof flared upwards at the corners, giving the high stoneworks the sublime appearance of a large snowy bird in flight.

"Neil! Neil!" came Ai's frantic cry from below on the path.

Springing to his feet, Macneil was ready for action as she ran up to him.

"Mounted samurais coming!" she panted. "One rides the same jet-black horse I wanted to kill.

"Look!" she said, jumping up on the rock where he had been sitting. She pulled him up behind her and pointed west to the plain around Morioka.

The plain was rimmed by wooded low hills enclosing the valley with a pine-green band. On top of one hill three miles off loomed a Buddhist temple, indistinct in the haze. Ai pointed to it.

"See that temple? Go there later, when the way is clear.

"Take these," she instructed, urgency tightening her voice. She thrust two sacks, the swords, her bow and quiver, and a bundle of clothing he had not seen before into Macneil's arms.

"Now find a place to hide. Quickly! They'll be here in a minute."

"But you. What about you?"

"I'll lead them away from you."

"No, I can't let you do that. We will fight them."

"Do what I tell you. Now!"

"Where will we meet?"

"At that temple, tonight." She pointed once more, then jumped down and darted off along the path toward the valley, carrying only her staff.

Picking up their gear, Macneil bolted along the crest for thirty yards until he found a hiding place that let him see the path Ai was running along like a young doe in full flight.

The mounted samurais charged into Macneil's field of vision, yelping and whooping like hoarse hungry hounds in hot pursuit of their quarry. Eleven of them, they made a nightmarish sight, their elbows flapping against their sides like the wings of rising birds of prey. Tied to a short bamboo pole on the back of one saddle was a blue banner with white stripes that snapped in their wake. The banner, Ai had told him, was that of the house of Lord Michinobu, the Christian-hating daimyo to the north.

From three other samurai saddles waved banners that looked like gigantic white ostrich plumes. All the riders had red and gold blankets under their saddles.

One samurai, mounted on a dappled grey, wore an aquamarine jacket that stood out against the others' dark armor.

The jet-black steed they had set free galloped second in the procession. All the samurais were armed with lances and swords and rode swiftly with a soul-withering intentness.

Halfway down the slope, one of them spotted Ai running along the road through the paddies half a mile ahead. His cry and lifted lance alerted the others, who spurred their horses in her direction.

Macneil held his breath and prayed for Ai; he did not see how she could possibly outpace the horses. Nor was there any concealment along the road through the flat fields.

But Ai was giving the samurais a good run. The horsemen gained little on her during the first quarter-mile; then two faster horses—the dappled grey and the jet black—pulled ahead, leaving the rest behind in the choking dust clouds roiled by their flying hooves.

Tearing his eyes from the running horses, Macneil looked to see how far Ai's receding figure had gone. But there was no Ai to be seen. Not even in the paddies, though he studied them and the entire area thoroughly through the spyglass. No farmhouse or bamboo grove or shrine stood near the road where she could be hiding.

She had disappeared.

The two leading samurais must have realized that when Macneil did. Leaning back on their reins, they skidded their mounts to a halt on the dusty road and spun around looking wildly this way and that. The warrior on the dappled grey had drawn his sword and brandished it in an excess of furious frustration.

The eleven horsemen started forward at a trot examining carefully both sides of the road. Three times they stopped for a more thorough scrutiny.

Suddenly, Macneil's heart rose in his throat. All eleven plunged off the road into the paddy water and surrounded something invisible to Macneil at that distance, even through the spyglass.

When at last they spurred their horses back onto the road, they were still empty handed. A brief council of war followed as their steeds pawed the dusty road.

Perhaps it had occurred to the hostile samurais that Lord Nobuoki's warriors might have spotted them from the ramparts of White Phoenix Castle and might even now be preparing to repel this unwelcome intrusion into Nobuoki's domain.

Whatever the reason, the samurais turned their horses' heads back to the north and began to withdraw, with many backward glances over their shoulders. They must have been as mystified as Neil was at the complete disappearance of their quarry.

Neil had no choice but to follow Ai's instructions and strike out for the Buddhist temple three miles away at the western end of the plain. Even though the distance was short, it might take Macneil all day to get there. He knew he would have to stay in the foothills rimming the Morioka plain, avoiding the roads and well-traveled paths. Dim forest trails would better suit his purpose, but if they did not lead to the temple, he would have to push through tangled brush and up and down the wooded slopes of the many hills standing between him and his destination.

CHAPTER 6

Seen from a distance the Buddhist temple rose out of the surrounding forest and dominated the top of the hill. Lower roofs to its right and left indicated the presence of detached buildings that supported the temple functions. Clearly it was much more than a simple roadside place of worship, and it lent to this end of the valley a sense of pervasive tranquility.

Below the temple, by the base of the hill, flowed a clear stream that Macneil forded in waist-deep water. He thought it wiser not to cross on the bridge he saw farther downstream toward Morioka. In the deepening dusk, with no one in sight, he stripped off his sweaty garments, rinsed them in the cool water, and gave himself what Ai called a crow's bath.

When reasonably clean, he sat by the brook and let the evening air dry his skin. Before it became too dark to see, he climbed the path to the temple above, forced twice to step into the shadows by a young blank-eyed farmer leading a one-eared ox and by a tottering old woman, hunchbacked from a life of stoop labor in the rice paddies.

At the top, he paused among five magnificent trees closely resembling the redwoods he had known at home, and watched dusk fall over the quiet old temple. From somewhere in its depths a bell tolled, the slow reverberations calling together the bonzes in their yellow robes. Maybe it was a summons to vespers or a dinner bell. Macneil had not had a proper meal since leaving *Phoenician*. Sinking slowly onto the grass, mouth watering, he recalled the wild game stews, the salmon baked in herbs, and the pit-baked chicken his sister Margaret had often prepared for him and their father in Oregon.

A dozen bonzes with shaven heads bowed shuffled from a building on the north side of the temple past the front, where each in turn rinsed his hands in a stone basin, clapped, bowed, and passed on to a hall on the south side, where lamplight flickering through the doors hinted at activity inside.

After they had gone, there was no sign of anyone else. The birds had ceased their caws and chatter to be replaced by a rising cicada chorus—incessant and sonorous, resembling the joyous cascading of a crystal waterfall.

While he waited for Ai, Macneil began to regard the Buddhist temple as a refuge, an oasis of peace after the violence of the past few days. From the main hall came the chanting of Buddhist prayers. Absorbing the song though not the meaning of the murmurs, he luxuriated in the serene atmosphere of the temple and let himself sink deeper into tranquility. As he watched through half-closed eyes, a second procession of priests, in black robes and white *tabi* socks, walked quietly from an inner building with hands clasped before them. From a stepping-stone walkway, they mounted to the veranda along the main worship hall, leaving their sandals on the polished planks and going inside wearing *tabi* only.

Now the temple grounds stood again in silence, broken only by the singing of the tireless cicadas. In the fading light, Macneil's eyes drank in the physical details. The construction timbers were huge, all in their natural state except where they were elaborately lacquered in dull red or covered with sheet copper ornamented with gold. The entrance with its broad steps was guarded by four monstrous figures carved in wood, the size of a man, clothed in garments that appeared to be blown about by a violent storm. On their feet were prehensile clawed toes and from their mouths protruded threatening fangs. Their heads appeared to be on fire, and they wore partial armor. Goggle eyes and mouths strained open to their widest in faces distorted by exaggerated expressions of furious anger.

The four companions guarding the temple appeared to be trampling on and otherwise grossly mistreating four other demons. All were more fearsome by far than any Macneil had ever seen, even on the hideous totem poles in Oregon.

"Neil-*san!*" came a faint whisper from the dark. Macneil's heart leaped.

"Ai!" He was dizzy with relief. "Where are you?"

"Over here. Don't come near me."

He detected a stench in the air.

"Why? What shall I do?"

"I came up here from the south," she said. "I found no streams. Did you cross one coming from the north?"

"Yes."

"How far?"

"At the foot of this hill." He must have used a wrong word, for it took her a while to understand.

"Near here?"

"Yes, right below us."

"Good. Start going toward it. I will follow."

"Let me walk with you," Macneil said.

"No! You mustn't come near me. Just go ahead to the stream."

He led the way down the path, stumbling now and then in the darkness under the trees. The foul stench wafted close behind.

At the side of the stream, Macneil sat on the rock where he had dried himself earlier and watched for Ai to appear. Away from the shelter of the trees, it was not so dark. An early rising moon added illumination.

From the darkness of the trees, Ai dashed to the stream. Pausing only to empty her jacket pockets at the bank, she threw herself into the water and splashed through the rapid current into the deepest part. There, she tore off her clothes as if they were afire and let them float downstream.

"Shall I bring your clothes back?"

Stiffly, she said, "Later."

Something was wrong, Macneil knew, but he was so pleased to see her again that he held his tongue and waited.

She must have stayed in the stream half an hour, dousing her head uncountable times and snorting to clear her nose and working at her ears with frantic fingers. Finally, she waded to the bank. Gathering up handfuls of sand, she scrubbed herself from stem to stern until Macneil thought she might have drawn blood.

By now, an hour had passed. In the faint light of the moon, her naked body was lithe and lovely and utterly desirable.

His legs began to cramp again, so he too slid into the cool, clean water where mounting passion drew him downstream to Ai's perch at the edge of the water.

"Stay away from me," she ordered.

Offended, he settled himself several steps from where she sat with the current lapping at her legs. She was still scooping handfuls of water and splashing them on her neck and shoulders and breasts.

"I didn't intend to touch you." His petulant words were awkward, but their tone got through to her.

In the light of the crescive moon, Ai turned and looked at Macneil, her face softening.

"That wasn't my meaning, Neil-*san*. Sit with me if you dare.

It's just that I thought the smell would drive you off."

"Smell?"

She looked surprised. "You smelled nothing?"

"Well, I did smell something pretty bad up by the temple. And on the way down here."

Ai snorted with disgust.

"Do you know what a *koyashi-dame* is?" she asked.

CHAPTER 7

"It's a pit in the ground where farmers store the *fumben* and *nyo* from their toilets. They pour the mixture on their fields to make crops grow better."

"My God!" Macneil blurted in English.

"What?"

"Go on."

"There are many such manure pits in the fields. I'll show you one soon. The thick liquid in the bottom is usually about so deep." Ai measured three feet with her hands.

"And you jumped into that?" He was incredulous.

Her delicate shudder was affirmation enough.

"But how did you breathe?"

Ai reached for her staff behind her on the bank. With a twist, she separated it into two parts. From the hollow center of one part dropped a smaller tube of bamboo, also hollow. After she had washed it well on the outside and sluiced water through it a half dozen times, she put one end of the bamboo in her mouth and sank beneath the surface of the stream. The breathing tube protruded a scant inch above the water.

After a moment, Ai surfaced spluttering.

"How long did you stay in the pit?" Macneil asked.

"Too long."

"And then?"

"Finally, I crawled out, but I thought they might have left a lookout on the ridge where we parted, so I lay there in the grass beside the pit until early dusk. Then I made my way here from the south."

Their conversation was still halting. For every word clearly understood, there were at least three or four that failed to do their job. Still, they managed somehow, and they were improving.

Sitting there in the water beside Ai, he felt the night air begin to chill him while a sparkling moon-mist enveloped the leafy tops of the bamboos. Why, Macneil wondered, would a simple rural girl like Ai carry a breathing tube inside her walking staff?

Then the humor of her earlier predicament struck him. He started to laugh boisterously.

Angry, Ai grabbed him by the hair with both hands, pulled him into the stream, and forced his head under the water.

Now she laughed at Macneil—but with him, too.

"We must find a place to sleep," she said. "Tomorrow I'll go into Morioka and steal clothing for you."

"Clothing? What kind?"

"The only kind you can wear to travel around Japan without arousing suspicion."

He wondered what such an outfit would be—and if it would really conceal his foreign identity. If it did not, Macneil would stand out like a four-masted opium clipper among outrigger canoes.

CHAPTER 8

Next day, Ai was more relaxed.

During her first days with the American, the wilderness nymph had been serious, watchful, suspicious. Now her doubts had apparently faded, and a warm friendly personality was beginning to emerge. She smiled often and sometimes touched him when they talked.

Macneil had donned the clothes she had stolen for him in Morioka. Seeing him wearing them, she collapsed in helpless giggles.

This new outfit comprised *geta* or wooden clogs, a dark gray robe with a blue *obi* or sash, a flute, a begging bowl, and a basket mask. The last item had triggered Ai's peals of laughter. The large hood-like headpiece completely concealed the wearer's face. But for two small holes in the mask, the person under it could not have seen where he was going.

Unknowing, Macneil put the basket mask on backwards and was groping around the clearing in the bamboo grove, stumbling over roots and rocks.

"Turn it around, Neil," she managed to gasp after laughing herself into a mild state of hysterics. "Then maybe you will pass for a *komuso*."

"What on earth are *komuso*?"

"Traveling priests. Beggars really. They belong to one of the Buddhist sects."

"But why do they wear these basket masks?"

"The priests take vows to make a silent pilgrimage for a year. During that time, they can say nothing. Their ideal is what they call 'faceless silence.' No one must see their faces or hear their voices."

"But how do they live?"

"They walk from town to town and beg—silently."

"How can one beg in silence?" Macneil scoffed.

"They just stand quietly in front of a house or shop until someone comes out and puts food in their begging bowl."

"Even if they have to stand there for an hour or more?"

"Well, sometimes they play their flute to call attention to themselves."

"Where do they sleep?"

"In temples or by the road."

"Aren't I too tall to be a *komuso*?"

"Now and then we see a Japanese man as tall as you," she said, "but not very often. Still, they are not so rare as to justify suspicion."

"How about you, Ai? What are you going to wear?"

In reply, she thrust an arm into the sack she had brought back from her foraging trip of the night before last and pulled out a worn black kimono.

Stripping down to her skin, she stood there apparently oblivious of her nakedness until she noticed Macneil studying her.

"You look at me as if you had never seen a naked woman before. Don't you see them in America?"

"Not often enough," he said. "Do you always expose yourself like this in front of men?"

This she would not answer, but instead gave him another studious stare from under half-closed lids.

Once the kimono and its wide heavy sash were wrapped round her, Ai stretched one arm down between her legs, caught hold of the bottom edge of the kimono in back, pulled it up through her legs, and tucked it under her sash in front. This brought the bottom of the kimono to above her knees and converted the lower part of the garment into makeshift trousers, leaving her legs freer for movement. Then she tied a faded black scarf around her head, concealing most of her short hair.

"Now you must become the silent priest who begs for food," she said, "and I'm a *bikuni* who begs at your side."

"A *bikuni*?"

Macneil looked up the word in two dictionaries. It meant "nun."

"Sometimes," she went on, "they beg for alms, and even— well, they do other things with their bodies to raise money for their temples."

She stripped off her kimono and, digging into the sack beside her, brought out her sewing packet and half a dozen cloth patches. With these she began to sew pockets onto the lining of her garment, again sitting tailor-fashion on the grass of the clearing in unabashed and absolute nudity.

"Sometimes, *ronin* disguise themselves as *komuso*," she said, taking out a needle and cutting off the right length of thread with her eyeteeth.

Here we go again, Macneil thought, reaching for his dictionaries, but she beat him to it with an explanation.

"*Ronin* are samurais who have lost their masters for some reason. They wander around looking for a daimyo in need of fighting men."

"Why disguise themselves?"

"Because often they are troublemakers not welcome in many fiefs. Anyway, people treat the *komuso* with caution and respect. They never know when one may be a *ronin* with two swords hidden in his sack. And, of course, they could not see a topknot if one was tied up under the basket mask."

Finished sewing, she put her kimono back on, picked up her staff, and prepared to leave.

"You stay here, Neil," she said. "I'll go into Morioka. My clan has a member there who is usually well informed. He might know something about your relatives. I will be back tonight. You stay out of sight."

"Can you find something for us to eat besides raw chicken?"

Most of the next day—a long one for him—Macneil spent thumbing through his dictionaries and worrying about Ai. Just before dusk she returned with her *furoshiki* cloth filled with cooked rice stolen from a farmer's pot—many farmers, she said, cooked rice outside their homes over brushwood fires—and a *daikon*, a white radish two feet long. These could be eaten raw, as Ai soon showed him. Macneil thought a taste for *daikon* was one that needed some cultivating. As hungry as he was, however, he hesitated not at all in alternating raw *daikon* bites with mouthfuls of rice.

"After dark, we'll go bathe in the stream," she said.

"What did you find out?" He was impatient to know.

"You were right."

"What do you mean?"

"Your family did come ashore near here. At least, two of them did."

Macneil's heart pumped faster, his mouth suddenly dry. "Just two?"

"Yes." With her dagger, she cut off two more inch-thick slices of *daikon*. "This is good for the digestion."

"Which two?"

"The two women."

God in heaven, what had happened to his father?

"Your father may have come ashore farther south," Ai said. "You did say they took separate lifeboats, didn't you?"

"Were Anne and Margaret all right?"

"Both were hurt—cuts, bruises, a broken leg."

"Where are they now?"

"We don't know."

"Well," Macneil said, springing to his feet, "what can we do now?"

"Tomorrow, you put on that *komuso* outfit and we'll go through Morioka to see the fisherman who found your women on the beach."

"Is the fisherman this far inland?"

"We may be in luck. He hauls his dried fish to Morioka once a month and sells them on the streets. He sleeps in a shack just outside town. He was seen on the streets yesterday with many fish left to sell."

"Will he tell us what he knows?"

"If he knows anything, he will tell us *all* he knows," Ai said.

For the first time, Macneil was able to travel over the roads of Japan openly, though he could not see as much as he wanted to through the two peepholes in the mask. Under it, the heat was stifling.

Ai led the way, walking with her staff. As they neared Morioka the traffic became heavier and they passed many large two-wheeled carts drawn by men in loin cloths. If the load was heavy rocks or timber, the cart was pushed by others as well. Bearers loped by carrying what Ai called *norimono* or *kago*—box-like enclosures suspended from a pole with enough room inside for only one cramped passenger. Farmers and mounted samurais made up the rest of the passersby.

Pack horses as well as pack cattle with four or six wooden buckets tied to frames on their backs were driven along by farm folk, the stench—all the worse for the hot sun and humid air—revealing what the cargo was.

With her staff, Ai pointed to a farmer emptying buckets into a stone-lined pit in the middle of his field. Sourly, she confirmed it was identical to the one where she had submerged herself.

They passed another solitary *komuso*. No words were exchanged—only slight bows.

San Francisco was the only large town the young American had ever seen, but Morioka was different. Its streets swarmed with people: vendors, porters, beggars, samurais, officials from the magistrate's office (identifiable, Ai pointed out, by the emblem on their short jackets), priests, coolies, housewives, children, and dogs. Children and dogs everywhere. And mothers with babies tied to their backs. The people—many scarred by smallpox—appeared contented and good-humored; some went out of their way to pat a child's head or to toss a food scrap to a dog.

Before a busy shop selling vegetables and fish dipped in batter and fried, Ai waited for Macneil to come up beside her.

"You might as well learn how to beg now," she whispered. "Get out your begging bowl and stand here."

He did as instructed. He was hungry, and a delicious aroma wafted to them from food frying in a large pot of bubbling oil.

Five minutes passed before the shop owner strode out with exasperation written on his face. He tossed fried green peppers, mushrooms, and tidbits of white fish into Macneil's bowl.

"Be on your way, priest. You speechless ghosts drive away my regular customers." He was a stocky, red-faced man with wall eyes.

Down the street, Macneil shared these delicious "alms" with Ai. They ate ravenously, licking the grease from their fingers.

Beyond Morioka, they found the shack they sought, only the fisherman was absent. Not far off was a graveyard with high tombstones crowded against each other, since only a small urn of ashes was buried under each stone. Land was too scarce to bury a corpse in a coffin.

"He may still be in Morioka hawking his fish," Ai said, walking among the tombstones and sitting down with the sinking sun at her back. "We will wait."

That suited Macneil. With palatable food in his stomach, he was more comfortable than he had been at any time since landing in Japan.

It was full dark when he awoke, having fallen asleep leaning against a black marble stone with two vertical lines of fancy *kanji* carved on the face. The fisherman must have returned, because a lamp was burning in his one-room shack

Ai was not beside him. She must have gone alone into the shack. He could hear an angry male voice rising in volume from within the shack across the road. Putting on his basket mask, he ran over to the crude dwelling, stopping just outside the door.

Ai's voice was not as loud as the fisherman's, but it was even more angry. "And you just left them lying there on the beach?"

"You impertinent bitch!" the fisherman shouted. "What I did and did not do is none of your affair."

"*Chikusho!*" Ai hurled at him. There was that word again.

"You said both were hurt and one had a broken leg, but you just left them there, without food or water or shelter?"

"Fool!" the man yelled, his voice even louder now. "They were just barbarian wenches. They were lucky I had to carry fish into Omoto the following day and could report them to the magistrate there."

There was a pause. Macneil could imagine Ai trying to control her temper.

"What happened to them next?" she asked.

"I told you to go."

"Just tell me what happened, then I'll leave."

"All right, then." His voice ranged from exasperation to rage. "That afternoon, the magistrate went there with two *norimono* and carted them off to Omoto."

That, at least, was what Macneil understood the fisherman to say. He was still missing about one word in every three so he had to guess at the meaning.

"And then?"

"What do you mean 'and then'? Do you think I had time to follow them? They were no concern of mine, those foreign sluts!"

Macneil's blood boiled. He took off the basket mask and his sandals.

"You must know what became of them," Ai persisted. "You probably loitered around the magistrate's office every day after that, hoping for a reward."

"Get out!" the fisherman shouted. "May dogs rape your mother!"

Hearing a scuffle, Macneil rushed in through the door.

The fisherman had grabbed a large bottle by the neck and was trying to hit Ai with it. She had raised her staff to ward off the blow.

Seeing Macneil without the basket mask, he gasped, "Another barbarian cur?"

With one leap, Macneil was on top of the powerful, scar-faced man, pounding him to the floor. At the thought of this brute's treatment of Anne and Margaret, rage welled up. He would have beaten the fisherman to death had Ai not stopped him.

"You won't learn anything from him if he is dead."

Picking up the bottle the fisherman had dropped, Macneil broke its neck off against a stone jar and touched the man's throat with its jagged edge. In his frantic struggle, the fisherman pushed himself upward, slicing open his own throat on the broken points. Blood flowed down one side of his neck.

"Ask him again what happened to them," he grated at Ai.

His answer was only a croak until the American pulled the jagged bottle away from his throat.

"One woman's leg wound became infected," the fisherman managed to gasp. "They said it would take a long time to heal and for the broken bone to mend."

"Which one was it?" Macneil asked.

"How do I know? They both looked just alike." The fisherman was growing pale.

"Where were they taken?" Ai asked, anticipating the next question.

"To Morioka. To the castle."

"Not to Omoto?" Macneil asked.

"Morioka is where the daimyo is," Ai told him. "They went there from Omoto."

"That's all we need."

"Kill him," Ai told Macneil tensely.

He was strongly tempted to follow her advice. Macneil knew he had been wrong in not killing the horses when she wanted to, and they had suffered for it. Still, he hesitated to take a human life.

"I can't do it," he said at last.

"Praised be God, the matter is no longer in our hands," she said. "Look."

The fisherman's eyes were staring blankly. He had bled to death.

CHAPTER 9

The bamboo grove covered forty acres. In the center they had found a small clearing that was secure and safe at this season.

During the fall, Ai explained, the townspeople would throng into the grove to dig bamboo shoots, which were tender, tasty, and grew at least two inches nightly. But the fall growing season for shoots had not come, so Ai and Neil felt safe staying for the time being among the bamboo.

Returning to the clearing that evening, they made a meal from the rice and dried fish they took from the shack of the fisherman, who was now buried in a horse manure heap behind his shack. They had also confiscated the small, vicious horse that pulled his cart.

If they left the horse there unattended, it was sure to be seen, and questions would be asked. And it was not out of character for Ai, in her new role as a *bikuni*, or prostitute nun, to carry the belongings of herself and her master on such a beast.

Right away, they put the horse, which kept trying to bite Neil, to good use. They packed all the fisherman's dried fish into four baskets and tied them to the horse's back. They added a large rice bag, a pot to cook the rice in, and a kettle to boil water for the tea Ai bought as they passed through Morioka again later that evening.

After dinner, Ai and Neil held a council of war.

"Do you think Anne and Margaret could still be inside the castle?" Neil asked.

"It's certain they were there at one time."

"I wonder if I should go ask for a meeting with Lord Michinobu?"

Ai looked at Macneil as if his hair were burning.

"You're insane," she said. "Nobody just asks to talk to a

daimyo, especially not a barbari...an American."

"Ai, do you really believe I am a barbarian?" He used the word *tojin* which originally meant "barbaric foreigner from China," but was now applied to all non-Japanese. An even more common expression was *keto*, defined in Neil's dictionary as "hairy barbarian."

Ai gave him a long careful look from under half-closed lids.

"Your silence tells me you do," he said, laughing.

"No, there *are* times, Neil, when I must confess you behave in an almost civilized manner."

Ai gathered up the bowls and chopsticks. He knew she would walk to the stream below the Buddhist temple to wash the utensils and luxuriate in her evening bath. Neil considered going with her for the thrill of watching her bathe nude, but he was tired and besides, she had not asked for his company.

"Tell me," he said, determined to settle this before she left, "what do *you* think we should do now?"

Standing, she looked down at him. "There's only one thing we *can* do. I must get inside the castle and look for your relatives. If they're not there, I must talk to someone who knows where they were taken."

"How will you do that?"

"I'll disguise myself as a scullery maid. The kitchen servants prepare all the meals and carry them to the castle rooms, so they should know if the women are there.

"But how do you get into the castle? Do you just walk through the gate?"

"That will be the hard part. I know how to do it, but we have to wait for bad weather—heavy rain, a storm, maybe even a typhoon."

"A typhoon?"

"This is the beginning of the typhoon season. Two or three strike Japan every year during these next two months."

She turned her back on Neil, and, singing a sad song about a maiden who died from unrequited love, Ai walked off into the darkness.

For the next twelve days, the searing summer sun baked the Morioka valley, while Ai and Neil studied the horizon daily, praying for heavy rain and high winds. To scale the walls of White Phoenix Castle, Ai said she would need the protective cover of bad weather. Since it was her life that would be at risk, Neil had to stifle his impatience and let her do things her way. Even so, the thought of what Anne and Margaret might be suffering behind those high stone walls made him lie awake at night gnawing his lips with frustration and anxiety.

Nor had he any notion where his father might be, if he was alive. Nairn could have landed on the coast near the two injured girls and gone to look for help. Or they might have seen his lifeboat being pushed further south by the storm winds. They might even have seen his lifeboat sinking and witnessed his drowning in the turbulent sea.

"When do you think the weather will change?" he asked.

"Ask the rain god," Ai snapped, weary from hearing the same question a dozen times daily.

Despite her occasional impatience, Neil suspected Ai was enjoying herself. She had made their camp in the bamboo grove half livable with the odds and ends she brought from her nightly foraging expeditions into Morioka. Although she never confessed it, he assumed she had stolen the food, clothing and utensils she fetched back.

Somewhere she had laid her callused hands on certain strange equipment she said would be needed to get into the castle. One item was a pair of black leather gloves with metal claws attached to the finger ends. A second was a light chain with an iron ball two inches in diameter welded to one end. Still another was a long strong cord with knots tied at intervals and a miniature three-pronged anchor at one end.

"Where did you get these?" he asked her.

"From a member of my clan in Morioka."

"The one you told me about?"

"Yes."

"Maybe I should meet him."

She merely laughed, shaking her head.

The waiting made Neil more irritable with each passing day. To pass the time he studied and practiced Japanese. When Ai was not washing or cooking or bathing or foraging, she drilled him. She built up his vocabulary and polished his pronunciation, which she said was "awful." She made him tell stories in Japanese. She would say, "Describe the Indians in Oregon." Or, "What goods did you sell at the trading post in Fort George?" Or, "I want to know about life aboard a whaling ship." Or, "What do you plan to do in Hong Kong?" Or, "Tell me about America."

On each topic, Neil spoke in Japanese as long as he could, with frequent corrections and more probing questions from Ai.

She seemed keenly interested in Anne. Her questions became embarrassingly blunt.

"Do you really love her?" she asked one evening at dusk while they sat together eating rice and dried fish.

"Yes."

"Have you ever seen her without any clothes on?"

Neil's ears burned red in embarrassment. He did not know what to say.

"Well, have you?"

"Ai, you—"

"Do I embarrass you?"

"Yes, you do."

"Have you ever done *omanko* with her?" Ai used a verb unknown to the American, but he could guess its meaning.

"We are engaged," he answered at last.

"Well, I hope you did."

"Did what?"

She used the same verb again.

"Why?"

"I wouldn't want you be a *dotei*."

Out came the dictionaries. The meaning was "male virgin."

"Once you told me American men kiss their women. We Japanese do not have such a strange custom."

"Oh?" He didn't know what comment to make.

"The man's lips touch the woman's? That is all?"

"Sometimes their tongues touch, too."

"Their tongues touch? How disgusting! The girl sticks out her tongue, the man sticks out his tongue, and they touch? Is that what you mean? Really?"

"Not quite like that."

"How then?"

"It...well, it's a little hard to explain."

"Show me."

Neil was acutely conscious of his vow to be faithful to his cousin Anne. *Still*, he thought, *it would be foolish to refuse since Anne's very life might depend on Ai's continuing good will and help.*

He drew Ai's face to his and with his fingers, he gently squeezed open her mouth and twirled his tongue around the tip of hers.

Suddenly, the blood was pounding against his eyeballs, while his vow to Anne faded. He and Ai entwined themselves in each other's arms. But when the rising hardness beneath Neil's abdomen pressed against her, Ai broke off the embrace and with a gasp backed away.

It's a damned good thing she has her clothes on, Neil thought. *Otherwise, I would have taken her on the spot, no matter what.*

Neil had been raised to believe in sexual fidelity to one's wife or lover. His father had drilled this principle into his consciousness while warning him time and again against the pitfalls faced by any male Macneil. (Neil wondered why the

Macneil females should not be as disastrously passionate as the males?)

His father had recounted to him often enough the scandals, wicked behavior, and atrocious misconduct of the Macneil men of past generations, the blame for which he laid at the front door of lustful blood. ("Aye, laddie, the good Laird has seen fit to put the pitfall of lusty blood in our paths," his father had repeated on countless occasions.)

There were times when Neil wondered if the sexual drive of his clan was actually as excessive as his father suggested, for Neil did not always feel inclined to set out in ardent pursuit of just any attractive woman who came into view. But there were other times, as at his first meeting with cousin Anne, when his desire was so overwhelming that the blood rushed to his head and made him dizzy.

It was such a feeling that had just flooded through him when he and Ai kissed, that despite his vow of fidelity to Anne, he was without moral strength in the grasp of this lust. If he was to remain faithful to Anne, then he would have to avoid close physical intimacy with Ai from here on. For a man and woman traveling alone together in the wilderness, it remained to be seen just how feasible that might be.

Neil needed to be able to understand Japanese as well as to speak it, so Ai talked at length about her people, their customs, and their way of life. Neil tried to guide her words into channels that would tell him more about herself.

At first, she was reluctant to talk much about who she was and why she was so good at disguises and feats of physical prowess. But he persisted, and bit by bit, her story came out.

She began with her family background. She said family honor was supremely important to the Koga family and vengeance was a means of upholding honor.

She often said, "Vengeance is a joy divine."

She told Neil about an ancestor who had been the daimyo of Arima, near Nagasaki in Kyushu. This Koga had fought for the Tokugawas at the battle of Sekigahara on October 21, 1600.

"He and his samurais won many honors," Ai said, "and the first Tokugawa shogun—Ieyasu—rewarded him by doubling his fief in size. But by then, my ancestor had already become a follower of our Lord Jesus Christ, one of many converts around Nagasaki. When Ieyasu outlawed the 'evil Christian sect,' as he called it, my ancestor refused to give up his beliefs. He swore he would never defile a picture of Jesus by stepping on it."

"The practice you call *fumi-e*?"

Ai nodded. "At first, the regulation was not strictly enforced, but as Ieyasu became more suspicious of the ultimate intentions of the Catholic priests, he showed no mercy in repressing the Christians."

Neil's father Nairn had often told him and Margaret that most wars and much of man's suffering had their roots in religion. Here was just one more example.

"When Ieyasu died," Ai went on, "his son Hidetada grew even harsher in his anti-Christian edicts. Finally, when nine Christians were crucified in Nagasaki, rebellion broke out in Shimabara, a peninsula not far from there."

Ai gripped Macneil's arm as she relived her story. "The Christians in Arima had united with other Christians living in Kyushu. Together, they raised 37,000 men and women, who fortified the ruined Hara castle in Shimabara. The shogun's army was commanded by a general named Matsudaira. It laid siege to the castle and tried to starve out the Koga clan and the Amakusa Christians, but they held out for many months. At last, in April 1638, Matsudaira mustered 100,000 troops and made an all-out assault on the stronghold. They overran it."

"And then?"

For a while, Ai sat silent, but her eyes burned with the tortured emotions she felt. "Many of the original 37,000 defenders had already died from starvation. Fewer than 30,000 remained alive." She looked down at her hands, adding in a low voice, "They were all slain."

Macneil felt himself, almost against his will, being recruited to support her cause.

"On orders from the Tokugawa, General Matsudaira wanted to crucify all the survivors, but he did not have enough wood for the crosses. Every tree within one *ri*," Neil knew a *ri* was about two and a half miles, "was cut down. Shimabara is a rocky peninsula, anyway, and there just weren't enough trees."

The thirst for vengeance so clearly written on Ai's face made it seem as if she had been there.

"On the peninsula, Matsudaira's men found a bamboo grove, even larger than this one." She gestured at the bamboo trees around them. "After chopping down all the trees, they cut each one up into lengths of half a *ken* each." A *ken* equalled six feet. "They drove these into the soil on all sides of the castle. Then they herded the survivors out into those fields and began to cut off their heads. Each head was impaled on a bamboo stake. Those waiting their turn to die were forced to carry the headless bodies down the slopes and throw them into the sea."

Ai paused, gathering strength to go on.

"In the end, no one was left alive to carry the corpses to the sea, so they were eaten by ravens."

Not knowing what to say, Neil held her hand, wondering how events of 215 years ago could evoke such strong emotions.

"The story was passed down from Koga generation to generation," she continued. "As far as the eye could see from the castle walls, it was said that the fields were covered with thousands of bamboo stakes each topped with a head. Among these, like taller trees growing in a field of corn, stood the crucifixion crosses for which Matsudaira's men had found wood. Many victims nailed to the crosses lived for several days."

Neil waited, wishing she had not started this tale.

"One piece of ground was called the Children's Field." With a shudder, Ai gave a soft, brief sob. "Only children's heads were mounted on the stakes in that field. Over the next few weeks, despite the sickening smell, many outsiders came from Nagasaki and even Saga—on orders from the Tokugawa authorities, who wanted the terrible cost of disobedience to be remembered forever—to view this great slaughter. It is said, however, that none would go near the Children's Field, even though the Tokugawa samurais on guard duty threatened them with severe punishment if they did not. The skulls stayed there on those stakes for many years after that."

"Ai, I am sorry."

"My ancestor was crucified there."

"The one who was a daimyo?"

"No, he was killed during the siege. This was another ancestor, Amakusa Shiro Tokisada, the general commanding the defending forces."

"Dear God," he murmured in English.

"It took him three days to die, the survivors were told."

"Is that why you were so ready to shoot the arrow at your brother?"

Ai nodded her bowed head, then drew a deep breath and stiffened her shoulders.

"Anyway, we Kogas lost all our holdings. Because we swore we would never defile Jesus' picture, those who were still alive packed up and left. There were only a few survivors, you understand."

"Where did you go?"

"To the Amakusa Islands."

"I'd like to see them some day."

"I'm sure you will, Neil. They are so beautiful. Hundreds of tiny green islands in a deep blue sea."

"Are they flat?"

"Oh, no. Mostly, they are like cones. The larger ones even

have mountains. They are just off the Kyushu coast. Our people have a saying, 'Who needs heaven when we have the Amakusas?'"

"What happened next?"

"According to stories handed down through the generations, the few Koga survivors gathered on the main Amakusa island, in the town of Ushibuka. The first thing they did was to swear eternal vengeance against the Tokugawa clan, including those Tokugawa relatives, the Matsudairas. They took an oath and wrote it down in blood and vowed they and all their descendants would never rest until the last Tokugawa was dead. When I was a child, I was shown the paper many times by my grandmother. It was a sacred object, and she cried whenever she showed it to me."

"What did your clan do? How did they live?" Neil asked, glancing up at the darkening sky.

"The Kogas became *funa-kainin.*"

"*Funa-kainin?*"

"It means 'boat and sea people.' The first *funa-kainin* were on the Kii Peninsula in the seventh century, then spread to the Amakusa Islands, near Nagasaki. They lived on boats anchored in secluded coves. I guess you could say they were outlaws. They lived a hand-to-mouth existence, doing whatever was necessary to survive."

"And the Kogas joined the *funa-kainin?*"

"Not exactly," Ai said. "The Koga clan remained independent, but we were so much like the *funa-kainin* that people began calling us that."

"And the Kogas all live in the Amakusas now?"

"Not all. We're scattered all over. We fish off boats in the Inland Sea and around the Seven Isles of Izu. Some farm in isolated mountain valleys, like the one I may take you to if we don't find your relatives in White Phoenix Castle."

"But I'm not sure I really understand what you do."

"I just told you, the Koga clan are—"

"I meant, what is it *you* do, Ai."

She gave Neil a long enigmatic look. "I've dedicated my life to taking vengeance on the Tokugawas."

The following night, he had gone to sleep early, thanking God for the two *futon*, or comforters, and the mosquito net Ai had confiscated. En route to Morioka, they had kept to the hills where the cooler temperatures discouraged mosquitoes from energetic nighttime activity. Here in the bamboo grove not much higher than the Morioka valley floor, however, the insects attacked in steady waves, like Matsudaira's legions crushing the Christians at Shimabara.

In mutual self-protection, they had laid out their two *futon* side by side, touching, so they could both sleep under the single mosquito net, supported by bamboo stakes.

When they had crawled under the net from opposite sides, both Ai and Neil had been laughing about a silly mistake he persisted in making in Japanese pronunciation. Try as he might to correct himself, he still failed to make the correct distinction between the long and short vowels. He had just said *koomon* when he should have said *komon*. The difference was important. What he intended to say to Ai was, "I'm lucky to have you as my advisor," whereas what he had actually said was, "I'm lucky to have you as my rectum."

Ai had laughed so hard they had cut short the language lesson for that evening and gone to bed. Still chuckling and in a gay mood, she had reached over, under the net, to touch his hand and say 'Good night' softly.

The Macneil carnal appetite never needed much encouragement, and her small unthinking gesture was more than enough to arouse it. Neil began to edge slowly across the empty *futon* space between them. He advanced an inch, then stopped to control his breathing. Another inch—and more breath control. The third inch and....

At that point, he fell asleep.

Just before midnight, Neil was dreaming about Anne Macneil. They were sitting on a grassy river bank in Oregon, and he was about to embrace his cousin. "Anne, dearest...."

A painful pinch roused him to full wakefulness.

"What the devil!"

Clearly angry, Ai knelt beside him. "I was about to awaken you with a kiss, but then you called me 'Anne.' "

"Forgive me, Ai," Neil pleaded, opening his arms. "Kiss me, anyway."

"Don't ever touch me again, you barbarian."

Neil fell back on his *futon*. "Then why did you wake me up?"

"We must go."

Neil could see lightning walking on stilts across the eastern sky, providing sporadic stage illumination for the Dance of the Winds being performed by the bamboos around them.

"Now is the time to enter the castle," she said. "If that Anne woman means so much to you, I will just have to find her."

Grimly, Ai added, "Then I can be rid of you."

CHAPTER 10

The road leading into Morioka was deserted at that late hour except for a post rider who came flying by, carrying a forked stick with a mail packet tied between the forks.

The lightning flashes stalked toward Ai and Neil, the rising wind howling a warning of the approach of the storm. Already, Neil had felt a few drops of rain on his hands but not on his face, which was covered by the basket mask.

A sudden wind gust tore the basket mask off and blew it into a rice paddy. He caught up with it beside a human manure pit like the one Ai had hidden in.

Neil was dressed as a *komuso* again, while Ai wore a dark jacket, loose breeches tied below the knee, and a scarf wrapped around her head—a different outfit from the one she wore in her disguise as a *bikuni*. In her hands, she carried another scarf, or *furoshiki*, containing several pieces of the gear she needed for what she planned to do. Her inner jacket pockets hid even more such items. Neil had brought his timepiece along and would have brought the Navy Colt, but Ai advised against it.

"If you're caught, just having a pistol could mean a death sentence. Firearms are frowned on in Japan. Not even the shogun's samurais carry them."

As before, entering Morioka was easy because the town was without gates or watchmen. But the castle was protected by moats and walls with guards at the four bridges across the main moat. The bridges led to the massive, twelve-foot high wooden gates at each entrance.

Except for harried dogs being pushed along by the rising wind with their tails between their legs, the streets were deserted. The rain came closer.

Wooden shutters had been pulled out from their recesses and closed across the windows and doors of the darkened shops. So, for the moment, there seemed little danger that Neil and Ai would be detected.

Even if they were seen, Neil was merely a harmless, silent *komuso* on some foolish nighttime errand with a stupid girl in tow. Ai had showed him how well she could pretend to be half-witted, with glazed eyes and open mouth and spittle bubbling at one corner.

"The castle is just ahead," Ai said, taking Neil by the arm and drawing him close. "What time is it now?"

He pulled out his Waltham timepiece and waited for the next lightning flash.

"Almost ten-thirty," he said. Neil had taught Ai how to tell Western time. The Japanese way was, to Neil, impossibly complicated. Their calculations started with nine in the evening, called the Hour of the Mouse. In place of timepieces, the Japanese relied on temple bells and candles with the hour level marked by a horizontal line.

"Midnight on your timepiece is when the next patrol around the moat is made," she warned. "Now follow me." She led him into an alleyway no more than six feet wide. This brought them to the castle moat so abruptly Neil almost fell over the edge. Without the protection of the houses lining the alley, he was now struck by the full force of the wind. Again, it lifted the basket mask from his head, though this time he grabbed it before it could be blown away.

"This way," Ai said. They ran along the moat to a cul-de-sac between what looked like a stable and an inn kitchen. Neil found he could stand in the darkened niche and look out across the moat and up at the gray stone castle wall.

As the full force of the thunderstorm hit Morioka, the rain pelted down in sheets, drenching Ai and Neil. For once, he was thankful for the basket mask, since it was large enough to serve as an umbrella, if he could only keep it on his head.

"Now is the best time," Ai said, removing the plain *jika-tabi* sandals she had been wearing and replacing them with a pair that had metal claws—like the claws in her gloves—imbedded in the soles. She checked her equipment once more.

"I must hurry," she said, "before the rain stops."

"You're going to climb *that* wall?" Neil was incredulous. "There's nothing to hold on to."

"You'll see."

"I want to go with you."

She was scornful. "Do you really think you could climb it?"

Neil peered through the blinding rain up at the almost vertical parapet.

"Well, I'm not sure."

"Even if you could, there's no need for you to go," Ai said. "Now, this is what you must do, Neil. It's very important, so don't fail me." She pointed up at a narrow window near the top of the towering wall. "Keep your eyes on that window. I'll go in and come back out through it. If it's still raining when I come back, then I'll be safe—I think. No one will be watching in rain this heavy."

Ai gripped Neil's arm with her empty hand.

"Ai," he said, removing his basket mask and taking her by both arms. "You shouldn't do this. If anything happened to you...."

"You needn't worry, Neil," she said, rising on her toes and putting her mouth against his. With her free hand, she squeezed open his lips and circled the tip of his tongue with hers. "There! Did I do it right?"

Before Neil could answer, she hurried on. "If the rain has stopped when I come back down, it will be easy for them to see me, so what you must do then, without fail, is to light the powder in these." She handed him two clay pots, each seven inches in diameter.

"What are these?"

"Smoke pots. The smoke will cover me for about five minutes, if the wind is right."

"Where do I put them?"

She pointed to two places along the moat, one on each side of where they stood.

"But you must leave here before twelve, when the patrol comes by. Remember that," she said.

"What if you aren't back by then?"

Something warned him not to let her go.

"I'll be all right. I may find a better way to get out of the castle. Anyway, we'll meet back at the bamboo grove."

"Ai, don't...," he started to say, but she was already over the edge lowering herself into the moat.

The sheets of rain swirled by the wind roiled the surface of the moat, but Neil was able to watch her progress part way across, until he lost sight of her in a squall. As she started up the wall, she was again visible during a lull in the rain, looking like a large black spider on the gray-white surface of the vertical stones.

Her agility amazed Neil. Aided by the claw-like metal attachments on her gloves and feet, she mounted the wall as if strolling casually along on flat ground.

During the two minutes it took Ai to reach the high window, she could have been seen from below, but Neil doubted anyone would be standing outside in this rain storm staring up at the castle walls.

The last he saw of Ai, she was squeezing herself through a narrow embrasure.

For the next hour and twenty minutes Neil took turns watching the high window in the castle wall, looking at his timepiece, glancing toward where Ai said the midnight patrol would come from, and trying to keep the basket mask on his head, the niche where he stood affording only partial protection from the gusts. When not so occupied, his thoughts turned to his family. If his situation was uncomfortable and risky, theirs might be far worse. He tried to tell himself he should not, without good reason, leap to the conclusion that Anne and Margaret were being mistreated, but his mind could not accept this optimism. The shogun forbade entry into Japan, so all who came were outlaws, no matter why they came. William Amanuma had believed completely the stories about American sailors being killed for setting foot on the sacred soil of his country. And Anne and Margaret were both young desirable women, adding to the temptation to abuse them sexually.

Setting aside such darkling thoughts, Neil shifted to Ai. How did she learn to climb vertical parapets like a fly? Where could she have laid her hands on things like gloves and sandals with metal claws on them?

He had already come to accept and respect her deep feeling that she had to pay her debts. In her tales, she always gave the highest honor to those men and women who had met their obligations, no matter how difficult the repayment had been. She called an unpaid debt an "intolerable burden," and the Japanese word for obligation—*on*— occurred so often in her speech that Neil knew it must dominate her thoughts. Probably it was a racial characteristic; certainly it was one that characterized her clan.

Midnight approached. Neil would have to leave this niche in only a few minutes. He shivered, wondering if Ai had been caught or injured—possibly mortally.

God, he prayed, let her show up *now*! His neck and hand muscles tensed as he strove to command her to appear.

But what, he thought, *if Ai has found Anne and Margaret? What if even now she is leading them through the dark passages to the escape window?*

Two minutes before midnight. Neil knew he had to go now— without Ai. But the rain had stopped; visibility had improved. She would be in greater danger.

One more minute, he thought. *Just one more minute. Please, Ai, show yourself now! Please, God, help her.*

Now it was midnight. He started to leave his niche, and found himself face to face with two guards on patrol around the circumference of the moat. Both wore straw rain capes and looked like twin hedgehogs, but much more dangerous.

"*Komuso ja nai ka!*" exploded the guard on Neil's right, seeing his outfit and recognizing his occupation.

The second guard laughed. "Why are you standing out here, priest? Do you think someone in the castle will toss you some scraps of food at this hour?"

"Maybe he needs a bath," said the first. "Shove him in the moat."

"No, let him go," growled the other. "These silent beggars are harmless."

Just then a gust of dying wind from the passing storm lifted the basket mask from Macneil's head and blew it skimming across into the middle of the moat.

"*Tojin da zo!*" The guard who had wanted to let Macneil go shouted they had found a hairy barbarian.

Kicking off his sandals, Macneil turned to run, hoping the guards' surprise would paralyze them long enough for him to escape, but one guard recovered his presence of mind quickly enough to slash at Macneil with his long sword as he dashed by.

CHAPTER 11

The sword made an excruciating gash in Macneil's left side. Spinning around, he grappled with the guard so that the man could not easily withdraw the sword entangled in the folds of Macneil's jacket.

Yelling for help, the second sentinel hopped this way and that behind the first, trying to get a cut at the American. Feeling the short sword under the first guard's raincape, Macneil pulled it out and stabbed him in the stomach. The guard toppled over the edge into the moat, his final cry fading to a gargle as the waters engulfed him.

Still gripping the short sword Macneil began slashing wildly at the second guard in the darkness. Macneil must have caught the man off balance, for he stumbled backward three paces before steadying himself and charging at the American with a ferocious cry.

Knowing he had little chance against a trained swordsman, Macneil threw the short sword at his assailant. It did no harm but slowed him for the seconds Macneil needed to turn on his heels and sprint off through the darkness. Twisting and turning, he dodged down the alleyways behind rows of shops and houses. His side felt as if a burning torch had been pressed against it. Wadding up his jacket as he fled, he pressed it against the wound to stanch the bleeding.

Behind him, he could hear the guard still yelling for reinforcements.

Down the silent alleyways, where there was no one to see him and say which way he had gone, Macneil darted first this way, then that, through the grounds of a temple, across a muddy vegetable patch, past a darkened bathhouse. Despite frequent shifts in direction, he tried to head generally northwest, the direction in which the bamboo grove and temple lay.

The farther Macneil raced, the weaker he became from fatigue and from loss of blood.

A madly barking, flop-eared brown cur pursued him fifty yards until he stopped, picked up a rock, and chucked it at the animal, which scurried off yelping, as if the rock had not missed.

On the outskirts of the town Macneil slowed his pace. He could hear no close pursuit. The darkened, unpainted homes with their thatched roofs were fewer now, interspersed more often with vegetable plots and yards for threshing rice. The lower left side of his outfit was drenched with blood. He needed rest. If only he could find a safe place.

Stumbling feebly on for half a mile, he came to a small Shinto shrine, with its characteristic *torii* gateway, on the right side of the road. Unlike the Buddhist temples, these Shinto shrines were often small and unattended, meant only to be places where the passing worshipper could stop to pray a moment and perhaps leave an offering to the gods.

Past the hand-washing basin, he staggered up the three steps to collapse on the porch. The interior was open on three sides but dark. Even in the dark, however, Macneil could see the row of wood casks, each holding about two gallons, lined up before the god shelf.

Crawling nearer, he was delighted beyond reason that he could read the four characters repeated on each—*Seishu ikkyu.* "Pure sake, first grade."

These casks held the seasonal sake offerings to the harvest god, given as a heavenly bribe for a bountiful rice crop. Since they were presents to the god, no Japanese would dare touch them, but Macneil was not Japanese. With his sailor's pocket knife, he cut the straw rope wrapped round one cask and feebly stomped in its top with his heel.

Back in Fort George, the Macneils had not held with drinking spirits, and aboard the whaler, Neil had given his daily rum ration to a friend. He knew, however, that alcohol gave a man strength, even if only temporarily. If he could rest here an hour and drink enough rice wine, he might find the strength to return to the bamboo grove before full light.

Cutting straw ropes from around other sake casks, Macneil used them to make a belt to hold his wadded-up jacket against his wound. Then, leaning back against a pillar, he determined to see how much rice wine he could swallow before striking out, without the protection of his basket mask, for the bamboo grove.

If he drank too much, he might pass out and be found here in the shrine in the morning. If not enough, he might not reach the hideout he shared with Ai.

CHAPTER 12

From Morioka south toward the Mikuni Mountains

During the four hours since dawn, Neil Macneil had staggered off the road whenever he saw a rider or foot traveler approach. *I'm spending more time lying in these fields behind stacks of rice-straw than stumbling along on the road,* he thought, but gave thanks he did not have to submerge himself in any of the many manure tanks he passed.

Finally, at mid-morning he reached the stream flowing by the hill on which the temple stood. By now his tormenting thirst had forced all other thoughts out of his mind, so he threw himself into the clear cool water with his clothes on, leaving only his bag of possibles on the bank. When he crawled dripping out of the current, he was sure the level of the stream must be two inches lower than it had been before.

Staggering now and then from weariness, blood loss and too much sake, Macneil climbed up the slope and past the temple to approach the bamboo grove from above and from the rear. He did not know just what he might find in their clearing, but he wanted a chance to see what was there before blundering into it.

As an energy source, the sake had proved efficient enough. In fact, once he got back on his feet, Macneil almost felt like running and even singing as he left the roadside shrine. One cask was empty, although he had spilled more than he drank. It was a great deal of alcohol for Neil, but it gave him the strength to move along the road at a swaying half-trot.

He reached the valley rim safely, but by now the sake had worn off. Dehydrated—and weaker than before—it was all Macneil could do to push his way wearily through the swaying bamboo until he saw the familiar clearing. Nothing had changed except that their precious mosquito net had been blown into the bamboo tops, where it hung like the blue web of a giant spider.

To one side huddled a small figure in dark jacket and trousers. Her face was hidden in arms folded over her knees, and though Neil could hardly believe it, she was crying. Her shoulders shook and he heard her sobs as he limped closer.

He was bleary-eyed from want of sleep and too much sake. The morning sun shining directly into his eyes made it hard to see clearly. Still, he was sure the crying woman was Ai, even though he had never imagined that a tough, self-possessed, and at times unforgiving person like her would ever break down and sob her heart out.

Macneil was quite close. He pushed aside two intervening stalks and walked in front of her.

"Ai," he said in a low, tired voice, "I'm back."

Eyes staring wildly out of her tear-stained face, Ai sprang to her feet. "Neil?" she gasped. "*Neil?* Is it really you? Oh, thank God, thank God!" She crossed herself.

"*Ore da,*" he said, using a masculine phrase she had taught him, meaning "It's none other." Reeling from fatigue, he added, "I think I'd better sit down."

"Are you hurt?" She flew across the short distance between them and clutched Neil to her like a mother clasping a lost baby to her breasts.

"Where are you wounded? Here, let me help you." The words poured from her mouth without pause for breath or answers. "What happened? Let me see the wound. I was sure you were dead when I saw the basket mask and a body floating in the moat. Sit here. No, it's better if you lie down. Now, show me."

Neil was overjoyed to stretch out on the cool grass still wet from the rain and to see Ai's lovely face and warm, parted lips so close. He could still taste the kiss she had given him last night.

She untied the straw belt around his waist with expert fingers and opened his jacket, her eyes darkening with concern when she saw the wound itself. "Lie still," she ordered, then dashed off toward the stream below the temple.

Neil was nearly unconscious when she returned with water and handfuls of moss and herbs and bamboo leaves. After letting him drink his fill, she produced a small oil-paper packet holding yellowish powder from an inner pocket, dusted it on the open gash, filled that with moss, and covered it with bamboo leaves.

"We'll leave it like that for a few hours to draw out the poisons, then stitch the edges of the wound." She added darkly, "If you die, it'll be from a hangover, not from this cut."

"Could you tell I've been drinking sake?"

"Of course. The smell. What happened?"

"What happened to you? I waited till after midnight."

"I was...delayed. Then, when I started to climb down the wall, I saw a dozen guards with torches and lanterns running this way and that alongside the moat. I knew they were looking for you. I had to wait a while for things to calm down. When finally I went down the wall and swam across the moat, I saw your basket mask and a body floating face down in the water. I didn't have time to examine it, because I heard guards coming, but I was sure it was your body."

"But what about Anne and Margaret?"

"They were in the castle for a while. One had a broken leg that had become infected. She couldn't be moved until it healed."

"And then?"

"The daimyo decided to send both to the shogun in Edo for disposition. But on the way to Edo, in the mountains south of here, *sanzoku* attacked the escort and kidnapped the two women from their sedan chair. No one knows where they are now." She had to explain that *sanzoku* meant mountain bandits.

"What do *you* think happened to them, Ai?"

"The *sanzoku* must have thought they were capturing wives of officials from Lord Nobuoki's fief, for whom they could get ransom. When they saw they had caught two foreign women instead, they may have killed them out of hand or decided to take them farther south or even west to sell them to another daimyo."

"And we have no way of knowing where they were taken or even if they are still alive?"

"You mustn't give up hope. When you can travel, I'll take you to our clan's valley back in the mountains. My uncle there has many friends in northern Japan. He may be able to learn something."

Only half awake, Neil began to tell Ai what had happened to him, but fell asleep before he could finish. He slept till evening, aroused only once by Ai who made him drink a vile-tasting herb mixture she said would hasten his healing.

When he woke, Ai pressed him for the rest of the story, and was astounded that alone he had returned safely to the bamboo grove. Her final comment was, "The gods must look after drunkards and helpless Americans."

The journey from Morioka to Ai's uncle's home in a nearly inaccessible valley of the Mikuni Mountain Range took twenty-six days. Under her care, the flesh wound in his side had nearly healed before they started out.

Leaving Morioka and its broad fertile valley behind, they kept to paths in the Ou Range foothills, leaving them to cross the Yamagata Basin with its opulent orchards, from which they ate their fill of a variety of pilfered fruit for two days.

After skirting Mounts Zao, Azuma, and Bandai, they veered from their due south course to a southwesterly one that skirted the ancient castle town called Aizu-Wakamatsu and followed the broad Tadami River to its juncture with the River Ima.

Within sight of towering Mount Hiuchi, the swift, clear River Ima rose from its source in a spring. There, Ai planned to leave the trail they had followed and start their long hike toward the mountains to the west. In their disguises as priest and nun, Neil and Ai expected no trouble along the way. Nevertheless, she avoided the barrier stations— the *sekisho*—on the main roads.

The packhorse—Ai had named her Hana—became one of them. The little animal had been mistreated, but under Ai's kind handling, Hana stopped biting and kicking within a week and became a useful and even friendly animal. She carried their *futon*, mosquito net, kettle, pot, food supplies, and the sack containing Neil's kilt, bagpipe, Navy Colt revolver, spy glass, stolen sword, and dictionaries.

All Neil could squeeze from Ai about her uncle was that he headed a *bunke* or branch of the Koga clan. She reasoned that he might have information sources who could point to where Anne and Margaret had been taken, saving months of aimless searching.

Rain poured down much of the way to the valley. After the first storm, Ai made a foraging expedition into a nearby town and returned with two straw rain-capes like those worn by the guards at the castle. The cape and his basket mask kept Neil dry enough during the day, while at night he and Ai sought overhanging ledges or caves or woods with dense overhead foliage.

This same rain falling on the mountains to the west raised the level of the rivers. Since there were few bridges, Ai and Neil often forded turbulent streams on foot, struggling to keep little Hana from being swept away.

"Why are there so few bridges?" Neil complained.

"The shogun discourages travel, especially between fiefs. That's also why the roads are so seldom repaired, except for the main highways with their many daimyo processions."

CHAPTER 13

"My kingdom for a map," Neil grumbled to Ai as they plodded along in the heavy rain with the packhorse Hana between them. Seven days had passed since they had reached the Ima River.

"What kingdom?" Ai asked. "Anyway, maps are forbidden."

"For what possible reason?" *Here is one more of those damned oddities,* Neil thought. He kept running up against them in this topsy-turvy country, where they mounted their horses from the right, beached their boats backwards, drew arrows on the right side of the bow, wrote vertically, and tied bells to cows' tails instead of around their necks.

"Only a few officials have them. The shogun doesn't take chances on maps getting into foreign hands."

"Even if they did, so what?"

"That would make it easier for you barbarians to invade Japan, as you already have done in China."

"How would a chit of an uneducated country girl like you know about China?" Neil didn't know much himself, but he was feeling out of sorts, thanks to the never-ending rain.

"We Kogas have a Chinese friend, a...uh, a pirate, I suppose you would call him. Sometimes his ships meet ours off southern Japan to trade goods."

"Smuggling? I thought it might be something like that." Neil still wanted Ai to say straight out whatever it was she and her clan really did in their hideout in the Amakusa Islands, but she did not rise to his bait.

During a brief rest in the late afternoon, Neil said, "We should make camp soon."

"First we must ford the river. After a heavy rain like this, the Ima rises faster than any other. If we don't cross soon, we'll have to wait until tomorrow—or even later."

What they were about to cross was a clear, fast-flowing stream that normally averaged thirty yards in width and three feet in depth. But the surging Ima River had turned ugly. As Neil, Ai, and Hana stopped at the edge of its turbulent, frothing expanse, Hana neighed and recoiled, pawing the air with thrashing forelegs.

"I think we can make it," Ai said, "but we'll have to hurry." They removed the *futon* and Neil's sack of belongings to lighten the load on the little horse, so that she would not drown if the current tumbled her off her hooves.

Ai led her by the reins while Neil stood against the horse's down-current side to support her with his shoulder if the raging river proved too strong.

Plunging in, they were instantly pounded almost off their feet by seething white water reaching to their necks. White-eyed, Hana reared and fought Ai, but once the horse was in the river, she had no choice but to press on. The river seemed to be rising with every passing minute.

So strong did the current become they spent ten minutes floundering and sliding on the slippery bottom rocks before they reached the far bank and were able to crawl up it. Shoving Hana to keep her upright had opened the nearly healed wound in Neil's side. He knew Ai would have to stitch it again.

Ai turned back to retrieve the *futon* and Neil's sack which were still on the other bank. Before he could stop her, she was in the white water again, fighting her way across. Suddenly she was swept off her feet and carried downstream in the gathering dusk. Neil saw that she was taking a bad beating as she was thrown against first one boulder, then another by the power of the torrent.

In the next instant, her head slipped under the frothy waves and she disappeared.

CHAPTER 14

Frantically, Neil ran alongside the river looking for a place to dive in. Finally, a hundred yards from where they had crossed, he came to a wider, shallower stretch where the force of the churning flood had abated. He was poised to dive in when Ai stood up unsteadily in knee-deep water near the far bank and signaled she was safe. After catching their breath, they both moved back upstream along the opposite banks.

But by the time they reached their starting point, the river had risen even more. A wave two feet high roared down at them from upstream, leaving Neil to wonder if a dam farther back in the mountains had burst.

The torrent was fearsome. Tree trunks and other debris bounced on the waves. Crossing the river again was out of the question for Ai. Barely visible in the dusk, she spread her hands in resignation. They would have to camp on opposite banks.

Next morning Ai was a sorry sight as Neil helped her ford the much calmer river. He made a second trip to retrieve their *futon* and his sack.

She was starving, dripping wet, and, Neil could see, mad at the world. To worsen her mood, she was covered with cuts, bruises, and scrapes from her head-on encounters with boulders. Where her skin was not lacerated, it was marked by swelling mosquito welts that she scratched vigorously.

After a cursory look around Neil's camp, she walked over to the nearest low tree branch and hung her clothing up to dry. All her clothing. Wringing water from her hair, she stood on widespread feet and lifted her face to the sun, a wilderness nymph turned sun worshipper, whose girlish nakedness set Neil's blood racing.

Finding a small jar of pungent salve in her belongings, she handed it to the American.

"Rub this on my mosquito bites." Curt and grumpy, she was obviously in no mood to brook any nonsense.

His powers of restraint were sorely tried. The mosquitoes had left their marks everywhere on Ai, but seemed to have found her breasts especially tasty. It occurred to Neil that he might, too. He found himself speculating what her reaction would be if he suddenly pressed his face to her bosom and licked those breasts with his tongue and nibbled at their delicate tips.

Touching one, he asked, "How did mosquitoes bite you here, Ai? Under your clothes, I mean." He felt her nipple respond tautly.

For a moment, he thought she would not answer, but finally she replied with scant civility. "I took off my wet clothes and hung them out to dry. I must have dozed off. That was when they bit me."

When Ai's clothes were dry, they loaded their gear on Hana and struck out along a narrow path next to the receding river.

At nightfall, they stopped in a glen off the trail and above the river. Ai made a fire, and boiled rice, mixing bits of dried fish and black seaweed in it. Neil watered the horse, letting her graze in the foot-high grass in the glen. As an afterthought, he hobbled her, though he doubted they could get Hana to leave them now, even if they tried.

After they ate in the early dusk, Neil noticed Ai looked longingly at the river. He knew what was coming.

"I'm going to bathe," she said. "You had better come with me."

"Maybe later. I'm pretty tired."

"Come on along; you need a bath," she coaxed, pulling him to his feet.

Reluctantly, he followed her to the river. The water was chilly but bracing. He let the current carry him ten yards downstream where he could not see Ai clearly, but she followed him.

"Come back, Neil. I want you beside me."

"Why?"

"We didn't have a language lesson last night. We can dry ourselves here on the bank while I tell you more about the polite and impolite expressions in Japanese."

"I don't feel like being polite tonight."

"*Anata wa do shita no?*" Ai asked, meaning "What's wrong with you?" but she used the pronoun *anata* for "you." Neil remembered her telling him women usually said *anata* when speaking to their husbands and lovers.

"Ai, I must talk to you seriously."

"Go ahead." She sat down six inches from Neil.

"Well, this is hard for me to say, especially in Japanese, but, well, I see you every day and many times you are...ah, without clothing, like now. This bothers me."

"You don't like to see me like this?"

"Of course, I do, but it's hard on me—I mean, being a man and well, like today, when I put salve on your...on your..."

"*Oppai* is the word, Neil."

"Yes. Well, I found I did not want to stop putting the medicine on your *oppai*."

"I know. You used up all my salve."

"Seeing you without clothes practically every day, Ai, is— well, it is having a very...ah, strong effect on me. You see, as a man, I want to..."

In the dusk, Ai brought her pert face and bright eyes close to his face. "But Neil," she protested. "I didn't think it would bother you. You and I are more like—like brother and sister, aren't we? In Japan, brothers and sisters—even whole families— bathe together. Why shouldn't you and I do so, too? Anyway, by now you should be accustomed to seeing me this way."

Neil ground his teeth in torment. Seeing this lovely wood-land sprite sitting naked beside him weakened his pledge to remain faithful to Anne. It started his heart pounding wildly.

With a moan, Neil reached for Ai and feverishly kissed her mouth, her throat, her breasts.

"Neil...Neil...oh!"

Her thighs opened. Her eyes closed, and a small sound of wonder came from her throat. Her hips rose in invitation.

Tremors of desire ran through him as he breathed, "Ai...Ai...I am sorry, but I can't help myself."

Just before the actual entry, however, he whispered, "Ai, are you a virgin?"

Abruptly, she drew back. "Does it matter?"

"No, except I thought, you know, if you *are* a virgin, it may hurt a little."

"Well, I *am* a virgin," she said, pushing him away from her. "And I'm glad you reminded me."

They were quiet and still for a moment.

"Neil, have you ever done *omanko* with a virgin? Do you know all about it?"

"Well, I think Anne was a virgin the first time."

"You *think?* Don't you know? Was there no bleeding?"

"It was hard to tell. We had so much mud on us."

"Mud?"

"It happened on a muddy river bank."

Ai made a contemptuous sound, then said, "The Koga clan

has a tradition that all their daughters must go to their marriage *futon* as virgins."

"I see."

"If I'm not a virgin when I wed, my husband can reject me and send me back to my father, who would lose face—and I would never be able to make a decent marriage after that."

"What do you mean by a decent marriage?"

"Oh, I could marry *someone*, I'm sure, but not anyone my father would accept as his son-in-law. What makes it worse is that I'm now my father's only child. If I produce no children acceptable to him, the Koga clan will die out. I'm his only hope. Do you see?"

"Then why the devil did you let me—"

"Let you go as far as you did? Oh, *anata*, I wanted you!" she cried. "I couldn't help myself, being alone with you in this beautiful place. We Japanese have a proverb about the hounds of passion. Well, those hounds were hot on my trail tonight, Neil. I couldn't shake them off."

"Has your father chosen the man you are to marry?"

"Yes."

"Do you love him?"

Her answer was a sudden explosion of breath. "I *hate* him!"

Later, under the mosquito net, Ai moved closer to Neil. "I'm sorry, Neil. Truly, I am. It would have been wonderful, I'm sure."

Curtly, he said, "Good night, Ai."

Moving still closer, she kissed him on the back of his neck, her tongue as soft and warm as a kitten's.

"Neil, I want to tell you how they bury a daimyo's wife, you being always so interested in Japanese customs."

"Well, how do they bury her?"

"In a crypt in a mausoleum."

"Oh?"

"After a seven-jade funeral."

"What does that mean?" Neil asked, becoming interested despite himself.

"When a daimyo's wife dies, they put a piece of jade in each of her seven body openings to pay her entry fee into Takamagahara, the Shinto heaven."

Neil was silent.

"Are you counting openings?" she asked, smiling.

"I'm sure a seven-jade funeral is very nice, but why are you telling me this?"

"I wanted you to know about the jade and the *seven* openings."

"I see." Neil rolled away, determined to go to sleep.

Two minutes, then three passed.

"Neil, if I should die while looking for your Anne, would you give me a seven-jade funeral?"

"I don't have even one piece of jade, Ai, so how could I?"

Ai sounded as bitter as Neil was earlier. "Well, even if you had seven pieces of jade, it wouldn't do me any good."

"Why?"

"Because you wouldn't know where to find all the openings."

Next morning, Neil awakened before Ai.

He made a fire, watered the pack horse, and walked into the brush to relieve himself. Then, he aroused Ai.

"You slept late," he said coldly.

"I couldn't seem to fall asleep last night," Ai said, rubbing her eyes.

"Was your conscience bothering you?"

"No, but I was troubled by a question. It kept me awake."

"What was it?"

"Tell me the truth, Neil," she said, coming to her feet. "Are all Americans as stupid as you?"

Next day, the trail along the meandering Ima River was flat, but the following day was the first of four during which they went steadily up and down mountains rising progressively in elevation. At places, the trail—if one existed at all—was so steep they transferred their baggage from Hana to their own backs. Then the little horse rubbed her nose against Ai's back and gave voice to a long, soft neigh that to Neil sounded like a shudder of relief.

From their height, they could see the Mikuni Range stretching out, peak after lofty peak, to the west and southwest in unending magnificence. The rain that had plagued them until the Ima River crossing had given up its pursuit. Now glorious summer weather, its heat tempered by the elevation, favored Ai and Neil for the rest of their journey. He shivered to think what it would have been like to climb these slippery mountain trails in a driving rain.

One morning five days later, after pulling and pushing Hana upward for an hour, they came to a tunnel, its entrance concealed by brush. Pushing through the foliage, Ai led the way inside. The tunnel was just high enough for little Hana to walk into, but Macneil had to stoop over to pass through the short, dark interior.

Suddenly, they emerged into brilliant sunshine. They had

reached the hidden valley that was their destination, the hide-
away of Ai's uncle and other Koga clan members.

CHAPTER 15

The mountain camp of the *funa-kainin*

From the east, a stream flowed into the isolated valley and forked halfway through it. Between its two branches stood eight buildings of varying sizes, all with thatch roofs. A dozen people moved about. Without his spyglass, Neil could not make out much about them.

The path from the mouth of the tunnel led off to the right along a ledge that broadened to take in a wooded area with thirty or so pine trees. From the trees, it wound down the steep slope into the valley far below.

"Is this your uncle's home?" Neil asked.

"Yes. His name is Tomoharu Koga."

"Let me rest for a few minutes. Then we'll go down and meet him."

"No."

"No?"

"You stay here." Ai started unloading Hana and making camp.

"Are you going to tell me why? I thought we came here to ask for his help in finding Anne and Margaret."

"That's right, but we in the Koga clan have sworn never to bring outsiders into our private places."

"I see."

"I'll go tell him about you and ask for his help, but you must stay here. It's a strict rule."

"When can he find out something?"

"Neil," she said, placing a hand on his arm, "be patient. I have other matters to be concerned with. No one here or in Amakusa knows about my brother's death."

"Sorry, Ai. I forgot."

"I have no other brothers. If father dies and I have no sons, they will have to make me head of the Koga clan."

"William Amanuma told me women were never allowed to become heads of anything in Japan."

"It has been that way under the Tokugawas with their Confucian ethics, but it was not always that way, nor is it with us *funa-kainin*. We are outside Tokugawa authority."

"Will you have new responsibilities at once?"

"My uncle here may think he should be next in line to head the clan after my father. He might even...but no, I won't even think that. Anyway, I'll have other things to worry about for a day or two."

Ai helped Neil set up camp and find a place to let Hana graze, then showed him where they could get water from a spring.

"Will your uncle and his people know I'm up here?"

Ai said they would.

Wondering how long he would have to wait, Neil said, "I wish I had something to do to pass the time."

Ai thought for a moment, then brought out three star-shaped pieces of metal from an inner pocket in her robe.

"Practice throwing these," she said.

"Throwing them?"

"Watch."

With flicks of her wrist so fast Neil could not follow the motions, Ai threw the three stars at a pine tree twenty feet away. All three stuck in the pine bark side by side in perfect alignment. Neil was dumbfounded by her speed and accuracy.

The stars were flat metal pieces six inches in diameter. Each had six needle-sharp points. When thrown, they spun through the air so at least one point had to stick into whatever the star struck. Ai said they could penetrate two inches into flesh but would kill only if they drove deep into an eye or a jugular vein. Neil was certain they would be most painful and possibly disabling.

"Don't worry about me," Ai said. "I may be gone two or three days."

For lack of anything better to do, Macneil spent the day practicing with the throwing stars, which had been constructed to make an eerie whistling sound in flight, as air went through the holes in the base.

By sundown, he had made fair progress. His accuracy was improving, but his arm muscles were sore, so he quit for the day. He took Hana to drink at the spring, then hobbled her in a patch of deep grass. When he returned to their camp, Ai was waiting, red-faced with anger.

"You're back sooner than I expected," Neil said.

"I'll spend the night up here." Her voice was cross, her words clipped.

"Trouble with your uncle?"

"Not yet," she said.

"Then what?"

"My father has sent the man I'm to marry. He's an older man from another clan branch. His name is..." she paused as if scorning to utter the name. "Iki. Shigeo Iki. My uncle says I must marry him soon."

"Are you reconciled to marriage?"

"No," she said. "I told you I hate him."

"Surely, you could refuse." Neil sat down next to her in the gathering dark.

"You don't know much about Japan yet, Neil. There's no question I will have to obey my father."

"Is there no way out of it?"

She was thoughtful for a moment, then said with a bitter laugh. "Only by fleeing Japan could I avoid this marriage."

"Did you ask about finding Anne and Margaret?"

"I told my uncle briefly about you and your search for them and what we learned in Morioka. I told him how you saved my life, so he understands the Koga clan is under an absolute obligation to help. Tomorrow, he will dispatch couriers to the fiefs where we have friends who will give us information. It may take a while."

Neil felt a flood of relief and hope.

"I'll never be able to thank you enough, Ai," he said, putting an arm around her shoulders.

After eating their evening meal, they sat on a ledge overlooking the valley and watched the half-moon rise. For a long while, they were both silent. Neil was lost in thoughts about Anne.

"I wish I could...," Ai began, then stopped.

"Could what?"

"Could leave Japan. Go somewhere. Go anywhere."

Her voice was suddenly plaintive. "Take me away somewhere, Neil?"

"If we had enough money, we could go anywhere, Ai," he said lightly. "I could take you to European capitals, to the Spice Islands, even to the Horn of Africa."

"I could get the money," Ai said seriously.

"You, Ai? How?"

After a silent moment, she said, "This is a secret of the Koga clan, Neil. Many years ago, a Dutch vessel carrying a gold shipment from Nagasaki sank off the Amakusa Islands. All hands were lost. My father saw it sink near the shore but in deep water. Too deep for divers to reach it."

"Are your people the only ones who know the spot?"

Ai nodded. "Just my father and me. Oh, Neil, if I showed it to you, do you think you could get the gold?"

"*I* might not be able to but someone in America or in Europe may have invented a way for men to go into deep water and bring things back up."

"If you did recover the treasure, would you—would you take me away from Japan?"

So eager, so pitifully intent were her eyes, Neil was obliged to promise he would. Only later did he realize he had not thought about Anne at all.

"Ai!" came a growl from behind them in the darkness. Neil almost fell off the ledge.

"It's Shigeo Iki," Ai whispered, rising slowly.

As Iki walked up to Ai, Neil could see him more clearly. He was, as Ai had said, older—about thirty-seven. His build was sturdy, his head partly shaven, and his face arrogant and badly pockmarked. He carried a long sword and was dressed in an open jacket reaching to mid-thigh. Other than that, he wore only a loin cloth revealing a half-healed wound on his left kneecap, which caused him to favor that leg.

Although he had a topknot, he did not carry a second shorter sword, so Neil doubted he could be a true samurai. His face was set in a deep scowl.

"Come back to the valley with me," he demanded.

"I'll stay here tonight," Ai answered, her voice mild. Neil knew well that tone of voice, which promised turmoil, possibly violence.

"Are you defying me?" he asked, his coarse voice rising.

"You are not my husband yet, Shigeo," she said.

"I will be."

"Until then," she said, "I will do whatever I like."

Neil moved up beside Ai, wishing his pistol were closer at hand.

"I will lose face if you stay here tonight with this barbarian." He spat at the American's feet.

"He saved my life, Shigeo."

"And that is the only reason I haven't already opened wind holes in his guts."

"Leave us be, Shigeo," Ai warned, a dangerous glint showing in her narrowed eyes.

He slapped her hard with his open hand, knocking her flat.

Without thinking, Neil struck the man with his fist. Delivered with all the American's strength, the blow probably broke Iki's nose, which gushed blood.

Shigeo Iki may not have been a samurai, but he was fast with his sword. Before Neil could move again, he had unsheathed that blade and raised it over his head.

CHAPTER 16

Snarling with rage, his eyes popping out of his head, Shigeo Iki set himself to deliver the fatal slash.

The flickering light from the campfire flashed on the raised sword as the American gathered himself to spring at Iki in an attempt to grapple him to the ground and disarm him.

From the corner of an eye, Neil saw Ai, a mere blur, unsheathe the knife in her sash and leap onto Iki's back. While her left hand yanked his head back, the fingers gouging into Iki's eye sockets, she touched the razor-like edge of her knife to his exposed throat.

Iki stopped dead in his tracks, as if he had been struck by a bolt of lightning.

"Drop the sword," Ai grated into his ear.

It fell to the ground.

"Now back off."

He obeyed, walking unsteadily, his eyes on the night sky above him, which was like the face of onrushing death. Ai clung to his back like a wildcat climbing a tree.

"Now, Shigeo," she spoke in that soft voice, "say it again. Just what was it you were going to do to this foreigner?"

"Nothing. Nothing at all, Ai."

"Come now, Shigeo. I heard you say something about opening wind holes..." Ai used the word *kaza-ana*. "...in his guts, didn't I?"

"I think you're wrong, Ai. I didn't say anything like that."

"Maybe it was just the wind blowing in the trees, eh?"

"Yes, that must be it. The wind blowing in the trees."

The night was perfectly still.

"Or maybe just meaningless wind from your mouth. Could that be it, Shigeo? Were you farting from your mouth again? That's a vulgar habit you have, Shigeo."

"Yes, Ai. Just a fart...from my mouth." Shigeo's voice was a mere croak, as the knife pressed deeper into the skin covering his windpipe.

Macneil thought her knife was already drawing blood, although he could not be sure, because the man's smashed nose was dripping blood over his chin onto his neck.

Ai dropped from his back to the ground but kept her knife at the ready. "Leave, Shigeo," she said. "I'll be back tomorrow. Maybe."

Pale and shaken, with hatred burning in his eyes, Shigeo stumbled back on his game leg to where he had dropped his sword. "Wait till after we're married," he blustered, recovering some of his bravado. "Then you'll learn your manners from a true Japanese and not from a barbarian dog."

"I would rather crawl under the *futon* with a snake than with you," Ai jeered as he limped down the dark path.

"You have no choice. Your father has already made his decision."

That night, Ai and Neil slept side by side. Although the elevation was higher, the advancing summer heat permitted mosquitoes and other insects to breed, so they still hung the mosquito net over them.

Neil wondered if Ai, after such a violent dispute with her fiance, would be more approachable. It was worth a try.

Ai gave Neil a lingering kiss as she got ready to descend into the valley the next morning. "Thank you so much," she whispered, bowing her head.

"Thanks? For what, Ai?"

"For what you did last night."

"I do not understand. *You* are thanking *me?*"

"In Japan, when a man gives a woman sexual satisfaction—in whatever fashion—it's good manners for her to thank him. Didn't Anne thank you for releasing her from her virginity on that muddy river bank?"

The very thought of a muddy Anne Macneil bowing and thanking him for what he had done to her convulsed Neil with wild laughter. "No, of course not," he finally managed to gasp.

Ai was first puzzled, then indignant. "What an ill-mannered woman you've chosen to wed!"

Sobering, Neil took Ai in his arms for another long kiss. "Anyway, what you and I did was wonderful, Ai." In a ragged whisper, he added, "I can't wait till you come back. Maybe then we can go further and I really will—what did you say?—release you from your virginity."

She gave him an impish look. "I've just had a marvelous idea, Neil."

"What?"

"Your Anne and Shigeo..." She paused to spit. "...seem to be well-matched. Maybe I could send him to look for Anne. Isn't that a splendid idea?" She turned to go. "And, oh yes, watch out for *mamushi*."

Neil did not think Ai's idea amusing in the least.

It so disturbed him he forgot to ask what a *mamushi* was.

Perched on a boulder in the warm morning sunlight, Neil watched the deadly sprite of the forests, as he knew he would forever think of her, making her agile way down the path to the valley, where eight men, not counting three instructors, were practicing the stealthy arts and skills of the *funa-kainin*. Closer to the main building, two boys were wrestling. Looking through his glass at them, he saw that they were not boys, but midgets.

As he followed Ai's downhill progress with his eyes, he shook his head in wonder at her talents and determination. In Neil's mind, there was not the slightest doubt she would have slit her fiance's throat last night if he had not dropped his sword when she ordered him to.

"How can he still want to marry her?" Neil asked himself.

Ai's skills with weapons such as the knife and throwing star and bow and arrow must have come, Macneil figured, from the same training being undergone by the eight men below. Shifting the direction of his glass, he studied them in turn.

They trained in the open space around the thatched-roof buildings, with their three instructors walking back and forth shouting and pointing. The teachers, men of middle age, carried bamboo rods with which they poked and lashed their students to rouse them to more strenuous efforts. The students appeared to be in their early twenties or younger. The training included archery, throwing stars, broad jumping, climbing the face of a vertical cliff, breaking boards with heel kicks, plunging stiffened fingers into tubs of what appeared to be sand, and swimming under water in a small lake.

At mid-morning, Ai walked out from the main building, stopped, and shaded her eyes to look up in Neil's direction. He waved, hoping she could see him. *Why*, he thought, *does life quicken its pace and colors became more vivid whenever I see her?*

Walking among the training sites, Ai seemed to be giving advice to the staff. From what Neil had seen her do, he knew she could well have been their superior in those skills.

At noon, she called everyone to her side and spoke to them for half an hour. All during the lecture, if that was what it was, she appeared to be demonstrating certain techniques, for she spun around, leaped, crawled, squatted, twisted, and went through the motions of throwing stars and drawing bows. She made the others, even the staff, imitate her motions and postures, tapping first one, then another with her bamboo rod— though Neil could not tell whether in praise or criticism. Like the others, Ai was dressed in a short blue jacket tied at the waist with a black sash, knee-length pants, and straw sandals. After their frenetic acrobatics of the night before, Neil was amazed she could move about at all.

At last, the lecture must have ended, for Ai led the others into a thatched-roof building.

Jumping down off the boulder from which he had been watching, Macneil stretched his stiff muscles, wishing for even half Ai's agility and skill, and set about making a small fire with nearly smokeless hard wood for his noon meal.

After eating, he took the three throwing stars from his pack and began practicing with them. The small clearing being hemmed in on three sides by pines, he threw the stars first at one tree, then at another on all three sides. He could hit a tree within fifteen feet, but his aim became less reliable when the distance lengthened to twenty-five feet or more.

In the middle of the afternoon, Neil napped and rested his throwing arm, then started practicing again and continued until dusk. He calculated that he had thrown the stars at least three hundred times, and that one-third of the throws missed the target tree and had to be retrieved from the brush beyond.

As darkness fell, tired and disgusted with missing so many, he left the stars sticking in the bark of the trees where they had last been imbedded. If his arm muscles permitted, he would begin practice again the next morning, so he thought he might as well leave them there as stow them away in his pack.

If his arm muscles were too sore, he could get out his pad and pencil and sketch the training facility in the valley below. Having neglected his sketching since landing in Japan, he felt the urge to record what he had seen—the crucifixion scene, the samurais in pursuit of Ai, the Ima River in flood, the death of the fisherman, Ai upon her return from an afternoon in a manure tank, and much else.

After his evening meal, Neil spread out his upper and lower *futon*, drank some water, and then sat and stared into the fire embers for a while, thinking about Anne. As always, he imagined her and Margaret undergoing privation, hunger, extreme physical discomfort, and even pain.

At last, he shook off these dark thoughts and rose to gather an armful of green firewood. With the smoke from the green wood, he hoped to be able to keep at bay the occasional mosquito. He would drape the mosquito net over the stakes at both ends of the *futon*, but the rough usage given the net had torn gaps on both sides through which the insects could get in. Ai had promised to sew up the holes, but she had not gotten around to it.

With the net in position and the green firewood producing a respectable cloud of smoke, Neil made a final inspection around the clearing, noting in passing the location of the three throwing stars that reflected the flames off their polished metal sides.

Flexing his right arm, Neil pulled one star from the tree bark and threw it across the clearing at the pine tree where another star was already imbedded. To his pleased surprise, it hit the pine not more than three inches from its mate.

More satisfied now with his progress, he lifted the mosquito net and crawled in between the two *futon*. On the verge of falling asleep, he remembered what Ai had said that morning.

"Watch out for *mamushi*, Neil."

Now what the devil was a *mamushi*? Given the surroundings, it seemed reasonable to suppose that a *mamushi* was a living creature, though whether animal or fowl or insect, he had no way of knowing. He started to get up and pore over his dictionaries by the firelight to see what he could learn but decided he was too weary.

Fatigue and sleep caught up with him.

Neil Macneil dreamt about a woman. Completely naked, she seemed to be lowering herself onto his *futon* and was about to stretch herself out beside him. Though he could not see her face in the darkness, Neil muttered, "Darling," and opened his arms to embrace her. As he did, he felt a painful pinch on his forearm and heard a hissed warning.

"Be quiet and be still, you barbarian fool!"

Tautly awake now, he knew danger threatened and that it was Ai there under the net warning him. Immobile, he waited for her to act.

Placing her fingers over Neil's mouth, she leaned down to his left ear and whispered, "There's a *mamushi* right beside you. On the *futon*."

He didn't dare turn his head to look.

Ai's voice was tense, low. "When I throw the *futon* over it, you roll toward me. Be quick! Ready?"

Neil blinked his eyes twice.

"Now!"

As she threw the left side of the *futon* over the right, he rolled toward her.

Clasping her lithe body to him, he rolled out from under the net and over to the edge of the fire, ending up on top of her.

"You're heavy, barbarian. Get off me."

"What happened? What's a *mamushi*?"

"Will you get off me?"

Neil rolled a little to one side, feeling the warmth of the fire on his back as he did.

Testily, she said, "Now you can also remove your arms."

"For God's sake, Ai, just tell me what a *mamushi* is."

"It's a *hebi*," she said. Neil knew *hebi* meant snake. "A *dokuja*," she added, but he did not know the word. "Its bite will kill you," she explained, so then he knew *dokuja* must mean poisonous snake. "Who were you dreaming about? You called someone 'darling!' You taught me that English word."

Contrite, he said, "You saved my life again, Ai."

"What color was the hair of the woman in your dream?"

The dream came back to Neil in vivid detail. Sitting up, he took her hands. "Her hair was black, Ai."

Her hands gripped his painfully. "Are you sure?"

Her glistening eyes plumbed the depths of his soul. At last, she made a throaty sound somewhere between frustration and satisfaction. Rising, she went looking for a stick.

"Don't get blood on the *futon*," he warned her, knowing what she was about to do.

She made another sound in her throat, this one closer to contempt. With the stick, Ai lifted the mosquito net, then turned back the *futon*.

The *mamushi*—about two feet long—slithered off the *futon* toward the surrounding pine trees. Ai waited till it was eight or nine feet away. Then, with amazing swiftness, she took a throwing star from an inside pocket and threw it at the gliding snake.

Catching the snake behind its head, the star pinned it to the earth. Bending over, Ai pulled the star free and at the same time gripped the still-writhing snake's neck. Her mood turning suddenly playful, she tried to hand Neil the snake.

"You keep it," Neil said sourly. "You probably have some use for it."

"As a matter of fact," she said, crushing the snake's head with a rock, "we put *mamushi* meat in a sake jar for six months and then drink the sake. It's a restorative."

"A what?"

"A restorative. It gives a man the strength to pleasure his wife three times every night."

Neil wondered how a virgin would know about such marital details. "What about you and Shigeo Iki? What happened?"

She skinned the *mamushi*. "My uncle has arranged a truce."

"So you made up?"

"I did *not* make up," she growled.

"But will you marry him?"

She didn't answer.

After examining both *futon* carefully to be sure no more *mamushi* were underneath, Ai lifted one side of the mosquito net and motioned to Neil to crawl under it. She followed and showed him how to tuck the net under the edges of the *futon* from the inside so no other unwelcome intruders would come calling that night.

Then, stretching out close by Neil, she pulled the *kake-buton* up over them. With her back to him, she settled herself for what remained of the night.

After a moment, however, Ai rolled over. "Neil," she said, her mouth only inches from his, "the bandits who kidnapped your women may sell them separately."

"I should think so," he muttered. "I doubt that anyone would want to put up with two concubines."

"We cannot be certain about that, either."

"Anyway, what's your point, Ai?"

"When we find one or the other—*if* we do—how could anyone but you tell them apart?"

"Well, Margaret is maybe an inch taller. Both have blonde hair, but Margaret's is a shade darker, I think. Both have blue eyes. Margaret may be five or six pounds heavier and has bigger...." He forgot the word for the female breast, so he reached over and touched Ai's. She slapped his hand away.

"*Oppai*," Ai said stiffly, "and I don't want you touching mine while telling me all about those of your precious Anne."

"Why does it irritate you when I talk about Anne?"

"I'll let you figure that out by yourself."

"Anne is prettier, although Margaret is pretty, too, but Anne is...well, she's...," he stumbled on, wishing he knew the word for breathtaking in Japanese.

"Nothing you've said so far helps at all, barbarian. We'll need something more definite if we are to tell the difference. Doesn't your darling Anne have six fingers or sharp-pointed ears or something like that?"

"Everything about her is nearly perfect."

"Including body odor and fish-belly skin color?"

"*Anne has no body odor!*"

"Did you ever bathe with her?"

"Of course not."

"In Japan, men and women often bathe together."

"We're not heathens. You are."

Even as he said that, Neil remembered that Ai was a Christian.

"It's better than not bathing at all."

"I told you, Ai..." Neil was beginning to shout. "...that Anne *bathes!* Quite often, I believe."

"And you can't think of a way to tell them apart?"

He forced himself to be calm and think. "Well, Anne does have that scar on her neck under her right ear. About as long as my thumb knuckle."

"Did she get cut in a drunken brawl?"

"She told me she fell off her horse while fox hunting. She was thrown into a clump of brush. The sharp end of a broken branch made a cut in her neck."

"Fox hunting? How odd! Do Scots eat foxes?"

"Of course not! We just chase them."

"Why?"

"Well, we put on red coats and white pants and take a drink called a stirrup cup and let some dogs loose. Then we mount horses and cry 'Tallyho!' or 'Yoicks!' and the chase is on."

"But *why?*"

"What the devil difference does it make, why?" Neil shouted. "We just do it!"

With that, they both subsided, and Neil took himself in hand and vowed not to yell at Ai again, no matter what the provocation. He already owed her too much ever to repay. And he might owe her much more before Anne was once again in his arms.

In the heat of the argument, Neil had forgotten their passionate intimacy of the previous night. Evidently Ai had, too, for when he laid a hand on her arm, she shook it off and moved toward the far edge of the *futon*.

CHAPTER 17

During the next two weeks, the hot summer sun beat down on Japan. In the lowlands, farmers worked their rice paddies and vegetable plots in the sweltering heat. At Neil's camp above the *funa-kainin's* hidden valley, however, the force of the sun was partly disarmed by breezes from the higher peaks to the west.

Only thrice did Ai make the climb up from the valley floor to bring Neil supplies. Each time, she seemed distraught and weary, but she would not share her problems with Neil. His questions about Anne and Margaret only seemed to sour her mood, but he had to ask. She had nothing to report.

When idle, Neil found himself thinking too much about his sister and fiancee and how they might be suffering, so he tried to fill every minute of his time. But there was only so much he could do after finishing the camp chores.

Neil devoted mornings to the throwing stars. Without many more weeks of practice, he knew he could not throw the sharp-spiked wheels as well as Ai, but after ten days, he could at least hit whichever pine tree trunk he aimed at.

He borrowed Ai's bow and quiver of arrows and shot the arrows at pine cones imbedded in soft earth mounds thirty or so yards away.

He found the Japanese bows were made so the point where the archer gripped them with his left hand was not in the exact middle of the bow but farther down. The upper portion made up two-thirds of the length of the weapon and the lower portion only one-third. The bows were so long that Japanese men, who seemed to average only about five feet, five inches in height, could not have held them in the exact middle without the lower end of the bow digging into the earth. He learned to let the arrow run along the right-hand side instead of the left.

"You people seem to do everything backwards," Neil complained to Ai after supper during her third visit to the camp.

Before the evening meal, she had given him more instruction in using her bow and arrows. On her two previous visits, she had returned to the valley by this hour, so this time Neil hoped she intended to spend the night with him in the camp.

"On the contrary, barbarian, you and your people do everything in ways just the opposite from what is proper and correct."

"And who decides what is correct?"

"Japan is where the sun rises and sets, and Amaterasu no Omikami, the Sun Goddess, dwelt here in these islands. What we do here should set the standard for you natives in primitive lands to follow."

"I thought you believed in the Christian God," Neil said. "Someday maybe you'll come to understand which is the civilized and which the savage culture."

A new look came into her eyes, as she moved closer to him. "And when will that be, Neil? When you take me to those far-off countries?" She dropped her eyes and sat beside him demurely, hands clasped on her legs.

"Your father expects you to marry Shigeo Iki. You cannot do that in Paris or London."

"I think...no, I *know* I would rather be in London."

"Well," Neil said, retreating into fantasy, "if you help me raise that treasure from the Dutch trading vessel sunk off your islands, I'll take you to London and Paris and..." He began ticking off the cities on his fingers. "...Rome and Berlin and New York and Glasgow—yes, by all means, Glasgow. Then San Francisco and—"

"And Fort George in Oregon?" she asked.

"Fort George, dear Ai, is not a city. You would hardly—"

"What did you say?"

"I said Fort George is not—"

"No, no, no. I mean about me."

"Oh, you mean, 'dear Ai'?"

Before Neil knew it, she was in his arms and clinging to him. "Please, please, *please!* Take me there, Neil," she pleaded.

"Where?"

"*Any*where! Just take me with you."

"I thought you were going to marry Shigeo."

"*Stop* talking about that oaf!" There were tears in her eyes. "Will you take me?"

"Will you show me the place where the ship sank?"

"Of course, but can you raise the gold?"

"Who knows? All I can promise is that when I reach Hong Kong—*if* I ever get there—I'll find out about the latest diving equipment. In this age of new inventions—the telegraph, the steam engine, the tin can—surely some new device will let us go down deeper in the sea than man has ever gone before."

Resignation came over her lovely face. "That will be least a year or so in the future, won't it?"

"I have to find Anne and get to Hong Kong before I can do anything at all. Please understand that."

Ai turned her face away. "And that will be too late for me, I'm afraid."

She was silent and morose as they prepared for sleep.

"Goodnight, Ai," Neil said when they were between their *futon.*

For several minutes, Ai said nothing. Neil thought she had gone to sleep, but suddenly she rolled over and let him put his arms around her.

CHAPTER 18

Eighteen days had passed since their arrival in the mountain camp. Neil had just finished his evening meal of rice, dried fish, and *miso* balls when Ai came running into the light of the campfire. She panted with exertion and excitement.

"Neil? Neil!" she cried. "Wonderful news! Your people have come."

His heart stopped.

"My people?"

"The Americans! The American fleet. They call them the 'black ships.' They're anchored off Uraga, near Edo. They have already been there for..." Taking her arms from around his neck, she counted the days on her fingers, little finger first. "...for maybe five or six days. We'll have to leave as soon as possible. You must get ready!"

"Wait, Ai, slow down!" Neil said, holding her close to restrain her excitement. "What do you...I don't understand at all. The American fleet? *What* American fleet?"

Ai gulped twice, breathing deeply. "Listen to me, Neil. Just listen, all right?

"The man we sent to Edo—''

"What man?"

"Damn you, listen! We sent a man to Edo, looking for a trace of your precious Anne."

"He found Anne?"

"No, no, NO! No one has found Anne, barbarian! Not yet, but what he *did* find was an American fleet off Uraga."

"Uraga?" Neil repeated. He thought he must have sounded stupid to Ai.

"Yes, Uraga. Shall I write the *kanji* for you, rock-head? It's a tiny port south of Edo. A fleet of huge black ships has come to ask the shogun—or the emperor, we're not sure which—to open

Japan to the outside world."

Neil's excitement grew as he realized what this meant. At last, his fellow Americans had come knocking at Japan's portals to ask, he supposed, for decent treatment for whalers and shipwrecked persons and for coal and provisions when needed. Surely they would also demand the release of all Americans now in Japanese custody.

William Amanuma had predicted this day would come, but Neil had not dreamed it would come so soon.

"When shall we go?" he asked.

"I thought it out on the way up here just now. Sit down." Ai led him to a rock ten feet from the fire. "I couldn't tell you this before, but the truth is, we had almost no chance of finding your women."

This shocked Neil. "What do you mean?"

"There are too many places where your women could have been taken, and our resources are too few to do much good. The shogun and many of the *fudai* daimyo are hostile to us and—"

"But I thought—"

"We *do* have some reliable people in a few fiefs, but not in many. Just think, Neil," she said, gripping his wrist, "There are 265 fiefs! We can't possibly—"

"All right, all right. I see your point."

"So, if an American fleet is knocking at Japan's closed doors, you should ask them also to demand the return of Anne and Margaret."

Dear God, how he longed to enlist that American fleet in his quest for Anne! Until now, even in his wildest dreams, Neil had never come anywhere near the idea of an entire American fleet coming to Japan.

"We'll have to reach Uraga as soon as possible," Ai said, pacing back and forth. "We learned that Perry—the American admiral—will not stay there much longer."

"How long will it take us?" The thought that the fleet might set sail before they could get to Uraga was intolerable.

"A couple of days. We'll go down the river by boat the first day. The current is fast with many rapids, so we can make good time. Besides, there are no barrier stations on the river."

"And then what?"

"We may have to do a lot of running."

"Couldn't we hire two horses?"

"A begging priest in a basket hat and a prostitute nun racing across the countryside on horseback?" Ai's snort was contemptuous. "Don't ask such foolish questions, barbarian. Only first-class samurais are allowed to ride horses. We can use them as pack animals, but that's all."

"I'd better get packed," Neil said. "I'll take my pistol and dictionaries and sketch pad and the kilt and bagpipe."

"Leave behind the infernal instrument that sounds like a cat being tortured."

"My bagpipe? Never!"

Ai shrugged. "You're the one who has to carry it."

"What should I do with what I'm wearing?" He pointed to the loose, knee-length trousers and the jacket he had worn aboard the whaler. On his feet were the straw sandals Ai had provided.

"Keep everything. Wear the priest's robe over your jacket. I'll get you another basket hat."

After Ai had gone, Neil threw more branches on the fire and set about putting together what he would take with him. He stowed the precious dictionaries in his sea bag, followed by the kilt and bagpipe. These alone almost filled the sack, but there was room for the pistol.

He laid out his *komuso* outfit, complete except for the basket hat. Then there were the three throwing stars. Two were still stuck side by side in a pine trunk just above head level. He stood up to get them.

As he did, he heard someone approaching on the path from the *funa-kainin* training camp below. It would be Ai, he figured. She must have forgotten something.

But it was not Ai who stepped into the light of the crackling campfire.

It was Shigeo Iki, with a scowl on his face and a burning anger in his eyes that told Neil he had not come just to bid the American a pleasant farewell.

A daimyo's castle southeast of Nagoya

The sun had been in the sky two hours when Anne Macneil slid open the door and changed her slippers. She was wearing a blue and white *yukata* robe with a flower and leaf design.

Margaret Macneil lay listless on her *futon* in the stifling room. A tray holding bowls of *miso* soup, rice, seaweed, and pickled cabbage had been placed on the *tatami* beside her. She had not touched her breakfast.

"I'll open the other shutter," Anne said, "and let a breeze through here." As she did, she looked out from their upper-level castle room at the bay to the north. On the beach below, fishermen's wives in nondescript garb spread tiny fish to dry on straw mats. From the castle courtyard rose a medley of the day's sounds: laughter, orders to hurry, clopping horses' hooves, a woman's shrill protest, the cries of children chasing each other. It was the same as the day before and the day before that. It would be the same tomorrow.

"Where did you spend last night?" Margaret asked.

"With the daimyo."

"Was it awful?"

"It was bad enough, I suppose," Anne said, sitting at the low table and pouring herself a cup of Margaret's breakfast tea. *Anyway,* she thought, *I endured it.*

"Did you go with the visiting samurai from Nagoya last night?"

Margaret nodded numbly.

"What happened?"

"He...beat me." Margaret's voice quavered.

Anne's heart filled with pity for her cousin, who had grown old long before her time. "Margaret," she said, "it's been two years and four months since we left Fort George."

"I know."

"And it's been almost two years since we were shipwrecked up north." Anne's eyes filled with sudden tears.

Sitting up on the *futon,* Margaret clasped Anne to her bosom. "Now we have only each other, Anne."

"I know," Anne said, wiping her eyes. "That's what I want to say. We must be brave, and we must adapt. We must *survive,* Margaret. I've given up hope that Neil or our fathers will ever find us."

"Oh, don't say that! We must cling to the hope that they will."

"But they may think we drowned," Anne said.

"Maybe my father didn't drown. He was still alive in the other lifeboat when we last saw him, wasn't he?"

"If he didn't drown, he may have come ashore, too, and now either be dead or in a prison."

"No, they wouldn't keep him. They only keep us to...use us. I think they would have mercy and let him go."

Anne laughed in scorn. "Let him go? I don't think these people know what mercy is. Besides, how would they let him go? Just shove him outside a castle gate? No, Margaret, we must face reality. We may be here for the rest of our lives, and we might as well make the best of it. We can moan and cry and feel sorry for ourselves or we can lift our chins and determine to try to get a little pleasure from our lives."

"Like *this?*" Margaret asked, shocked. "Why, Anne, we're no better than those women on the San Francisco streets who live by selling their bodies."

"If you mean whores, Margaret, then say whores. There's no room for the speech of refined young ladies in a place like this."

CHAPTER 19

Iki's first grated words—"*Kono chikusho*"—confirmed his visit was no social call. By calling Macneil a four-legged beast, he left no doubt he intended the American serious harm. His right hand gripped the sword at his waist.

Backing away, Macneil moved nearer the pine tree with the two throwing stars stuck in its bark. He wished he were closer to the pistol in his seaman's bag, but a *shiriken*—ah, ha!—he had remembered Ai's word for the deadly stars—would have to do.

"Ai is only going to show me the way to Edo," Macneil said. He stepped backward, nearer to the pine. "She will be back. Ai and I—we're only friends."

Iki growled. "You have made me a laughingstock among our clan." He advanced. "You have thrown mud on my face. No true samurai could tolerate such an insult to his honor."

"You're no samurai," Macneil jeered, seeing it was useless to continue appeasing him. "You have no daimyo master. You don't even carry two swords. And where did you get your family name? I'm sure no daimyo gave it to you."

Iki's blade flashed in the firelight. The taunt about his family name had hit a tender spot. Peasants and merchants had no right to family names unless they were given to them through a special dispensation by the daimyo they served. Ai had a family name only because her family had been both samurais and daimyos, until the Shimabara Rebellion.

As Iki advanced, Macneil retreated farther from the fire, hoping his senses guided him well. He took another step backward, and his back came up against a tree trunk. He prayed it was the pine he sought.

"What...what are you going to do?" Macneil let a quaver enter his voice. "Look, I'm helpless. I have no weapons." He raised his arms overhead to emphasize his helplessness.

"I'm going to spill your canine guts on the ground, you fish slime. With you dead, Ai won't leave here and I won't lose face."

"But what will you do with my body?" Macneil asked. "When Ai finds it here tomorrow morning, she'll know you killed me."

Macneil groped in the semi-darkness above his head for the stars.

"Not far from here is a cliff that drops straight into a thick forest no one ever goes into. I'll toss you over that cliff. In a week, badgers and foxes will have eaten your stinking hairy flesh and carried off your bones."

He stood only ten feet from Macneil.

That's close enough, Macneil thought. *One or two more steps and he'll charge.*

"I'll throw your belongings down after you," Iki went on, carried away by his clever plan. "I told no one where I was going, and there will be no trace of you. Ai will believe you could not wait for her, that you started for Edo on your own."

"But she will know better than that."

At that instant Macneil's exploring fingers touched the throwing stars.

Snatching them from the bark, he hurled one at the mask of hate that was Iki's face, catching the charging *funa-kainin* in the left eye. One of the needle-like points penetrated his eyeball. With a horrible groan, Iki dropped his sword and wrenched the star free. Blood flowed from his eye socket.

By then, Macneil had sent the second star on its way after the first.

The second struck Iki in the throat, on the Adam's apple—what the Japanese called "Buddha in the throat"—stopping his groans. His voice was a faint choking rasp as he tottered this way and that, disoriented in extreme pain.

Macneil dodged around him and snatched up his sword. Iki had dropped to his knees in the praying position and was trying to pry the second star from his throat.

Macneil raised the sword in both hands and brought it down with all his strength on the back of the bowed neck.

The sword sliced through flesh, nerves, and bone. The head dropped off neatly. Blood spurted from the neck as the torso toppled forward, splattering the pine needles that made a soft carpet beneath the trees.

Tossing aside the sword, Macneil grabbed Iki's feet and pulled his body into the trees.

Untying the long sash from around Iki's waist, Macneil looped one end around the man's feet, tying the other end to his own waist. He forced his way into the head-high brush under the trees fringing the camp site, dragging the body behind him. He crashed through the tightly woven thicket and stumbled along for five minutes, then untied the sash from his waist, and picked up a fallen branch, using it as a cane to probe his way through the clinging foliage and the darkness.

Abruptly, the branch lost contact with the ground two feet ahead. He inched forward until his right foot found the cliff. By then, his eyes had grown more accustomed to the dark, and he could half see, half sense a vast emptiness. Retracing his path, he found Iki's body and dragged it to the cliff.

Macneil rolled him over, and without waiting to hear him fall, fought his way back through the dense brush to the camp. Besides the blood, the only traces of Iki were his sword and his head. Macneil struggled through the clutching foliage once more to drop them over the cliff.

When he got back to the camp, a reaction to the bloody incident set in. Neil was exhausted and sickened by another death. Shaking, he sank to the ground by the fire.

After a while, he got slowly to his feet and walked about collecting the bloody pine needles, which he carried deeper into the surrounding woods. He sprinkled fresh dirt over the spot where Iki had bled, and carefully went over the entire camp, seeking anything he might have overlooked, any clue to tell others Iki had been there and died there. Even though the man said he had told no one where he was going, he was sure to be missed and sought tomorrow.

Satisfied, Macneil stretched out under the mosquito net and tried to sleep. Tomorrow, he would race to catch the American fleet at Uraga. Hope and excitement filled him at the thought that he would at last be taking positive action that could lead to Anne and Margaret's rescue.

His last thought before sleep overcame him was that he had done Ai a kindness by killing the brutish lout she was to have wed.

CHAPTER 20

Beyond Edo to the port of Uraga

It was almost dusk next day when their boat reached the *shukuba* or post station town of Konosu. Ai and Neil had come more than half the distance to Edo. The two boatmen—one standing in the bow, the other braced at the stern—had guided them through the many rapids and swift currents with consummate skill. Often, they barely averted what appeared to be certain collisions against midstream boulders with deft, powerful shoves of their bamboo poles. In high spirits, they shouted warnings and encouragement back and forth all day while Ai and Neil sat huddled in miserable silence in the deep mid-section of the twenty-six-foot craft.

The leaping, racing rapids crashing against the boulders made conversation impossible, while Neil's new basket hat and the high sides of the river craft combined with the curtain of spray to ruin any chance he might have had to see the countryside they passed through.

But the *komuso* cape and the basket hat, while limiting visibility, protected Neil from the drenching Ai got. Like a sulky half-drowned kitten, she huddled before him, scowling at his comparatively dry and more comfortable condition.

The boatmen had expected Ai and Neil to part company with them just beyond the town of Konosu, but, although the land was flat thereabouts, the river current was nonetheless faster than a man could walk.

"If we leave the boat here, we'll have to sleep somewhere, even if only for a few hours," Ai said in a low voice.

"You're right," he said. "We'd be better off to sleep aboard while the boat is floating on toward Edo with the current."

Ai bargained again with the head boatman. Neil saw her pass him an oblong gold coin. Nodding, the man gave her change in silver *bu*. He agreed to pole them down river through the night, but refused to go further the next morning, no matter what the enticement.

Dry and rested after the extra night aboard in calm water, they felt the boat nudge its prow into an earth bank at Tatebayashi early the following morning. The boatman in the stern used his pole to steady the craft against the bank so his passengers could step ashore with ease. Having poled all night, both men, clad only in *fundoshi* or breechcloths, had exhausted the exuberance with which they had ridden through the rapids the day before and now appeared sodden with fatigue.

Neil and Ai breakfasted on rice and *miso* soup aboard, courtesy of the boatmen, who also gave them four rice balls peppered with sesame seeds to eat later in the day. Neil had spoken no words within their hearing at any time during the voyage down river. He kept his silence under the basket hat until he and Ai were well started on their way along the road toward Edo.

Despite the curious looks the boatmen had given Neil, Ai did not think they had any genuine suspicions that the pair were other than what she had told them: a mendicant priest on a pilgrimage accompanied by a serving woman.

Ai and Neil spent a few minutes tightening belts, straps, and sashes for the final leg of their race to Uraga and, if the American fleet was still at anchor there, to Commodore Perry's four black ships.

"I wish I could throw away this damned hood," Neil grumbled.

"We would get no more than one *ri* without it."

Ai tied Neil's sea bag more securely to his back, so his arms would be free for what lay ahead. In her hands, she carried only the short fighting staff Neil had seen her use in training her *funa-kainin* apprentices. She wore straw sandals with a thong between her big toe and its neighbor, leggings, indigo-hued pantaloons tied just below the knee, a light-blue jacket, a sash, and a large scarf wrapped around her head covering, when adjusted, much of her face. Since Neil too wore a hood, no one who saw them now would recognize them again from their faces.

They started off at a fast pace while Ai described their route.

"We have to cover twelve *ri* as fast as we can, Neil-san. The road is flat and reasonably straight most of the way, but we will have to make two detours to avoid the *sekisho*—the barrier stations. I can guide us around all the villages and towns along the way except one. When we get to that one—Kawaguchi—we'll have to go straight through. Going around it would take too long, and I'm afraid our time may be running out."

"What if we don't get there before the American ships leave?"

"I haven't given much thought to that," she muttered. "I suppose we would have to find a fishing boat to take us to Amakusa, where you would have the Koga clan's protection." Her face brightened as if she liked that prospect.

A pang of guilt chewed at Macneil with this reminder about her fiance's fate, followed quickly by the pleasing thought that never would Ai have to spend her nights on a *futon* next to the gross Shigeo Iki.

"Anyway, we *will* make it," Ai said. She quickened her pace.

For the first hour, the two ran for twenty-five minutes, walked for ten, then ran for another twenty-five. At that early morning hour, the road was deserted, although the farmers were up doing their chores or had gone into the fields around the farmhouses dotting the plain. For the first hour of their race, Neil was even able to remove his hood without fear he would be recognized as a foreigner.

Traffic on the road increased toward mid-morning, forcing Macneil to replace the hood. A few broad-wheeled carts piled high with produce lumbered toward the next town, being both pushed and pulled by farmers in loincloths. Palanquins or *kago* came swinging along, the porters always increasing their pace as they neared anyone to impress viewers with their passenger's importance.

A wandering minstrel playing a discordant melody on a bamboo flute strolled along at a slower pace than the others. Pack-horses, pack-oxen and luggage porters jostled against each other for the right to the center of the rough road. An occasional samurai, probably too poor to afford the convenience of a horse or sedan chair, strode swaggering past. Everyone gave the warrior's left side a wide berth, it being a deadly insult to brush against his sword—his very soul.

Next on the danger scale to the samurais' swords were the pack-horses' mouths, for the overburdened little beasts would bite viciously and for no apparent reason if given the chance, as Neil learned to his indignant regret.

The pack-horses reminded Macneil of their faithful Hana. When he had the chance, he panted to Ai, "What did you do with our horse?"

"I gave orders she was to be well cared for."

The women in the fields, the samurais, the porters, the farmers carrying their vegetables to market—almost everyone, in fact, but the post runners—wore headgear of startling shapes and sizes, mostly flatter and broader than Neil's hood. Many were like oversized, upside-down bowls made with plaited bamboo and tied to the head by an elaborate arrangement of thongs.

It was becoming apparent to Macneil that hats in Japan served two purposes—one, to warm the head in winter and take the place of an umbrella and two, to help conceal the wearer's identity. Even those few who did not wear such headgear usually wrapped a cloth or a scarf around their heads and part of their faces.

In Neil's two brief months in Japan, he had learned that conceal-ing identity was a major worry for almost everyone, probably fostered by the shogun's omnipresent network of spies. The wide-brim straw hats and heads wrapped in cloth, the sedan chairs in which the passenger could become invisible behind drawn curtains, and the houses protected by high walls for those who could afford them were all evidence of this deep-rooted, self-preserving desire to keep one's identity and activities hidden.

Ai always slowed their pace to a walk as they neared anyone, explaining that if a *komuso* and his serving woman were seen running down a road, people would assume a fire or a local disturbance such as a rice riot was taking place and set out in pursuit just to witness the spectacle.

When the sun was high overhead, Ai handed Neil a rice-ball, halved one for herself, and halted at a farmer's well only long enough to fill their canteens, which were cut from a bamboo section. The farmer tried to charge Ai for the water, but she said something Macneil could not hear that so shocked the man that he backed off on tremulous bandy-legs with an anxious bow.

By then, Neil was too exhausted to ask what she had said, but he wondered if she had mentioned the *funa-kainin* to intimidate him. Normally, Japanese men, even peasants, would not tolerate such impertinence from a mere snip of a girl.

Throughout the long, hot afternoon Ai led the way, alternating the pace often. They walked, trotted, loped, and at times even ran at full speed, depending on her judgment of the danger posed by those close enough to watch. This repeated slowing down and speeding up was more tiring than rhythmical, steady movement would have been.

By mid-afternoon, Neil's tongue had swelled to fill his mouth, and his back ached where the sea bag had bounced against it all day. The muscles in first one arm, then in the other, pained him from holding the hood in place on his head, and sweat poured from him in torrents that rivaled the Tone River.

The journey in the bouncing, careening river boat now seemed a luxury compared to the suffering this day had brought. He thanked God there was no water shortage, for he had emptied the canteen so often Ai had begun to make cutting remarks about his being not only a barbarian but one without any grit.

"My God, Ai!" he panted, "How can you...just keep...running like...this?"

Just as the setting sun touched the serrated mountains rimming the vast plain on the west, Neil's burning leg muscles began to cramp. Whenever they stopped, his muscles bunched into tight balls, inducing agonized groans from under the hood.

The first time, Ai drew Neil quickly into the shelter of a roadside shrine half-hidden in a grove and massaged the knotted calf muscles. She also made him swallow a thimble full of salt to replace what he had lost through perspiration.

As dusk descended softly over the plain north of Edo, the road traffic thickened. Farmers who had gone that morning to the town ahead to sell their produce were returning home, along with tax collectors, *ashigaru* militia of the local daimyo, and vendors of herbs and patent medicines.

Ai pulled Neil to his feet. He was too spent to protest. "That is Kawaguchi, the town we can't avoid," she told him, nodding toward the spread-out collection of houses and shops still at least two miles south. "But once we have passed through it," she said, "it will be full dark and Edo will be only four and a half *ri* beyond."

Macneil doubted he would still be conscious at the end of those eleven miles.

As Neil and Ai ran past the last house in Kawaguchi, he had a premonition that Commodore Perry might already have issued the order for his four black ships to weigh anchors at dawn tomorrow.

This tormenting notion gave him the impetus he needed to overcome the accumulated fatigue of the day. For the first time, he found himself running ahead of Ai.

And he stayed ahead along the remainder of that long, dark road to Edo.

CHAPTER 21

They found the American fleet still at anchor in the quiet waters off Uraga.

Neil and Ai could see the riding lanterns of four ships from the top of an unattended *hinomi-yagura*. They had climbed the fire tower in the fishing village beyond Edo, which they had skirted at a tired, stumbling run. Even Ai was near collapse.

Climbing the stairs to the tower top set Macneil's calf muscles cramping again, so he halted halfway up to let Ai's fingers work their magic. He was in such agony that he was tempted to drive a knife into the knotted muscles to relieve their rigidity.

Ai pulled Neil up after her to the platform atop the tower, where he crumbled in a heap of gasping lungs and spastic muscular contractions. From the towers wardens watched for fires when they weren't patroling the night streets clacking together two pieces of resonant wood, chanting *"Hi no yojin! Hi no yojin!"* ("Be careful of fire! Be careful of fire!")

Drawing her close to him when he was able to sit up, Neil said, "Look, Ai! Those four shapes! They're the black ships. American ships!"

The four dim silhouettes floated a hundred yards offshore. The night was moonless, so without the riding lanterns they would not have known the ships were there.

Ai strained her eyes to make out the shadowy American fleet.

"Have you ever seen such large sailing ships before?" Neil asked.

"I've seen the Dutch trading vessels—one at a time—sailing past the Amakusa Islands on their way to Nagasaki, and I saw one with a different flag that might have been British or Russian," she said in a small, awed voice, "but I've never seen anything like this. *Never!* Four of them—and so *huge*.

"Look, Neil-*san!*" Ai gripped his arm. "One has a chimney in the middle of its deck. Does that mean they have a fireplace below deck for the crew to warm themselves?"

"You really are a silly country girl. That's a *steam*ship, my dear. The fire below deck is in a big oven. It makes steam which moves the..." He made a circling motion with his hand, since he didn't know the word for paddle wheel. "...and that pushes the ship forward."

The truth was that he had never seen a steamship either, but he had heard about them.

"We should rest up here for a while," Ai said, breathing deeply the cool moist sea air. "The ships won't leave before dawn, if then."

"What about the fire warden?"

"When the warden comes back this way, we'll hear him long before he gets here," she said. "Besides, we're doing no one any harm."

Neil welcomed the respite. His muscles burned in fiery torment, and he kept stretching and bending his legs to keep them from cramping again.

"Just think what it must have been like when those black ships came sailing in here. Our *suppa* told us that—"

"*Suppa?*" Neil asked.

"Our confidential agent. The man we sent to Edo. That's where he was when the ships arrived."

"What did he say?"

"He said everyone in Edo believed Japan had been invaded. The whole city was in terrible chaos. Bells tolled all night. Women shrieked; children cried. Men piled their belongings in carts and fought through masses of frightened people to flee the city. Armed samurais on war horses clattered hither and yon. Old people fluttered this way and that like wild marsh birds scared by a sudden intruder. Horror-stricken women put babies on their backs and sought protection in temples, only to run back to their homes when they saw the priests were no more prepared for the crisis than the barber or the nightsoil collector. To bolster their confidence, firemen paraded through the streets singing brave songs in chorus, though there were no fires. In fact, Edo's one million people stayed out in the streets all night, ready to run to—"

"Is that the number of people in Edo, one million?" Neil asked, thinking that this small port at their feet must have seen even more frantic, hysterical activity than Edo as the curious residents fought back their fears and ran to congregate along the coastline to stare wide-eyed at the four black monsters out there. What could have passed through their minds as they looked into the gaping mouths of the gigantic cannon pointed right at their flimsy homes?

Ai nodded. "And what made it worse, the *suppa* told us, was that a meteor..." He didn't understand that word until Ai pointed up into the night sky and made a falling motion. "...a meteor with a red wedge-shaped tail plummeted down that night. The people knew it had to be connected with the invading fleet and the awesome, mystic power you foreign devils possess...." Ai reached up and touched his cheek. "...so they rushed to burn incense at altars and pray for deliverance from such evil."

Suddenly, the most terrible realization since hearing of his family's shipwreck flooded through Neil. He was actually leaving Ai, and might not see her again. Ever.

"Ai," he began, clearing his throat, "I'll go aboard tonight and when the commodore hears my story, he and I will probably come ashore tomorrow to see the shogun together."

Her voice a faint whisper, she said, "I will not be here, Neil-*san*."

Sudden tears burned his eyes. "You will go back to the mountains?" he asked.

"No. The day before we left, I received a message from my father. He wants me to go back to Amakusa right away."

"Something about your marriage?"

"He seems to have forgotten about that for the time being," she said, and Neil detected a thankful note in her voice. "Something more serious. Amakusa is in the province of Higo, and the daimyo there has always left the Koga clan alone. Of course, he knew about us and has even given us special—ah, assignments over the years."

"Well, what has happened?"

"The shogun has heard Christian rituals are still being performed in Amakusa by the many hidden Christians there."

"So he has decided to put teeth in the anti-Christian laws?"

"He has ordered the Higo daimyo to mount an expedition against all Christians in Amakusa, including us."

"And your father wants you there to fight at his side?"

"I will do that, of course, but he also needs me to go to Amami-Oshima to buy firearms."

"Where is that?"

"Amami-Oshima lies between Kyushu and Okinawa. It's in the Satsuma domain. The chief port is Naze. Many years ago, the daimyo of Satsuma—the most southern fief in Kyushu—received special dispensation from the shogun to import weapons at Naze."

Neil stood up. "I might as well see if I can get out to the flagship."

At that hour, well past midnight, Uraga was quiet. After eluding a patrol of three lantern-carrying *doshin*, they found their way to a breakwater of large rocks sheltering six fishing boats, one hardly larger than a rowboat. Ai pushed Neil down behind a pile of fishing nets and went off to rouse a fisherman.

Soon she came back leading a bandy-legged, leather-faced man of fifty with a white band around his head. He was smiling and bowing every other step, so Neil knew Ai had either given him another oblong gold coin or had made a threat about his personal safety and *funa-kainin* vengeance.

His was the smallest of the craft. In three minutes, he had freed it from its mooring and shipped his stern oar. Then he stood waiting, still smiling and bowing, for Neil to come aboard.

"Ai..." Neil began, removing the basket mask and putting his hands on her shoulders. "I can't just leave you like this. I must know that some day we'll meet again."

"Some day, when you come back to take me to all those wonderful places you told me about, Neil-*san?*" In the semi-darkness, she lifted her face to his, and he could see the tears glisten in her eyes just as she must have seen those in his.

"Ai, I promise that—"

"No!" she said, putting a hand over his lips. "Don't make a promise that's not in your heart."

She was right. If Neil found Anne, they would marry and live in Hong Kong. Where would there be a place for Ai?

"Ai, my dear," he said, drawing her closer, "I'll promise you this. I promise we will meet again. We will meet somewhere more than once, perhaps many times, and we will know each other for a long time. I promise you that."

Ai crossed herself. "I pray to God you can keep that promise." Then she shook her head as if to remind herself of where they stood and what they were doing there.

"Keep your *komuso* outfit on until you come alongside the flagship," Ai said. "Take off the hood and cape just before you climb aboard. And maybe you had better call out in English before you start up the side of the ship."

"I must know how to find you," he whispered, his heart crumbling.

Reaching inside her jacket, she drew out a scrap of paper. "Here's the name of a village on one of the Amakusa Islands. Go there any time and ask for 'Kampachi,' the man whose name is also written on the paper. He's a fisherman as well as the village headman—the *nanushi*. Just say your name's Neil. Otherwise, he'll tell you nothing. Then wait. Someone will come for you. I'll arrange it. And if you ever go to the port of Naze in Amami-Oshima, ask for Ueda-san, who sells provisions to ships. Remember his name: Ueda. He acts as confidential agent for the Koga clan there." She handed him several gold coins. "You may need these."

"And if you ever go to Hong Kong," Neil said, "remember to ask for my uncle, Neville Macneil. He'll know where I am."

"One more thing."

"What, Ai?"

"Teach me how to kiss, just once more?"

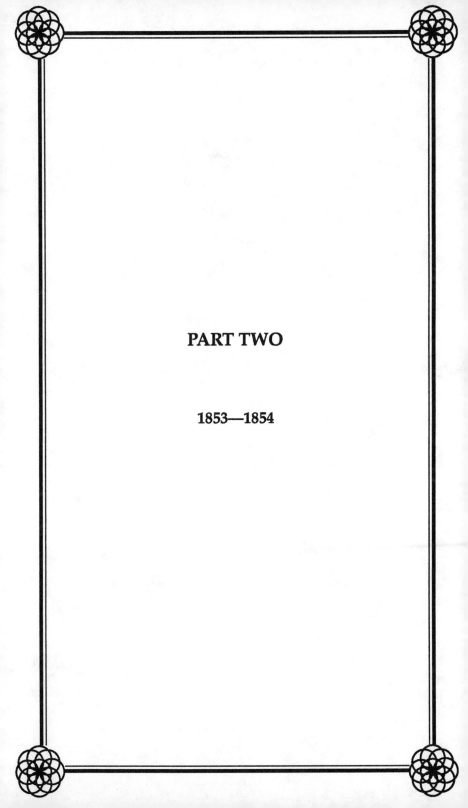

PART TWO

1853—1854

CHAPTER 22

Aboard USS Susquehanna

Neil Macneil stood outside Commodore Matthew Calbraith Perry's cabin on his flagship *USS Susquehanna*, waiting for the commodore's flag lieutenant to summon him inside. It was the next morning, and the creaking of the sail winches and the running about and shouting on deck warned Macneil the fleet would soon depart. Already the flagship anchor had been raised. Her steam was up, ready to force the side-paddles into their rotary motion.

If he didn't make his plea to the commodore in a few minutes, it would be too late.

Last night, Macneil had first asked, then demanded to see Perry as soon as he came aboard, but the deck officer did not believe a word of his story. Over Macneil's bitter protests, two marines had dragged him to a room used to store uniforms and locked him in for the night.

An hour ago, an old salt had at last unlocked his door and handed him a breakfast tray with eggs, bacon, ship biscuit, and coffee. It was the first time he had coffee and bacon in the two months since leaving the whaler.

The old sailor stood before Macneil watching in wonder at the speed with which the young American ate.

"I could go fetch ye more, laddie," he said, "but they tole me to haul you up to Old Bruin's cabin soon as ye finished them vittles."

"Old Bruin?"

"Thet's what the sailors all call the commodore, cause he's allus acting like an ole wounded grizzly what's mad at the hull dad-blamed world. When he gets his hackles up, every man jack in the fleet knows it."

Macneil finished the last bite and rose to follow the sailor up on deck. "What happened while you were at anchor here?" he asked. "Did Perry sign a treaty with the shogun?"

"It won't do ye no good to be asking the likes of me such questions, young feller," the sailor said over his shoulder as he led the way up on deck. "There was a power of palavering going on and giving of presents back and forth, but nobody ain't tole us ordinary able-bodies what was decided." Then, after a moment of thought, "Fer what it's worth, scuttlebutt has it the fleet'll winter in Hong Kong and come back here early next year. An' thet suits me right down to the ground. I'd a heap druther cozy up to the heathen Chinee than these here Japan-ers any day of the week."

The commodore's cabin door opened, and the flag lieutenant—a tall, slim young man with his mouth set in disapproving lines—beckoned to Macneil. "The commodore can spare you a few minutes now."

From behind his desk, Matthew Perry glared at Macneil. Even seated, he was a large imposing man. He had black, bulbous eyes set in an angry red face.

Fixing Macneil with a chilling stare, he bellowed, "Well, state your business."

"Sir," Macneil said, speaking as calmly as he could, "three members of my family were shipwrecked off the coast of this country. I think they're still in Japan, held here against their will. As an American, I respectfully ask you to send a message to the Japanese telling them about my relatives and asking for their aid in finding them."

Perry slammed the desk with the palm of his hand. "Absolutely no," he shouted. "I will neither delay our sailing nor will I send another message of any kind to the mikado."

"You haven't been dealing with the mikado, Commodore."

"And pray tell me, sir, with whom *have* I been dealing?"

"You've been dealing with the shogun and his ministers."

"Aren't the shogun and the mikado one and the same?"

"By no means, Commodore," Macneil said, stepping closer to the desk. "The mikado is the emperor and is shut up in a palace in Kyoto. Although he is revered, he has very little to do with running this country. The shogun is Iemochi Tokugawa, the fourteenth in his line, who rules Japan from his Edo castle with a hand as cruel and dictatorial as ever governed anywhere."

"And how do you know all this?"

"I've had two fine teachers—William Amanuma and Ai Koga."

"And I suppose that next you'll be telling me you speak this impossible tongue?"

"I'm a long way from being fluent, sir, but I can speak some and understand about half what's said."

Perry harrumphed twice, then asked for a fuller explanation of Macneil's family's fate—and of what he was doing in this forbidden country.

Macneil went into detail about his origin, his family's reported fate, his illegal entry into Japan and his adventures and mishaps while making his way from northern Honshu to Edo and then Uraga, omitting only the deaths for which he and Ai had been responsible.

"Well," Perry said, "you are an American if what you say is true, and I owe you the protection of your country's navy, so I will give you passage as far as Hong Kong. If your uncle is there, he can take care of you after that."

"My family are Americans, too. Don't they deserve your protection?"

"I believe you told me your cousin had lived in Scotland and was on her way to join her Scot father—your uncle—in Hong Kong."

"That's true, sir, but my sister Margaret and my father Nairn Macneil were living in Fort George when Oregon became a U.S. territory, just as I was, so they are as much American as I am."

"Dammit, young man, your persistence fatigues me. American though the lot of you may be, I'm not going to upset the delicate balance of our negotiations with these damned Japanese for the sake of people who may well be dead."

"I told you, sir," Macneil said, his voice and temper rising, "that Anne and Margaret are very much alive. They were captured by bandits on their way south from Morioka, long after the wreck of *Eliza Grayson*."

"I have a list here," Perry said, pointing to the documents stacked on the left-hand side of his desk, "of thirty-seven Americans who have landed on the shores of this heathen land over the past ten years. Some may be dead, for they were whaler hands—a notoriously drunken lot—and if they tried to treat the Japanese in the same high-handed manner that they have long treated the natives of other Pacific islands, they may have learned to their regret that such arrogance served them ill. These damnable samurais would not brook such an attitude, as I'm sure you will agree if you have had the experiences with them you claim to have had."

"What I've told you is true, Commodore. Every last word of it."

"Scratch me for a Turk, sirrah, *will* you hear me out?" Perry's shouting brought his flag lieutenant running through the cabin door.

"Listen well to me, Macneil," Perry said, "for I will say no more on this subject, and Lt. Warren there will witness my decision. I will *not* delay the departure of this fleet for an instant. I will *not* send a message of any kind to the shogun or the mikado or whoever the Goddamned high panjandrum is who lives in that castle in Edo."

Macneil's hopes crumpled, as his face must have done.

"But," the commodore's voice dropped, "I'm not entirely insensitive to your distress or to the plight of your loved ones. Therefore," he said with a heavy sigh, "when the fleet has passed through the sea between Shikoku and Honshu...."

"The heathens call it the Setonaikai, sir," said the flag lieutenant.

"We will proceed to the Straits of Kammon and then, passing through them, turn south toward Nagasaki for a brief visit to that port where the Goddamned Dutchmen and heathen Chinese have controlled all foreign trade in and out of this island empire since the invention of time. And while— "

"Controlled is hardly the word, Commodore," interrupted Lt. Warren. "The Dutch and the Chinese are completely under the thumb of the Japanese and continually humiliated and harassed."

Again the commodore's hackles rose. "Your acquaintance with the situation in Nagasaki is commendable, Lieutenant, and I shall bear it in mind—along with *other* matters—when I submit your next fitness report to Washington. In the meantime, you will favor me, sir, by allowing me to choose my own words in speaking to this young man."

Perry fixed his protruding eyes on Warren for a full twenty seconds before turning back to Macneil.

"While at anchor in the port of Nagasaki, I will turn over to the shogun's representative there a supplemental petition asking his benevolence in finding your family and dispatching them to Hong Kong by the earliest means feasible—and in good health. I will append a description of all three of them, which you can prepare and give to Lt. Warren by this time tomorrow, so that there will be time for me to have it re-written in a more formal—and perhaps more schooled?—hand."

Stiffly, Macneil said, "I write quite legibly, I am told."

"Maybe you do, Macneil, maybe you do at that." Perry said with resignation.

For the first time, Macneil spotted a glint of humor in the commodore's eyes.

The flag lieutenant pushed Macneil through the cabin door

back out on deck. The side-paddles had begun to turn slowly. The hands not otherwise engaged below or aloft crowded the railing to wave farewell to the crowds lining the shore to watch the departure of the fleet. A flotilla of small craft carrying tradesmen selling odds and ends backed water to avoid the currents and undertows created by the huge paddle wheels of *Susquehanna*.

Standing at the rail, Macneil wondered what he had accomplished. The commodore had promised to submit a petition to the shogun's representative in Nagasaki, but without the force of a signed treaty behind it, the petition might well be ignored. And the signing of the treaty could not take place before the fleet returned to Edo next year, *if* the shogun was willing to put his seal on the document at all.

With a sigh, Macneil concluded that no action was likely to be taken on a petition until next year. The thought was intolerable. He might have been better off casting his lot with Ai and her *funa-kainin* clan.

He wondered where his woodland sprite was now. Probably already on her way back to the Amakusa Islands, maybe even now on one of the many junks and fishing boats he could see headed for the mouth of Edo Bay.

Macneil's first duty—and love—was to Anne Macneil, but he owed much to Ai Koga, too.

He wondered if he would ever repay that debt or even see Ai again.

CHAPTER 23

Through the Inland Sea to Nagasaki

Like gulls on the wind, the American black ships, led by *Susquehanna* with its blue stripe at gun-port level, sailed serenely into the Inland Sea. They passed the gigantic Naruto whirlpool and went on through the many islands dotting the narrow body of water between Shikoku and Honshu.

During much of the voyage, Macneil stood at the rail, either sketching the islands and the fishing boats or watching the millions of large jellies floating just under the surface. In that green world, their living-lace tentacles of blue, pink and lavender trailed behind or beneath them like the swaying hair of native beach dancers.

At dusk, the ships approached the Kammon Straits, with the port of Shimonoseki to starboard. The sun was setting directly ahead of the fleet in a brilliant display of gold and red.

Through a glass, he could spot the 18-pounder batteries protecting the approaches to Shimonoseki, gun crews standing ready beside their cannon. Although none offered the fleet any harm, some among the crews could be seen making motions in the air with their hands. The old sailor who had served Macneil breakfast—Hardy—said they were shaking their fists, but Macneil argued that, on the contrary, they were waving hello.

Beyond Shimonoseki, the fleet lowered most of the sails, while those with steam power banked their engine-room fires. With only flying jibs and fore-skysails aloft to maintain headway, the ships drifted south under a clear sky and a rising full moon.

After dark, Macneil stood at the bow for an hour, looking at the sky. Had it not been for the slap and splash the waves made against the hull, he thought, he might have been able to hear the tinkle of the stars.

At first light next morning, all hands clambered aloft to

clap on full canvas. As they passed the Kujuku Islands to port, the wind died, but picked up again as they turned toward the mouth of the Bay of Nagasaki.

Something ominous about the weather disturbed the sailing master as well as Captain Adams and Commodore Perry, who clustered around the barometer at the stern.

"I don't like it one bit, sir," Adams said to Perry.

"And neither do I," Perry said. Turning about, he shouted, "Heco! Joseph Heco! Find that young man and send him to me instantly."

Joseph Heco was the fleet interpreter, a Japanese sea waif like William Amanuma, who had been hired in Honolulu by the commodore. In Macneil's judgment, his English was miserable.

"Heco!" Perry bellowed when the bowing young Japanese was still fifteen yards from him. "When is the typhoon season in these heathen parts?"

"*Taifu* season, sah?" Heco said, bobbing his head. "Already, it is begin."

Perry waved the interpreter away, then said to Adams and the sailing master, "I'd like more sea room if we get caught in one, stab me if I wouldn't."

"Amen to that," said Adams.

"Well, let's see what happens," Perry said. "We'll drop our hooks at the bay mouth and signal for a pilot and a port official to come out."

The fleet anchored in the lee of Pappenberg Island, with Ogami Point on the west and Megami Point on the east. Atop both promontories were manned gun batteries with six three-pounders on each.

All afternoon, the fleet waited for someone to appear. Macneil passed the time pacing the deck and worrying about Anne, Margaret and Nairn. Finally, lacking anything better to do, he fetched his pencil and sketching pad from his cabin and spent the next hour on deck drawing from memory profiles and full-face views of Anne.

"Now, there be a true beauty, young feller," old Hardy said. He had come up to stand beside Macneil at the railing. He pointed at the sketches with a pipe he had fashioned from driftwood. "Did you dream her up?"

"No, she lives," Macneil said. "At least, I hope she does."

"I wager she'd fetch a pretty price in these islands. Some Japan-ers have a strong appetite for white women."

Macneil shuddered.

"I suppose 'tis the same the world over," Hardy mused. "Men a-lusting after that which be different, I mean. Like those

Japan-er girls what gets sold in Tonkin and Burma and even in Macao."

"I haven't heard about them," Macneil said, moving to the old tar's other side to keep the acrid tobacco smoke out of his nostrils.

"It's a brass-bound fact, lad, or I wouldn't say it. Families in the Amakusa Islands south of here sell their daughters to rich Chinese."

"But I thought no one could leave or enter Japan," Macneil said. "How do they manage it?"

"Easy enough, I've heard. They put 'em on fishing boats what takes 'em to the port of Naze—that's south of Kyushu— where Chinese pirates pick 'em up and deliver 'em to the buyers. It's been going on for a long while and the panjandrums wink at it, I'm guessing. Too many people and too little food in these parts, anyway. I've heard they've even got a school in the port of Naze what teaches them pitiful little creatures how to proper pleasure a man."

A cry from the masthead interrupted their conversation.

"Barge two points off the bow," the lookout at the mast called down.

"Advise the commodore on the double!" the deck officer ordered a seaman.

Perry took his time appearing, so all hands on deck had ample time to watch the approach of the large, flat-bottomed barge carrying officials in stiff-shouldered ceremonial robes and small lacquered hats perched on their heads and tied under their chins. The sharp-featured man standing in the prow of the barge with his shoulders thrown back was dressed in a wide-sleeved blue brocade jacket, shining black lacquer clogs and baggy golden trousers.

When the barge came alongside *Susquehanna*, aft of the port side-paddle, the men on deck threw out a line which the rowers of the barge ignored while keeping the barge steady in one place with deft oar movements.

"*Doko no mono ka hayaku ie!*" The Japanese magistrate in the baggy golden trousers demanded to know who the men aboard *Susquehanna* were.

In a tremulous voice, Joseph Heco, who had preceded the commodore on deck, began to explain this vessel was the flagship of Commodore Perry of the U.S. Navy, the fleet had come from Uraga through the Inland Sea, in Uraga the commodore had met—

Rudely, the magistrate broke in to tell Heco he had heard nothing from Edo about such a visit, only Dutch and Chinese ships were allowed to enter Nagasaki Bay and this fleet should haul anchor and set sail immediately.

Heco, who was kneeling on the deck looking down at the magistrate, bowed deeply upon hearing these arrogant orders. Standing back from the railing, Perry asked Heco what had been said.

Heco softened the impact of the magistrate's impertinent words and stammered to Perry that these Nagasaki officials had heard nothing about the visit of the fleet to Uraga. They deeply regretted, he went on, that they could not offer the fleet the hospitality of the port.

In growing irritation, Macneil listened to Heco interpret the general meaning but not the actual tenor of the magistrate's words.

Perry's response was mild. "Tell him all I want to do is to hand over a letter for him to send to Mr. Masahiro Abe of his government in Edo."

In interpreting this, Heco, who constantly winked with both eyes alternately, used words appropriate for inferiors when speaking to superiors.

"I cannot accept such a letter," growled the magistrate. "Be off with you. We want no more barbarians here."

"What was that?" asked Perry, still standing back from the railing.

"He say very sorry, sah. Pureeze to forgive him, but he no can accept youah rettah."

"Harrumph," Perry growled. Looking at the crew around him, he caught sight of Macneil and motioned him to his side. "It's looks like an impasse, Macneil. I cannot force this man to take the document."

"But, Commodore," Macneil protested, "the interpreter— that Heco—he's making it sound as if you are a servant or an insignificant underling. Don't let him get away with this! That Japanese bastard even called us barbarians."

In an instant, it became plain why Matthew Perry was called Old Bruin throughout the fleet. As quickly as a golden grizzly just coming out of hibernation, he flared into anger.

"What was that?" he roared. "Barbarians, are we? God rot his heathen slanty eyes! Barbarians, are we? You there, Heco! You tell that arrogant little bastard he is nothing more than a maggot-covered piece of shitty flotsam and I'll sink that barge of his if he's not out of my cannon range in five minutes. No, by the breath of God, make that *three* minutes!"

In trembling terror, Heco prostrated himself on the deck, "Pureeze, Commodore! I no can say frotsam. What is meaning this word?"

Before this linguistic tangle could be solved, the magistrate had turned his contemptuous back on *Susquehanna* and ordered his oarsmen to row the barge back into Nagasaki bay.

Still in a frothy rage, Perry spun on his heel, took Macneil by the arm and half dragged him into his cabin. There, he poured himself and Macneil a glass of port. He cursed steadily—and, Macneil thought, with commendable inventiveness—through two glasses of the wine, then calmed down enough to say, "I'm sorry, young man. I know how you must feel. I had hoped that if our letter reached the authorities in Edo, they might find your family and have them waiting for the fleet when we come back next year."

"Sir, please listen," Macneil said. He knew he was on the point of begging but could not help himself. "Anne and Meg, they're so young, so innocent. Can't something be done? Couldn't we stay at anchor here a while longer? We might call upon the Dutch in Nagasaki to intervene."

"I can't, son, and I'm truly sorry. The weather glass is falling, and I want to be out in open seas if a typhoon hits. You must see I can't risk the safety of an entire American fleet."

Slowly, Macneil bowed his head.

In the mildest voice Macneil had heard him use so far, the commodore said, "You can come back with us next year, if you like, Macneil. I could appoint you interpreter for the fleet in that wretched Heco's place."

In the falling dusk that evening, the fleet—under both steam and sail—pushed south on a course for the Formosa Straits and from there to its winter anchorage at Hong Kong. The crew was exuberant. Though they had missed shore leave in Nagasaki, they could look forward to longer periods of recreation on land—between occasional training cruises—in Hong Kong.

In a state of shock, Macneil leaned over the stern railing, ignoring the bells signaling the evening meal and looking through damp, tortured eyes at the west coast of Kyushu as it slipped past, only a nautical mile off the port side.

"Ye've missed your dinner, laddie," said the wrizzled Hardy, clapping a fatherly hand on Macneil's shoulder.

"I'm not hungry."

"Troubles?"

"Aye."

"Might be I could help ye?"

"I'm afraid not, Hardy, but thanks. It's about that girl whose face I was sketching. She's there, somewhere," Macneil said, nodding toward the Japanese coast.

"Dear Holy Mother of God!" the old sailor breathed. "And to think what I said to ye about the Japan-ers a-lusting after white women."

"It's all right. I knew that already." He could have added, "*And I've lusted after one of their women, too,*" but he refrained.

Off to port, they saw a chain of islands in the dusk.

Hardy pointed at them with his pipe. "They be the Amakusa Islands, son. The ones I was telling ye about. Where they get the girls from the poor families to sell to rich Chinamen."

"I remember, Hardy." Macneil also remembered that in those islands Ai Koga had been raised. There the *funa-kainin* of Ai's father Heihachiro still held out in hidden island valleys, plotting against their eternal enemies, the Tokugawa clan.

When he had finished his pipe, Hardy said good night. The young man from Oregon stayed at the rail only a short while longer.

He knew what he had to do.

CHAPTER 24

The Amakusa Islands south of Nagasaki

In the warm water of the East China Sea, Macneil had swum far enough to see the dark mass of an island loom directly ahead, though the moon had not yet risen.

Tied around his neck was a waterproof oilskin bag holding his precious dictionaries. He had left his pistol, throwing stars, sketch pad, kilt, and bagpipe in a sack by old Hardy's hammock, with a note directing him to deliver them to a merchant named Neville Macneil in Hong Kong.

Neil asked Hardy to inform his uncle that Neil had left *Susquehanna* to go on with the search for Anne and Margaret. If his uncle heard no further word from any of them, Neil suggested prayers be offered for their souls.

Glancing back over his shoulder, Macneil saw the running lanterns on the *kurobune*, the black ship fleet, as it sailed serenely south, bound for Formosa and Hong Kong. The last ship in line was still not far off, tempting him to swim after it. Hard though a sailor's life might be, Macneil knew it would be better than what awaited him ashore: sleeping in the open in the rain and cold, eating uncooked radish and raw chicken—or nothing—his life at risk every day.

But when he thought of Anne and Margaret, alive somewhere in these islands, he knew that every day they might be suffering unspeakable indignities and mistreatment. Every day, every *minute* was to them important.

How could he idly pass the winter in Hong Kong waiting to resume the search for them in the spring?

Ahead, he heard the waves lapping on rocks and sand and saw their sparkling phosphorescence, like the lights of a distant village.

When his feet at last found sandy bottom, he was sure he had landed on an island in the Amakusa group.

On the sandy beach, Macneil collapsed, too tired to crawl an inch further. The tropical night held the promise of a full moon. No lights from houses. Stillness. And stars. Only the gentle lapping of the waves. Removing the oilskin bag from around his neck, Macneil stretched out on the sand and scooped some over him with his hands. In the early morning hours, it would be chilly.

The urge to scratch a mosquito bite on his cheek woke Macneil up.

His clothes were clammy from sea spray and early dew. Removing his trousers and shirt and heavy stockings, he rinsed them in the surf, which was pounding the shore with more vigor than last night. He spread his clothes to dry on an outcropping of black volcanic rock.

He washed himself and stood naked in the morning sun waiting for the salty moisture to evaporate. Then he dressed, put on his sandals and climbed over the rocks and through the heavy brush to the top of the hill. There, he could see that this cone was all there was to this small island, except for the beach where he had slept and another, more protected, sandy strip on the southern shore.

Though the island rose only two hundred feet above the sea, the view from the top was magnificent. A much larger and higher island loomed to the north. Many smaller ones sprinkled the sea to the east. Beyond them he could see what he assumed was the mainland of Kyushu itself—a low, dim bar of earth, darker than the sea, backed by far-off mountains. Macneil's island seemed to be the southernmost in the Amakusa archipelago. The distance to its nearest neighbor he guessed was about two miles. Although he knew the name of the island Ai called home, Macneil had no idea which of the many it was.

Though no one lived on Macneil's island, many others were doubtless inhabited, but at this distance he could not tell which were and which were not.

Fishing craft and coastal transports were visible along the outer limits of his vision, but they could not have sighted Macneil even if he had any way to signal them.

Sitting on a rock at the top of the hill, Macneil pondered his situation. He decided what he would have to do was find the Amakusa *funa-kainin*, explain to Ai's father who he was, and wait for Ai to come.

To find the *funa-kainin*, or the island where they lived, Macneil first had to get off this island and swim to one that was inhabited.

Hunger twisted Macneil's stomach. He had eaten no dinner the night before nor had he been able to bring any food with him from *Susquehanna*. But even that hunger was not as severe as his thirst. Macneil carried no canteen and could see no fresh water source on the tiny island. The sky was as clear as a baby's eyes, with no promise of rain. The late summer sun was already blistering his bare back and would quickly suck out what little moisture was left in him. He would have to have water soon.

Circling the top of the hill, Macneil looked down the slope and at the shore on all sides, thinking he might sight a rain-water pool somewhere.

But there was none.

On the point of giving up the search, he saw something bobbing on the surface of an inlet almost completely cut off from the sea by surrounding rocks. It was a wooden cask with writing on it.

Could it contain water? Japanese fishing boats had to carry water, and there was no reason their water casks should not resemble those Macneil had seen elsewhere, as this one did.

But, of course, it might be empty.

He crashed down through the brush and over the rocks to the inlet. As he was about to leap from one boulder to the next, the rock under his right foot crumbled, and he lost his footing, plunged forward, and caught his leg in a crevice.

At the last instant, his ankle came free, saving the bone from snapping like a twig. Even so, his ankle was badly wrenched and the pain ran up his leg as if molten metal had been poured through his veins.

He fell ten feet, the undergrowth breaking the full force of his fall, but bruising and scraping him in a dozen places.

For a while, he lay where he had fallen, trying to recover his senses.

After ten minutes, he remembered the floating cask and cautiously crawled out from the brush and down the slope to the water line. The cask was still bobbing gently on the protected water of the tiny cove. As he crept into the water, the salt stung his wounds, but he hoped that might promote healing.

He stretched out his hand and took hold of the cask. On it were the same *kanji* he had seen on the smaller casks in the roadside shrine near Morioka. This one held about ten gallons. From its weight and the sloshing noise inside, he could tell it was almost full. Was it sake? Or had some fisherman filled an empty sake cask with water?

The wooden plug in the bung hole refused to budge. It must have been pounded in place with a heavy mallet. In growing desperation, Macneil got out his sailor's knife and at last managed to prize it free.

Cupping a hand, he poured out the clear liquid and tasted it.

He had found ten gallons of sake, in a cask like those Japanese seamen offer to the god Kompira when they pray for calm seas. In five minutes, Macneil had swallowed a pint or more.

In less than an hour since he had climbed to the top of the island, his predicament had changed from bad to worse. He still had no food, and, with his throbbing sprained ankle, he could not hope to swim to a neighboring island. He now had liquid to drink, but how well it would quench his thirst—or for how long—remained to be seen.

Since he could not possibly shoulder and carry the sake cask to the other beach where he had slept last night, Macneil decided to crawl into the water and work his way around the island, paddling and floating from rock to rock, to retrieve his clothing and oilskin bag.

By the time he reached the other beach, it was late afternoon. Thirst dominated his every thought. He cupped his hands and drank from the cask again and again, even though he knew alcohol was dehydrating. Stretching out on the narrow sand strip, he eased his ankle, which was throbbing with excruciating pain, into the gentle surf. The sun still burned down from its westerly course. Painfully, he gathered seaweed from the wet rocks within reach and covered his exposed skin. Again, he spread his clothes on a rock to dry.

Macneil's head swam from the sake. Pain enveloped him. His eyes closed. He wondered how far away—or how near—Ai was.

But his last conscious thought was, *What will become of Anne and Margaret if I die here?*

CHAPTER 25

Next morning Macneil's right ankle was swollen to twice its normal size and hurt so badly his leg jerked with each throb. He wondered if he had broken the ankle bone. When he felt for a break, the agony drove away his exploring fingers. He relieved his thirst temporarily with more sake, the only possession he had more than enough of. His head hurt.

Ai had told Macneil rice-wine came in several grades. Did the Japanese sacrifice only the cheapest grade—the head-splitting variety—to the god Kompira? Could a god have a headache?

Perhaps to show his resentment of Macneil's commandeering the sacrificial cask of sake, the storm god had turned churlish and sent scudding oyster-gray clouds and fretful winds to toss the surface of the sea. Macneil scanned the horizon for nearby fishing craft but sighted none. Even if he had, he did not know how to signal them. He had brought nothing to make a fire with—only a knife that would cut kindling.

From the surrounding brush he cut four half-inch limbs. With the limbs and cloth strips ripped from his shirt, he bound his ankle as tightly as he could. If a bone was broken, he would have to keep it immobile.

Macneil's hunger had grown to an implacable prowling beast in his belly. He tried to eat the dark berries he found on a low bush, but they were so bitter he spat them out, downing another half-pint of the sake to wash away the taste.

Below the surface of the water in the tiny cove he found many spiny, purple sea creatures that might have been edible, but he couldn't crack open their walnut-size cores. Small fish flitted back and forth, taunting him to try to catch them. He had more sense than to make the effort.

How he survived until the rain started twenty-four hours later, Macneil did not know. *I suppose the sake has food value,* he thought, *even though the alcohol keeps drying me out.*

At the first raindrops from the sullen clouds, Macneil turned over on his back and lay with his mouth open. When the shower became a downpour, he was able to swallow half a mouthful of water every few minutes.

Having no way to store the water, he continued to swallow the rain until it backed up in his throat.

This blessed rainfall, however, carried with it a supreme danger. It was a harbinger of the typhoon Commodore Perry had worried about. All morning, the winds and waves grew stronger. The surrounding boulders protected him from the direct force of the seas, but the water level within the cove rose so that Macneil was now half-floating in it and in danger of being swept through the narrow mouth of the cove into the open sea.

If he stayed there, he would probably drown. Macneil had to do something quickly.

Pouring out all the sake, he plugged the cask and tied it to his chest with what strips of cloth remained from his shirt. Setting aside his two dictionaries, Macneil filled the oilskin bag with air, tied the mouth closed so it would serve as a buoy, and attached it to the back of his belt. Regretfully leaving his sandals and dictionaries, he floated out from the comparative calm of the cove into the violent sea lashing at the island.

His first impulse was to turn back instantly and hope for survival within the cove, but Macneil had heard of typhoons whose mountainous waves had swept over entire islands, swallowing houses and humans, trees and temples—everything—in their path. He had to take one risk or the other.

He chose the open sea.

The ache in his head was Macneil's first concern.

He touched a place just above the left ear. It was swollen and as sore as a carbuncle, even more painful than his throbbing ankle. When he tried to shift his position, he found several pangs vying with one another for dominance in his neck, shoulder and ribs. Believing unconsciousness to be by far the preferable state, he did not resist when he felt himself sinking back into the misty grayness from which he had briefly emerged.

Nagasaki

Pain—sharp, searing pain—brought him around. He was being carried in something resembling a hammock slung underneath a stout pole. How many men carried the pole, he could not see. He knew they had to be going uphill, for he felt himself continually sliding to the lower end of the sling.

When they reached their destination, Macneil was dumped from the sling and dragged through a small opening into a large cage. Other tattered men stood around him, silent. Macneil's eyes blurred and he could not see their faces clearly. The pain pushed all other thoughts from his mind. All he wanted was to close his eyes and rest—if possible, to sleep. Perhaps even to die.

When he woke, someone was holding his wrist. His vision was clearer. Beside him a wispy man with a straggly beard was taking his pulse. A doctor? He took the pulse on Macneil's other wrist, on both sides of his throat, at the elbows, just in front of the ears, in his armpits, and just inside his knees. When he saw Macneil's half-open eyes, he grinned and began tapping him here and there.

Whenever Macneil groaned the man said, "*Ha!*" and nodded wisely, as if he had known all along that spot would be painful. He devoted his attention to Macneil's rib cage and collarbone, to his ankle and head wounds. He rubbed a salve on the abrasions and the cuts, explaining to the others the salve was his own formula, mixed from ground deer horns, powdered snakes, dried dog testicles, and ripened child's urine.

He called an assistant who had been kneeling just outside the cage and told him, "If this barbarian stays in this filthy place, he will soon die. We must move him to a temple. Go tell the jailer."

The trip from the cage to the temple sent agony through Macneil with every jolting step of the porters. He prayed for unconsciousness again, but the trip was short.

Inside the temple, he was carried up a flight of stone stairs to a room with a *futon* laid out on the reed matting and two acolyte priests in attendance. Macneil was lowered to the *futon*— a heavenly, merciful softness.

The doctor, whose head was shaved, said to an acolyte, "Have a woman bring hot water. Tell her to wash the barbarian. Remove his trousers and burn them. Then fetch a *yukata* for him to wear."

When Macneil was washed and naked, the doctor and his assistant bound his ribs, ankle and collar bone. The doctor told the chubby, middle-aged serving woman, "Many broken bones. Keep him as still as possible until he heals."

"How long will that be, sir?" she asked.

"Maybe six weeks," he told her, closing his bag. "I will come again tomorrow."

Macneil's next clear memory—it may have been the following day or the following week—was of two samurais who came into the temple room and sat beside his *futon*. One spoke to him in Japanese, the other in a language Neil thought was Dutch. Dazed, weak, and feverish, he answered neither of them.

Macneil understood only a few words of the Dutch and about half the Japanese. He had decided, during those brief moments when he could think clearly, that he should not admit to understanding Japanese.

It would be wiser, he reasoned, to appear to be a complete stranger to Japan. If he spoke any Japanese, questions would be asked about where and how he had learned the language. He might explain that what little he knew came from sea waifs like William Amanuma and Joseph Heco, but pretending not to know any Japanese at all might be to his advantage if this lulled his captors into speaking freely in his hearing. He might pick up information that would save his life or help him to escape or even set him on the trail to Anne and Margaret.

The two samurais—he guessed them to be junior officials— sat one on each side of his *futon* and did not appear to be upset about their inability to communicate with him. In fact, they laughed about it.

Sipping the tea brought by Chizu, the chubby serving woman who had become Macneil's regular attendant and nurse, one samurai said, "It must be just as the magistrate said. This fellow is nothing more than a sailor off one of the black ships."

"When his bones mend, we can throw him back in the prison cage and wait until another foreign ship comes by," said the second. "They can take him to a southern port like Hong Kong."

"Do you think he's just an ordinary sailor?"

"I suppose he is. He was wearing nothing but an old pair of trousers when the fishing boat picked him up."

This information gave Macneil an idea. He waited for his chance.

"Where did they find him?" asked the first samurai, the one with the pock-marked face.

"Floating in the surf at the tip of the Shimabara Peninsula, right below the Hara Castle ruins. The storm waves were throwing him up against the rocks. That's what caused his injuries."

"He's lucky to be alive."

Macneil made the motions of writing.

"Look, what's he doing?"

"I think he wants to write something."

They clapped their hands. Chizu opened the sliding door and crawled inside.

"Bring paper and brush and ink. Be quick."

When she had fetched the writing materials, Chizu dipped

the ink stone in water and rubbed it against the slate slab to make the ink called *sumi*. Kneeling, she propped Macneil's head up on her knee. Taking the brush in his left hand, he drew a picture of *Susquehanna* flying the U.S. flag. Drawing with his left hand was awkward, but it was the best he could do with a broken right collarbone and sprained wrist.

"Ah! We were right. Look, it's one of the black ships. The main one, I think. He must mean that was his ship."

Coming closer, the pair watched intently as Macneil sketched himself wearing a naval officer's uniform, with epaulets on his shoulders, a dress saber hanging from his sash, and a tricorn on his head.

They looked at the prisoner with new respect.

"He's an officer! I'm sure of it. Only officers wear those tassels on their shoulders. It's the same with the Dutch on Dejima."

"We'd better tell the magistrate. He won't want us to put this officer back in the cage with those common criminals, even if he is only a barbarian."

"But this one's a criminal, too."

"A criminal?"

"He violated the shogun's law by coming ashore, didn't he?"

"Maybe it was an accident."

Already Macneil was drawing his next sketch as fast as he could. It showed Macneil and two other officers drinking from bottles. They stood on a ship's deck. By drawing stars and circles around his own head in the picture, Macneil indicated he was drunk.

Then with a few more quick brush strokes, he made his two drinking companions disappear from the scene. He showed himself staggering toward the railing. He sketched the arrival of darkness and the huge waves of the typhoon. Last, he drew himself falling overboard.

"He got drunk and fell into the sea. That's it!" Laughing, the samurai with the pock-marked face slapped his knee twice as if to confirm the correctness of this obvious analysis.

"I agree. Well, we must report to the magistrate."

They took the sketches and left. Macneil wondered about his punishment. Entry into Japan, whatever the reason, was forbidden and illegal. William Amanuma had told him such illegal entry was often punished by death.

CHAPTER 26

Nagasaki

The room where Macneil spent weeks recovering from his injuries occupied part of the second floor of the Daihian, a building attached to the Sofukuji—the Good Fortune Worshipping Temple—near the center of Nagasaki.

Obviously, his spacious quarters were not intended as a jail for prisoners, though he was a prisoner beyond any doubt.

Macneil seldom saw a priest. His needs were tended to solely by Chizu, a widow whose farmer-husband had been killed in an *ikki*, a peasant revolt, near the town of Isahaya. With their tiny farm confiscated, she—a childless woman of middle age—had been forced to do menial work in the nearest city, Nagasaki. Her face was as plain as a bowl of rice, her skin ruddy and chapped, her teeth snaggled, and in her nondescript indigo robe and faded red sash, she looked rough and unkempt. But she was also cheerful, clean, kind, and wondrously active. She regarded the young American with the proprietary air of a mother hen hovering over an injured chick.

Chizu's outstanding characteristic was her talkativeness. Her tongue clattered so much Macneil wondered how she could breathe. Her verbosity arose, he decided, not so much from the need to communicate thoughts as from a desire to fill the air space around her. As yet he had given her no reason to suspect he understood more than a handful of rudimentary words, but perhaps she believed that if he heard Japanese speech often enough, he would come to understand it naturally.

If so, she was not entirely wrong, he decided. The more he listened to her running commentaries, the more he thought he understood them.

Four times the doctor came to examine Macneil, changing the bandages and giving Chizu more salves and ointments to apply to his cuts and scrapes. The two samurais who had first interrogated him came again, bringing with them Meinheer Joseph Henrij Levyssohn, head of the Dutch trading mission on Dejima in Nagasaki harbor. A small, short man with a brick-red face, deep ridges in his forehead, thick auburn hair, and full, sensual lips had been brought along to act as interpreter.

After the three visitors had arranged themselves around Macneil's *futon* and Chizu had served them bitter tea, the taller samurai cleared his throat, unrolled an official document, and began to read from it. Occasionally, he would stop to explain the formal written words in more colloquial Japanese so the Dutchman could understand. Although Levyssohn had lived on Dejima in Nagasaki for twenty-seven years, he had no knowledge of written Japanese, and his spoken Japanese was pidgin, at best. His English, Macneil soon learned, was not much better.

But hearing the formal Japanese read, then its explanation in colloquial Japanese, and the Dutchman's translation to indifferent English, Macneil got the gist of the document clearly enough.

It said the Magistrate of the North—Nagasaki had two magistrates who took turns ruling the port—had investigated and had found that this naval officer had fallen overboard from his American warship while drinking, had been caught in a typhoon while adrift in the sea, and had been washed ashore unconscious and was injured on the rocks. Even though he had violated shogunal law by coming ashore, the fact that he was unconscious and injured suggested extenuating circumstances. This officer therefore was to be kept in the Daihian at the Sofuku Temple until he recovered and a foreign vessel could be found to take him away from Japan. He was not to be treated as a criminal.

What was really significant about the magistrate's document, however, was the last part: "Inasmuch as the shogunal administration in Edo has been asked by the United States of America to open certain ports to foreign trade, and inasmuch as our city of Nagasaki with its long foreign commerce history will surely become a port to be opened, we deem it wise and prudent to encourage certain of our younger officials and scions of leading families to spend time with this American officer, when he has recovered sufficiently, to learn his language and the customs and history of his country. With this in mind, we hereby authorize visitors to his room in the Daihian."

The document closed with, "Be it so ordered, Magistrate of the North."

When the paper was held up before his eyes, Macneil could see the magistrate's square red *han* or seal under his title.

The samurais departed first. The Dutchman stayed just long enough to add in awkward English, "You are very lucky young man. You be good, then will be put on ship. Take you other place. Yes, lucky. Very lucky." With a smile, he swallowed the rest of his tea and followed the two samurais out.

While Chizu gathered the tea paraphernalia, Macneil reflected that one of his earlier plans to go to a magistrate and ask for help in finding Anne, Margaret and his father would now be absurd. How could he possibly explain that he, an officer of marines in the U.S. Navy who had fallen overboard drunk, just happened to have three relatives lost somewhere in Japan?

But he was much encouraged by what the Magistrate of the North had written about opening the ports. Once the ports were open and foreigners could move freely about Japan, his search and rescue attempts should become less difficult.

After three or four days, Macneil's life on the second floor of the Daihian eased into a routine. At four o'clock in the morning, the temple dwellers were aroused by a gentle bell that gave out the most peaceful, soothing sound imaginable— beautifully deep and melodious. It did not shake or startle the sleeper into abrupt wakefulness but insinuated itself ever so slowly into his sleep-drugged unconscious mind, so that waking became a pleasure, almost an act of devotion.

So leisurely did each hum succeed the one before it that the half-aroused listener assumed the previous loving peal had been the last, and he would be about to return to slumber when the next trembled through the air above the temple grounds. Its susurrus would ease into the sleeping chambers of high and low alike, assuring all of Buddha's grace and benevolence.

Often enough, Macneil did go back to sleep. There was no reason for him to get up or even to be awake. The priests and the temple visitors may have had their breakfasts earlier, but Chizu did not bring his until around seven o'clock, just after she had carried off his toilet bucket.

Macneil was given only two meals a day, breakfast and supper, although at noon Chizu often brought tea and o-nigiri— rice-balls speckled with vegetable bits—to tide him over.

Breakfast and supper varied little. There was the ubiquitous white rice—of which Macneil could have all he wanted— pickled vegetables, seaweed and salted fish. In the morning, Chizu served him miso-shiru, a cloudy soup containing tofu cubes, which, though almost tasteless, were nutritious. In the evening the soup was always a clear broth, containing small objects of unknown origin.

The diet was monotonous and uninspired. Macneil longed

for bread and fresh fruit and beef, but he knew he was lucky to be given what he got, for it sustained and nourished him during his recovery. And it was surely better than the roots and berries and possibly raw chicken he might have been living on—with Ai?—had he been back in the mountains. He prayed Anne and Margaret were eating as well as he was.

Except for the noon tea and food she brought Macneil, Chizu seldom came to his room again until early evening, when she fetched his supper. At first, she fed him herself, but gradually he learned to use chopsticks with his left hand, since his entire right arm was bound tightly to his body to immobilize the mending collar bone and to protect his damaged rib cage.

In addition to her commentaries to the world at large, Chizu "taught" him a dozen words in essential Japanese—words for rice, water, pain, toilet, cold, hot, and so forth. Macneil already knew them, of course, but had to pretend he did not.

After dinner, Chizu brought embers in a pan to light the wick in the oil inside the circular, paper-shaded night lamp or *andon*.

Few Japanese—his nurse-maid managed to convey—ever slept in complete darkness.

From the deep cupboards built into two sides of Macneil's room Chizu brought forth the upper and lower *futon*—the wadded quilts—and a bag filled with bean hulls used as a pillow.

By the end of the second week, the constant pain had gone, at least when Macneil stayed motionless. At the end of the third week, he forced himself to crawl across the reed matting to one of the two windows where, with Chizu's help, he pulled himself up to a sitting position and, leaning his left elbow on the window edge, watched the scene below.

One window faced Nagasaki Bay, the other the center of the town. Since the temple was built on a slope at slight elevation above the bay, both windows afforded a broad view of Nagasaki life. As Macneil grew stronger and could use his right hand, he made sketches of what he could see with the paper and ink Chizu provided.

At first, Macneil contented himself studying the panorama of the bay and its shipping, the countryside and the city itself. He judged Nagasaki to be two miles long and three-quarters of a mile wide. He counted forty-two temples and shrines, but this number did not include the Sofuku Temple, of whose complex his building was a part, since it stood on the blind side of the room.

From his two windows, Macneil could see three main thoroughfares passing by his temple or originating from it. One was lined with shops, the second with lower-class dwellings, and the third—according to Chizu—with the homes of samurais, officials, and wealthy merchants.

When at last he was able to sit and sketch without much pain, Macneil would choose a scene to draw that day and spend the first hour scrutinizing it—the movement of the people, their dress and activities, and their conduct toward each other. Next, he would put a tentative outline of the scene on paper.

He found that with the *fude* or brush he had to draw quickly or the paper would absorb too much ink and allow the brush strokes to blur, so he persuaded Chizu, now a close ally, to procure a pencil—a rare item in Japan.

The street lined with residences of samurais and officials was divided by a rock-lined gutter two feet wide. Chizu liked to talk about this gutter and the clear-water stream running through it. In the stream swam multicolored carp, their bright hues visible even from Macneil's temple window.

Chizu said she had witnessed two sword fights between samurais living along that street, the cause being that one warrior's sword had brushed against another's in passing.

The magistrate's solution to this potential danger to public tranquility had been to dig a trench down the middle of the street, with north-bound pedestrians walking only on one side and those headed south restricting themselves to the other—with the water-filled gutter between them.

Along this upper-class street little could be seen of every-day life, since each house was enclosed by a high wall. On the street of lower-class dwellings that ran off to the left from the window overlooking the bay the view was more mundane, detailed and revealing.

For example, when the weather was warm enough—as it was now—many families bathed outside their houses in the street. These families owned wooden tubs three feet deep—just large enough to hold one bather. The tubs—one for men and one for women—were dragged out from under the eaves of the house and filled with hot water. When the water reached the right depth and proper temperature, the wife would call her husband, who then walked out from the house totally naked except for a wispy hand towel covering his genitalia. Pausing a moment to glance around and bow to any neighbors in sight, he would ladle out enough water to soap himself with, then rinse off and climb into the tub for a protracted immersion.

The other male members of his household would follow his lead in order of age, skimming off the surface film of dirt with a hair sieve. The soaking time of each bather lessened with descending rank in the family. The women washed in their own tub. Not all families had such tubs, but used the neighborhood *sento* or public bathhouse, whose tall, distinctive chimney Macneil could see two streets over.

Next morning, the bath water of the previous evening was used for laundry and to dampen street dust. Care was taken— Chizu had lectured—to wash the men's and women's clothing separately, for the men would throw away any garments found to have been "defiled" in the female tub.

Even then, the wooden tubs were not entirely emptied until evening when the next bath had to be made ready. The half-empty tub provided a handy source of water for use as a weapon against neighborhood fires whenever they might occur, which was all too often.

Macneil's observations and Chizu's description of the street of shops provided the material for Macneil's most interesting sketches.

All the shops were open in front, though some had a short curtain draped from a horizontal bamboo pole that one pushed aside to enter. Most of the shops doubled as homes, the shop-keeper and his family living in the rear or above. Customers removed their *geta* or clogs on the street and stepped up to the reed matting of the shop floor, where they sat and allowed clerks to bring them any merchandise they wished to examine and consider.

Shops dealing in egg-shell china and other porcelain were most numerous, though Macneil could also identify others offering swords, curios, lacquer ware, cloth, masks, dolls, toys, sugar figures, tobacco, scrolls, umbrellas, tooth powder, pomatum, pillows, and bed quilts. Many products were individually wrapped in paper that, according to Chizu's continuing monologue, had the price and even the quality written on it.

One shop Macneil watched with particular attention sold birds in cages and fish in jars. Most of its patrons were people returning from visits to the temple. Usually those who bought the birds in their little bamboo cages opened the cage doors on the spot and let the captive fowl fly away to freedom. Those buying the fish walked off with their purchases, reportedly to release them in ponds or rivers on their way home. Adherents to this gentle religion thus set free the imprisoned creatures to earn a reward for their kindness in the next world.

But every evening at dusk, the shopkeeper and his two daughters wandered through the temple grounds with nets attached to long poles. Often the freed birds were so accustomed to life in a cage that they seemed lost after release. Instead of flying off to the mountains around Nagasaki Bay, they perched forlornly in nearby trees as if saying, "Please tell me what to do next."

They fell easy prey to the nets of the shopkeeper and his daughters. No doubt they were soon sold again, so life for them became a cycle of release and capture, freedom and imprisonment.

Margaret used to say Neil had a calendar in his head, for he always seemed to know the day and month without consulting an almanac or even pausing to count. Each morning upon awakening in Nagasaki, his first thought was, *Today is the such and such day of such and such month.*

The morning of October first—almost four months after his first landing in Japan—Macneil went through the usual calendar exercise in his mind, but promptly realized that on this very day the whaler *Phoenician* was standing by off the northern Honshu coast awaiting a signal from him. Captain Hiram Stillwell would no doubt wait as long as he had promised, but then would regretfully depart.

Although he continued to sit by the window and look out at the passing scenes, Macneil could not bring himself to do any sketching that day. Chizu noticed his depression and tried to jolly him out of it, even bringing him what for her was doubtless a great delicacy—a skewer of broiled sparrow, including the bird's head. Since she must have spent money she could ill afford for this treat, Macneil had to eat it, but swallowing the wee bird's parts only deepened his gloom.

Neil looked forward eagerly to the visits of students who wanted to learn English from him because he wanted to learn more about Japan from them.

As the Dutchman Joseph Levyssohn from the island of Dejima had explained, the Council of Elders had recently advised the shogun to build up the coastal defenses of Japan and simultaneously encourage his people to learn as much about the Western barbarians as possible. This policy would prepare the nation both for war and for peace. Part of the plan called for language training, of which Nagasaki would become a focal point. The shogun "wished" that many of his ambitious, intelligent young samurais would learn English and, through the medium of that tongue, acquire the superior technology of the Western world. In the fief of Nagasaki, as in most others, the shogun's wish was *"Tsuru no hito-koe,"* to speak was to command.

CHAPTER 27

One week before his first English class, Macneil was moved from the second floor of the Daihian to a room on the first. Though he would miss seeing the lovely autumn colors on the hillsides from his two upper windows, the first floor location more than compensated for that loss.

Not only was it larger, but the new space also had an attached bath and separate open-pit toilet. For reasons he did not understand, the downstairs room had none of the fleas that had plagued him above.

The door to his new quarters stood close to the entrance of the Daihian, permitting Macneil to see for the first time the armed guard on duty there day and night. Until recently, his physical weakness would have prevented him from leaving, but now that he had regained some of his former agility, the Nagasaki magistrate must have decided to take precautions against his unauthorized departure.

Another possible explanation was that the guard stood there not to keep Macneil from leaving but to protect him. In her daily running commentary to the world at large, Chizu had mentioned the heated debate taking place in Japan over whether to open the country to the Western world.

One side held that Japan had no choice, since the Western nations were much stronger. Those opposed maintained that the sacred soil of the gods' homeland would be defiled by the hairy barbarians' feet and this defilement should be resisted to the death. Accordingly, Macneil's presence in the Daihian, which was not a secret, might motivate advocates of the latter view to dispose of a barbarian already polluting their soil.

The first evening in his new room, Macneil's meal also was a notch better than those he had been fed upstairs. Fish, both raw and grilled, was added, as well as a piece of fruit—tonight, a loquat. Two more candles had been furnished, though they still sputtered fiercely and gave off the same acrid odor.

When Chizu had heated the water in his large *hinoki*-wood bathtub, Macneil luxuriated in the finest bath he had taken since the summer evening when he and Ai had found a hot spring in the mountains en route to the *funa-kainin* training camp and had cavorted in it together.

Ai had insisted he scrub her back and she his, explaining that bathing and back-washing were national addictions in Japan, where a class of people called *sansuke* made washing the backs of others their lifework. Ai had made scathing comments about any civilization so backward as not to nurture readily available *sansuke* in large numbers.

Shortly after Macneil had climbed into his hot tub in the Daihian, Chizu entered the bathroom and made him climb back out and sit on a low stool on the wooden floor while she performed the same *sansuke* duties. After that, he soaped thoroughly, sluiced the soap off with water ladled from the tub, and again immersed himself in the hot water to soak, relax and think about the joys of a reunion with Anne.

Macneil's English class began at two o'clock in the afternoon. On the first day, only four students came, but this number increased quickly until it reached fourteen. None of them knew a word of English, though a few had a smattering of Dutch. Macneil was able to obtain from Meinheer Levyssohn on Dejima the same kinds of dictionaries he had used in studying Japanese under William Amanuma. One was English-Dutch and the other Dutch-Japanese. With these, he planned to teach his fourteen samurais English, while continuing to pretend he knew only a few words of Japanese himself.

In age, the students ranged from twenty to twenty-nine. On arrival, they placed their long swords on the sword rack in the entryway of the Daihian and entered their teacher's room carrying only their short swords, fans and writing materials. They were all dressed in the usual samurai garments. The tops of their heads were shaven, with hair growing on the side, in back, and in a narrow strip toward the rear of the crown. This strip was greased with camellia oil, then tightly drawn upwards and backwards, and tied in a topknot.

Just before two o'clock each afternoon, Chizu would set out the low tables, floor cushions, charcoal braziers, and tea cups and kettle on a hibachi. When the students were all assembled, Macneil would take his place and sit crosslegged facing them on the *tatami* mats. When he inclined his head in a nod, they bowed deeply.

Macneil had never been in a classroom of any kind in his life, though his father had taught him and Margaret the English classics, the Bible and their sums. Despite his inexperience, he managed during the first several months of instruction to teach his pupils the ordinary English greetings, names of commonplace objects, basic action verbs, and the construction of simple declarative sentences.

Their attitude toward him was an odd mixture of hauteur and respectful obedience. On the one hand, they had to respect the young Oregonian as their teacher, always an honored role in Japan. On the other, they could not forget they were samurais and their teacher merely a barbarian. Their eagerness to learn, however, was so strong that the respect due Macneil as a teacher soon won out over their samurai presumptions of superiority. And it was this very eagerness to absorb knowledge that enabled them to learn much faster than he had expected.

Each day, after two hours of instruction and drill, Chizu would serve tea, together with the rice-crackers, fruit or bean-paste cakes the students often brought along as gifts. After tea, the Macneil School of English would close for the day. The samurais—usually no more than eleven or twelve came any one day—would depart, each leaving a few silver *bu* coins in a bowl Chizu had set just inside the door.

Macneil had not expected payment for what he was doing, but Chizu explained it would have been unthinkable for the samurais to accept instruction without reimbursing him somehow.

After the first two months, the students had learned enough to communicate at a rudimentary level, so Macneil decided to introduce an hour of English conversation after tea. This idea was greeted with enthusiasm. Though what they said to each other in the beginning was often ridiculous, they did, after a while, begin to make remarkable progress.

One student suggested they all adopt American names and pretend they were a group of Americans or Englishmen chatting over tea.

Everyone readily agreed to this except Osamu Ito, whose father, the daimyo of the Kii fief, had sent his son Osamu to be the fief's *kiki-yaku* or agent in Nagasaki.

At twenty-nine, Ito was the oldest pupil, and the most important, since he was next in line to succeed his father in Kii.

Since Nagasaki was under the shogun's direct control, certain favored fiefs were allowed to maintain offices there to participate in the trade with the Dutch and the Chinese, though the shogun always made sure his profits were larger than anyone else's.

Because the Kii clan was a loyal Tokugawa adherent, one of the *fudai*, there was a rumor that Ito might be called to Edo to take an important post in the shogun's government, at least as long as his father still lived and headed the clan at home.

Since he was still unmarried, Ito had brought his slightly older sister with him to Nagasaki to run his household. Ito himself was short and squat, arrogant and—Macneil suspected—vicious, if given cause. He always spoke in rough, discourteous Japanese and never smiled, perhaps because his face had been scarred in a sword duel. The scar twisted the right side of his mouth into a permanent snarl. Obviously, he believed himself a cut or two above the others. And, according to Japanese definitions of social status, at least, he probably was.

At the other end of the spectrum from Osamu Ito stood a big, strapping fellow with warm eyes, a wide mouth and a marvelous set of teeth. Though he tied his hair in a topknot like all samurais, he shaved less hair from the top of his head than the others and so appeared younger. A few years older than Macneil, he was the most open and friendly of the samurai pupils, and perhaps the smartest.

This likable samurai came from the fief of Tosa, famous for fighting men and fighting dogs, and served as its agent in Nagasaki. His name was Shintaro Sakamoto. His intimates called him "*Shin-san*," but Macneil had given him the American name Thomas. He liked being called Thomas and insisted the others always call him that.

Thomas proved himself to be Macneil's most ardent pupil. He absorbed Western knowledge quickly and seemed attached to the American personally. Often, he would stay after class to ask if there were any errands he could run for Macneil.

Having settled the matter of names, Dennosuke "James" Inomata made the proposal that instead of tea they all drink sake. This idea was met with approving shouts, and thereafter the students took turns in bringing two or three *issho* bottles of *seishu tokkyu* (pure sake, special grade) to class for Chizu to warm and have ready to serve after the two hours of instruction.

At first, Macneil was doubtful about the introduction of alcohol into his classroom, fearing that the conversation sessions would degenerate into drunken arguments, but his doubts were erased when he saw how it turned out. Under the influence of the rice-wine, the students, except Osamu Ito, grew more friendly and relaxed. They lost their shyness and hesitation in speaking English, and as a consequence made faster progress.

To learn more about their country and language, Macneil asked them questions in English and listened carefully to the discussion they always held among themselves in Japanese before answering.

One afternoon in late fall, Macneil asked his class in English:

"How many fiefs are there in Japan?"

A flurry of Japanese conversation followed:

"Fief? What is that?"

"*Han*, you dolt."

"The teacher wants to know how many *han* there are in Japan."

"Well, how many are there?"

"Both *tozama* and *fudai* fiefs?"

"Of course!"

"There are 265, I think. How do you say that number in English?"

"We can't tell him the exact number."

"Oh, what the devil! The country will be opened to trade with the West, anyway. What difference will it make if he knows?"

"You will see what a difference it makes if you are caught and have to commit *hara-kiri*."

And so it went. Each evening when he was alone, Macneil thought up four or five such leading questions to ask the next day.

But he didn't always have to resort to such subterfuges, for many of his questions were answered in candid detail, without devious prompting. One evening Macneil wanted to know, "Why do the Japanese not want to have anything to do with Westerners?"

In Japanese, among themselves, the students mentioned the three reasons Macneil had heard from William Amanuma: the invasion by the English ship *Phaeton* of Nagasaki Bay in 1808, the rampage on the Kyushu coast by the American whaler crew in 1824 and the early shoguns' belief that the Western powers wanted to conquer Japan and make it a colony. Osamu Ito, however, offered an explanation new to Macneil but evidently well-known to the students. "We had better not mention that one," said Thomas Sakamoto to the others. "It is not only offensive but also ridiculous."

As might have been expected, however, Ito was not to be put off by any fear of offending Macneil. A certain priest and scholar of the eighteenth century, Ito said, had taught that though the Japanese were descended from gods, Westerners traced their ancestry to cats and dogs—a theory widely believed and for good reason, he said.

The students peered at Macneil as if fearing a wrathful explosion, but he only stared at them in silence for a moment. Then he said "*Wan-wan*"—the Japanese equivalent of "bow-wow."

The class laughed uproariously. Several clapped their hands and called for Chizu to bring on the hot sake. In a less tense atmosphere, they traded jokes with each other for the next hour.

During a later session of sake drinking and joking, Macneil's students began to tease their teacher about what they assumed to be his long abstinence from sexual pleasures.

One started off by asking in halting English:

"Chizu-san, she your wife?"

Chizu—who was twice Macneil's age—almost spilled the sake she was pouring, but managed to laugh as loudly as the others.

By then, Macneil had told his class he had been raised in the Oregon Territory among Indians, so one pupil—Tsunenosuke "Adam" Namura—asked:

"How many Indian wife you got?"

The class found this question hilarious, especially when their teacher answered, "More than I could count."

With a lecherous grin, another suggested, "I think better we send back-washer to teacher Macneil."

"No, thanks. I have Chizu-san. She is a very good *sansuke*," Macneil said.

"No, no. teacher! I mean real *sansuke* girl. Pretty. Young. She wash you *every*where."

The class howled with laughter.

When he thought all the humor possible had been wrung from the situation, Macneil tried to find another topic to capture their attention, but the class seemed captivated by the idea of sending their teacher a back-washer. They swore they would do so just as soon as they could find a *sansuke* pretty enough to deserve the honor.

One pupil—Keijuro "Robert" Ogawa—earnestly advised the American to remember that after the girl had washed his back, she was expected to pretend to be shy and would resist advances from him. This would be merely a device to make herself more desirable, and later she would charge more for her services.

After the students left, Macneil asked Chizu, with whom it now seemed safe to use more and more of the Japanese he had learned from Ai Koga and William Amanuma, about the *sansuke*.

"Public baths all have *sansuke* who wash backs," she said. "Most are men. But *yuna*, who are bathhouse prostitutes, also wash backs. Your students were talking about the *yuna*."

"Do you think they really will send one here?"

"I don't know. Do you want them to?"

"No, but would it insult them if I sent the *yuna* away?"

"It might."

"Is it true what they said about the girl pretending to be shy to make herself seem more desirable?"

"Some *yuna* will do that. Some will at first even pretend to be shy about going into the bathroom with the customer. Of course, it's nothing but play-acting."

Macneil hoped the idea of sending a bathhouse prostitute to his room was a sake-inspired joke. Being honest about it, he did not want to have to wrestle with temptation, for he did not know who would win.

With no attractive women near at hand, Macneil found it much easier to be faithful to Anne Macneil.

CHAPTER 28

As their study of English progressed and Macneil's friendship with all the samurais but Osamu Ito deepened, it dawned on him that they might become allies in his search for Anne and Margaret.

The fourteen Japanese men came from eight clans, most lying to the west of Kyoto in central Japan. If all fourteen agreed to help look for the two lost women, it would be a good start, though, of course, their eight clans made up only a small fraction of the 265 fiefs in Japan.

Macneil gave the matter much thought, but several dangers were involved, the paramount being that a pupil might report the American's request to the magistrate in his home fief—or in Nagasaki.

By then, however, Thomas Sakamoto and Macneil had become close enough that the American believed he could trust the Tosa samurai if no one else, so Macneil laid out the matter before him. He also showed the samurai sketches he had made of Anne and Margaret.

Hearing Macneil's story, Sakamoto bowed deeply and said in formal Japanese, "Teacher, I take it as an honor you have entrusted me with this confidence. I will not betray you. I know that neither of your women is in my fief of Tosa. My father is still active in our daimyo's castle and we would know if such women were there. However, I promise to keep my ears standing erect and make discreet inquiries."

As he stood to leave, he looked again at Macneil's sketches of the women. "Did you draw these?"

"Yes."

"I wonder if you would be kind enough to draw my picture?"

"I would be happy to. Come by in the morning."

At the hour agreed on, the Tosa samurai appeared in a light green *hakama* or divided skirt with thin vertical stripes, a sky-blue surcoat and a dark gray *juban* or undergarment with a silk brocade purse tucked in its fold. He held a pipe in his hand and they agreed he could bring his long sword with him into the room for a realistic effect.

When the others saw the sketch of Thomas, they too asked for portraits—they used the word *e*—of themselves. After Macneil had sketched most of his pupils, they asked if they could bring their friends and relatives for the same purpose and he agreed.

Takanosuke Shige brought his aged parents, the mother so feeble she had to be carried. Another student brought his betrothed, a girl who seldom stopped giggling. Still another, his two children. Only one brought his wife, about whom he was most derogatory, calling her his *tonsai* or pigwife. Two others brought geishas.

Even Chizu asked Macneil to draw her face. To reward her for her friendship and loyalty, he gave her a face better than the one which God—or Buddha—had originally granted her. The new image pleased her so much that she joked she would use it for *0-miai*. When Macneil asked what that meant, she explained she would let a marriage broker use the picture to arouse the interest of possible husbands.

Osamu Ito, as ever the proud and distant one, disdainfully posed for and accepted the American's portrait of him. Later he showed it to his older sister, who wanted one made of herself.

All who came for their pictures insisted on adding to the coin bowl inside the door, ignoring Macneil's protests that he wanted nothing for his art.

He had entered the fifth month of his captivity and was beginning to despair that a foreign vessel would ever call at Nagasaki. Not even a Dutch ship had entered the harbor and the Dutchman Meinheer Levyssohn was said to believe that pirates or storms were responsible.

A game to which his students were addicted was called *Hyaku-nin Isshu* or One Hundred Poems. It was a card game Macneil never tired of watching. The poems were short, only thirty-one syllables, and the students apparently knew them all by heart.

The bottom half of each poem was written on a card and placed face up on the tatami. A reader would then recite the entire poem while the players competed to see who could find the bottom part of the poem first. Quickness of hand and a thorough knowledge of all one hundred poems were the requisites for winning.

Some knew the poems so well that they could begin reciting the bottom half as soon as the reader uttered the first one or two words of the poem. Even so, the players still had to find that bottom part first. The winner, of course, was the one who had collected more bottom-half cards than any other when the last poem was read.

Usually, *Hyaku-nin Isshu* was played at the New Year, but Macneil encouraged his students to play it at any time. He added a new twist to the game by having the young samurais translate the poems into English. Even though the resulting translations were awkward, they bettered the American's understanding of classical Japanese. In time, he even memorized many of the poems himself, in both Japanese and English, having listened so often to the recitations.

One afternoon after class, "Douglas" Iwase and "Louis" Moriyama fell to arguing about recent fighting in the Amakusa Islands. Apparently, the shogun in Edo had ordered the daimyo of Higo to stamp out all remaining hidden Christians in Amakusa. A samurai force had been dispatched there and had swept through the islands, demanding that the inhabitants perform the act of *fumi-e*—stamping on an image of Jesus Christ.

When this happened, the peasants in the islands rose up in rebellious wrath and smote the Higo samurais several mighty blows.

Reinforcements sped to Higo from other Kyushu clans and the rebels were at length put down, with fearsome losses on both sides. Many rebels were executed out of hand, but the shogun extended amnesty to others, knowing that if he denuded the islands entirely of their population, no one would be left to raise rice, catch fish, and—most important—pay taxes.

Macneil burned with curiosity about the *funa-kainins'* fate, but that was one question he could not ask. Nor was their fate ever mentioned, though he led the conversation back to the Amakusa revolt as often as he could.

During this discussion about the battles in Amakusa, one pupil, Yoichiro "Steven" Nishi, asked, "I wonder how those peasants could inflict so many injuries on the samurais from the other Kyushu clans?"

"Didn't you hear?" asked Rokuro "Louis" Moriyama. "They used rifles."

"Rifles? Peasants with rifles?"

Macneil was listening attentively, for he remembered Ai Koga saying her father wanted her to return to Amakusa, then go to the port of Naze in Amami-Oshima to buy weapons for the *funa-kainin*.

"What dirty tactics!" spat another pupil.

"Dirty? Why dirty?" Macneil asked.

"Swords, spears, even bows and arrows are the weapons of honorable men, teacher" came the reply. "If peasants are permitted to use firearms, the whole world will be turned upside down. Don't you see? The peasants might then defeat samurais in battle. Our whole social structure would suffer an upheaval."

Several agreed. Thoughtfully, Takaaki Daigo from the Satsuma clan said, "You're right, of course. But what can we do about it? The Western world is forcing us to open our doors. How can we resist without modern weapons?"

"I heard that the Portuguese brought firearms to Japan about the middle of the 1600's," Macneil said, "and that you Japanese learned to make matchlocks in large quantities."

"That's true," said Sakushichiro "Randolph" Uemura. "At the Battle of Nagashino in 1575, Lord Oda drew up his 3,000 matchlock-men in three ranks and had them fire in succession. While one rank was shooting, the other two were reloading. The success of this tactic convinced many they should use firearms."

"But then a reaction began to set in," Daigo of Satsuma said. "The daimyos foresaw that if they gave their peasant-militia firearms, the samurai class would gradually be destroyed by ignorant, uncouth farmers. Within sixty years after that battle, all firearms were either destroyed or locked away. No more were made."

"Anyway," Thomas Sakamoto said, "whether the shogun signs the treaty with America or not, it is now certain Japan will be pushed into the international arena. But it will take us one or two decades to learn how to make firearms again."

Later, Macneil thought about the Japanese not being able to manufacture firearms. If he could enter that business, it would give him the wealth he needed to expand his search for Anne, Margaret and Nairn.

CHAPTER 29

Still no ship came to anchor at the mouth of Nagasaki Bay, though the coast lookouts had reported several that passed them by.

Macneil's despair deepened and hopelessness darkened his mood. His sketches grew somber. He studied less and drank more sake.

His constant concern about Anne and Meg showed in his face. Seeing this, without knowing why, the language students tried to cheer him up.

Late one afternoon, Thomas took the American aside after the others had left and said, "Teacher, five pupils intend to give you a present." With his usual wide grin, he spoke in unsure but improving English.

Wearily, Macneil glanced at him and asked, "And just what would that present be, Thomas?"

"You remember about back-washer?"

Macneil's heart sank. In his glum mood, such a woman was the last thing he wanted, but he worried about the repercussions of a flat refusal.

"Do you mean a real *sansuke*—or a *yuna*?" Macneil asked.

"Both kinds wash backs, but this will be a *yuna*—so she will do other things, too."

Macneil tried to think of a way to ward off this unwanted favor.

"I haven't seen her, but they tell me she is most unusual," Thomas said, pulling at his lower lip. "Very pretty and new to the business."

"Who are the five pupils?"

"Namura, Motoki, Iwase, Nakayama and Nishi."

"Well, tell them thank you, but I'm not interested."

"Please, teacher, I promised I not tell. Forget I told you this.

I just wanted you to have warning."

"Thank you, Thomas. In that case, I'll say nothing."

A week passed. Macneil forgot Thomas' warning. He continued with his English classes—though without enthusiasm—and did occasional sketches for friends of his pupils and even one for the head priest of the temple. Evidently, Macneil's India ink portraits were being well received, for the requests kept coming though he tried to limit them to three or four a week.

In his growing despair, Macneil preferred to sit at his prison window and stare out gloomily into the gathering Kyushu dusk and think of Anne and pray for her well-being. Sometimes memories of Ai crept in, too—uninvited but welcome.

One evening—it was now the thirteenth of January, seven months since coming to Japan—he was sitting at his window drinking sake and thinking dark thoughts. Chizu had taken away the dinner tray, laid out the *futon,* heated his bath, and left for the day. When Macneil could no longer distinguish the outlines of the statues and trees in the temple grounds, he picked up the sake bottle and retired to the bath to soak and drink—and try to forget. Staggering, he almost dropped the bottle on the bathroom floor.

He was no sooner immersed in the liquid warmth than he heard a female voice from his room. *"Gomen nasai"* —"Excuse me."

Unsteadily, Macneil climbed out of the *hinoki*-wood tub, used a small towel to absorb the water running off him, and put on a light robe.

Just inside the closed sliding door that was the entrance to Macneil's room knelt a willowy creature in a light-green kimono and a persimmon-colored sash. Her hair was done up ornately with two tortoise shell combs holding the curling whorls in place. Through his sake-induced mental cobwebs, made thicker by his hot bath, he suddenly remembered what Thomas had told him.

This *yuna*—bathhouse prostitute—was not exactly what he would have described as beautiful, but she did have fine aristocratic features and marvelous skin. And what made her more appealing was that she had not blackened her teeth or shaved her eyebrows. Macneil guessed she was in her early thirties, but it was still hard for him to be sure about Japanese ages.

"Forgive me," she said in soft-voiced Japanese. "Are you alone?" She looked this way and that around the room.

By then, the charcoal in the brazier had burned low, and Macneil was getting chilled standing there still damp from his bath.

"Yes, I'm alone, but I'm getting cold," he said in her language.

She bowed in apology. "*Sumimasen. Sensei no seito no ane desu. Shozo wo o-negai shimasu. Mochiron haraimasu kara.*"

What his visitor said and what Macneil thought her words meant did not exactly coincide.

The first problem was that the American did not know the word *shozo*. And while he was aware that the verb *haraimasu* meant to pay and he had learned a similar verb *araimasu* meaning to wash, his ear did not catch the initial '*h*' in the former so he thought she meant, "I will wash" instead of "I will pay." The second was that he confused the two *ane:* one was a blood-related elder sister, while the other was a word used in the nighttime entertainment business by younger geishas when addressing an older one, by younger male patrons of houses of assignation when talking to the older women of the house, and when summoning a waitress in a restaurant.

What this woman of aristocratic mien actually said to Macneil was, "Forgive me. I am the elder sister of one of your pupils. I came for a portrait. Of course, I will pay."

What he *thought* she said, however, was, "Forgive me. I am the elder sister (in the sense of being a woman employed in a nighttime entertainment place) of one of your pupils. I came for a *shozo* . Of course, I will wash."

"Fine," Macneil said, still not knowing just what '*shozo* ' meant. Anyway, he was desperate to get warm again. "Now I must get back into my bath. It's very cold in this room."

"Shall I wait out here?"

"No, come into the bath with me. We have to do it there, of course."

Now it was her turn to look strangely at the American. "But I can't go into the bath dressed like this," she protested, indicating with a graceful gesture of her slim hands her elaborate kimono.

"Well, take off your clothes then," he told her sharply. Macneil was too chilled to allow further pointless discussion. Hurrying back into the bathroom, he left the door open for her to follow—if she wanted to. His teeth chattering, he sank into the steaming water.

Macneil had decided he would let this *yuna* wash his back, after which he would give her several silver coins and send her packing. And he would make her promise to tell no one the details of their meeting.

Looking out through the bathroom door, he could see that the *yuna* was slowly—*very* slowly—removing her clothing. She was doing so with considerable reluctance and indecisive reflection as she took off each garment.

When finally only a chemise-like garment—the *nagajuban*—remained, the *yuna* latched the room's outer door from the inside, then turned to approach the bath with the utmost hesitation, as if two forces were dragging her in opposite directions. *She's playing this game of shyness to the hilt,* Macneil thought. *Maybe even over-playing it a little.* But then he recalled Thomas saying she was new to the business.

With a bow, the willowy *yuna*—taller than most Japanese women—stepped down onto the wooden boards forming the bathroom's floor.

"You had better take that thing off, too," Macneil said.

Blushing, she cried, "But then I would be totally...well, without anything on."

"Of course, you will. That's the best way to do it."

For a moment, it seemed she had changed her mind and was going to leave. Suddenly, however, the doubts left her face and she smiled. "Oh, I see now. You want to do the *shozo* with me nude."

Macneil nodded, wishing she would get on with the back-washing preparations. He would worry about the *shozo* later.

Standing up she turned her back, removed her last remaining garment, and hung it on a wooden peg beside Macneil's *dotera* robe. Turning back toward him, she sat down on a low wooden stool, her knees pressed tightly together and her arms folded over her nicely formed breasts. She had a mole on her left kneecap.

Stepping out of the bath, Macneil sat on a stool with his back to her. After waiting for half a minute—during which time she did nothing, he handed her the soap and a *tawashi* or scrubbing brush. "You might as well get started," he said.

"Start...what?" Her voice was low and tremulous as if she were nervous.

"Washing my back, of course."

With a smile, she said, "I had heard you Westerners have very strange customs, but I had no idea just how strange."

Nonetheless, she started washing his back—with gentle hesitation at first, then with increasing speed and vigor.

When she had ladled hot water from the bath over Macneil, she moved her stool around so that her back was turned to him. Obviously, she now expected him to perform the same service for her. Since Macneil had done this for Ai in the hot spring in northern Japan, he supposed it was required by custom.

While washing her back, Macneil could not stop his hands

from wandering beyond the limits of what would be strictly defined as a "back." He washed her arms and shoulders, her neck, her breasts, her stomach, and her legs as well.

Reminding himself that she was, after all, only a *yuna*, he washed the inside of her thighs and then her private parts, paying them particularly close attention. These washing motions had a disturbing effect on the *yuna*. Her eyes closed, her mouth fell open, and her breath came in short, shallow gasps, punctuated by occasional soft moans.

Macneil sluiced the lather away and pulled her into the wooden tub after him. He found that if she sat on his lap facing him with her legs wrapped around his waist, they both fitted into the tub neatly. While he taught her elementary kissing, her fingers were busy inserting his male part into her female cavity.

Believing that decency mandated he know her name before the final stages were reached, Macneil asked her what it was.

She answered, "Katsu...ko...oh!"

"My name...is...Neil."

"I...I know. Oh...oh! Now, now, I'm *coming!*"

Actually, in Japanese, she said, "*Iku wa yo!*" or "I'm going!"

When she had "gone," Katsuko laid her head on Macneil's shoulder, pressed her lips against his neck, and relaxed against him like slowly melting wax. In the warmth of the bath water, the lassitude coming on the heels of satisfactory coition lulled both into a state of half-sleep for five minutes or so.

Then Katsuko's hips began to move ever so lightly, bringing Macneil's grenadier into the stiff and erect posture of attention once more.

She whispered against his neck, "*Atashi ga suki na no?*" ("Do you like me?")

He assured her he did. To him, it seemed the gentlemanly thing to say.

"*Honto?*" she asked.

He vowed he had spoken the truth.

In a moment, they repeated the previous performance and then, after a more extended respite, during which Macneil really did go to sleep, they did it again.

Just before "going" for the third time, with the bath water sloshing around in the tub and splashing out on the floor, Macneil heard a knock at his outer door, followed by the sounds of someone trying impatiently to enter. He ignored this summons until Katsuko and he were thoroughly drained. During this time, the knocking continued unabated. If anything, it grew louder.

Wearily, Macneil disengaged himself from the *yuna*. Donning his *dotera*, he went to unlatch the door.

In burst Thomas and Chizu.

"Is someone with you?" Thomas asked while Chizu hastily latched the door again from the inside.

"Why, yes, there is. What's the excitement?" He and Thomas were speaking English.

Thomas gripped his teacher's arms in the intensity of his interrogation. "What's her name?"

"It's Katsuko. Don't you remember? She's the *yuna* you said was coming to visit me."

Thomas struck the side of his head with the heel of his hand.

"This means serious trouble, teacher. She's no *yuna*. That's the elder sister of Osamu Ito."

"Dear God in Heaven," Macneil breathed, growing faint. He might as well have ravished a niece of the Tokugawa shogun.

"She may have left word at home that she was coming over here," Thomas said. "If she did, Ito could be on his way here himself."

CHAPTER 30

"Chizu," Thomas ordered, "tell that woman to get out of the bath and dress quickly. Say her brother may be on his way here. You help her."

Still not fully understanding all that had happened, Macneil asked Thomas, "What does *shozo* mean?"

"Portrait."

"Oh, my God! She came over here to have me sketch her, but I thought she was the bathhouse prostitute the students were going to send me."

"We must get her out of here. Right now." Thomas left to stand guard at the temple gate.

Led by Chizu, Katsuko came into the room trying to cover her nakedness. Chizu helped her dress, for tying the heavy *obi* or sash in back was a chore no woman could do alone.

Dressed, but with her hair still in disarray, Katsuko sat down at the low table, casting fearful glances at the door. Chizu started to comb her hair back into its previous fashion.

While Chizu's fingers flew about their task, Macneil got out his sketch pad and began in wild haste to draw Katsuko's face.

To complete the sketch and to dress Katsuko's hair took fifteen minutes. "Run hire a sedan chair to carry this lady home," Macneil told Chizu. "Take some coins to pay the bearers with. And when you see Thomas, ask him to come back in here. Tell him we're ready for Ito any time."

As Chizu hurried out, Macneil called after her, "And tell the guard in the entryway that *no one* came to see me this evening. Give him money to buy his silence."

When Katsuko Ito and Macneil were alone, he felt acutely embarrassed. Not knowing what to say, he drew her into his arms and kissed her. It was a long kiss. She did not seem anxious to go.

"May I come to see you again?" she asked.

"Of course, but don't let anyone know you're coming."

"My brother has to visit our father in Kii soon. He should be gone at least a month. I'll let you know."

He led Katsuko Ito to the door with an arm around her shoulders and told Thomas, "Chizu has gone to fetch a sedan-chair. Will you kindly escort this lady to the chair and tell the bearers where to take her?"

Smiling at Neil over her shoulder, Katsuko serenely left the room and walked toward the entryway. Marveling at the way she had recovered her poise, Macneil thought, *Maybe this is the style of Japanese nobility.*

For the next several days, Macneil watched for an angry reaction from Osamu Ito. If the Kii samurai learned of his sister's unescorted visit to Macneil's quarters, he would surely have suspected the worst, and Neil was afraid he might storm into the Daihian with drawn sword and armed lackeys at any time.

To Macneil's relief, however, nothing like that happened, and in class Ito gave no sign he disliked the American any more than he always had.

Macneil's affairs fell back into their tedious routine of teaching, study, sketching, and long sessions of despair and contemplation in the evening bath. The liaison with Katsuko had added brief excitement—and pleasure—to Macneil's life. While deeply regretting his infidelity to Anne, he nonetheless found himself wishing Katsuko would come again. Not that he imagined himself falling in love with the tall aristocratic woman, but the boredom and frustration of making no progress at all in finding Anne and Meg were eating away at his sanity. *If only a ship would come,* he thought a dozen times each day.

In his desperation, Macneil considered escaping from the Daihian, which he could have done, and making his way to the *funa-kainin* stronghold in Amakusa. But with the recent fighting there it was possible that Ai Koga and her clan had been wiped out. If he found no one there, he would be at a dead end.

The odds seemed to favor biding his time and waiting for a passing ship. Surely one would sail into port soon. Never before in his memory, Thomas told Macneil, had so many months passed without a Dutch or a Chinese ship entering the harbor, or a ship of another nationality at least trying to enter.

About that time, Osamu Ito departed on a month-long trip to Kii to visit his father, the daimyo, having postponed it several times for one reason or another. His sister Katsuko was left to run the house they rented on a slope overlooking the bay. With her in the house lived three servants—a groom, a maid and a cook—and Katsuko began to send them to their *futon* early. Afterwards, she would take a sedan-chair to the entryway to the Daihian, where she gave a coin to the guard to insure his silence, and came to Macneil's door, which he always unlatched about that hour.

The Nagasaki winter, usually mild, was now upon the city. Once snow fell, a rarity delighting the children. The chilly evenings bothered Katsuko and Macneil little, however, for they would either immerse themselves in the hot bath or snuggle between heavy *futon* wearing *dotera,* a winter version of the summer *yukata* robe. Their relationship was a congenial, sedate one, not a wild, passionate romance. Despite Osamu's ferocious nature and appearance, the Itos were genuine aristocracy, with the blood of emperors in their veins. Because of her aristocratic manners and language, Katsuko fascinated the American. And it seemed he was of interest to her as a foreigner whose customs, beliefs and manners were often the opposite of her own.

One night early in their relationship, when they held each other between the *futon,* she whispered, "Whenever I'm with you, Neil-san, I feel as if I'm visiting a foreign country."

"What do you mean?"

"It's as if I'm in a place where the rules we live by in Japan no longer apply. It would be hard for you to believe all the restrictions that govern us."

"Even daimyo families?"

"Especially us. Did you know we can't marry without the shogun's consent? Maybe that is why we have to find love before such a marriage. Even our clothing must meet certain strict specifications. How we speak to our superiors and inferiors and even the depth of our bows are dictated by the shogun. And he has spies from his *metsuke* bureau everywhere who report on all we do. We can't even repair a hole in our castle wall without his permission."

"And you couldn't marry just anyone you happened to love?"

Covering her mouth, Katsuko laughed as heartily as he had ever heard her laugh. "One of the reasons my brother Osamu has gone back to Kii," she said, "is to help our father arrange an advantageous marriage for me."

"You're about to be married?"

"Not right away. Maybe not for a year or so, but soon, no doubt. I am already well past the prime marriage age, but my father wants me to marry as high as possible to strengthen the position of Kii. He has rejected many proposals because he is always looking higher. Of course, I don't really care," she said, her face a study in distaste. "I would rather stay single than marry just anyone selected for his wealth or influence."

"Maybe your father wants you to marry the emperor," Macneil joked.

"No, there's no chance of me marrying the emperor, since I am much older than he. I'm closer in age to the shogun, and, of course, the Ito family is one of the three branch families of the Tokugawas. Several shoguns have come from our family as well as brides for the shoguns and even occasionally for the emperors."

Katsuko snuggled closer. "There! That's enough family history for one evening. Now you tell me: who are the foreign women in those two sketches?"

Macneil knew she meant the two sketches of Anne and Margaret he had made to show to Thomas. He hesitated, considering how to answer. Since there could be no permanent relationship between him and Katsuko, the truth should not make her jealous. And if she married someone high in the ranks of Japanese officialdom or aristocracy, there was always the chance she might one day help him in his search. He decided to tell her the truth in detail.

The story excited her interest, being the kind of sad love tale so many women relish. After some thought, she said, "I'll try to help you find your sister and the other woman. I'll write to my younger sister in Kii and tell her the whole story."

Groaning, Macneil said, "I wish you wouldn't do that. Your sister will be there in Kii in the same house with your brother."

"My sister hates Osamu. She would never tell him anything."

"Still, if you tell her the story in a letter, it might be read by someone else."

"Do not worry, Neil-*san*," she said. "What if Osamu does find out about your two lost women? What difference would it make to him?"

Her wriggling around on top of Macneil distracted him from further worries for the time being, but he still didn't like the idea.

About two months later Thomas came bursting into Macneil's room during class.

"*Sensei!*" he cried, "A ship! A ship!"

Macneil leapt to his feet.

"Already in the harbor?"

"No, no. Not that close yet."

"Where then?"

"North of here, off the Chikuzen coast."

"What kind of ship?"

"The lookout said British. It's a surveying ship, sailing south along our coast."

"Has it entered port anywhere in Kyushu?"

"No, and it probably won't."

"When will it pass the mouth to Nagasaki Bay?"

"If it keeps its present speed, the day after tomorrow."

"That doesn't give us much time." Macneil walked nervously around the room that had confined him so long.

"Thomas, will you go see the magistrate and get his approval for me to leave? I'm sure he'll be pleased to be rid of me."

"How will you get aboard the British ship?"

"Can't we take a small boat out to one of the islands at the mouth of the bay and signal the survey ship when it passes? I'll even row out to intercept it if need be."

When Thomas had gone, Macneil ended the class, cautioning his pupils that it was far from certain he would be able to board the survey ship. Two of them left to procure more sake, and they were in the midst of a bacchanalia when Thomas returned.

"He said it's all right," Thomas reported. "And you were right. He is glad to be rid of you."

That evening Chizu packed Neil's few belongings, and he gave her most of the contents of his coin bowl. Thomas left to arrange a boat for the morrow and to procure provisions in case they had to stay on the island more than a day. They would carry water and an axe in case they had to cut wood for a signal fire.

Macneil slept fitfully, but was up early to be ready. When he stepped outside the Daihian for the first time in six months, the plum trees were in bloom, a harbinger of spring in Japan. He wanted to run and shout, to dance a fling. He gave Chizu three *bu* coins and told her to buy a bird at the bird seller's and release it as far away as possible.

Carrying her bird cage, Chizu went with Thomas and Macneil to the dock and watched as they got into the skiff propelled by a stern-oar. Macneil kissed Chizu on the top of her graying head, sending her into a fit of giggling. "I'll be back," he promised. "Be sure I can find you if you have to go elsewhere."

Kami-no-Shima was the name of the tree-covered cone of rocky soil just outside the mouth of Nagasaki Bay. Since it had no beaches, they landed among surf-pounded boulders and clambered over them to the dry slope above, dragging the skiff after them.

Next morning, Macneil and Thomas scrambled up the hill

to take up their lookout duties. The path they followed came out of the trees to pass along the edge of a sheer cliff. From there, it was a straight drop of a hundred feet to the rocks below.

They looked out over the dark-green sea. Clouds drifted southward. The morning breeze blew crisp and cool from behind them. The balsamic aroma of the pines wafted up from below.

Thomas bowed his head and made the sign of the Cross.

Macneil was amazed. He asked if the Tosa samurai was a crypto-Christian.

Thomas waited a minute until he had finished his silent prayer, then answered, "Yes, I am."

"Why did you wait till now to let me know?"

"I have always kept it a secret. We may be the only Christian family in all of Tosa province. When you told me Ai Koga was a Christian, I decided to tell you—at the right time. I may be able to get in touch with the Amakusa *funa-kainin* for you, through mutual Christian friends."

Macneil told Thomas about the agent for the *funa-kainin* in the free port of Naze in Amami-Oshima. They agreed that failing other means, they would try to send word to each other through him.

"Have you ever been to Naze, Thomas?"

"Once. On business for my clan. It's under the Satsuma administration and they are touchy about any interference in their territories."

"Is Satsuma entirely independent of the shogun?"

"No, not entirely. If the shogun wanted to, he could probably muster enough troops to force his will on Satsuma, but why should he? The Satsuma people pay lip-service to the shogun and their daimyo observes the ritual of spending every other year in Edo. After all, Edo is a far more interesting and exciting place than Kagoshima. The women of the flower and willow quarters are prettier and more accomplished, their necks are longer and whiter, the best eels are raised near there in Urawa."

"You were talking about the port of Naze."

"So I was. Well, the shogun has no official representative there, so the Satsuma authorities use it as a free port. They let people and ships come and go as they like. They collect duty on goods entering Kagoshima from Naze, almost as if Naze were in a foreign land."

"Why did you make the sign of the cross at this spot?" Macneil asked.

"After the repression of Christians long ago in Shimabara, the daimyo of Hizen rounded up thousands of suspected Christians, loaded them into barges, and brought them here. They were all forced to jump from this ledge down onto those rocks below."

Later that day, Steven Nishi rowed out to the island to bring Macneil a letter Chizu thought might be important.

Steven stayed only long enough to tell them that more news of the fighting in Amakusa had been received in Nagasaki. Twenty-six of the rebellious peasants captured in the fighting had been tried and crucified upside down. Three had been women.

Dear God, Macneil prayed, let Ai Koga be alive and well.

Promising to come again the following day, Steven left. There being still an hour of daylight remaining, Thomas and Macneil trudged back up the path to their lookout post, where Macneil tore open the letter and tried to read it. It was written in the *sosho* or grass-writing style and in difficult epistolary language. He might have understood much of it in the standard *kaisho* style and even some in the intermediate *gyosho* style, but grass-writing was far beyond his ability.

He handed it to Thomas. "Who is it from?"

"Katsuko Ito."

"Would you read it and tell me what it says?"

While Thomas was reading the long letter, Macneil glanced out to sea. There, under full sail, ran southward the three-masted British surveying ship at a fast clip.

"Look, Thomas! Look!" Macneil cried, "There she is!"

The "lime-juicer," as the sailors aboard *Phoenician* would have called her, looked magnificent with the golden orb of the westering sun behind her.

"Do you think I can catch her?" Macneil started down the narrow, rocky path at a half-run.

"Maybe," Thomas panted behind him.

At the bottom of the path, where they had dragged the skiff up on the rocky shore, Macneil began throwing his scanty belongings aboard. Thomas tried to help, but Neil said, "I can do this alone. Tell me what's in that letter."

"I can tell you that while we row out to intercept the ship."

"No, Thomas. You had better not go out there with me. Alone, I am sure they'll take me aboard, but if they see a samurai with me, they might take you prisoner or even open fire on us. Let me have the skiff. You stay here. Steven can pick you up tomorrow."

"I want to go out there with you, to see you safe aboard."

"Please, Thomas. There's no time." Macneil finished stowing his gear. He started pulling the light skiff across the rocky ground to the edge of the sea.

"All right. Katsuko says first of all that she's pregnant and that you're the father." He started pushing the skiff while Macneil pulled. "Second, it's too late for an abortion, so she had to tell her brother, and he knows who the father is. Come on, just one more shove and we'll have her in the water."

"What else does she say?" Macneil climbed into the skiff.

"Her brother has completed arrangements for her marriage next year, which means she will have to be sent to an isolated place like Sado Island to have her baby, where the birth can be kept secret."

Wading into the water, Thomas started pushing the skiff through the deepening water out of the tiny cove. "Osamu Ito has sworn to take revenge on you. And he is being called to Edo to take a high position in the shogun's government."

"Anything else?" Neil saw that the water was up to Thomas' waist.

"Her last line was 'If they had given me a choice between a mansion in Edo and a room in the Daihian in Nagasaki, I would have chosen the Daihian.' "

"Thomas, I count you as a good friend. I have given you my uncle's name and the name of his company in Hong Kong. I'll come back soon. In the meantime, God bless you."

"And God bless you, too, *sensei*." Giving the skiff one last shove, the Tosa samurai straightened up and yelled his farewell, "*Go-kigen yo! Iza-saraba!*"

Macneil was paddling too hard to do more than wave briefly back over one shoulder.

With six hundred yards of choppy sea between him and the survey ship, there was at least an even chance Macneil would not intercept it in time. Already, he was beginning to consider what to do if he failed to board the Britisher. Rather than return to the tedium of the Daihian, and the danger he was sure to face now that Osamu Ito knew of his sister's seduction, it might be better to turn the skiff south toward the Amakusas, praying that Ai was still alive, and was there.

Macneil was still at least a hundred yards from where he should have intercepted the fast-moving survey ship when she passed beyond that point. Standing in the stern of the unsteady skiff, he shouted until he was in danger of turning his throat inside out.

"Dear God, help me, for Anne's sake," he prayed.

CHAPTER 31

East China Sea

In despair, Neil Macneil had stopped rowing. He knew he had lost his chance of catching the ship now.

As he stared at it, time and motion seemed to cease. It was a full minute before he realized this was not just a trick of the imagination. There were no more frothy ostrich plumes on the waves. Suddenly, the wind had died.

Now, the ship moved only in a silky roll, her canvas flapping idly from the gentle motion of the sea. For the moment, the survey ship was becalmed.

Grabbing the stern oar again, Macneil began to row. Five minutes, ten minutes passed, when all he was aware of were the sounds of his labored breathing and the plunk-and-splash of his oar.

Then came the cry of the lookout across the remaining distance, "Small boat off port!"

Thank merciful God, he thought, *they've seen me.*

Once past Nagasaki, the British survey vessel *Mariner* closed in toward the Amakusa Islands and slowed her pace. Under only her mizzen-skysail, she wore her way south along their western shores, taking occasional soundings to fill in blanks on the Admiralty charts partly completed by earlier surveyors.

On the fourth day after Macneil had been lifted aboard HMS *Mariner*, the ship stood off the west coast of Satsuma, the southernmost fiefdom on Kyushu. From there, Captain Palmer St. James told his American passenger, they would run south parallel to the line of islands—Amami-Oshima, the Ryukyus, the Senkakus—that led like stepping stones to Formosa.

Mariner would follow the coast of Formosa farther south and then veer west for Hong Kong.

The southern coast of Satsuma—the last of Japan proper—slowly disappeared in the distance, ending Macneil's ten months in that country. His thoughts were as much with Ai as they were with Anne and Margaret.

For what little he knew, all three of them might be in captivity, or dead. And Katsuko Ito was pregnant with his child, the object of her brother's wrath, and probably on her way to a long period of exile until she gave birth.

That evening, Captain St. James asked Macneil to dine with him in his cabin for the third time. *He must find me as strange and fascinating as I find him*, Macneil thought. Certainly, they were compatible, for by the end of their first evening together, they were laughing and joking like old friends.

Captain Palmer St. James was twenty-four, only two years older than Macneil, and as dark as the American was blond. Otherwise, they might have been kinsmen. They were of the same height and physique. They had the same lean faces, blue eyes and high noses. Even the same wavy hair, though Palmer's was black as night.

Palmer St. James would have passed for what was commonly called "black Irish," but if he was, his mother, now deceased, must have ventured outside the sacred confines of marriage at least once, for his lineage, he said, could be traced back many generations through the purest English nobility and landed gentry.

Palmer's father, Darcy St. James, was the ninth Earl of Oxbridge. Addressed as "Lord St. James" in the House of Lords and while on his 83,000-acre estate in Sussex, he was Admiral St. James while performing his duties as Vice-Lord of the Admiralty. Oxbridge Hall was built in the seventeenth century and had ninety-one rooms. The Earl also owned a brooding, pseudo-Gothic castle in Scotland to which the family went only for pheasant and grouse shooting. The town house in Belgrave Square pleased Palmer more, as it did his brother, Colonel George St. James, Light Cavalry, age twenty-six, heir presumptive to the title.

The immediate family also included Virginia St. James, age twenty-three, whom Palmer characterized, albeit with a hint of affection, as "barking mad."

As a loyal Scot who had never really forgiven the English for what they had done to Bonnie Prince Charlie, Macneil's father Nairn did not approve of the English upper class. Even he, however, would agree that the unmatched courage and equanimity under fire of their elite officer class had won for England its overseas empire.

Macneil had been prepared to dislike Palmer St. James, but the past four days aboard his ship had shown the American that a spark of friendship could be struck between two men of entirely different backgrounds.

Macneil's first appearance on the white holystoned deck planking of *Mariner* must have given her captain a shock, for the American was bearded, barefoot, and dressed only in a light Japanese robe. He had introduced himself as Neil Macneil, lieutenant of marines, late of *USS Susquehanna.*

Palmer St. James' only comment had been, "Fancy that."

Macneil fully intended to reveal his true identity later, but decided to wait until they reached Hong Kong, where it wouldn't matter if he was thrown overboard as an impostor.

Dressed in a spare pair of the Englishman's white breeches and a shirt from ship stores, Macneil had dined with him each evening and had drunk a good deal of his port, to which he was not at all accustomed. Tongue oiled by the wine, Macneil spun his host tales of growing up in the wild Oregon Territory and six months of confinement in a Nagasaki temple, with no mention of intervening adventures. St. James had matched Macneil glass for glass and tale for tale with his own accounts of going to sea as a midshipman at fourteen, the land battles in which his older brother George—whom he idolized—had fought, and the mad-cap antics of his little sister Virginia.

Virginia, it seemed, had recently scandalized English society—and not for the first time. During the past summer, Lord Darcy St. James had allowed her to give a dress ball at the family seat, Oxbridge Hall: a mammoth granite pile facing a long reflecting pool bordered by what were said to be the tallest poplar trees in England. As the warm summer evening wore on, more and more guests spilled from the main ballroom out into the cooler air around the reflecting pool. A battalion of butlers followed with trays of champagne glasses.

One of Virginia's young friends, Lady Clarissa Howard, in a moment of wine-inspired perversity, dared her hostess to swim naked across the pool. Virginia thought a minute, swallowed her sixth glass of champagne, and told a butler to fetch a candle, which he did, shading its flame carefully with his hand against the mild breeze. As he turned back to his other duties, Virginia drew a deep breath and set fire to her dress. The female guests began to scream and the males to shout.

With the sangfroid of a Charlotte Corday on her way to the guillotine, Virginia stepped out of her burning, hundred-guinea gown and her smoking lacy lingerie, the scantiness of which sent titillations of delight through the lords and ladies. As the last garment touched the ground, she plunged into the pool and swam across it.

Later, her friends asked her, "But, Virginia darling, why didn't you simply jump into the pool with your dress *on*? That would have put the fire out quite nicely, wouldn't it?"

"But don't you see?" Virginia had replied—and her words still echoed throughout London society, "that would hardly have been sporting."

Slapping the thigh of his long right leg in exasperation, Palmer had said, "She's dotty, I tell you. Mad as a coot."

The captain's quarters on *HMS Mariner* were situated under the poop at the after-end of the quarterdeck and had a day cabin that extended the width of the deck at the stern, commanding a fine view through the aft windows. These quarters had their own head, a night cabin, and a dining room. The entryway, guarded day and night by a marine sentry, led out onto the quarterdeck by the wheel. One side of this deck was used exclusively by the captain.

Macneil's quarters were little more than a spare hammock stretched between two posts in the cabin of First Lieutenant Owen Poore. Neil avoided Poore's company as much as possible, fearing if they compared too many notes, it would become evident he was no more a marine officer than a Cheyenne brave. As a consequence, Macneil spent much of his time talking to the crew in the wardroom or visiting Palmer St. James whenever the captain allowed him underfoot.

After a fine dinner of salted beef roast that evening—the captain had an overflowing larder and wine chest bought with his private funds—the two sat late over port, listening to the creaking spars and tackle overhead and the groaning timbers below as *Mariner* rolled this way and that in a quartering sea.

Having pulled off his knee boots, St. James had his stocking feet propped up on the dining table, from which his best cabin pewter had just been cleared away. The smoke from his cheroots wafted past Macneil's nose on its way to freedom through the aft windows.

"To President Pierce," St. James toasted, lifting his glass.

"To the Queen, God bless her," Macneil said, returning the courtesy.

"I 'spect, old boy, you'll be re-joining your ship in Hong Kong?" The captain's eyes were half-closed as he rolled the port over his tongue.

"I expect so, yes, if *Susquehanna* is still in port." Macneil hated to deceive a friend, as Palmer St. James was fast becoming, but if he told the captain the truth now, he might change course for the port of Naze in Amami-Oshima, less than a day's sailing away, and drop the American off there without so much as a by-your-leave.

"We'll nip on down to Hong Kong in no time, my dear fellow." Palmer spoke with the nasal twang typical of the English aristocracy and gentry. "*Mariner* has completed her surveying chores for this voyage and I only hope the Senior Officer on Station there will assign me to a fighting ship and more exciting duties. Surveying bores me witless, you know."

"Pity, that," Macneil murmured.

"Pray, tell me more about your six months in that prison." Palmer poured out two more measures of port, in which Macneil was already awash. "S'truth, I'm fascinated by these Orientals."

St. James asked dozens of questions about the Japanese, on whose shores he had never set foot, though he had sailed up and down their coast for months. He wanted to know about their coastal batteries. Neil told him what Thomas had said about their number and location in southwestern Japan and the size and age of the guns and what Macneil had seen for himself in the Straits of Shimonoseki and near the mouth of Nagasaki Bay.

St. James nodded with satisfaction. "Splendid! Even with these puny nine-pounders on *Mariner*, I'll wager I could take out one of those batteries in three salvos. No protection for the gun crews, you say? They'll learn from bitter experience, I fear."

When they had finished the bottle of port, St. James went up for a stroll around his private deck. Macneil started to turn in, but when he saw that a ship's lantern still burned in Owen Poore's cabin, he decided to take a turn through the ship while waiting for his cabinmate to retire for the night. Poore was a talkative sort and asked as many questions about a marine officer's life aboard an American ship of war as his captain asked about exotic Japanese ways.

On the gun deck of *Mariner*, five seamen were smoking their pipes, this area forward of the galley being the only place aboard where the men were permitted to smoke because of the fire hazard. Beyond them, the manger was in plain view, with its goats and sheep and hogs, though with the voyage nearing its end, only a few were still left uneaten.

When Macneil returned to his cabin, Owen Poore was snoring in his bunk. Hanging his shirt and breeches on a hook screwed into a post, the young American hoisted himself by the overhead line, then eased his body into the swaying hammock, which was a little too short for him.

Next morning, the first thing Neil heard was the shrill and quaver of a boatswain's pipe and the lookout's call, "Ship ho!"

In five seconds, the man aloft followed his first call with a second, "Ship fine off starboard quarter and closing, sir!"

With sunlight flooding the tiny cabin, Macneil could see that Lieutenant Owen Poore was not in his bunk. Over the clatter on deck, he heard a goat bleating, and then the cannonade-like beating of a drum, calling the complement of the surveying vessel to quarters.

CHAPTER 32

"Masthead there!"

"Aye, sir."

"Can you read yon vessel?"

"A big 'un, sir. A two-decker."

"Captain," broke in Lieutenant Pennington, "she'll be *Wolodimir*, 58 guns. On Vladivostok Station. Only non-British man-of-war that size in these waters."

"Russian, eh?" said St. James. "I'll speak to her captain. See what news he has from Europe."

Macneil had come up on the quarterdeck.

"Helmsman," said the captain, "pray set me a course to come alongside her."

"Aye, aye, sir."

"Ah, there you are, Macneil. Fine morning, what?"

"Good morning to you, Captain." Macneil watched *Wolodimir* less than a mile off starboard. She was even larger than *Susquehanna*. With her 58 heavy cannon, she could blow *Mariner* out of the water, but she was a sailor and not a steamer. As a screw frigate, little *Mariner* could augment her sail with steam and probably out-distance *Wolodimir*, even though she was of shallow draft and designed for surveying work, not speed. Her six nine-pounders, as St. James had pointed out with regret, could do little more than vanquish pirate junks.

Ship inspection had been completed before the Russian vessel was sighted. St. James had been on the point of ordering gunnery practice. The tanned seamen on deck were barefoot and stripped to the waist, with bandannas tied around their heads to protect their ears from the blasts and to keep sweat out of their eyes.

"Haven't had news from Europe since we left Hong Kong three months ago." St. James told the American beside him.

"Mayhaps the Russian captain will join me for a light repast and some Portuguese amontillado. I laid in a few casks in Lisbon on the way out last year."

Only seven hundred yards separated the two ships.

Turning to a seaman, St. James said, "Make a signal. Say I—"

"By God's breath, Captain, wait! Look!" The sailing master pointed.

"Christ save us!" exploded the first lieutenant. "She's opening her gun ports. All of 'em!"

With icy calmness, St. James said, "My word, I do believe you're right, Mr. Pennington. The insolent fellow may be planning something underhanded." He added, "And *Mariner* with nothing more than nine-pound popguns. Jove, I do wish I had a proper fighting ship."

Could it be the huge Russian man-of-war was going to fire on *Mariner*? Macneil looked around. The crew divided their attention between *Wolodimir* and Captain Palmer St. James, who stood relaxed on the quarterdeck. He was dressed in clean white breeches and white silk stockings. From his waist hung his sword with its gold hilt. His frock coat with its epaulets had just been removed in anticipation of heated physical activity.

In the gangways the Royal Marines had been drawn up, wearing red jackets, white crossbelts, trousers of blue, and high black headdresses with scarlet plumes. Lieutenant Owen Poore strode from one gangway to another inspecting the uniforms and equipment of his small contingent, whose main duty in a sea battle was to clamber up into the shrouds and fire their muskets at the enemy's gun crews.

Seeing Macneil about to leave the quarterdeck, St. James said, "I shall be glad of your company. As a fellow officer—even though a colonial—you should derive a certain pleasure and mayhaps even some instruction from observing how your British cousins handle a ship in battle. But whatever our Roosky friends have in mind, I shall not favor them with much opportunity to use those guns, especially not the forty-two-pound carronades I can see through the glass."

He handed Macneil his fifteen-inch brass telescope, then turned to give orders. "You will favor me, Mr. Pennington, by shaking out all the reefs. Then hoist skysails and studding sails, set fore and maintop, and crack on the flying jib and the main royal."

"She's within easy range, Captain," called down the lookout.

"Indeed," said St. James, taking back his telescope. "Ah, yes, Mr. Pennington, you might also order a full head of steam on the boiler just in case her intentions are not honorable, as now appears likely."

Abruptly, *Wolodimir* disappeared from view in a mass of smoke as she loosed a broadside at the survey ship.

"For what we are about to receive..." the captain murmured in the naval tradition. Then he said more loudly, "We will clear for action, if you please, Mr. Pennington."

Where all had been calm and comparative quiet, suddenly *Mariner* was transformed into a veritable bedlam. The salvo from *Wolodimir* took her square. A noise Macneil had never heard before or had never even imagined, as if the sails had all been ripped asunder at once, clawed at his ears. It was the roar of the Russian shot whistling through their rigging.

Pennington shouted to St. James, "She's firing double shot, sir!"

Even Macneil could tell that, for double shot struck the hull with a one-two thud, the interval between the two impacts being nearly indistinguishable. One-two, one-two, one-two. *Mariner* shuddered with each double thud, as did the American.

It was terrifying experience, but Macneil stood his ground by St. James. He wasn't going to let this proud aristocrat of an Englishman see him flinch in the face of enemy fire.

The boatswain came running up. "Permission to issue grog, Captain?"

"Denied," said St. James. "It's too late for Dutch courage now, sir."

Smoke from a second salvo enveloped *Wolodimir*. This one was even better aimed than the first and when it struck *Mariner*, a cloud of splinters and fragments from the bulwarks together with bits of torn hammocks rose, while shot-cut rigging fell. After crashing through the bulwark, a smoking thirty-two pound cannon ball rolled across the deck toward a powder scuttle. At the last possible instant, a barefoot powder boy, about thirteen years old, kicked it overboard.

The fore-topsail plunged into the slings; the jib sheets were shot away.

Mariner was now picking up speed as her screw began to take hold, even though a third salvo from *Wolodimir* smashed to splinters all boats but the jolly boat. This metal deluge knocked over three of the six nine-pounders and wreaked havoc among the crew and the marines. The decks were slippery with blood, and the screams of the wounded, some of whom were rolling about with arms and legs torn off, formed an agonized crescendo.

"Smartly now," St. James, icier than ever, ordered. "Cut

that wreckage away."

The gunnery lieutenant ran up. "Sir, permission to open fire?"

"By all means, Mr. Burke, fire as you bear!"

Turning to Macneil, the captain said, "Our three remaining nine-pounders won't even make the Roosky blink, but it will buoy up the crew to think we're doing something."

Trying desperately to maintain a demeanor as cool as the captain's, the American asked, "But why should a Russian warship attack us, Palmer?"

"I haven't the foggiest, my dear fellow. Why, indeed?"

Lieutenant Poore sprang up the six steps to the quarterdeck and when he was no more than five paces from Captain St. James, stopped and half-turned to point with his left arm toward the Russian two-decker. As he opened his mouth to speak, a non-explosive shot from one of the enemy's heavy guns struck him in the side, and Owen Poore, quite literally, disintegrated. Body fragments flew every which way, but none fell on deck at the spot where he had been standing. Gore and blood spattered the captain and Macneil, droplets interspersed with gobs.

"I believe we have lost Mr. Poore," St. James observed, wiping blood from his eyes with a white silk handkerchief.

Later, when he inspected the grisly litter of the fight, Macneil found odds and ends of what must have been his former cabin-mate's skin, one piece with hair attached, stuck to the inside of the bulwark around the quarterdeck. He also found a finger driven into the wooden railing like a nail hammered into the wood. He did not know what to do with it, so he left it in place.

With the damaged spars and canvas cut away and the screw revolutions building up toward their maximum, *Mariner* was at last zigzagging out of firing range.

After bursting through the gun deck, a Russian round shot had swept away the siding of the manger where the livestock were penned. The nanny goat kept by the officers for her milk had raced up on deck, only to have a shell fragment take off her front legs at the knees.

A seaman—the one who milked her daily—gently lifted the weakly bleating creature in his arms. Passing below Macneil, he carried her to the rail.

With tears streaming down his cheeks, he heaved the nanny goat overboard.

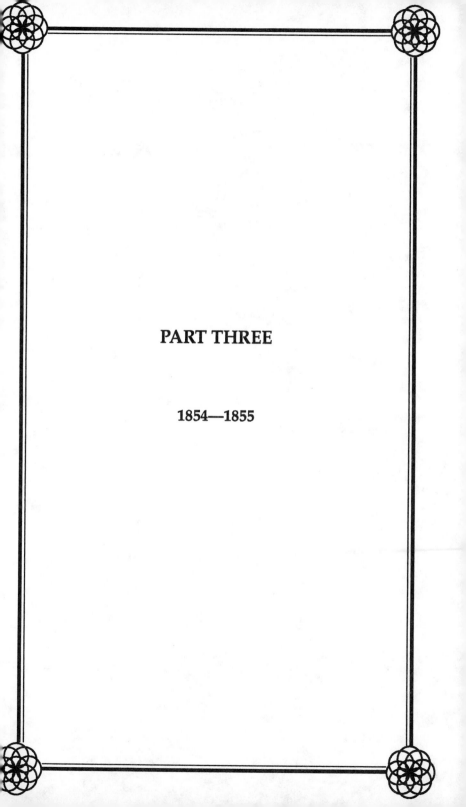

PART THREE

1854—1855

CHAPTER 33

Port of Naze

Although she suffered no irreparable structural damage from the enemy salvos, *Mariner* needed extensive repairs as well as time to tend her wounded. Propelled only by her screw, she limped toward the port of Naze on Amami-Oshima. With her damaged rigging and shattered masts the survey ship looked like an unsteady sea gull emerging tousled and battered from a fight with two truculent pelicans.

After doubling the lookout, St. James stayed on deck the rest of that day and till mid-morning of the next, when Amami-Oshima was sighted. He also took the precaution of dousing the sea-lanterns throughout the night.

The Russian two-decker was not seen and presumably had not again sighted *Mariner*. Owen Poore—what little could be found of him—was buried at sea sewn into a hammock. Four other corpses were prepared for burial in the same way, with roundshot added. These and others soon to die constituted what the captain called the "butcher's bill."

One wounded seaman had screamed almost continuously since the sea fight. The third mate, who had a smattering of medical experience, said the man would not survive to see the harbor at Naze. His prediction proved correct.

Except for the captain, the *Mariner* officers all discussed possible reasons for the unprovoked attack. St. James kept his own counsel, glowering at the sea behind *Mariner* with angry dark-blue eyes.

Daring once to intrude on his private deck, Macneil said, "Palmer, those two lookouts can see farther than you. Why don't you rest and eat?"

He got no reply.

"I'm sure you'll find the Russian again someday," Macneil said later, "when you command a ship of the line."

"I dare say I will, laddie," St. James said through clenched teeth. "A ghastly business, really. Owen Poore was a friend of mine. His father was the vicar of a parish on our Sussex estate. Owen was older by several years, but I've known him since boyhood. I'll have to go see his father when I'm next home." His voice hoarsened, and he said no more.

Macneil cast around for a way to change the subject. "I've been meaning to ask you, Palmer. Do many Englishmen become ship captains at the age of twenty-four?"

Turning from his pacing of the deck, St. James ambled over to Neil's side. "There have been twenty-one-year old captains, though I'm confident the average age when they first attain captaincy is much higher."

"What did you do to earn your rank at twenty-three?"

"You're thinking, old boy, that when your governor is Vice-Lord of the Admiralty, ascension up the naval rank ladder is swift and almost automatic, what? I'd rather fancy that, and by my word, I'd like to say it's true. It's what many want to believe, so let them, and be damned to them, I say."

"Obviously, then, such was not the case?"

"Fact of the matter is," he said, cupping his hands to light a cheroot with a lucifer in the light breeze from the island ahead, "I was made captain before the governor became Vice-Lord."

"I see."

"Oh, I readily admit that as an admiral and member of the House of Lords, he was able to influence important persons to give my record more than passing consideration, but what really counts in the Queen's navy is what we call 'friendly interest.'"

"Friendly interest?"

"Aye, it's a term used to refer to the unofficial opinion held of you by senior officers, usually the captains of vessels you've served on. They pass the word around. 'Watch old Smythe's cub, he's a comer.' Or, 'Damnedest thing, sir. That lad stood there at the railing—mind you, the ship was sinking fast—and calmly directed lowering the boats while older men quailed and threw themselves overboard.' That sort of thing."

"And you did such things?"

"Really, Macneil, it wouldn't be fitting for me to comment on such matters," he said, turning away. "Suffice to say that as this 'friendly interest' accumulates, your climb up the ladder quickens."

"Will you stay in the navy? I mean, always at sea, seldom at home."

"Oh, I say, it's not that bad. You see, at any given time, more than half our naval officers are on half-pay, which really isn't half-pay. It's more like three-quarters pay. You're on half-pay when you're not on active duty aboard a ship at sea. The admiralty doesn't have that many active vessels, except in time of war, so more than half of us have to be ashore doing whatever we like and drawing about three-quarters of what we would be receiving on active duty."

St. James paused to study the enlarging hills of Amami-Oshima through his brass telescope.

"But to answer your question," he said, shutting his telescope with a series of clicks as the four sections entered each other, "I suspect I'll stay in the naval service. I've got a good start on promotions, and it's a sporting sort of life if you're single and have a roving eye. But you—a marine officer—should know that, shouldn't you? At any rate, my brother George will inherit the title when our father dies, and I'll have to make my way somehow, don't you know? Frankly, I'd like to serve out here in the Orient as long as I can. Demmed fascinating place. In Hong Kong, I'll introduce you to one of the reasons for my fascination. Her name is Hut'ieh Gonzaga. Her father was Portugese, her dam Chinese. She's what is commonly called a 'pretty Portugee.' Very young but quite luscious, I assure you."

"Are you learning Chinese from her?" Neil asked.

"I'm trying, but it's devilish hard."

"How about Portuguese?"

"She speaks that tongue indifferently, I'm afraid. Hardly remembers her father. Chinese is her native lingo, but her English is almost as good. She went to a finishing school of sorts in Hong Kong—the Diocesan Girls' School—a place where poor Eurasian girls are given free educations by nuns who are also missionaries," said St. James with a laugh.

Macneil looked at him.

"I was laughing at those poor missionaries. They go to great trouble and expense to educate and elevate those girls, who, upon graduation, are quite proper, chaste, and well-schooled in morals and the social graces." He laughed again, louder this time. "Then, if they have any looks at all—and most Eurasians seem to be a cut above average in appearance—the girls are snapped up by wicked wights, like myself, as mistresses. The missionaries can't stop it, though they bewail it loudly and threaten all concerned with hellfire and damnation. In fact, their school is commonly called the 'Nuns' Riding Academy.' "

St. James studied Macneil for a moment. "If you weren't so demmed eager to hurry back to Japan on *Susquehanna*, I could arrange for you to meet one of the recent graduates of the academy, with temporary matrimony in mind. Hang me if I don't think you could have your pick of the lot, with your flat stomach, legs just right for high boots, and that devil-may-care look the ladies seem to go dotty over."

"Palmer," Macneil said, "I've told you about my Anne and how I feel about her. How could I, in good conscience, enter into a state of 'temporary matrimony' with such a woman?"

"Merely a suggestion, old chap. Nights can be very lonely on Far East station."

"Those same nights would be just as long for Anne."

"For your sake, I hope they are."

Mariner was now much closer to Amami-Oshima, whose coastal features had begun to take on personality.

"Mr. Pennington," St. James said to his first officer, "pray reduce screw revolutions to three hundred." To the helmsman, he said, "Take us in through yon passage, if you please." He pointed to the space between two islands now looming large directly ahead of *Mariner*.

"By the mark, six and a half," the linesman bawled.

And two minutes later, "By the mark, six!"

"Well, this is not time for me to be idle," St. James said. "I must take *Mariner* into port and arrange for her repairs."

Amami-Oshima—the back door to Japan—was a small group of islands, almost tropical in climate, that lay halfway between Okinawa in the Ryukyu or Loochoo chain and the southern tip of Kyushu, being if anything somewhat closer to Okinawa. It did not have one distinct harbor equipped with docks for loading and unloading. Instead, the vessels that called here anchored in any of several inlets and had their cargoes lightered off. With no officials on hand to collect tariffs on goods or assign dock space, docking was an easy, informal arrangement.

Mariner had no cargo to discharge but instead needed repair facilities. Of timber, Amami-Oshima had aplenty. That was obvious. From his observations in Nagasaki, Macneil assumed Japanese carpenters had no match as craftsmen.

The repairs needed by *Mariner* were nearly all above deck: shattered bulwarks, rent sails (she carried her own extra canvas), broken spars and masts, torn or frayed lines. Given the materials, all these could be done while the ship still floated. There should be no need to careen her on one of the glistening white beaches, in any case a monumental task.

Easing his way in among the islands, the captain found a protected inlet he liked. The anchor—the "hook," as St. James called it—was lowered with a prolonged rumble, as if the ship and its crew were heaving a collective sigh of relief.

The jolly boat took the first officer Mr. Pennington, the

carpenter and carpenter's mate, and Macneil ashore, where four fishermen had gathered to watch. They had passed the town of Naze itself as *Mariner* wended its way into the anchorage, and Macneil asked one of the fishermen to show them a path leading back to the town. Showing no surprise at being spoken to in Japanese—though Mr. Pennington appeared thunderstruck—the fisherman not only pointed out the path but offered to lead the party around the promontory and through the low hills to the town, a distance of one-quarter mile.

In the small town of Naze, they paid their fisherman guide a silver Mexican trade dollar from Mr. Pennington's pocket and explored the main street while searching for a lumber yard and local carpenters. The street was lined with shops resembling those of the street Macneil had observed from his temple window in Nagasaki, though the merchandise these shops sold was sometimes quite different.

Here in Naze, Macneil found more products—toys, statues, cloth—of obvious Chinese origin and more tropical fruit. In particular, the stores that sold birds and beasts as pets caught his eye.

These pets included tiny, long-haired dogs with eyes like saucers and almost nothing in the way of a nose, long-bearded goats, mandarin ducks, shy, darkness-loving nightingales, baby bears, pheasants with gold or silver plumage, and red-faced, apoplectic monkeys.

One shop sold nothing but toy *kara-jishi*, frightening mythical creatures with a dog's face and a lion's body. Hundreds of them in many sizes, colored red and yellow, were aligned on shelves—like a child's nightmare on a stormy night.

Children and dogs abounded, with extremely agile chickens. They also saw a team of street tumblers with lion masks, a sword-swallower, jugglers, albino ponies regarded as sacred—overfed and waddling fat, and a group of eight street musicians making the most unearthly noise—a squeaky orchestra of fife, drum and stringed instruments, each player apparently seeking with the greatest diligence to drown out the noise of his neighbor—and, against reason, succeeding.

A trio of remarkable top-spinners detained the party longer than anyone else. They so impressed Macneil that he gave them one of his hoarded silver *bu* coins, and asked them where he could find timber and carpenters.

The *Mariner* men spent an hour talking to three carpenters squatting on their heels and constantly filling and refilling their small metal pipes. They understood each other badly because of the local dialect, so the carpenters agreed to go aboard *Mariner* and see for themselves what had to be done and the officers would then buy whatever timber the carpenters said would be needed. Pennington gave them ten Mexican trade dollars, which they bit and pronounced sound, as a down payment on services to be rendered, and they all left for the ship.

The following morning Neil sought out Mr. Ueda, the man Ai Koga had said was the confidential agent in Amami-Oshima for her *funa-kainin* clan.

Ueda was not at all hard to find. Everyone in business in Naze seemed to know everyone else. It turned out that Ueda was, among other things, a ship chandler, giving Macneil a reasonable excuse to call on him.

Ueda received Macneil in his living quarters in the rear of his open-front shop, at the east end of the main street. Kneeling in the entryway, Macneil bowed and told Ueda his name and the name of his ship.

At Macneil's first words in Japanese, the cloud lifted from the agent's face, and his smile widened. Before Macneil could go on, he clapped his hands, called for tea, and announced to whoever was in his kitchen that an *erai o-kyakusan*—a "great visitor"—had deigned to call at his home.

Momentarily disconcerted by this outrageous flattery, Macneil struggled on. "My ship will need supplies. I would like to bring our purser here and introduce him." He didn't know the word for purser, so he said "the man who buys food."

Ueda, who was in his fifties, heavy-set, and with short-cropped, gray hair, drew in his breath deeply and said, "I will be honored to provide whatever you need." Settling back on his haunches again, he asked, "How long will you be here?"

"We estimate twelve days."

"Plenty of time," he said, producing an abacus and letting his fingers dance over its beads. "Yes, yes. Plenty of time. Please do not worry. I hear you're already trying to buy timber elsewhere." His Japanese was easier to understand than the carpenters'.

"Yes," Macneil said, sipping the tea with a slight bow, "we found carpenters yesterday."

"I know them," Ueda said, putting away his abacus. "I will talk to them and make sure they give you a good price. You should have come to me first. I would have given you the cheapest price." He paused, then asked cautiously, "Judging from the amount of timber you need, it sounds as if your ship was heavily damaged. A storm, perhaps?

"A Russian ship—*Wolodimir*—attacked us without warning. *Mariner* is only a survey vessel. Our nine-pounders would do no more damage to the Russian's sides than hailstones on a tile roof. We still do not understand why we were attacked."

"Then you do not know?"

"Know what?"

"England is at war with Russia."

Macneil said he was astounded at the news and the speed with which it had come to Ueda's ears.

"We keep informed," the *funa-kainin* agent said. "Many small ships come here from China and from Southeast Asia. They transship their cargoes here to Satsuma. It enrages the shogun, who wishes he could collect tariffs and control this back door to his country, but even the Tokugawas walk carefully when they deal with the Satsuma clan."

Macneil had heard about bellicose Satsuma before. "Why is that?" he asked.

"They're a war-loving clan," Ueda said. "More than forty percent of their people are samurais. That figure is unheard of, except for the Tosa and Aizu clans."

From the depths of Ueda's house came the screams of female laughter. A brief scowl flitted across his face. "Those girls! Never do they take their lessons seriously."

"Actually, I came to see you about another matter, Mr. Ueda."

Ueda bowed his head. "Any way I can be of service. Please tell me without reserve."

"It concerns the *funa-kainin* clan of Amakusa."

Blanching, Ueda looked back over his shoulder. He spoke in a low, strangled voice. "What do you know about them?"

"Please rest easy, Mr. Ueda. Let me explain."

Macneil told him that he and Ai Koga had been of service to each other north of Edo last summer. When they parted, she had given him Ueda's name as a person to see when the American needed to reach her.

As Macneil spoke, some of the alarm and tension left Ueda's face, but not all of it.

"But you are a Westerner," he said. "How could you have been in Japan's interior last summer?"

"Believe me, Mr. Ueda, what I am telling you is true. Later, in Nagasaki, I heard about the fighting in the Amakusa Islands. I became worried about Ai Koga. She means a great deal to me. All I want to ask you is—have you any word about her? Is she safe and well? If she is, could you send a message to her?"

After studying Macneil's face for a long moment, Ueda seemed to make up his mind. "All right. I will answer your questions. First of all, Ai is safe."

Thank God for that, Macneil thought.

"But she is not well."

Macneil waited.

"No, I won't send her a message from you."

Macneil's heart shriveled.

"But I will do something better than that." Ueda smiled. "I'll take you to her."

"Take me to her? But I can't go back into Japan again. They wouldn't let me."

Ueda's smile widened. "You won't have to go anywhere. She is right here in my home, at this very moment."

CHAPTER 34

Macneil could hardly believe his ears. Ai Koga here in Naze! Elation flooded through him, and his face flushed with happiness. He ached to see her immediately.

"You said she isn't well?"

"I must tell you what happened before I take you to her." Ueda stood up to close the sliding *fusuma* around the room. "On orders of the shogun, the daimyo of Higo sent an expedition to annihilate the hidden Christians in the Amakusa Islands. In the fighting Ai was captured, and tortured. They tried to make her reveal the location of the *funa-kainin* hideouts in Amakusa, but she wouldn't tell them. She was imprisoned in Higo castle where they must have done terrible things to her. She has never told anyone what tortures they used."

Dear God, Macneil thought, *while I was resting comfortably in a Nagasaki temple and carrying on with Katsuko, Ai was being tortured.*

"Her father sent three of his best men to steal into the castle at night and rescue her. Two of them were killed."

"Was she badly hurt?"

"Not from the escape, though her body was torn and mangled from the torturing. Even before she had fully recovered, she joined her father's rebel band again. They captured a Higo cannon and turned it on the enemy, but they didn't know much about artillery, it seems. They must have used too much gunpowder. The cannon blew apart. Part of the barrel struck Ai in the head. For a week, she was unconscious. More than half the *funa-kainin* were killed in that and other battles. Today, less than a hundred survive. They are hiding in remote valleys in Amakusa until this trouble blows away."

"But what about Ai?"

"Her father Heihachiro sent her here on a fishing boat. That was a month ago, and she is still not well. The doctors—if you can call them that—here in Amami-Oshima cannot do anything for her."

"Couldn't you take her back to Kyushu, perhaps to Nagasaki or Kagoshima?"

"She's now listed as a *tazune-mono*..." A wanted person was what he meant. "...by the shogunal authorities. Even the Satsuma clan would probably turn her in. She can't return to Japan at all."

"But what's wrong with her? Is it a wound that will heal in time?"

Ueda's eyes were deeply troubled. He sipped his tea before answering. "She's blind."

Ueda's rambling house was constructed in three levels against a slope. The bottom level served as the office of his ship chandlery. The top level was the family's sleeping quarters, and there was a kitchen on the first level, behind the chandlery office. The second-level rooms were the source of the joyous female laughter Macneil had heard earlier.

Through a corridor alongside the rooms on this level, Ueda and Macneil passed to reach the third level, where Ueda said Ai was now convalescing.

The *fusuma* were half open as the two men slid along in slippers over the highly polished natural woods of the corridor floor. Macneil could see into each of the three rooms in passing. Around low tables in each sat a half dozen or so girls who looked to be only fourteen or fifteen, though they may have been older.

In each room, an older woman was lecturing the girls while showing them illustrations and certain small objects that Macneil could not identify in those brief glimpses. Whatever the subjects being taught in these classrooms were, they had captured the enthusiastic attention of the pupils, many of whom listened with mouths agape and eyes glistening. They appeared even more eager to learn than his samurai pupils of English had been.

On the third level, Ueda slid open the *fusuma* and signaled to a serving woman to withdraw. The room was dark, but Macneil could detect a form lying on a *futon* under a light cover.

"Ueda-san?" came a weak voice.

"Yes," Ueda said, leading Macneil to the side of the *futon*. "Ai-san, do you remember the letter you gave me to send to the Westerner in Hong Kong?"

The dark head nodded in the dimness.

"I'm sorry to say I still have not been able to find a trustworthy ship captain who is going to Hong Kong."

"Oh?" Deep disappointment dwelt in that one word.

"But, I can do something better than that," Ueda said, taking an envelope out of the deep pocket in his sleeve. "I will hand the letter to him directly myself."

There was a spark of life and interest in Ai's voice as she said, "Oh, are you going to Hong Kong, *ojisan*?"

Ojisan, Macneil knew, meant "uncle" but was also used to older men who are close to one's family, even though not blood-related.

"No, I will give it to him here in Naze."

Instantly, this brought her up to a half-sitting position. "He's coming *here*?"

Gently, Ueda said, "He *is* here, Ai."

"Oh...*oh*! Neil-*san* is *here*, in Naze? Oh, *ojisan*, how wonderful! I'm dying to see him." A cloud descended over her face. "I mean, I want to *talk* to him right away. Will you ask your wife to help me with my hair and a bath?"

Her eyes were open but sightless. A heavy bandage was wrapped around her head. Tears rolled down her cheeks.

"He's right next to you."

"Neil? Neil? Here? Where...*where*?" Her voice was a gasp, but her face glowed. She explored the space around her with her hands. Macneil took hold of one.

"I'm here, Ai."

Ai was thin, wan, disheveled. Cuts and bruises were visible on her neck and hands. He yearned to hold her in his arms and protect her from any future harm.

She pulled Macneil toward her and touched his face. "But you aren't...are you really Neil-*san*? *You* have a beard, but he didn't."

"I'm Neil, all right," he told her with a laugh. "I grew a beard while confined in Nagasaki." Macneil heard Ueda quietly leave the room. "If I kiss you, the beard will scratch."

With a flash of her old self, she ordered, "Then scratch away, barbarian!"

Neil Macneil went back to *Mariner* nightly to sleep in Owen Poore's cabin, which he had taken over, but spent all the next three days sitting beside Ai in her darkened room. Despite frequent headaches, she was in better spirits. They talked and drank sake and become almost merry at times. Neil recounted all that had befallen him at least twice. Each time he came to the part where he jumped overboard from *Susquehanna* to swim ashore on the Amakusa Islands, she clapped her hands in delight.

"Really, Neil-*san*? You jumped off the ship to come looking for me?"

His confirming he had done exactly that seemed to give her inordinate pleasure, so he did not point out that his purpose in finding her had been to ask her help in rescuing Anne and Margaret.

After three days of reunion, Macneil knew he had to face up to a difficult decision about Ai. If he left her here in Amami-Oshima, it seemed possible—perhaps even likely—she would be permanently blind. If she returned to the mainland of Japan, she would be sought as a wanted outlaw. Besides, there might not be proper medical help for her in Japan, either.

In fact, Macneil had no assurance that proper medical help could be found for her anywhere, but he had to do something.

The question was—what? *Mariner* was not his ship, nor was it even an American vessel. Other than a handful of gold *koban* and silver *bu* coins earned in Nagasaki, he had no money. He knew not if his father was still alive. His only hope was his uncle Neville. If he could just take Ai to Hong Kong.

Palmer St. James had been quite decent about offering Macneil—a fellow naval officer—passage to Hong Kong, but would he extend the same courtesy to a blind Japanese woman?

Macneil's only hope was that he and Palmer St. James had become fast enough friends during his short stay aboard *Mariner* that the captain would help him find the best medical treatment for Ai.

Instead of going ashore with the contingent on pass their fourth morning in Naze, Macneil waited till Palmer St. James had inspected the ship and the wounded below deck, assigned duties for the day to the officers, reviewed the progress of the repairs and taken his obligatory stroll fifty times around the perimeter of his private deck. Then he confronted him.

"Palmer, there's something I must tell you."

"Fire away, old boy, On a brilliant morning like this," he waved one hand around him expansively, "I can't fancy what could justify such a ferocious scowl. But then, you Scots have always been a moody race."

"I came aboard *Mariner* under false colors," Macneil blurted. "I'm not an American officer of marines."

"Steady on, laddie," Palmer said with a smile. "Do you really think I didn't know that? Within five minutes—even less—of the time you first trod my deck, I knew you had never spent a day in the military service of the United States or any other nation. My word, Macneil, I'm not a complete idiot, you know."

"But why then, did you...did you...?"

He took Macneil by the arm and guided him to a corner of the stern where there was less chance they would be overheard.

"Well, for one thing, you seemed a likable sort. I knew your true story would come out sooner or later, and in the meantime you presented no danger to my ship. Besides, I was looking for a new dinner companion. I was bloody bored hearing the same old tales over and over again from my officers."

A sense of relief flooded through Macneil, and he thanked God that Palmer St. James was proving to be a friend. But now he had to test that friendship even further.

The whole story took nearly an hour, for they were often interrupted by officers and sailors approaching the captain on one errand or another, but at last Macneil had given Palmer the unvarnished truth in full detail, bringing him up to where matters stood when he left Ai's room the previous afternoon.

"I can't just leave her here, Palmer. You see that, don't you? If only I could take her to Hong Kong, maybe a doctor there can find out why she is blind and tell us what treatment there is, if any."

"The cause was the blow to her head, of course, when the cannon exploded," St. James said. "I've seen and heard of other cases like that, but I'm no medical officer. We'll bring your Miss Koga aboard and put her in Owen Poore's bunk. You can see to her needs, if you will."

"Of course."

"Just one thing. Rather personal, but I'd like to know."

"Anything Palmer."

"Just what is this woman to you? Judging from what you've told me, I thought you would go to the ends of the earth out of love and devotion to the other lady, your cousin."

It was a question as hard for Macneil to answer as it apparently was for Palmer St. James to ask. Turning away to gaze at the two low green hills that separated *Mariner* from the town of Naze, Macneil contemplated his own feelings. It didn't matter so much what he told Palmer, but Macneil wanted the true answer for himself, and he wasn't at all certain he knew it.

At last, he turned back to Palmer. "I love Anne Macneil more than life itself, Palmer. I will never give up my search for her. Never!" He paused. "But if Anne were not alive—God forbid—I do believe I would be in love with Ai Koga."

"Puts you in a bit of an awkward spot, doesn't it, old boy?"

"What do you mean?"

"I mean the obvious, Neil. You'll have to be in the same cabin with her all the way to Hong Kong. We've no other cabin space."

"But she's—"

"Blind? To be sure, she is. But most boudoir activities, I do believe, are carried out in darkness."

"Palmer, I'll bunk with the crew if you like."

"Oh, I assure you, old chap, it matters not a hang to me. Fornication without let or hindrance is my motto."

"Ai and I have often been alone in darkness and in isolated situations," Macneil said stiffly. "I have given her an occasional kiss."

"An occasional kiss, you say? Aha! We must compare notes on the Japanese style of osculation versus the Chinese."

"You refer to Hut'ieh, I'm sure."

"Despite her youth, she is one of the world's most sensuous women, I warrant you. Completely given over to sensual coupling in many rather bizarre forms. A kiss to Hut'ieh is no more than a handshake."

Macneil broke off the interview before more embarrassing revelations could be made and promptly left ship to advise Ai of her pending voyage to Hong Kong.

She was overjoyed. It was like being with the old Ai again. "Oh, Neil-san, you have kept your promise. Remember? You said you would take me to see all those places you told me about and now...." But then, her face fell, and she closed her sightless eyes. "But now, I won't really be able to *see* them, will I?"

"You'll see again, Ai," Macneil said, holding her thin, weak body in his arms. "I'll make sure you do."

As Macneil left her room, he found Mr. Ueda waiting outside in the corridor. Ueda led the way along the corridors and down the stairs toward the first level as Macneil told him his plan to take Ai to Hong Kong for medical attention.

As they passed the three "classrooms" on the second level, one group of young pupils burst into laughter. Macneil looked in through the half-open *fusuma*. The girls were huddled around a low table. One had her hands tied behind her and her face bent over a bowl of noodles. She had sucked a long strand of buckwheat noodle halfway into her mouth. With facial contortions and moans, she was struggling to do something with the slippery noodle.

"What in the world is she trying to do?"

Ueda laughed. "She's trying to tie a knot in a noodle using only her tongue and lips."

"Why should anyone want to do a thing like that?"

"Those girls," Ueda said, "are all *karayuki-san*."

Macneil remembered that *karayuki-san* were the young virgins sent to rich Chinese, mostly in Southeast Asia.

"All of them come from Amakusa, where life is hard and the peasants are among the poorest in Japan," Ueda said. "To keep from starving, they sometimes have to sell their daughters. I buy their girls, train them, and then sell them in Tonkin and Singapore and Chochin—places like that.

"It's really not a bad thing for them, Macneil-*san*. They go on five-year contracts. Half the money paid in advance and half after five years. The advance money is a significant sum and often keeps their families from starving. What they bring home with them is enough for a dowry. They are not often mistreated, according to what I have heard. Some even want to go on living with their Chinese masters after their contracts expire. The Chinese usually let them live easy, luxurious lives. Sometimes the Chinese even fall in love and marry them, even though only as second or third wives."

"You said you trained them. Is that what tying a knot in a noodle is all about?"

"You're right, Macneil-*san*. Any girl who can tie a knot in a noodle with her tongue can also arouse wonderful sensations in a man's *ichibutsu*." This was a Japanese word for penis, literally meaning "one-thing" or "The Thing."

Macneil did not know whether to be repelled or fascinated.

"To be sure, we teach them much more," Ueda said. "Much more, indeed! But it is not an easy business, Macneil-*san*. You see, they must arrive at their destinations as virgins. The Chinese are sharp businessmen. They conduct an immediate physical examination. If the girl's hymen has been broken, back she comes! Just like that," he said, snapping his fingers. "Teaching these *karayuki-san* a little something about music and singing and poetry is one thing, but teaching them how to give a man the utmost pleasure in bed—such extreme pleasure that he will believe he has died and has arrived in paradise—while leaving their hymens intact and never permitting them to have any actual practice is quite another, believe me."

"I had only a quick look, but they all seemed rather pretty."

Ueda rewarded Macneil with an exaggerated wink. "Of course. I can't send the Chinese buyers *kara-jishi*..." Macneil recalled the hideous "lion-dog" toys he had seen in a shop earlier. "...for what they pay. I make more money from my *karayuki-san* girls than from my naval supplies and from—"

"And from your business as agent for the *funa-kainin*?"

Again the hasty, furtive look over his shoulder, the lowered voice. "Be cautious, Macneil-*san*, please. Even here in Amami-Oshima, the shogun has friends. But to answer the question: yes.

When needed, I sometimes lend Heihachiro Koga and his clan a helping hand."

"They pay you, don't they?"

"Not in gold or silver."

"Then how?"

"They pay me by insuring that the *karayuki-san* girls reach me safely. Two batches a year. Two or three dozen in each batch. Six months of training for each. I have much overhead, so I must deal in large numbers."

"Well," Macneil said, "I hope you approve of my taking Ai Koga to Hong Kong."

"Of course I do. I will cooperate in any way I can."

"You should inform her father."

"Ai has already told me she wants to dictate a letter to her father, perhaps tonight. I'll make an extra copy and send them to him by different routes, in case one doesn't reach him. The Higo authorities are very touchy these days. They strip and search all travelers from and to Amakusa at the barriers."

Before leaving, Macneil went back up for a brief consultation with Ai. He knew she had told her father about his search for Anne and Margaret, so he asked her to remind him in her letter that Macneil was still looking for them and that he would come back to Japan as soon as possible.

Groping in the semi-darkness of the room, Ai reached out and touched Neil's bearded chin. "Did you think I would forget something as important to you as that, Neil-*san*? I'm only sorry I cannot go back myself to help in the search—and to take our revenge on Higo and the Tokugawas. Just as soon as I get my sight back, I will return. Then we'll see. They'll pay in blood, I swear it."

CHAPTER 35

From Naze to Hong Kong

"Sail ho!"

"Where away?"

"Dead ahead, sir."

"What ship?"

"She's three-masted and she's a *two*-decker, sir!"

Pandemonium broke out on deck. The drum beat to quarters. The boatswain's pipe sent seamen flying into the rigging.

Not yet two days out of Naze, Macneil thought, *and a ship that could be Wolodimir heaves into view. Could our luck be that bad?*

Calm and icy as ever when on the deck and in command, Palmer St. James ordered the sailing master, "Look you to those top-sails. They're not drawing well."

"Aye, captain."

"Bend on the colors, Mr. Pennington, if you please."

"Immediately, sir."

"Do you think she's the Russian again, Palmer?" Macneil asked.

"It's a huge ocean, old boy, and lots of bottoms float on it."

This time, with *Mariner* in top sailing condition and ample fuel for her boilers, they could probably stay out of harm's way if the winds did not follow *Wolodimir* too strongly.

Mariner was not built for speed, but she should be able to keep ahead of the distant three-master, thanks to steam power.

Palmer St. James divined the American's thinking. "We're entering the steam age, Neil. The admiralty expects to have 218 steam warships two years from now."

"Then sailing ships will be things of the past?"

"Not quite. Some of those magnificent vessels will be around for quite a while yet, I fancy. For one thing, wind is free. For another, the sailers can be very swift. Take your Yankee clippers and our tea clippers. The fastest hulls afloat. A tea

clipper can sail from a China port to London in as little as one
hundred days. Some have covered as much as three hundred
miles in a single day, with a good wind behind them. Can you
fancy that, Macneil? *Three hundred miles!* They pass ordinary
merchant vessels like a greyhound passing a snail. Never have
I seen a more beautiful sight—not even Hut'ieh when she steps
out of her bath—than a tea clipper under full sail flying south
from Madagascar."

"Why the emphasis on speed?"

"The tea, my boy, the *tea!* The freshest tea is the best. Picked
young, the tea leaves are carried to England at top speed."

"She's flying the Union Jack, sir," came the call from the
masthead.

On deck, wild cheering broke out. The men rushed to the
railing to see their sister warship.

Fixing his glass on her, St. James pronounced her to be
Conqueror, 48 guns. "We'll run alongside of her, if you please,
Mr. Wiggins," he said to his sailing master, then turned back to
Macneil.

"Many Englishmen should curse the ill wind that blew in
Emperor Shen Nung's garden."

Lieutenant Pennington stepped up smartly, his tricorn
tucked under his left arm. "Sir, how shall I signal *Conqueror*?"

"Favor me, Mr. Pennington, by going below to my cabin
and looking up her captain's name in the Active Duty List."

"Aye, sir."

"Then, when she is near enough, make to *Conqueror* we are
Mariner, give her my name as captain, and say I'd deem it a
distinct honor to be allowed to pay my respects."

"Certainly, sir."

"This time perhaps I'll be more successful at getting news
from Europe," Palmer said to Macneil. "I especially want to
know details about the go we're having with Russia, the one
your Mr. Ueda told you about."

"Well, he's not exactly my Mr. Ueda, you know."

"Come now, Neil. No false modesty, if you please. Obviously, you have a way with these Japanese, speaking their lingo
the way you do. In five minutes, you seem to have them eating
out of your hand. Devoted servants for life and all that. Saints
help us if you learn Chinese. I swear I'll have to put a chastity
belt on Hut'ieh whenever you're skulking about."

"What were you saying about tea?"'

"Ah, yes, the Emperor Shen Nung, right? Well, some leaves
from a tea bush blew into his pot of boiling water. They turned
the water orange-red and gave off a delicate aroma. When it was

no longer boiling hot, Shen Nung tasted it. He liked it so much he ordered this 'tea' to be served to him every day. He called it *cha*, and the Rooskies, by the way, now call it *chai*. Your friends the Japanese call it *cha*, and our British workers call it *char*. Fascinating, what?"

"But why did you say it was an ill wind that blew the leaves into the boiling water?"

St. James pounded his right fist in his left palm. "Because, damme, Englishmen have become absolute slaves to tea!"

Palmer paused to study *Conqueror* again through his glass.

"Problem has been," he went on, "China would not buy anything from England in return. By and large, the Chinese were self-sufficient, or at least thought they were. They took the position that if we were properly humble and appreciative—the old nine kowtows act—they would deign to sell us their tea for our silver, but we had no goods they particularly wanted.

"The upshot was, the British treasury was being drained at a tremendous clip. Either we had to prohibit the importation of tea, which might have caused the floors of Parliament to run red with the blood of the honorable members, or to find something the Chinese wanted as badly as we wanted their tea."

"Opium," Macneil said.

"Aha! For a colonial, you are well informed."

"You forget my uncle is a Hong Kong merchant. He deals in opium, among other things."

"Yes, yes, by all means. So you said, I believe. Anyway, a little opium had been grown in China, long ago, but now it was found opium could be grown more cheaply in British India and in a quality better suited to the Chinese palate than any other. Foreseeing this might be the only product to reverse the flow of gold and silver out of England, we nosed into the opium trade, took much of it over, and prayed the Chinese would become as addicted to the drug as we are to tea."

"And it worked, didn't it?"

"As you say, it worked. Splendidly, in point of fact. Now, the shoe was on the other foot. The Chinese faced a situation worse than the one we had faced, since opium is far more harmful and addictive than tea. The long and short of it was that China tried to stop the importation of opium by seizing and destroying British cargoes of the drug in Canton. That set off the Opium War. We needed a nearby base for our ships, so we built one on a sparsely inhabited island called Hong Kong. We won the war. The opium trade resumed. China ceded Hong Kong and Kowloon to us, and we made Hong Kong our major base for the China trade. And there you have it. Far East commercial history in one quick easy lesson."

That evening, blessed by a smooth sea and mild following breeze, *Mariner* and *Conqueror* sailed along on a south-south-westerly parallel course within fifty yards of each other. Macneil watched as the cutter took Palmer St. James, in full regalia, across that narrow strip of intervening sea and heard the shrill and quaver of him being piped aboard. Neil could see the Marine Guard on *Conqueror* snap to present arms and the assembled officers uncover their heads.

Earlier, in response to the first signal from *Mariner*, Captain Luard had confirmed it was he who commanded HMS *Conqueror*, a 48-gun ship of the line, and asked if he had the honor of addressing the Captain St. James who was son of the Right Honorable Earl of Oxbridge, Darcy St. James, First Lord of the Admiralty?

Palmer had signaled back that although he was indeed the son of Darcy St. James, his father was only Vice-Lord of the Admiralty, not First Lord.

Macneil was standing at Palmer's side while the signals officer read the reply in the pennants being hoisted to her masthead: "Correction. Now First Lord of Admiralty. Congratulations. Pray, dine with me."

Macneil didn't talk to Palmer when he returned to *Mariner* late that night, whistling jauntily as he climbed the ladder.

He saw the captain the next morning, however, when they welcomed aboard a short, portly officer with a magnificent moustache and a worn black bag.

Palmer called Macneil to his side and introduced Dr. Aloysius Sutton of *Conqueror*, who had agreed to offer a medical opinion on Ai's condition.

This he did forty minutes after beginning his examination.

"I won't bore you, Captain St. James, with the Latinate names, but this young woman has suffered a severe lesion to her optic nerves. There's a surgeon in private practice in London—Sir Horace Winthrop—who has the best hands in the business. There's a fifty-fifty chance he could restore her sight, but I doubt anyone else could. You should get her to him with all possible speed, sir. With every passing week her chances of recovery will grow slimmer. Those nerves atrophy if not used."

After Palmer had taken the surgeon to examine the wounded below deck, Macneil told Ai the British doctor had advised an operation in London and thought she would regain her sight. At first, she was thrilled at his news, but then she sobered. "But how will I get there, Neil-*san*? Is there a chance?"

"Leave everything to me, Ai," he said with a heartiness he did not at all feel. He had to get her to London quickly and for that he needed money to pay for her passage and for the famous surgeon's services. Macneil could not possibly go with her, for he assumed he would shortly board Commodore Perry's *Susquehanna* in Hong Kong for the return voyage to Edo.

Even if he raised the money—perhaps from Uncle Neville—who would go with Ai and stay with her before the operation and afterward? For all Macneil knew, there might not be even one person in all London—or England, for that matter—who knew a word of Japanese.

CHAPTER 36

"We'll raise Hong Kong by tomorrow evening," the navigation officer informed St. James.

"Increase the number of revolutions, Mr. Pennington," the captain said. "I'd like to anchor before dark. That will give me time to report our arrival and then have the evening free for...ah, other activities."

"Right you are, sir," said Pennington, turning aside to hide his grin of understanding. Pennington too had a Eurasian mistress tucked away somewhere in Happy Valley, St. James had told Macneil.

Having just passed the Chinese port of Amoy off to starboard, *Mariner* was sailing south through the Formosa Strait. After taking leave of the survey vessel off the Senkaku Islands, *Conqueror* had turned back north to search for *Wolodimir*. Palmer St. James gnashed his teeth at not being the fortunate captain of *Conqueror*.

The skies were clear. The wind stood in *Mariner's* favor. With the prospect of leave in their home port, the crew was exuberant. A few sang snatches of a rollicking seafarer's chanty.

For Macneil, the past week had been one of satisfaction and contentment. He was trying to teach Ai as much English as possible during the voyage to Hong Kong. With her quick mind, she was doing well. Mr. Pennington came down twice to sit and visit with her, and the captain came once.

Working from Ai's instructions, Macneil helped the cook prepare the Japanese food Ueda packed in a hamper for her.

"Enjoy it while you can," Macneil said. "I doubt you'll find any of these things in England."

"Then, I shall have to become a fine English lady," she said. "Would you like that, Neil-*san*?"

"I don't care what you eat or what you wear in London. All

I want is for you to be the same Ai that was with me when we made our run for Uraga and the black ships."

"And the same Ai who hid in the manure tank?" She held her nose at the memory.

Even though he tried, Macneil could not put other concerns completely out of mind. First, there was the matter of his family. He had to be in Hong Kong when Perry set sail for Uraga again. He was concerned about Katsuko Ito and the child she was carrying. His first offspring was due to enter this world in October. How would he or she be treated? Macneil could only assume the child would be sent somewhere for adoption. Would he ever see it?

That afternoon, they sighted a pair of junks locked in close embrace two points off the port bow. The larger of the pair was from Shantung, the junks of the several coastal provinces of China each having their own unique characteristics of construction. The smaller was of Fukien origin. As the English ship drew closer, it became apparent that the larger of the two was the attacker, a colorful war junk whose two visible cannon were painted bright red. It flew a long white banner on which was painted in black a writhing fire-breathing dragon designed to strike fear into the hearts of all who saw it. On its prow were drawn two huge eyes whose purpose, Palmer said in an aside, was to spy out prey.

Grinning, St. James said to his first officer, "Britannia to the rescue."

"Aye, sir," said Mr. Pennington, signaling to the boatswain, who instantly produced on his pipe a series of indecipherable squeaks that galvanized the crew in the way a ferret's sudden arrival would energize a colony of mice.

The drummer boy, only eleven years old, came rattling up the gangway holding the leather drum straps in his teeth while trying to shrug his shoulders into his jacket. With hair tousled and jacket unbuttoned, the boy slid to a halt in the middle of the main deck. Then, drawing a deep breath and squaring his shoulders, he began his rat-a-tat-tat, rat-a-tat-tat beat to general quarters, which he would continue until the boatswain or an officer of the deck ordered him to belay.

One of the legends of the British navy concerned the drummer boy aboard Admiral Horatio Nelson's flagship *Victory* at Trafalgar. The lad, forgotten in the heat of battle, had continued to rattle out his ruffle to arms until the fighting had ended and an eerie quiet had settled over *Victory* at Lord Nelson's death. It was only then that the drummer boy's indefatigable persistence in the performance of his duty came to the crew's attention.

Doubtless, the pirates had seen *Mariner*. They might even have got away except that in their eagerness to secure their booty, those sea vultures had attached a large number of grappling hooks and lines to their prey's bulwarks and rigging, a contrivance that became a trap, preventing their escape. Nor were their two old cannon, which were fixed in place, of much use against the nine-pounders of *Mariner*.

"Is this our fight, Palmer?" Macneil asked.

"You see that pennant?" Palmer asked, pointing to a long white flag with two black diamonds waving from the mast of the smaller Shantung junk.

Macneil nodded.

"That means the shipowner operates out of Hong Kong and has leased land there. That alone gives him the protection of the Crown. Strange as it may seem, that, sir, is a British ship."

St. James lay *Mariner* alongside the pirate junk, now caught in the middle, and tied her to his ship with grappling hooks. Through his speaking tube, he called on the pirate captain to surrender, but Macneil wondered if that squat individual in the baggy, red silk pants with only one ear understood a word said to him in English.

"Prepare to board," St. James shouted over the tumult and cries of defiance.

But before the boarders could be lined up for the jump across to the pirate's railing, Red Pants' villains defied them by attacking first.

From the capacious holds of the pirate junk poured forth a wild-looking tide of Chinese, Malayan and Lascar cutthroats armed with pistols, cutlasses, lances, and krises. They swarmed over the deck of *Mariner* in a snarling, yelling torrent.

"Mr. Pennington," called St. James.

"Sir!"

"Have the marines step up out of the gangways, if you please. Instruct them to fix bayonets and repel boarders."

But before he could reach the marine color-sergeant standing at attention and awaiting orders on the main deck, Pennington was cut down by the slash of a Malay kris.

"I'll tell them, Palmer!" Macneil yelled, leaping down onto the main deck.

At least fifty pirates had dashed aboard *Mariner* in those first few minutes and were slashing and thrusting at the British crew. Now they faced the line of marine "lobsters" who advanced on them with fixed bayonets while the ship officers fired from the upper deck into the attacking enemy mass.

Evidently, a steadily advancing line of British marines—

affectionately called the "bloody bollocks" by the crew—was something outside the pirates' experience. Their threatening cries and their flailing slashes with kris and sword aroused no more reaction in the granite-faced marines than a squawking sea-gull would have caused by attacking the Rock of Gibraltar. "Repel boarders!" had been their orders, and although two of their number had already collapsed on the deck dead or dying, they would do exactly that, or follow their comrades in death.

Indecision showed its face among the pirates, despite the threats being shouted at them by their chieftain in the red pants, a vicious rogue who cried out and jigged in glee whenever he saw a Britisher fall.

Macneil raced back to Palmer's side to see if he could be of any further help while keeping one eye on the gangway leading down to Ai's cabin. Palmer had a two-barrelled pistol in his left hand and a sword in his right. Macneil was reloading the pistol for him when he heard the captain cry out in pain and rage.

A Lascar in a loin-cloth had attacked the captain with a lance. The point penetrated Palmer's right armpit and pinned him to the mast. Macneil had only one pistol barrel loaded, but he fired that one at the Lascar just as he was on the point of disemboweling St. James with a curved-blade knife.

Dropping the pistol, Macneil jumped over the pirate's body to help the captain, who was cursing mightily and struggling to free himself from the lance, his efforts only enlarging his wound. Macneil took hold of the lance by the shaft end and planting his feet, pulled it loose.

Even as the lance came free, Macneil felt a sharp sting on his back. Spinning around, lance in hand, he found himself facing Red Pants himself, in whose hands flashed a heavy scimitar the pirate was about to bring down on Macneil's head. Before he could do that, a marine ran up behind the pirate chief and clubbed him to the deck with his Enfield musket butt.

"Good show, that!" called Palmer weakly. "We'll clap the scoundrel in irons and hang him in Hong Kong."

Their chief's fall took the remaining bellicosity out of the boarders, who now dropped their weapons on the deck and looked about them for avenues of escape. Three of them jumped into the South China Sea.

Mariner's "butcher bill" was six dead and fifteen wounded, counting the captain. With no doctor aboard, they had to press on to Hong Kong as quickly as possible. The captain of the rescued Shantung junk came aboard and tried to kiss St. James's feet in gratitude.

Palmer waved him off, charging him to bring the captured

pirate junk into port at Hong Kong and report the location of its anchorage to the senior naval officer on station as soon as feasible.

Palmer's wound was ghastly to look at, mostly because he had widened and torn its edges jagged in his efforts to free himself. No vital organs had been harmed, but his right arm would be incapacitated for a good while, during which time he would doubtless not be fit for sea duty.

As soon as Macneil could break away from the turmoil on deck, he ran down to Ai's cabin. She was sitting on her bunk with her mouth set grimly and her sightless eyes fixed in the direction of the door.

"Ai, it's Neil," he said, speaking in Japanese. "It's all over now. There's nothing to worry about."

"Are you all right, Neil-*san*?" She stood up and opened her arms.

She embraced Macneil, her hands meeting over the painful spot on his back. It reminded him of the sting he had felt on deck just before turning to confront the pirate chieftain with one ear and red pants.

She heard Macneil's gasp, though he had tried to stifle it.

"You're hurt! Oh, Neil-*san*! Call someone, *please!* I feel blood. My fingers are sticky. Please call someone!"

"Relax, Ai-san," he said, pushing her back down on the bunk. "There are men on deck far more badly hurt than I. I'll have it tended to later. I just came down so you would not be alone." He had just finished telling her the details of the fight with the pirates when he was summoned to the captain's cabin.

St. James was lying in his bed drinking wine and smoking a cheroot. Except for the heavy bandage on his upper right arm and shoulder Macneil could see no signs of damage.

"Sit down, laddie, and join me in a glass of port. Pour it yourself, if you will. I find myself a trifle dizzy if I stand."

"To the Queen," Macneil toasted.

"God save her," the captain said. "Well, I've been thinking, Neil, and I've decided on a course of action I hope will please all concerned."

Neil waited.

"As soon as we dock in Hong Kong, I'll report myself wounded in action to Admiral Stirling and request relief from active duty until I am declared fit for sea duty again. He will, I'm sure, approve. When he does, I'll buy passage for two on the next tea clipper to London."

"Two?"

"For myself and your Miss Koga, of course. With any luck, we should leave in a couple of days, maybe even the same day. I will have largely recuperated, I'm sure, during the voyage home. There, I'll get myself certified fit and then see the governor about command of a fighting ship."

"And Ai?"

"I promise you, Neil, before I do anything else, I'll take her to the surgeon Dr. Sutton recommended—what the deuce was his name? Sir Horace, ah, Winthrop?—and get her sorted out one way or the other. Find rooms for her, hire a woman to look after her, all that sort of thing."

"Palmer, I haven't much money right now."

"Never mind that, old boy. I'll take care of things, and we'll work it all out later."

"But sooner or later, you'll be going back to sea, and Ai speaks little English."

"I'll spend the entire voyage home teaching her, old fellow. Give me something to do."

"And if she doesn't regain her sight, she'll be in a terrible fix alone there in England."

"I said you're not to worry. In fact, I have an interesting proposal to put to you. You look after my Hut'ieh Gonzaga in Hong Kong—see her rent gets paid, she has money for food, that sort of thing—and I'll look after your Miss Koga in London."

He drained his glass of port. "*And* when I go back to sea, I'll put Ai under the personal care of none other than Darcy St. James. Would that satisfy you—having her being looked after by the Vice-Lord—no, by Jove!—the *First* Lord of the Admiralty?"

Macneil shook hands with St. James on that agreement.

CHAPTER 37

Hong Kong

Delayed by the capture of the pirate junk, *Mariner* reached Hong Kong one day late, but fate compensated for the delay by accelerating the pace of events on the morning of arrival.

Moored in the middle of the stream between Hong Kong and Kowloon, *Mariner* had hoisted signals that she carried dead and wounded. Hardly had the rumble of the anchor chain faded than three surgeons and a crew of medical orderlies were climbing aboard.

St. James had his wound dressed and certified by a surgeon first so he could be on his way to report to the senior naval officer on station. Before he had finished struggling into his frock coat, however, the crew of *Mariner* were surprised by the arrival, accompanied by much pomp and ceremony, of that same senior officer, Admiral Sir James Stirling. Seldom did an admiral come calling on a mere captain.

"He too knows the name of the new First Sea Lord," Macneil whispered to Palmer while helping him up the stairs to the deck.

The details of Palmer's sick leave were quickly settled, and when Admiral Stirling's launch with its blue flag had been piped away, Palmer had himself lowered in a boatswain's sling to his own jolly boat. He headed for the Hong Kong shore.

"Get Miss Koga ready," he told Macneil as he left. "There's no telling when the first tea clipper will sail, for there seems to be a god's plenty of them." He gestured with his left hand at the crowded harbor around them and the dozen sleek-looking "greyhounds of the deep," looking restive among the more mundane plodders of the sea-lanes. "I'll be back aboard before noon, I'm sure."

After assuring himself that Ai had breakfasted and knew what was happening, Macneil let a surgeon stitch and bandage the shallow cut on his back, then tended to his own packing—the work of ten minutes.

Back up on deck with sketch pad in hand, Macneil waited for Palmer's return. He would have liked to go ashore right away to look for Neville Macneil, but he could not take the chance that Palmer St. James might find a clipper ready to set sail that same day for the Cape of Good Hope and London, and that Ai would not be ready to leave with him.

The Hong Kong harbor was a scene to delight any artist's eyes. It offered variety, color, life, and movement and was so filled with masts and spars it looked like a forest of trees with sails for foliage. The distinctive junks from the Chinese maritime provinces vied for space with differently constructed craft from Singapore, Java, the Philippines, and Siam. All were shaking out their sails to dry from the drenching shower that had washed the white decks of *Mariner* clean as the survey vessel eased its way earlier through the traffic and confusion to its anchorage. Square-rigged sailing ships—many of them clippers—towered above the trading junks, while market boats laden with provisions from the mainland rudely nosed their way toward shore, demanding right of passage with clamorous cries and discordant bells. British men-of-war floated haughtily at their moorings, confident in the superiority of their empire and the weight of their cannon.

Macneil had done four sketches of the harbor, Kowloon, Victoria Peak, and a junk from Hainan when Palmer returned, shortly before noon.

"Neil, thank God you're about," he cried while being assisted up the ladder and onto the deck. "I've got them." He waved two passage vouchers at the American. "Is Miss Koga ready? We've not a minute to lose. *Ariel* is already shaking out sail, and I still have to introduce you to Hut'ieh."

In no time at all, St. James and his gear were stowed in the jolly boat, and Macneil was guiding Ai down the ladder. Palmer called up his farewells to the officers and crew of *Mariner*, who, breaking ranks and regulations, had crowded the railing to shout huzzahs.

Ai had no sooner settled in her seat than the oarsmen pushed the jolly boat away from the oaken sides of the vessel. Macneil felt a twinge of regret in leaving the survey ship. For three of the most adventurous weeks of his life, the stout little ship had been home to him.

They were rowed to *Ariel*, only six mooring buoys away, where they deposited Ai, her luggage, which was not much, and Palmer's gear. Then the captain and Macneil made haste for the

Hong Kong side of the harbor, where they climbed up onto the dock.

"Don't move till I return," St. James ordered the boat crew.

Walking as fast as Palmer could manage, they struck out eastward. In ten minutes, they came to a side street of nondescript frame and stone houses, some large and others quite small. The dwelling they entered, on the right-hand side of the street, was built in two stories, with what seemed to be four rooms below and three above. Palmer St. James had rented the upper three rooms for Hut'ieh Gonzaga. The rent was three guineas a month, which seemed high to Macneil but which Palmer said was not bad considering the booming port's housing shortage.

Stomping up the rickety staircase to the second floor, Palmer called out "Hut'ieh!" on every other step of the way. At the head of the stairs, she exploded from her room and ran into his arms, crying in joy, raining kisses on his head and face.

"Palmer, my darling! Oh, my darling! How I love you! Quick! Into our room. I must show you how lonely your beloved has been. Come, come!"

"Easy there, little one," said St. James, laughing. "Look behind me."

"Oh, I'm so sorry! How shameful of me! I did not know—"

"This is Neil Macneil, my dearest. I'm off to London, and he will take care of you while I'm away."

"Palmer, what is this bandage?" she cried. "Are you hurt? Yes! You are! You're wounded, that's what. Oh, Holy Mother of Jesus, save us today! My lover is *wounded*." She burst into tears.

Hut'ieh was tiny. Her eyes were large and limpid and dark, with extremely long eyelashes and heavy eyebrows.

As she wept, her face quivered with emotions—trembling lips, flickering eyes widening and narrowing almost in cadence with her breathing, nostrils that flared bunny-like.

She was dressed in a black skirt and white blouse that looked like a girls' school uniform, and probably had been. This may have enhanced her youthful appearance despite healthy breasts that shifted this way and that under her thin blouse, but Macneil judged her to be fifteen.

When the impact of Palmer's statement that he was off to London had overridden her distress over his wound, her wailing increased.

"But what..." she sobbed "...what will become of *me*?"

"There, there, my dear. I told you Neil Macneil here will look after you, didn't I?"

She stopped crying. With a sniffle, she looked up at him

with widening eyes and half-open mouth. "Palmer, does that mean—do you mean you're *giving* me to him, that he will be my lover?"

Turning, she fixed on the young American a gaze of frank and curious appraisal. No longer a bawling child of fifteen, she was now a self-possessed, calculating woman.

"Never, dearest, never!" Palmer protested.

With an abashed grin, he turned to Macneil. "Neil, pray wait for me outside. I'll be a few minutes. There's a good chap."

He was as good as his word. As they hurried back to the dock and the waiting jolly boat, he gave Macneil his address in Sussex as well as Hut'ieh's address in Hong Kong, saying he would write to Neil in care of her. He also told Macneil how much money to give her and on what days of the month.

"How old is Hut'ieh, Palmer?"

For the first time since Macneil had known him, Palmer St. James appeared embarrassed. "Well, that's rather...that is to say, well, confound it, if you must know, she's sixteen...but quite mature for her age, as you must have noticed."

"Hut'ieh—'Butterfly'—seems like a strange name. Is that the one her parents gave her?"

"No, that's the name I gave her."

"What made you choose a name like that?"

Again, the embarrassed hesitation. "Uh, this is just between us, old boy, right?"

"Of course."

"You noticed her long eyelashes?"

"Yes."

"Well, she's got a little—what would you call it, a lover's caress?—whereby she uses those eyelashes to...ah, how shall I express it...well, let me speak bluntly, dammit! She flutters those eyelashes against one's John Thomas, an incredibly tantalizing sensation, take my word for it, chappie. It's a well-known technique among Chinese courtesans. They call it the 'Butterfly.' "

Then, before Macneil knew it, he was helping St. James into the jolly boat. "Say goodbye to Ai for me," he said. "Tell her I'll write and I'll be praying for her. Tell her...." Macneil stopped, at a loss for what else to say, but by now the jolly boat had pulled away. He could only wave and stare out toward *Ariel* in the stream.

It must have been the salt in the sea-breeze that caused his eyes to water. Yes, he was sure the breeze was the cause. Turning away, he set out to find his Uncle Neville.

CHAPTER 38

The sticky Hong Kong midday heat embraced him in its wet arms as Neil pushed through the jostling, clamorous throngs of Chinese and Europeans, of Buddhists, Christians, Parsees, and Jews. With no sense of destination, he wandered down streets and alleys where cowsheds, pigsties and stagnant pools of water vied for space with busy shops and proper offices.

The strident shouting on the streets and the din of boat traffic from the harbor overwhelmed him. So many strange and wondrous sights kept turning Macneil's head that an hour passed before he took himself in hand and concentrated on finding the Hong Kong offices of Macneil Brothers, Ltd.

Forced at last to the realization that he would not find his uncle's hong, or trading company, by this hit-and-miss method of walking up and down the noisy, confusing streets, Macneil began to speak to men whose top hats and jackets suggested they were merchants. Several ignored him, doubtless because of his nondescript clothing and unshorn locks and beard; three had not heard of Macneil Brothers, Ltd; one did not understand Macneil's English words at all.

In addressing the next five passers-by, he asked if they knew the whereabouts of a Mr. Neville Macneil of Macneil Brothers, Ltd. Four professed ignorance, but the fifth, a red-faced, portly man dressed in a high-collar shirt, a waistcoat, a top hat, and a suit of black cloth, scowled at him with suspicion for a moment, then said, "Keep going straight till you come to the two-story building with the apothecary shop on the first floor. You'll find Macneil on the second floor, I believe."

The stairs to the second floor were rickety and dangerous looking, though the brick building looked new. On the second floor were three large counting rooms, each with a flock of Chinese sitting on stools before desks piled high with shipping manifests and banking documents. Macneil went into the middle counting room, but no one paid him the slightest heed.

Walking over to a Chinese in a black gown with skull cap and pigtail, Macneil touched his arm to get his attention and asked for Mr. Neville Macneil. The man turned from haranguing a younger Chinese and pointed toward the door of an inner office.

As Macneil approached, he saw in a corner outside the office his own sea bag, which he had entrusted to the sailor on *Susquehanna* to be delivered to his uncle in Hong Kong.

As he started to knock on the closed door, he heard bickering voices from within, one of them loud, the other muffled.

"But dammit, d'ye nae ken more 'an half oor wee profits come fra' opium? We *canna* gi'e it up."

In the heat of their seething argument, the disputants ignored Neil's knock, so he pushed the door inward and stepped into the small room. A thin, stooped man with pure white hair was seated behind a desk. This must be Neville Macneil, the uncle Neil had never seen. Nearly concealed behind the now open door to his right stood the second man.

"Uncle Neville?" Neil asked the man behind the desk.

"Aye, Neville Macneil it be, but am I yer ooncle?"

"Yes, sir, I think you are."

Blanching, the older man rose. "But...but there be but twa bairns on earth who can call me ooncle."

"And I'm one of them," Neil answered with a broad grin.

"Neil? Ye're *Neil*?" he croaked, rushing out from behind his desk in a shuffling gait.

Tears shone in his eyes as Neville held out his arms. Neil embraced him.

"Have you heard naught of Father?"

"Ye...ye dinna ken tha'...?"

Dear God, Neil thought, *don't let him say that Father is dead.*

"He's not...is he?"

"Nae wha', ye daft loon. Joost look behind ye!"

Neil looked.

There stood Nairn Macneil, tall and gaunt with sandy hair, looking just as he had when Neil had last seen him, boarding *Eliza Grayson* bound for Hong Kong.

For three solid days, the Macneils talked.

They talked in the offices of the hong. They talked on the veranda of the Hong Kong Club, where British merchants in short pants gathered in the early evening to air their crotches and drink stengahs under creaking punkahs. They talked in restaurants and in taverns like Lap Tat's. They talked in the small frame house Neville Macneil had built behind Queen's Road during his first year in Hong Kong, well before the great fire of 1852 and the law mandating only stone and brick houses. They talked in the small boat, called a walla-walla, in which Neville, ailing though he was, took his brother and nephew on a tour of the harbor. They talked until late each evening and went to bed regretting the day did not have more hours for conversation.

They stopped talking only when they were forced to find quarters for Neil. Neville's living space had been ample for him and his two Chinese servants, but cramped after Nairn Macneil had arrived to share it. So Neville's comprador, his top Chinese employee, made inquiries and found two rooms in the home of a middle-aged Italian widow, whose Irish husband had died the previous year of one of those many malignant fevers for which Hong Kong was infamous. Because her husband, a sea captain, had left her with little but their four-year-old house, she let rooms and taught singing, Italian style. According to this Madame Keogh ne'e Togliatti, she had been one of the brightest stars in the Milano Opera Company firmament until her impetuous seafaring husband had swept her off her feet and carried her away on his ship to this "pesthole of disease and depravity."

To the validity of the widow's claims to fame, Neil could not attest, though it was plain her voice was one of great volume. Luckily, she bellowed only when giving lessons, which was seldom—and then only in the middle of the day.

Even so, customers at the Wanchai Steam Bakery across the street sometimes reported to the constables that someone was doing unspeakable things to a cow on her premises.

Once the rent for the first month was paid, Neville instructed his comprador to buy certain furnishings for Neil's two rooms while Nairn took his son to a new store called Lane and Crawford's, where he bought him tight-fitting trousers, a jacket, a high-collar shirt, and a top hat. The getup was so outlandish and such a contrast to the odds and ends Neil had worn since leaving Oregon that he refused to walk the streets wearing it until his father persuaded him that all proper European merchants in Hong Kong wore similar clothing.

Finally, Nairn dragged Neil to a Chinese barber shop with the fanciful name of "Tonsorial Parlour of Insignificant Profit," where the young man lost two pounds of hair, including an entire beard.

"Wi' tha' beard," Nairn explained, "ye micht be mistooken for a pirate."

During the past year alone, Nairn said, pirates had attacked merchantmen and trading junks more than seven hundred times up and down the South China coast, from Amoy in the east to Macao in the west. In a single punitive raid on a pirate's lair on Hainan Island, British men-of-war had captured seventy-four of the villains. They were all sentenced to death, but the faint-hearted British authorities, being Christians, could not bring themselves to publicly execute seventy-four pirates in a stroke, so they handed them over to the Hong Kong Association of Chinese Businessmen, who had fewer qualms about dealing out justice.

The seventy-four pirates were beheaded and considered themselves lucky at that, for more imaginative methods of punishment were often employed by the Chinese. These refinements included, but were not limited to, public torture, tongue ripping, genital crushing, thumbscrews, beating to death, the bastinado, flesh slicing, and pouring molten lead into the ears.

For common misdemeanors, Chinese felons were flogged outside the jail, between the Anglican Church and the cricket grounds, on holidays, when the righteous could flock to observe and cheer. The British authorities pretended not to notice such barbaric practices, while the Chinese scoffed at the weakness of the religion and justice of the "red barbarians" from the West.

Leaving the barber shop, the father and son had chanced to pass a used book store where a four-volume set of old books called *Angeria Gorin Taisei* caught Neil's attention. A glance at the contents revealed the set to be an English-Dutch-Japanese dictionary. It had been compiled in Nagasaki between 1811 and 1814 by an interpreter named Shozaemon Motoki and the Dutchman Blomhoff, and had been printed in Batavia. The price was reasonable—in fact, dirt-cheap—so Neil borrowed five coins from his father and bought the set.

No discovery could have pleased him more, except finding Anne herself. With this dictionary, which contained far more words than his other dictionaries, he might begin to make real progress in his Japanese studies.

Neil still needed a teacher to help with pronunciation and comprehension, but this set of books would be invaluable in building his vocabulary.

Neil's one great disappointment in his first days in Hong Kong was learning that Commodore Perry's fleet had set sail thirteen days before Neil arrived. "Commodore Perry promised to let me go back to Edo with him, aboard *Susquehanna*," he told his father and uncle. "He said he would hand over a letter about Anne and Margaret to the shogun's government."

That being impossible now, Neil had to consider other means.

"If Perry signs the proposed treaty with the shogun, that means several of Japan's ports will soon open to trade and Americans can live and work there," he said. "When that happens, I want to go to Nagasaki immediately. With your approval, I could open a branch of this hong, and go on with my search from there."

"Agreed," Neville said, and Nairn nodded his head emphatically.

Neville was not well. He had been taken with consumption not long after reaching Hong Kong, and the disease had worsened with time. Because of it, his face had an unhealthy pallor, his shoulders were stooped, and his hair and mutton-chop whiskers were white. He was thin to the point of emaciation and looked ten years older than his brother Nairn instead of only three. Frequent coughs racked his body, and his handkerchiefs were often flecked with blood. He walked with a cane, as if fearful a breeze might topple him.

What had happened to Nairn since his son last saw him in San Francisco boarding *Eliza Grayson* bound for Hong Kong came out in bits and pieces during their three days of nearly non-stop talking. "Were it not for oor oars breaking, we too would hae followed the lifeboat with the twa lasses in it to shore," Nairn said, and related how the lifeboat he was in, being oarless, had been swept by winds and the current southward on a course parallel to the coast. In the storm, he had lost sight of the other lifeboat and *Eliza Grayson*.

For five weeks, Nairn and the three sailors with him drifted south, subsisting on rain water and provisions thrown hastily into the boat before they started for the Japanese shore. At length, the boat had drifted to an uninhabited island in the Bonin chain, where they lived by eating seabird eggs, turtles and fish while fashioning new oars from fallen trees.

Neil watched his father while he spoke, taking deep pleasure in the sight of his cheerful, open countenance, his full head of reddish hair, his glittery blue eyes, his tall spare frame.

In the Bonins, Nairn and the three sailors had stepped a short mast in their lifeboat and had used a scrap of canvas to fashion a tiny sail. With that and their new oars, they were able to push on to a point somewhere north of the Philippines, where they were picked up by a Spanish schooner that carried them to the small port of Aparri on the northern coast of Luzon. They slept on the beaches, scavenged and begged for food until the captain of a Chinese trading junk agreed to deliver a message to Neville Macneil when next he dropped anchor in Hong Kong.

When Neville got the message, he sent the hong ship *Rainbow* to Luzon to fetch back his brother and the two surviving sailors, the third having died of malnutrition and an unknown disease before they were picked up by the Spanish schooner.

Like almost every other European in Hong Kong not working for his government, Neville had plunged into the opium trade, where the profits glittered too brightly to be ignored. In his own Calvinist way, Neville was scrupulous in both personal and financial matters, but he was indifferent to moralistic reflections on addictive drugs, especially those used mainly by the heathen Chinese.

Nairn opposed the opium traffic vigorously and had already lost friends among the British community in Hong Kong because of his outspoken convictions.

"But opium," Neville told Nairn, "is th' inbound staple of trade, maun. Dinna ye ken there be eighty clippers in th' business? Eighty, maun! *Eighty!* Seven thousand tons sold to the heathen through Hong Kong last year alone."

"We ought to be looking at other goods," Nairn had replied, his voice rising.

"And wha' wad ye suggest?" Neville asked with heavy sarcasm.

"Ginseng, coal, sea otter skins, putchuck, even Chinese emigrants to the Australian gold fields...an' lucraban seeds an' tobacco an' silk an'...," Nairn paused to cast about in his mind for more. "Then wha' aboot seal fur, spices, gum copal from Zanzibar, an' even gold from Japan if th' Hollanders'll sell us some?"

"D'ye na ken I've thot of 'em all an' many, many more, maun? I'm telling ye I'd be wi' nary a shilling wi' out thae opium. One season's profits frae opium alone earned me enough to buy *Rainbow*, did it nae?"

On and on the argument went, until Neil remembered what his samurai pupils in Nagasaki had advised him to do.

"Has either of you thought about arms?"

"Arms?"

"Aye, buying and selling arms. Firearms and bullets. Weapons. Warships. Cannon."

"To whom?"

"To the Japanese, of course."

Neil told them about his students' recommendation and explained why he believed Japan would soon be a prime arms market.

Thoughtful, Nairn looked out the second-floor window of the newly built Hong Kong Club where the three were having their customary glass of heavy Spanish sherry before lunch. "Arms? Why, they're almost as bad as opium."

That remark perversely put Neville squarely on the opposite side of the argument. Neil shut his mouth and let them argue it out. After all, Neville owned sixty percent of the shares of the hong and his father forty.

In the hong office on the fourth day after their reunion, the comprador Lin Tze-hsu came padding up to Neil. "Man has message for you."

"Show him in."

"I took message."

"Well, what is it?"

"Man named Chiu A Po begs you come see him in jail."

"Who is he?"

"Very famous, very bad pirate. British ship *Mariner* capture him."

So, Neil thought, *it's Mr. Red Pants.*

"Just that?" Neil asked. "Just go see him in jail? Nothing more?"

"He wants sell something you. He says very important. He says you be very happy."

"No, I see no reason to see him."

"He meet head-cutter today. He must see you now or be too late."

"Head-cutter?"

"Chiu A Po have head cut off today."

CHAPTER 39

Not wanting to take Lin Tze-hsu away from his work at the hong, Neil asked Hut'ieh Gonzaga to accompany him as interpreter to see Chiu A Po. Dressed in her black skirt, black hose, and white blouse, she clung to Macneil's arm and chattered happily all the way to the jail. With bangs over her forehead and two pigtails hanging from above her ears, she still looked fifteen years old, or younger.

"I hope you don't mind my asking, Miss Gonzaga, but just how old are you?"

Her face took on an impish look.

"Do you suspect, Mr. Macneil, that I'm too young to be the mistress of a British navy captain?"

Her bluntness flustered Neil, who could think of no appropriate response.

She laughed. "Never mind. I'm seventeen...well, almost seventeen...and I'm very good in bed."

She looked up at Neil to gauge his reaction, which was shocked disapproval.

"Please call me Hut'ieh," she said.

"If you'll call me Neil."

"All right...Neil. Did Captain St. James tell you exactly why he calls me Hut'ieh?"

"No, he didn't."

"That's odd. I was almost certain he would. Are you quite sure?"

"I'm quite sure."

"He did tell you! He did so, didn't he? Oh, that villain!" She jumped behind Neil and began tickling his ribs. "Tell me the truth, Neil. Palmer told you, didn't he? I'll never forgive him, the scamp. Oh, shame on him! Shame, shame!"

Both were laughing as he broke free from her hands.

"Really, Hut'ieh, he didn't tell me."

"Liar, liar!"

"Cross my heart. But if it's so important, why don't you tell me yourself?"

"Indeed, I shan't! Never, never!"

"You'd better or else..."

"Or else, what?"

They were walking along a deserted road toward the harbor, so Neil grabbed her and began tickling her. His right hand rubbed over her left breast, which was firm and large and covered only by the thin fabric of her blouse. Shrieking with laughter, she struggled to free herself.

When Neil stopped, she stood still for a moment, then, looking up at him, said more seriously, "Tell you? That's out of the question. But someday, sir...mind you, I said someday, I just might show you."

Neil stepped away from her quickly. Never had he intended to have a conversation like this with her.

The jail, if it could be called that, was not the one operated by the British authorities but rather a temporary arrangement of bamboo cages lashed together by the Chinese businessmen of Hong Kong. The inmates were those pirates the British were squeamish about executing in large numbers without the customary tedious process of law. As the group that had suffered the most grievous losses from pirates, the Chinese businessmen felt no such qualms.

Nor did they feel any obligation to provide comfortable accommodations for their prisoners. The Chinese attitude was, "These lice in the pubic hair of society will die in a few days. Why waste money coddling them during the little time they have left?"

From a distance, the cages Hut'ieh was leading Neil to bore a resemblance to those where he was briefly housed in Nagasaki, but the resemblance lessened the closer he got.

These cages were built over a stagnant shallow pond that stank and bred mosquitoes by the thousands. The "first floor," the largest bamboo cage, housed a dozen criminals of several races. The floor, the sides, and the top of the cage were made of bamboo poles spaced four inches apart. If the pirates squeezed themselves together, all could lie down at the same time. On top of the bottom cage were stacked two more cages, each smaller and confining only two inmates each.

As they walked up to the six jailers lounging around the pond hawking and fighting off mosquitoes, a commotion arose from the cages.

It took a moment for Neil to realize what was happening. Since the cages had no toilets, the men in the second and third-level cages had to defecate and urinate down through the bamboo poles of their floors. If well aimed, the excreta fell through the three levels into the water in the shallow pond. Otherwise, it bounced off or stuck to the bamboos below.

The present commotion was caused by the upper-level pirates calling out warnings to their fellows to step aside and those below them casting up curses at the first signs of descending pollution.

Hut'ieh spoke to the head jailer for several minutes. He sent one of his assistants clambering up over the cages to the third-level where he unlocked a door and brought down an inmate, Mr. Red Pants himself—Chiu A Po.

The other jailers removed the manacles from the pirate's feet, then crowded close to prevent any possibility of escape. Chiu stretched his arms above his head and looked around him in good humor.

"Ask him what he wants with me," Neil told Hut'ieh.

She and Red Pants talked in Chinese, a tongue in which the Eurasian girl sounded formidable—almost mannish.

Neil grew impatient. "Hurry, Hut'ieh," he urged. "I'm sure this is a waste of my time, anyway."

"Be patient, Neil," she said, reaching back to touch a delicate hand on his arm. "This is just beginning to get interesting."

The pirate was doing most of the talking with dramatic gestures and occasional chuckles and pleading looks at Neil. At last, Hut'ieh put up her hands as a sign to him he had said enough. She led Neil a dozen paces away from the pirate and his ring of guards.

"He wants to sell you a guaranteed virgin."

"What?"

"He says you can examine the girl yourself to be sure she's a virgin." Her eyes were sparkling and the guards, who were watching the American, began to chuckle, too.

"He needs cash money for alcoholic drink and for Three-Chop Tsai."

"Tell me slowly and clearly what this is all about," Neil ordered.

"The pirate Chiu A Po, who was captured by Palmer and turned over to the Chinese businessmen of Hong Kong for execution, has a *karayuki-san*..." Her Japanese pronunciation was odd, but Neil recognized the Japanese word for the girls sold by poor peasants in Japan to rich Chinese merchants and mandarins. "...that he intended to deliver to a buyer in Tonkin. Since Chiu can't make delivery, he will sell her to you."

"But why did he think of *me*?"

"Because she is Japanese and because he heard you had tried to question some members of his crew in Japanese."

"You said he needed cash money for drink and for...who?"

"He wants to stupefy himself before the execution, so he must have liquor. Then, he wants to give squeeze to the head-cutter—a fellow called Three-Chop Tsai."

"It seems strange to want to give money to the man who cuts off your head, doesn't it?"

"If the head-cutter gets his squeeze, he'll do his job in one quick slash. But if he doesn't get such a bribe, it will take him..."

"...three strokes of the blade," Neil finished for her, the light dawning at last. "And, of course, that's why he is called Three-Chop."

"Here he comes now," Hut'ieh whispered.

"Here who comes?"

"Three-Chop."

A burly Chinese, naked from the waist up and wearing a wide low-cone hat like many Neil had seen in Japan, came strutting up to the bamboo cages followed by a noisy crowd of admirers.

"You mean...surely, you don't mean right here? And *now*?"

"If you really want the virgin girl," Hut'ieh urged, "you'd better do something fast."

"You little fool," Neil hissed at her. "Of course, I don't want the virgin girl. But then, neither do I want this man to suffer needlessly."

Hut'ieh smiled knowingly.

Spreading a reed mat on the sandy ground and digging a hole in front of it, the guards prepared the execution site. Macneil could see that Red Pants was watching him anxiously.

"Here," Neil said, shoving a Mexican trade dollar at Hut'ieh. "Have a guard buy him a bottle of liquor, any kind. And find out how much squeeze he needs to give Three-Chop."

Hut'ieh hurried over to a guard and spoke to him. The man ran toward a provisions shop down the road. She then talked to Red Pants, who took a paper from a pocket in his voluminous baggy pants and handed it to her. She came back to Neil.

"How much money do you have?"

Neil showed her the contents of his pocket—two gold *koban*, six silver *bu*, eight Mexican trade dollars, and about ten copper coins the Chinese called "cash."

Taking a gold *koban*, Hut'ieh said, "I'll try to bring back some change."

By this time, the guard had returned with a bottle of evil-looking yellowish liquor, which Chiu A Po started to gulp.

Hut'ieh went from Chiu to the head-cutter, who waited patiently at one side, his arms folded over his chest. A heavy curved sword dangled by a thong from his right wrist. He accepted the money from Hut'ieh with a benevolent smile, as if he had just sold her a loaf of bread or a melon.

Back at Neil's side, Hut'ieh placed something in the palm of his hand, closing his fingers over it.

"There," she said. "I made a good bargain for you and got some change besides. That piece of paper is the deed to the virgin girl and the address where you can find her. She's in the home of a relative of Chiu's."

A guard came running up carrying a small wooden tub with three inches of what looked like dirty sea salt in the bottom. Red Pants was pouring down the liquor with all possible speed. Already, his eyes were glazing and a silly smirk distorted his pockmarked face.

The crowd, growing by the minute, began to shout and move in closer. They jostled each other for the better places, as if attending a carnival. Like excited forest creatures, a gaggle of children ran in and out among the adults' legs.

"Let's get out of here," Neil said. "We've done what we came to do."

"No," she said sternly. "You're Chiu's benefactor now. You cannot insult him by not watching how he dies."

Even as she said those words, Chiu upended the bottle, drained it, and raised the empty bottle in salute to Neil. Feebly, Neil waved back.

The moment had come.

With the exception of Red Pants, all the participants in this drama, including the onlookers, seemed to know their roles well. With that silly grin still on his face, Red Pants staggered one step this way and another step that way, looking as if he expected to be congratulated.

Three of the guards forced him to kneel on the reed mat. Two tied a rope to his hands and pulled back on it. A third grabbed his queue and tugged forward till his head was directly above the hole dug in the sand. The nape of his thick pitted neck was exposed.

Now, Chiu was still but for his laboring chest.

Stepping forward, the head-cutter looked round with a superior smile. He must have known all eyes would be glued on him and wanted to prolong his brief moment of glory.

Neil's heart was pounding, his teeth were clenched, and his fingernails dug into his sweaty palms. Her mouth half open, Hut'ieh clung to one arm and held Neil in place.

A tense silence came over the crowd as if everyone had stopped breathing on cue.

"*Chi'iang pi!*" someone yelled.

"Off with his head," interpreted Hut'ieh in a whisper. Three-Chop raised his heavy sword. The sun glinted on its blade. Then, with a massive grunt, the head-cutter did his job. The sword flashed down with a soft whirr and struck the nape of Red Pants' neck with a thud.

It was a neat cut. Three-Chop had earned his squeeze and was already wiping his dripping blade on the dead pirate's red pants.

The guard whose job it was to pull forward on Chiu's queue staggered back and held up the head for the cheering throng to see. Neil could swear Chiu's eyes were open and his lips twitching in a grimace of distaste at what had just been done to him. When the guard began to swing the head back and forth like a child's toy on a string, the onlookers fell back to avoid being spattered with blood.

The two guards behind Chiu pushed his headless body, twitching like a fresh-caught fish, forward so that the neck—that gurgling stump of decapitated dreams—pumped blood into the hole in the sand. Another guard joined them and the three began to knead the body and tread on it to force the blood to empty faster.

This acted as a signal for the crowd to surge forward with exultant cries and dip their hands in the gushing blood.

"They're holding coins in their hands," Hut'ieh whispered. "They believe bloody money will multiply."

An old man pushed through the others to dip a half loaf of bread in the blood collecting in the hole.

"The old fool believes it will help him live longer," Hut'ieh said.

The man holding Chiu's head stopped swinging it back and forth and handed it by the queue to another fellow, who dropped it—with blood-bubbles frothy on its lips—into the small wooden tub half-filled with sea-salt and started off somewhere with it, grinning like a butcher's dog.

Thoroughly disgusted, Macneil asked Hut'ieh. "Now, what's he going to do with the head? Use it as a soup bone?"

"Don't be silly, Neil. I declare, you do say the strangest things. He's going to put it up on a pole as a warning."

"But why the salt?"

"To preserve it longer, of course."

Crossly, Neil asked, "Are we free to go now?"

"Of course, Neil. I'm sure you're quite eager to go inspect your new property. Who in his right mind would want to spend the rest of this exhilarating day in my company when he has just bought a virgin slave?"

Neil was so put out with Hut'ieh and her nonsense that he refused to speak at all till they got to a dock, where she waved to a walla-walla boatman to row over to them.

"Now what?" Neil growled.

"You're like a peevish old bear, Neil. I'm only trying to help you. Would you rather take me home first?"

"I'm sorry, Hut'ieh. It's not your fault, but it's not mine, either. I've had to witness a horrifying execution, and now I find myself burdened with a *karayuki-san* that I don't want."

"Be of good cheer, Neil. Remember, she's a virgin."

Exasperated, he exploded. "I don't care if she's a virgin or not. I'm not marrying her!"

"You don't have to marry her to bed her, do you?"

"It's a mistake trying to talk to you," he said, and retreated into a sullen silence as they climbed down into the gently bobbing walla-walla that the boatman used his stern-oar to keep pressed against the dock stanchions.

"Where are we going?" he asked at last when they were halfway across the bay.

"Your new property is on the Kowloon side." She gave additional directions to the boatman.

The stench from the harbor adding to his surliness, Macneil reflected on the English meaning of Hong Kong: "Incense Harbor." Maybe they had so named it because of the huge amounts of incense that would be needed to blot out all its obnoxious odors.

What on earth could he do with this *karayuki-san* they were now going to fetch? Already he had committed himself to Hut'ieh's upkeep, which he really could not afford, having not yet received even a ha'-penny in wages.

He had his own quarters to maintain. Now, on top of those two outlays, was he to be expected to pay the room and board of this *karayuki-san* until he could figure out how to get her back to Japan—and off his hands?

CHAPTER 40

Other than abandoning the *karayuki-san* on the Hong Kong streets, Macneil had no choice but to take her to his rooms. Even so, his intent was to return her to Japan as soon as possible.

She told him her name was Tomi, that she had come from the Amakusa Islands—Ai's home–and that she had been trained in Mr. Ueda's *karayuki-san* school in Naze. Neil's plan was to return her to Ueda, but before he could look for a Naze-bound vessel, his uncle and father called him to a business conference in their office.

"I like yer idea aboot arms an' warships, laddie, so we're sending ye to the Crimea," Neville told him.

"*Rainbow* can tak ye down to th' Straits of Sunda where ye can pick up anither ship to the Red Sea," his father said.

Their words came as a complete surprise to Neil. It was only four weeks since Palmer and Ai had taken ship for London.

"That's where Great Britain and Turkey and—who else, France?—are gathering their forces to fight the Russians, isn't it?" Neil asked.

"Where there's wars," his father pointed out, "there's discarded weapons to be picked up on the battlefields by scavengers, or bought from the stores captured by the victors."

"But it's too soon to sell arms to Japan," Neil protested. "We don't even know if the open-port treaty will be signed."

"It's worrth th' gamble, son," his father said. "Anyway, we can sell th' weapons to some o' th' warring sultans down in th' Malay States or Timor or maybe Bali."

"We'll gi'e ye letters of credit ye can cash with my agent Isaac Krakower in Constantinople when ye need—" Neville broke into an attack of coughing. His face turned livid. He signaled to his brother to do the rest of the talking.

Nairn took his son outside to permit Neville to recover.

Since it was close to noon, they decided to walk over to the Ship and Turtle on Queen's Road for a midday meal.

"Yer ooncle's nae doing so good, ye ken, laddie," Neil's father said, as they pushed through the street crowds. "That's one o' th' things he wanted to tell ye aboot. He's made oot a will. Had it done by a solicitor, all legal like."

At the restaurant, a Chinese waiter brought them local beer and took their food order under the vigilant eyes of the retired English sailor who owned the tavern. It was a wild and rowdy place at night, but served solid English fare at reasonable prices during the day. Neville and Nairn had been trying to talk the proprietor into learning to prepare haggis, the Scottish national dish, for the many Scots in Hong Kong. The idea of cooking anything in the lining of a sheep's stomach, however, was a mental barrier the man had yet to overcome.

While they waited for their meal, Nairn reminded his son of the terms of the business agreement. Nairn owned forty percent of Macneil Brothers' stock, and he had made out a will dividing his shares equally between Neil and Margaret. If Margaret were no longer living, Neil would inherit all of Nairn's shares. Neville had willed his sixty percent to Anne, his only child. Neil knew all of this, but he was surprised that Neville had arranged things so that in the event of his death, Neil would control his sixty percent until Anne was rescued. If Anne were never found, or if it could be proved she had died, the sixty percent would become Neil's. If Anne were rescued, and if she and Neil married, she would hold the sixty percent in her name, but Neville expected that she would assign Neil effective control over her shares.

Suddenly, Neil Macneil found that he had prospects of becoming a merchant of some means. If Anne and Margaret were both dead, he would eventually, in the normal course, own one hundred percent of Macneil Brothers, Ltd.

If both Anne and Margaret were rescued, and Anne married someone else, Neil would hold only twenty percent of the company, but even so, it seemed probable he would continue to manage the hong after Neville's and Nairn's deaths, if they preceded him. The death rate among Europeans in Hong Kong was so high—twenty percent of the British soldiers and sailors had died there in a recent year, he was told—that there was no predicting who would pass on first.

But Neil's concern was not so much with his inheritance or who would have effective control of Macneil Brothers, Ltd. His mind was set on returning to Japan and resuming his search for Anne and Margaret.

"Ye'd better tend to yer packing," his father told him over their meat pies. "*Rainbow* will leave day after tomorrow. She'll load 'er tea in Foochow an' set sail withoot coomin' back here at all. We'll gi'e ye instructions an' money an' th' letters o' credit tomorrow."

Despite his concern about Anne and Margaret in Japan, Neil felt a surge of exhilaration. His first mission for the hong! Off to distant parts to buy weapons. A chance to see the Middle East, and maybe to watch battles being fought.

"We'll go over to Mr. Lane's store this afternoon an' buy ye some more clothes an' a proper travel kit," Nairn said. He hesitated, then asked, "An' who'll be taking care o' yer twa women whiles ye're gone?"

"I'll just have to leave them some money for food, and I'll pay their rent for four or five months in advance," Neil said. "If they need more, they'll know where to find you. Can I get an advance on my salary from the hong?"

Nairn promised to set up a drawing account for his son with the Chinese who kept the cash ledger in the counting room.

Tomi had a hot bath ready for her new master when he returned to his rooms that evening. While he was eating the fried fish, rice, and vegetables Tomi had pickled in brine in a small wooden vat, Neil reflected that his trip to the Crimea solved for the time being the question of what to do with her.

Big for a Japanese girl, Tomi was at least four inches taller than Ai. In no sense was she fat, but she had a healthy, strong body and had already done man's work pulling in fishing nets at her home in the Amakusa Islands.

Tomi had heard often of the *funa-kainin* clan who lived in the secluded Amakusa valleys and even of Ai Koga, a heroine to youngsters throughout the islands, but she had never met her in the flesh. She envied Neil for knowing her.

Tomi had bold features, sparkling, inquisitive eyes, generous lips, and high cheekbones. She had large breasts—very large, Neil thought, for a girl of eighteen—and she had no more compunction than Ai had about appearing before him naked, such as when she went in or out of the bath just off one of Neil's two main rooms. Like Ai's, her devotion to cleanliness was obsessional.

For the first few days she was with Neil, Tomi—her full name was Tomi Uchida, with the "Tomi" meaning wealth—was terrified of the young American. (Uchida was a surname given her by Ueda in Naze, her family being of the class called *hira-byakusho* or peasants without surnames.) She acted as if she fully expected he would at any time fall upon her and devour her down to her little toes. When Neil tried speaking soothing words in Japanese to her, she broke into tears at the outlandish notion that a hairy devil of a barbarian could speak the same tongue that her fellow fisherfolk and peasants in Amakusa spoke.

After that, Neil said only what was necessary to her. He went out and bought three heavy Chinese quilts that he thought she could use in place of *futon* and dropped them carelessly in the room where he planned for her to sleep.

"I will let her live with me until I can find the means to return her to Japan," he told Madame Keogh.

"We will-a see," the landlady said. "It make-a no matter to me. One person, two person. All-a same rent." She nudged Neil in the ribs.

"You same sly dog lak-a my husa-band, eh?"

Neil had given up protesting to others that he had not installed an eighteen-year-old mistress in his bachelor quarters.

On the first night Tomi came to stay, he bedded down early, being tired and out of sorts. He closed the door and climbed into bed.

Soon, the door opened softly and in came Tomi, dressed in the indigo kimono she had been wearing when Hut'ieh and Neil went to get her. The conversation with Hut'ieh came back to him.

They had left the house of Chiu A Po's relative with Tomi walking fearfully with bowed head three paces behind her new master. "You are now the proud owner of a genuine slave girl," Hut'ieh said.

"Stop that," Neil said.

"Tell me, good sir, when will you hold the official inspection?"

"What the devil are you chattering about?"

"Why, the hymen inspection, to be sure! How else will you know that she is a genuine virgin?"

"And if she is not?"

"I'm sure I can sell her for you. Those *karayuki-san* girls, even with broken hymens, fetch pretty prices in these parts."

From the merry glint in her eyes, Neil could see that this was a field Hut'ieh fully intended to harvest for a long time to come.

Tomi slipped quietly into Neil's room, lit the wick in the night-lamp with a lucifer, and commenced to prepare herself for bed. She removed her kimono, then her other garments. Folding them all neatly on a chair, she knelt on the carpeted floor and bowed deeply to her master's apparently sleeping form.

Again, Macneil noticed that Tomi was taller than Ai and larger—but not at all fat. There was not an ounce of non-muscle flesh on her except a little on her breasts and hips. The word that occurred to him was "luscious."

She came around to the other side of his bed and bowed again, standing this time.

Then she stretched herself out beside him.

Time passed—five minutes, maybe longer.

Suddenly, the situation struck Neil as being funny. He struggled to keep from laughing. Turning his head a little, as if in his sleep, he slitted his eyes open. In the dim interior, he could see that Tomi was lying on her back, her knees drawn up and legs spread slightly apart.

This is foolish, Neil thought. He pretended to wake up. "*Tomi-san*, what are you doing here?" he said in Japanese.

"I was taught at the school in Naze to sleep by my master's side and await his pleasure," she said in a faint voice.

"This bed is very narrow," Neil said.

"Not if one person is on top of the other."

"Well, I'm tired," he said, "and I have no intention of sleeping on top of someone or vice versa, so you go sleep on those quilts I bought."

"*Kashikomarimashita*," she said, which meant something like, "To hear is to obey." "But there is one brazen request I must make of my honorable master."

Invariably, she called Neil "*danna-sama*" or "honorable master," as in, "Will the honorable master have his honorable dinner now?"

"Well, what's this brazen request?" he asked.

After some hesitation, she said, "It is the matter of the contract."

"Contract? What contract?" His impatience with her was plain in his choice of Japanese words.

"Have I angered the honorable master?" Her words were as soft as thrush wings in the forests of spring.

"No, no, you silly wench. It's just that I don't know what you're talking about."

"You have deigned to buy me and my body for five years. Now, I must send the contract—with the honorable master's seal or signature on it—back to that man Ueda-*san* in the town of Naze. He will send it and a certain sum of money on to my parents in Amakusa."

"Now wait, wait," Neil said, raising himself up on one elbow. "Let's understand each other, Tomi-*san*. I'm *not* going to buy you for five years or for any number of years, so I see no reason to sign a contract. I might send some money if your family is in urgent need, but—"

Tomi shifted her body up against Neil's and clutched his arm. "*Danna-sama*, please do not deign to utter those cruel words. I *must* have the signed contract. Without it, my family will lose face."

"I was about to say that I'm going to send you back to Naze and then to Japan on the next available ship, with some money."

She protested. "My parents could not accept the money if their daughter has done nothing to earn it."

Neil was amazed. "You mean they wouldn't take the money just as a gift?"

"Not unless I have earned it."

"Even if their other children don't have enough to eat?"

"There's always the *kozute-yabu*," she said, reminding Neil of the forest with many tiny skeletons he and Ai had seen in northern Honshu. That was one of the *kozute-yabu* where unwanted babies were left to die.

"Dear God," he said aloud.

"Does my honorable master wish me to join the *Jashumon*?" *Jashumon* was Japanese for the "evil Christian faith."

"Then you're not a hidden Christian?"

"Some Amakusa people are Shintoists—and others are Buddhists. A few are both. By no means are all of us hidden Christians."

Neil thought for a while. At length, he said, "All right, I'll sign a contract, and I'll send some money to your parents. A little now, and more later. Even so, I will not keep you here for five years. That's out of the question. I'll send you back to Japan long before that."

Tomi's voice was lower and calmer now. "Thank you. Now, will the honorable master examine me?"

"Examine you?"

"In the contract, the master will have to confirm that he examined me and found me to be a virgin."

"How do I examine you?" he said.

"Feel me."

"Feel you?"

"Yes, honorable master."

"Feel you...where?"

He heard a low chuckle. It was the first sign of humor he had observed in her. "I doubt that the honorable master will find my hymen..." She used the Japanese word *shojo-maku* for hymen. "...in my ear or in my mouth."

Neil felt himself blush. This was preposterous.

He began in a severe tone. "Tomi-*san*, I'm *not* going to feel you *anywhere*. Maybe, when I return from the Crimea, I'll have a Hong Kong doctor examine you. If he assures me you are a virgin, both he and I can sign a certificate to that effect."

Her voice was low but quite positive. "By then, I may no longer be a virgin."

"What do you mean? I won't be here."

"I must speak frankly to my honorable master, to whom I have now entrusted my life and the welfare of my family in the Amakusa Islands," she said, moving still closer to Neil and taking his hand. "For the past year, I have had a...a hot tingling in my loins. It is a wet, bothersome sensation. It makes me want to move my hips up and down and back and forth and press my legs together."

With extraordinary strength and firmness of purpose, Tomi guided his hand to the most private of her parts, where she pushed his middle finger into her vagina.

Though Neil had never knowingly touched a maidenhead (sometimes, he wondered if Anne had been a virgin when they mated), what he now felt at Tomi's entryway was without doubt a membranous obstruction of some sort.

"Will the honorable master now agree I am a virgin?"

"That I will," he said with a sigh. "That I will."

CHAPTER 41

From South China to the Crimea

Now that *Aksehir* had cleared the Bosporus, the captain of the merchant vessel began shouting orders in rapid, menacing Turkish to the masthands. They responded by clambering up through the rigging. Behind lay Constantinople. Ahead was clear sailing across the Black Sea to the Chersonese Peninsula in the Crimea and the port of Balaklava.

As far as Neil Macneil knew, no other person aboard this ship carrying supplies to the Turkish forces in the Crimea spoke any English. The voyage promised, therefore, to be silent and lonely, albeit comfortable. But the sea around the ship was by no means lonely, for a stream of vessels plied back and forth between Constantinople and Balaklava transporting troops, horses, supplies, and arms to the British, French and Turkish armies gathering their forces on the peninsula, where they were certain to clash with the might of Czarist Russia.

In Constantinople, Isaac Krakower, a Polish Jew who had offices in European cities as well, had given Macneil money and had arranged his passage on *Aksehir*. If Neil bought the arms he sought, he planned to consign them to Krakower through a Balaklava freight forwarder, so they could be transshipped from Turkey to Hong Kong.

Neil had spent only four days in Constantinople, but it had taken four months for him to sail to where he now was from Hong Kong. Never had he dreamed the trip would be so long or so tedious. By now, Palmer St. James and Ai should have reached London already and Ai's operation should have been performed. Palmer might even be pacing the foredeck of the warship he so deeply craved to command, seeking Russian targets on the high seas.

The four months had been filled with days of pacing the

decks of ships or rocking along on a camel's back, his thoughts shifting from Anne to Ai and back again. The four months had been filled with impatience, too. If the pending Crimea battles had already been fought, Neil might be too late to buy any captured or abandoned arms.

Four months ago, he had boarded the hong ship *Rainbow*, with her gleaming paint work and brass. A narrow band of four colors—red, white, green, and blue—was blazoned around her hull eight feet above the water line. A truly magnificent ship, she had been built as an opium clipper by Smith and Dimon of New York City for Messrs. Howland and Aspinwall. From them his uncle Neville had bought the graceful, feminine vessel.

Leaving Hong Kong, *Rainbow* had sailed up the China coast to the Min River mouth. From there, she followed its twisting 25-mile course upriver. En route she passed through tall canyons of trees—so close monkeys jumping from one side of the river to the other sometimes stopped for a breather in the top rigging of the tea clippers. After cautiously navigating the danger-ridden chow-chow currents of the Min, *Rainbow* had reached the Pagoda Anchorage in Foochow.

The hong flagship had hauled both opium and tea, but on this trip she would carry only tea to England, then fill her holds with chests of opium balls in India on the return trip. In Foochow she took on 1,230,900 pounds of tea—over 600 tons. First, however, fifty tons of kentledge—scrap iron—and one hundred tons of beach pebbles were stowed below as ballast. Next came a floor of planking and then the straw-covered wooden tea chests and half-chests, all packed tight to keep them from shifting at sea. First into the holds went the inferior teas, then the better grades atop them. All the chests were hammered into place, and more pebbles were forced into the space between the hull and the straight sides of the chests.

Finally, a covering of canvas and split bamboo was laid over the top layer of chests, a river pilot was brought aboard, and the sampans that had carried the tea out from the Pagoda Anchorage docks began slowly to move away from *Rainbow* like a myriad of suddenly indifferent water bugs.

Back down the Min River the ship had inched her way with wilted sails through the gorge of forests, the shrill cries of parrots piercing the ears of the people on board from both sides. When at last they had dropped their river pilot and headed out to open sea, Captain Hugh Chatham had ordered every shred of canvas on *Rainbow* raised. She had responded with a will, putting her shoulder down and surging ahead, as spray rose jubilantly over the figurehead and back onto the deck.

On this first leg of the voyage, Neil came to appreciate Palmer St. James's passion for sailing ships, for *Rainbow* was a gold-plated wonder. With her mainmast standing 140 feet above the deck, she carried more sail than a 74-gun warship. With her stunsails—what seamen called the studding sails—clapped on extended yards, she looked like a great white, many-winged bird in full flight.

The first day, *Rainbow* ran 292 miles. On the next, 301. The trip to the Sunda Straits she made in only twenty-one days. Every day, the spray splashed up in a continuous roar from the wave-breaking bow, while the bang and thunder of the hard-bellied sails made conversation difficult. Neil learned the marvelous excitement of sweeping past ordinary merchantmen, whose crews stood transfixed at the rails and gaped at the speed of the tea clipper.

Sadly, Neil had to leave *Rainbow* in the Sunda Straits, where their paths parted. There, Malayan sampans raced out from shore to sell chickens, ducks, pigs, coconuts, woven mats, shells, and even monkeys and caged sparrows.

After waiting six nail-chewing days in Tandjungkarang, Macneil was at last able to buy passage on a slow trading-dhow out of Java to Ceylon and then to Aden and finally up the Red Sea to the port of Suez, with long stays in each port.

In Suez, he had no choice but to join a camel caravan that plodded on north to Port Said, over never-ending sand dunes through which it was rumored a mighty canal would one day be dug. With the wind blowing the sand with abrasive force every day, Neil wondered if such a canal would not fill up and revert to smooth, trackless desert within a year.

But at last the long journey was over, as was the much shorter one across the Black Sea on *Aksehir*.

Now, in the early evening, he found himself approaching the insane bustle that was Balaklava, its yellow lights blinking wickedly like a tawdry whore luring the weary seafarer.

CHAPTER 42

The Crimean Peninsula in Russia

Balaklava was a small port at the southern end of the Chersonese Peninsula. There were two other ports in the Crimea where the British could have landed their forces, but these had been assigned to their French allies. Through this port had and would come the supplies and arms that the British needed to capture the vast deep-water harbor of Sevastopol, only seven miles to the north on the west side of the peninsula.

To reach Balaklava, *Aksehir* would have to wend its uneasy way up a narrow deep inlet not unlike the Min River at Foochow. The captain waited until the following morning to make the passage in the safety of daylight.

Once a pretty little fishing village, Balaklava had also been a summer resort for the wealthy residents of Sevastopol. Nestled among vegetable gardens, the green-tiled houses were covered in season with flowers such as clematis and honeysuckle. These would have grown in lovelier profusion, however, had the houses not lay in shadow most of the day from the towering hills and cliffs surrounding the inlet.

The arrival of the war god had changed entirely the appearance and character of Balaklava. The British admiral running the port—a decrepit, half-senile man named Boxer—had no system at all for unloading, stowing and transporting army equipment and stores to the heights overlooking Sevastopol. As a result, the harbor was hopelessly jammed, with the docks so overloaded two had already collapsed from the weight piled on them. Provisions were beginning to rot. The narrow roads were so deep in mud and blocked with overturned wagons that starving horses died in their harnesses from the exertion of trying to extricate themselves.

Farther up the peninsula, the slaughter yard for the British forces lay across from the upper end of the inlet, past which the road to Sevastopol ran. Daily, its tons of offal were either tossed into the still waters of the inlet or left to stink in the sun, attracting—as one British soldier told Macneil— "all the flies in southern Russia as well as most of those in Asia and Europe."

What had been a pleasant, neat resort had been turned into squalid, ugly chaos over which a miasma of throat-grabbing stenches hung like a tenacious London fog in December. First, the British troops had raped the gardens of the port, then trampled down all other vegetation in their rush to loot the vineyards. To cook their half-spoiled meat and boil water for their tea, they had torn down the fences and ripped up the board-walks, then carried off doors, shutters, roofs, and even walls of the houses.

Wading through the mire of the roads—some with cannon balls stacked like melons alongside them—Macneil learned first that there was nothing vaguely resembling a hotel where he could stay. This forced him to buy a small conical tent from a cross-eyed Armenian wearing birch-bark boots and leggings. The man also promised Macneil to procure blankets and food for him at outrageous prices. Other civilians like Macneil were doing the same. They had no choice.

Neil spent the rest of the day wandering around Balaklava. He even walked two miles north of the town to the hamlet of Kadikoi, where Lord Lucan, the commander of the British cavalry division, had established his headquarters. In Macneil's mind was the thought that he might talk to an officer about buying captured weapons, if there were any. By the time he got near the row of officers' tents, however, his clothes were so muddy he feared being thrown out on his ear if he tried to enter one of them.

Back in Balaklava in the early evening, he found the cross-eyed Armenian waiting for him. The man had pitched Macneil's tent, built a campfire and laid out a clean red blanket over a filthy gray one. Feeling beholden, Macneil invited the Armenian to share his meat and beans and black Russian bread. In vile English, the cross-eyed fellow managed to ask Macneil his purpose in Balaklava. Macneil told him he had come to buy discarded or captured arms.

With a huge smile, the Armenian told Macneil a battle had already been fought along the river Alma, north of Sevastopol, and he knew where to buy some of the rifles captured there. Pleased this business of buying arms promised to be relatively easy, Macneil negotiated with the Armenian to obtain for Macneil Brothers, Ltd., one hundred twenty "practically new" rifles. Neil was proud of arguing the Armenian down to less than half what he had first demanded.

The fellow wanted the money in advance. Macneil refused. Resigned, the man promised to leave the rifles in back of the American's tent that night and come by for his money in the morning, after Macneil had examined the arms in daylight. With that understanding, he slipped off into a night filled with the sounds of drunken brawls and boisterous singing.

The next morning, Macneil was kicked awake by two of the 800 British marines that occupied the town.

"On yer feet, guv'ner," said one.

Only half awake, Macneil croaked, "What the devil!"

"Up with yer now, there's a good gentleman."

Macneil could barely speak, much less think. "Just tell me what it is you—"

"Whut we wants? It's them fancy new Enfield rifles we wants, that's whut. Ye orta be ashamed o' yerself, sir, stealing from us poor, downtrodden redcoats." The first marine winked at the second and roared with laughter. "Get dressed now, and we'll let ye go pay yer respects to Lord Scarlett himself. Mebbe he'll hang ye. Who knows?"

Shocked into instant wakefulness, Macneil knew he had learned his first lesson in buying arms. Never buy weapons whose ownership is in doubt.

They marched him over the same two miles he had walked yesterday, past hundreds of northbound cavalry mounts loaded with supplies and boards for temporary shelters. He arrived outside Lord Scarlett's tent muddier, if that was possible, than he had been the day before. One of his captors told a sergeant why he had been brought there. The sergeant informed a cavalry lieutenant, who entered the tent and reported to someone inside that the two marines had caught a civilian in illegal possession of 120 new Enfield Pattern 1853 rifled muskets, .577 caliber. An unintelligible discussion followed.

In three minutes, the lieutenant stepped back through the tent flap, eyed Macneil distastefully, and said to the two marines, "Have him shot."

Macneil closed his eyes in shock.

"But...but," he stammered, "I *bought* those rifles!"

"A likely story," the blond lieutenant sneered.

"It's true, damn you!" Macneil cried.

"Have you a receipt?"

"I'll get one this morning. I haven't paid the money yet. This Armenian fellow told me they were guns captured at the Battle of Alma. I haven't even looked at them yet."

The officer laughed. "Someone just found boxes of brand-new Enfield rifles lying about on the battlefield, waiting to be picked up by scavengers, eh?" He snorted, then ordered, "Take him away."

CHAPTER 43

As the marines spun him around, Macneil heard a voice from inside the tent: "Wait! By Jove, I know that fellow."

The tent flap was pushed open, and there stood Captain Palmer St. James of the Royal Navy. Right behind him was an equally resplendent cavalry officer who, judging from his resemblance to Palmer, could have been none other than Colonel George St. James, his older brother.

The lesson Macneil learned about buying arms cost him less than he feared.

Though the 120 new Enfields were confiscated, he did not pay anything to the cross-eyed Armenian, who was caught and shot in Neil's place.

Palmer had assured Colonel George St. James that Macneil was a man of his word. "An honest sort, even though a colonial of Scottish forebears," were his exact words. The colonel had reported that opinion to Lord Scarlett, who had invited Macneil to dinner by way of apology for the "discourtesy" of almost having him shot.

Before dinner, Neil took Palmer aside.

"Well?" he asked, anxiously.

"Well what, old boy?"

"Damnit, Palmer, you know what I'm talking about. What about Ai? Did she—"

"Did she have her operation? The answer is yes, she did."

"And?"

"And when the surgeon removed the bandages in a dimly-lit room on the fourth day, she blinked several times, looked up at me and said in English, 'I see you.' "

Neil lowered his head and gave thanks to the Almighty.

Harrumphing in his best naval captain's manner, Palmer said, "And now about Hut'ieh. Is she all right?"

"She's perfectly all right, Palmer. Or she was when I left Hong Kong. I've paid her rent and left her money for expenses.

She can go to my father if she needs more."

"You found your father? Excellent, old chap, excellent!"

Neil told Palmer about his father and uncle, the Macneil hong, the execution of Chiu A Po, the acquisition of the *karayuki-san* Tomi Uchida, the trip upriver to Foochow, and the long journey to reach Balaklava. He was eager, however, to know more about Ai.

"Where's Ai staying?"

"I've found rooms for her near Belgrave Square. The First Lord promised to have someone look in on her now and then. What a marvelous creature she is, Neil! Bright as a penny. She's taken to the Queen's English with a fearful intensity of purpose. I've introduced her to several friends who will make sure she's all right. I bought her a wardrobe, and she was being invited to some topdrawer homes when I left. She'll be quite the rage, old chap."

Neil tried to imagine the Ai he knew—the woodland nymph who could let fly three fatal arrows in five seconds and threaten to cut the throat of her fiance to protect her American friend—dressed in the latest London fashions and gracing the salons of the elite. Somehow, he could not connect the two women in his mind.

"Palmer, I know all this is costing you much more than it costs me to care for Hut'ieh in Hong Kong. I'm on salary now, and I can afford to pay you in installments."

"Nonsense, Neil. Perish the thought. Our family's invest-ments in Lancashire and Birmingham textile mills and Belfast shipyards are paying handsome dividends, I'm told. You take care of Hut'ieh, and I'll look after Ai, each in his own fashion. That was the bargain, and I insist we stick to it. The First Lord has gone dotty over your young lady. First thing we know, he'll be contesting you for her affections."

"Look here, Palmer, Ai is a fine girl, and I owe her my life, but it's Anne who is my fiancee, and I haven't the slightest intention—"

"Yes, yes. I've heard all that before, but this Anne you speak of would have to be truly extraordinary to be in the same class with 'that splendid Miss Koga,' as I heard someone call her."

"How's your wound?"

"Much better," Palmer said. "Can't lift anything heavy yet with this arm, but I can raise a glass to my lips quite well—and with admirable regularity, thank you."

"And your command? I believe you were going to ask the First Lord for a larger ship, a man of war."

Palmer's look of joy was a thing to behold. "And I've got it, Neil! The Admiralty gave me *Warrior.*"

"*Warrior?*"

"Our first all-iron warship, old boy. She carries sail plus, mind you, a 5,470-horsepower steam engine. Even with 34 guns, she did nearly fifteen knots in her trials. She's got two stacks.

"She's being fitted out in Portsmouth. I'm to take command in two months."

"So, in the meantime, you just thought you'd take some leave and amble out to the Crimea to see what brother George was up to. Maybe you'd even try to get into the action yourself, eh?"

Disappointment replaced the pleasure on Palmer's face. "Georgie was willing enough to let me have a go. He doesn't give a fig for their damned silly regulations, but Lord Lucan wouldn't budge an inch. Dash it, I practically got down on my knees and begged the blighter to let me take a temporary commission in George's Hussars, but he's such a bloody stickler." Palmer walked off two paces, then turned back. "I should have gone to Lord Cardigan instead. He's not very bright, and he usually says yes to any proposal."

"Cardigan?"

"He has the Light Brigade. George's regiment is part of it."

"And Lord Lucan? Just what is his role?"

"He's the cavalry commander under Raglan. He's over both the Light and the Heavy Brigades. Scarlett's the commander of the Heavies"

"So what do you plan to do?"

"I suppose the best I can hope for is to watch what happens," Palmer said. "At dinner tonight, I'll ask Lucan for permission. He won't refuse that." He paused, then said, "I say, old fellow. Come with us tomorrow why don't you? I'll get Georgie to lend us a couple of mounts and we can at least see the fun."

"The fun? What on earth are you talking about, Palmer? What's going to happen tomorrow?"

"Haven't I told you? Well, the blasted Rooskies—25,000 of them under Count Liprandi—are trying to get round behind our forces encircling Sevastopol. Our overall commander, Lord Raglan, has assigned Lucan's cavalry division the task of driving them back. In support, there will be a battalion of Highlanders—your people, what?—and the French Chasseurs d'Afrique."

"Can they do it?"

"They're badly outnumbered, but with the Deaths to lead them—"

"The 'Deaths'?"

"The 'Death or Glory' men, you know. That's what we call the Light Brigade."

"Where will the fighting take place?"

"We can't be sure, of course, but Lord Raglan's command post was set up today on the Sapoune Ridge six miles north. It's on high ground overlooking two valleys with another ridge in between. On our maps, we've called them the North and South Valleys. Our Turkish allies man six redoubts on the heights between the valleys. Lord Raglan believes the Russians may set up their guns at the end of the North Valley as well as on the high ground to the west."

"So we might get to see a cavalry charge at the Russian guns?" Neil said.

"Never, old boy. Even a sailor knows that cavalry never charges up a slope at artillery, not without strong infantry support, and we doubt that the reserve infantry division can reach those valleys in time to provide that support."

CHAPTER 44

Neil and Palmer climbed to Lord Raglan's command post at an elevation of 600 feet on the Sapoune Ridge. Macneil had the feeling he was looking down at an irregular, uneven chessboard. All the knights and pawns stood in place, awaiting the hands and wills of the master players. He wished he had brought along a sketch pad and pencil.

"Keep in mind, Neil, that we can see most of it from up here, but those chaps below can't see nearly as much," Palmer said as they dismounted.

They edged into the circle surrounding Lord Raglan, the commander of all the British forces in the Crimea. A small man who had lost an arm at Waterloo in 1815, Raglan had not commanded troops in action since then. He frequently wore civilian attire, but even in uniform, he favored a white, floppy-brimmed civilian hat with a colorful scarf tied around the crown with its ends hanging down over his neck.

Palmer saluted, introduced himself and Macneil, and started to retire when Raglan exclaimed, "Jove, you're the First Lord's second cub, aren't you? Come to see brother George in action, eh?"

"I'd really like to be down there on the field with him, m'Lord," Palmer said, stepping forward again. "If only you would give me a thirty-day commission or even just your permission."

Raglan laughed. "Nonsense, m'boy. The First Lord would keelhaul me if anything happened to you on my field of battle. Be content to watch what happens like the rest of us, there's a good fellow."

General Airey, Raglan's second in command, stood alert at his superior's side. Aides-de-camp, subordinate commanders, French and Turkish officers, couriers, and even other civilians milled about. Scattered among them were seven officers' wives who had brought along picnic hampers and were spreading out tablecloths on this flat space atop the ridge.

Neil and Palmer had arrived just in time, it seemed, for they could already detect movement among the colorful bodies of men within their view.

Briefly, Palmer explained the situation. The North Valley stretched out before and below them in a rectangle. At the far end, aimed toward them, were the Russian guns. Beyond the guns, the reserve Russian cavalry waited. On the west, to the left of Palmer and Macneil as they looked down, stood another Russian battery, its guns pointing into the North Valley from that side. In a depression, between the two observers and that battery, was hidden the French cavalry—the Chasseurs d'Afrique. The east side of the North Valley, off to their right, was formed by what the British called the Causeway heights.

Six redoubts or temporary fortifications lay atop Causeway and had been held by the Turkish allies. In these redoubts were placed British guns, lent to the Turks by Lord Raglan. Russians pouring down into the South Valley, which lay beyond the Causeway, had attacked the Turkish redoubts earlier that morning. Despite valiant resistance by the Turks, the Russians had driven them out of the fortifications and down the ridge south toward Balaklava.

At the lower end of the North Valley, almost directly below Neil and Palmer, stood to horse Lord Lucan's cavalry. This division was made up of the Light Brigade, under Cardigan, and, behind it, the Heavy Brigade—"heavy" referring to the size of the horses and the men upon them—under Scarlett's command.

Off beyond the cavalry division and between it and the Causeway now stood at ease a farther forlorn looking battalion of Highlanders.

"It's the 93rd," Palmer said, "under Sir Colin Campbell."

Neil could see them clearly through the telescope he and Palmer shared. They wore red coats, white crossbelts, darkish kilts—Neil could not distinguish the tartan—high busbies with white plumes, and red hose under white leggings. Their colors enhanced the chessboard effect of the scene.

The Highlanders were serenaded by three bagpipers. Even at that distance, with the aid of an easterly breeze, Neil could faintly hear the soul-stirring skirl of the pipes. Their tune was "Scotland, the Brave."

Invigorated by the martial music and a racial memory of Scotland's misty highlands, Macneil cried, "Now that's where I'd like to be!"

"It's too late to join them now," Palmer said, pointing to the Causeway heights. Russian cavalry had appeared atop the heights and were racing down its slope to attack the nearest enemy body, the Highlanders' battalion.

Coolly, their officer in charge—it must have been Sir Colin Campbell—dressed his lines to the right flank and ordered his front rank to kneel and prepare to fire.

The Highlanders were using muzzle-loading Minie rifles, Palmer said, which could be fired only about twice a minute but were accurate and deadly up to 350 yards.

When the Russian cavalry came to within that many yards of the Highlanders, a sheet of flame shot out from the Scots' front rank, followed by a slowly rising cloud of smoke. The second rank stepped forward and knelt to fire, then rose to reload while the first rank walked four paces between them to kneel and fire. From Neil's distance, this long, thin line of red, tipped with the flashing steel of their bayonets, appeared to be moving slowly forward in measured steps.

The effect on the charging Russian cavalry was devastating.

The first volley from Campbell's men had slowed the Russians, and the second brought them to a halt. Thereafter, the Russians looked like a reeling punch-drunk pugilist being knocked backwards by the steady, relentless blows of an invisible opponent. Their dismay and confusion were plain.

Finally, the Russian commander ordered his men back up the slope to the ridge along the Causeway heights, where they milled about while medical orderlies ran down to the scene of the slaughter to rescue the wounded. One Highlander raised his rifle to fire at the rescuers, but Campbell dashed over to knock down the barrel with his sword.

Neil could see considerable frantic activity around the captured British guns in the redoubts atop the ridge. He thought the Russians were trying to shift the cannon so they could fire down on the Highlanders in revenge. Lord Raglan, however, who stood about twenty feet away, evidently believed the Russians were on the point of removing the guns and hauling them back with them as their cavalry retired to the north. At that distance and among so many milling horsemen, it was difficult to know which was true.

In any case, Raglan seemed inordinately fond of those guns—only twelve from among the 190 he had transported to the Crimea.

They all heard his anguished cry. "Look! The blackguards! They're making off with my guns!"

General Airey, second in command, strode up to Raglan as Neil and Palmer edged closer. "Your orders, m'lord?" asked Airey.

Very excited, Raglan said clearly in his high-pitched voice, "Write this down, Airey, and send it to Lord Lucan. 'Lord Raglan wishes the cavalry to advance rapidly to the front— follow the enemy and try to prevent the enemy carrying away the guns.' "

"But he didn't say *which* guns," Neil whispered urgently to Palmer. "There are also guns over there and there—and there."

He pointed toward the Causeway heights, then to the far end of the North Valley, and finally to the Fedyukhin heights forming the west wall of the valley.

"Instead of 'front,' it looks more like the 'right flank front' to me," Palmer said.

Certainly, Neil was in no position to say anything to anyone about what seemed to be a serious oversight by Lord Raglan. Nevertheless, a deep uneasiness drove him to say to Palmer, "Can't you talk to him? Those orders are too vague, aren't they?"

"I agree, laddie, but I fail to see how a sailor who is only a guest here can tell a field marshal his orders are too vague."

General Airey finished scrawling the dictated dispatch to Lord Lucan. He looked around for an aide-de-camp to carry it down the hill to where Lord Lucan and Lord Cardigan sat on their horses on this side of the Light Brigade. This brigade was made up of the 17th Lancers, the 4th and 13th Light Dragoons, and the 8th and 11th Hussars—the last being Colonel George St. James's regiment. George was easily identified by his rough-haired terrier Jemmy who was running back and forth in wild excitement around the feet of her master's gray stallion.

Before Airey could select an aide-de-camp to carry the message, a panting, disheveled captain wearing a lance cap raced his horse up to Airey's side and blurted, "Let me carry it, sir. *Please!*"

"That Nolan," Palmer muttered. "He's a silly ass. He's done a book called *Cavalry, Its History And Tactics* and thinks he knows more than anyone else about the use of mounted soldiers in battle. He's possessed with the odd notion that light cavalry, if it charges at sufficient speed, can carry anything before it."

"Do you know him?" Neil asked Palmer.

"We've lifted a glass or two together."

"Then intercept him, Palmer! Ride down the hill with him and tell him the message is too damned vague!"

"I rather doubt it would do any good."

"Do it, Palmer! At least, it can't do any harm."

Abruptly, the Englishman made up his mind. Leaping on his horse, he rode off at an angle to Nolan's direction of advance and caught up with him as the captain was beginning to descend the slope.

Leading his horse, Macneil walked over to the edge of the slope and watched Palmer St. James talking earnestly to Nolan as they rode downhill side by side. Finally, St. James turned around and spurred his horse to scramble back up to where Neil waited.

"Well?"

"I told him," Palmer said grimly.

"Good. Did he agree to tell Lucan exactly what Raglan meant?"

Palmer looked perplexed. "What an odd chap Nolan is! I

don't think he was really listening to me. He kept saying this was the Light Brigade's best chance to prove his cavalry tactics are correct. He had an insane look in his eyes. I do wish Airey had given the message to an aide-de-camp instead. Somehow, I don't quite trust that Nolan fellow. I suspect he's half mad."

Sharing the telescope, they watched Nolan make his way down the rough terrain of the slope. Beyond doubt, the man was a superb horseman, if nothing else. He galloped up to Lord Lucan. They could see him salute, hand something to Lucan, and wait for the cavalry division commander to read it.

Lord Lucan must have asked Captain Nolan a question, for Nolan pointed toward the Russians and said something in reply.

"Palmer!" Neil cried. "Nolan's pointing toward the Russian battery at the end of the North Valley. He's *not* pointing toward the guns on the Causeway heights at all." He handed Palmer the glass so he could see for himself.

"He's still pointing the wrong way," Palmer said. "The man's touched! What the bloody hell is he trying to do? Surely, he's not telling Lucan to charge the guns at the end of the valley!"

After reflecting for a moment, Palmer said more calmly, "But Lucan's no fool. He'd never mount a cavalry charge over open ground against massed cannon. Not without strong infantry support. He can see all that turmoil around the Causeway redoubts. Surely he will know those are the guns Lord Raglan wants recovered."

Neil's own nervousness was growing. "But Lucan may not be able to see those redoubts, Palmer. It's just as you said before. He's far below us, and that rise stands between him and the Causeway."

"We'll know in a minute," Palmer said. Already Lucan had ridden across the short distance between him and Cardigan— they were related by marriage but were bitter enemies—and must have given him Lord Raglan's orders.

Spinning about, Cardigan loped his mount to the front of the Light Brigade. Pausing for a brief moment, he straightened his back, then raised his saber to signal his brigade to move forward.

Faintly, Neil could hear, on this sunny morning, the officers dressing the lines. Three lines, each about four hundred yards apart. They stretched out sideways two hundred yards—one-fifth the width of the valley.

The 17th Lancers and the 13th Light Dragoons made up the first line, the 4th Light Dragoons and the 11th Hussars—George's men—the second, and the 8th Hussars the last. George's regiment, in the middle, rode gray horses and wore red coats with high black fur busbies on their heads. The lancers and the dragoons also had on coats of red, but the lancers wore lance caps and the dragoons spiked, visored helmets.

"What do you mean, 'we'll know in a minute'?" Neil asked.

"Well, four or five minutes." Palmer said. "If the brigade is going to charge the Causeway redoubts—as they should—they'll have to angle off to the right very soon now. If they don't turn, that will signify they're going right down the middle of the valley toward the wrong guns, in the direction Nolan pointed."

"Can't we do anything?" Neil asked.

There was nothing Palmer could say, nothing he, or anyone, could do now. Fate had tossed the dice. They could only wait to see whom the roll favored.

Lord Cardigan, with sloped sword and resplendent in his uniform and its trappings, rode well in advance of the first line. A large ruby-like gem adorned his horse Rodney's forehead. Whenever the lancers and dragoons tried to close up behind him, he waved them back with his sword.

Lord Lucan had not moved from his original position and no longer had any control over the Light Brigade.

No longer able to bear the suspense of waiting idly, Palmer spurred his horse over to Lord Raglan's group, with Macneil right behind him. Just as they pushed their way through the circle around Raglan, cries of dismay rose from the spectators. Even the seven wives showed that they knew enough of military tactics to understand what was happening.

Lord Cardigan had now ridden past the point where he should have turned half-right and directed his brigade off at an angle toward the slope up to the Causeway heights. Everyone held his breath, giving Cardigan one or two more minutes to make the turn. By then, however, it was obvious he would not do so. Instead, he was leading the Light Brigade straight down the valley toward the Russian batteries a thousand yards away.

Cries of anger and consternation rose. "Dear God, the bloody fool's going at the wrong guns," Neil heard a woman wail. "Peter, for the love of God, turn back!" she screamed down into the valley. Peter must have been her hapless husband.

"The man's insane!" shouted Raglan. "I'll have the idjit court-martialed and shot. I'll—"

"Doubtless, m'lord," they heard the cooler General Airey say, "Cardigan is only following the orders of Lord Lucan."

Raglan would not be soothed. "Then I'll have Lucan shot," he stormed. "Make a note of that, Airey—'Lucan to be shot.' D'ye hear me? Why, the man's throwing away the Deaths."

No one had the nerve to tell Raglan that at least part of the fault might be his own. Recklessly, Neil blurted out, "Your order didn't say *which* guns, m'lord!"

Raglan looked at the American as if he had just witnessed the invention of the wheel. "But," he sputtered, "surely Nolan *knew*, didn't he?" He looked wildly around him for support of that opinion.

He got none.

"Nolan's an absolute ass, m'lord," said a major off to one

side with a glass of champagne in his hand. "P'haps he *wanted* Cardigan to charge those guns at the end of the valley. Prove his silly tactical theory, and all that rot."

Raglan looked bewildered, then stricken as the realization of what may have happened sank in. "Surely not! Dear God, surely *not*," he pleaded with his eyes uplifted.

"Maybe we could reach George in time," Neil said tensely to Palmer, drawing back away from Lord Raglan.

Pale as a corpse, Palmer said. "Bless you, laddie, but we'd never make it. Look you, Cardigan is already signaling for the brigade to move forward at a trot."

St. James explained that in cavalry charges like this, the riders started out at a walk for 400 yards and then increased the pace to a trot for another 400 yards. Finally, over the last 200 yards in the enemy's front, they moved forward at a gallop: the all-out charge.

The Russian batteries knew this, and so they had the foolhardy British charge figured to a nicety. This speed of advance gave them time to fire nine rounds of solid shot or shrapnel while the enemy cavalry was walking, three solid shots or canisters while they were at a trot, and two rounds of canister while they were coming on at a full gallop.

Now, the Russian guns to the front as well as on the Causeway heights to the right and the Fedyukhin heights to the left were steadily belching their rage into the ranks of the sedately trotting Light Brigade, wreaking terrible havoc on the men and horses.

"God, make them charge!" Macneil cried. "If that's what they're determined to do, then make them do it."

"If they did, old chap," Palmer said with bitter resignation, "they'd use up the strength they need for the all-out charge at the far end of the valley."

In all three lines, great holes opened. The officers on the flanks kept pushing the troopers in toward the center to fill the holes and present a solid front. With her tail wagging impudently, the terrier Jemmy trailed her master George.

Near Macneil, some of the wives wept and called out their husbands' names. Two prayed for divine intervention. Tears flowed down the faces of three of the officers Neil could see.

"Those magnificent men—and their poor horses," Palmer fumed. "All because some Goddamned fool bungled."

The light breeze had shifted around to the north and was carrying the smoke from the Russian guns toward the Light Brigade. Its officers dressed the lines for the last 200-yard gallop to the death-dealing batteries.

At a dead run, the first line pounded into the rolls of smoke and disappeared from sight. The second line, with George and little Jemmy and one other colonel in the lead, had fallen farther behind because of the difficulty in threading their way through the fallen men and horses of the first line.

Just as George St. James plunged into the battle smoke, his horse was struck by enemy fire and collapsed in a heap. George lay caught under the animal.

"The devil take Lord Raglan and the whole damned British army!" Palmer shouted, spurring his horse forward. "I've got to help my brother."

Though it wasn't Neil's fight or even his war, Palmer St. James had been a good friend, so Neil had no choice. He followed Palmer down the treacherous slope as fast as his horse could gallop, riding down into and scrambling up out of six gulleys along the way.

It must have taken Neil and Palmer ten or twelve minutes to reach the spot where they had seen George St. James fall. During those long minutes, the entire brigade had disappeared into the advancing blanket of smoke, attacked the Russian batteries, and then been driven back by Russian cavalry held in reserve behind the guns.

Without infantry support or means to spike the enemy guns, the British survivors of the charge had no choice but to retire. Already, a few were coming back out of the merciful smoke, limping, leading injured horses, carrying sorely wounded comrades, crawling, hobbling, holding on to their horses' tails for support. Looking neither left nor right, Lord Cardigan rode proudly before them, untouched by enemy fire or any apparent concern for the condition of the men he had led into hell.

The smoke, the cries of the wounded men, the neighing of dying horses, and the pandemonium made an unforgettable impression on Neil Macneil. To make matters worse, the Russians were now running down from the barricaded heights on both sides of the valley to bayonet the wounded and strip their bodies.

Neil and Palmer dashed this way and that in the slowly dissipating smoke looking for George. At last, it was Jemmy's barking that led them to where the colonel still lay inert under his dead horse.

"Is he alive?" Neil asked.

"I can't tell," Palmer said, his voice a half-sob. He kneeled beside his brother, whose tunic was torn in back and changed in color to a darker red, and pulled him out from under the horse's neck and head.

Neil turned George over and examined him. The colonel's breath rasped out of his mouth in short bursts, his eyes were closed, and the three holes in the front of his tunic indicted he had been hit by grape shot.

"He's still alive, Palmer. Let's put him over the saddle of my horse."

Palmer's armpit wound from the sea battle with the pirate junk prevented him from being of much help, but Neil managed to get George up and crossways on the saddle. Just as he did, a Russian Cossack came charging out of the smoke on a huge white horse. Leveling his lance, he drove its point into Palmer's thigh.

Jemmy attacked the Cossack's horse, while Palmer yanked out his pistol and shot the Cossack in the throat. Pulling out the Russian lance, Neil tied Palmer's belt around the upper part of his leg and boosted him into the saddle of his own horse. Handing him the reins of the stallion with George draped over its back, Neil said, "Lead my horse and hurry back to the medical tents. You may still save your brother."

"I can't leave you here alone, old fellow," Palmer gasped, almost falling out of the saddle.

"Go, you fool!" Neil yelled. "You'll drop unconscious in another few minutes, and then you'll be no blamed good to anyone!"

Neil slapped his horse on the rump and sent it trotting off in the right direction.

As he looked around for a horse for himself, another Russian scavenger came running at him on foot.

This one wielded a rifle with a fixed bayonet, which was pointed at Macneil's stomach.

CHAPTER 45

Macneil started to turn and run, when he saw a pistol in the belt of the Cossack Palmer had shot in the throat. Thank God, the weapon—unlike his own—was loaded and primed.

Just in time, he spun about and snapped off a shot at the onrushing scavenger when he was but eight feet away. A red hole appeared in the Russian's chest.

Beyond the Cossack, other Russian scavengers could be seen through the drifting smoke as in a phantasmagoria, hurrying from body to body, bayoneting one, robbing the next.

Needing more ammunition, Macneil leaned over to snatch the leather bullet pouch from the shoulder of the owner of the pistol. By some miracle, the Russian was still alive. His eyes snapped open when he felt Macneil pull the pouch off his shoulder. Clutching at the pouch, he tried to say something, but no sounds came forth. Kicking the man's hand loose, Macneil ran staggering toward the rear.

Within fifty yards, he caught up with the two horses, which had come to a halt. Palmer was slumped over the saddlehorn of Neil's mount. Yelping, the terrier Jemmy danced about. Putting the pistol in his belt and the bullet pouch over his shoulder, Macneil scooped up the little dog in one arm and grabbed the reins of the two mounts in the other. He started toward the rear as fast as he could risk going without causing the two unconscious men to slide off the horses.

They were beginning to emerge from the smoke, but still had a considerable distance to go through the din of the suffering men and horses and debris littering this valley of death.

"What the bloody hell are ye doing here, guv'ner?" asked a member of the 17th Lancers who limped along beside Macneil, using his saber as a crutch. "How did the bleeding nabobs get a civilian mixed up in this awful mess?"

Macneil was too tired and distracted to answer. Before him, through the clearing battle smoke, he could see the line of medical orderlies, surgeons, farriers, and officers awaiting their return.

When he was within shouting distance, Macneil cried out, "Many more back there on the ground! Hurry! Russian scavengers working among them." His voice was no more than a croak, so he had to swallow before speaking again. "They're killing the wounded," he said. "They're looting the bodies."

As if in verification of Macneil's words, the sound of shots came from behind him, along with the cries of the wounded.

Eager hands reached out to lift Palmer and George St. James down from their horses. Others tried to push the American down onto a stretcher, but he clutched the two pairs of reins and pressed on. He was determined that these two animals should be cared for. They were little more than bones and tautly stretched skin from weeks of inadequate fodder, and the race down the slope had exhausted them to the point of collapse.

All the farriers were busy loading their pistols and running off into the smoke to shoot the suffering horses. The unceasing screams from the mounts threatened to drown out those of the men, except for one persistent human screecher who dominated them all.

Taking a swig of water from a medical orderly's canteen, Macneil shouted at the backs of the disappearing farriers, "Watch out for scavengers! They're all over the field."

Glancing back, he saw that Palmer and George were receiving the close attention of two surgeons, under the watchful eye of the terrier Jemmy. He pushed on farther toward the rear with the two horses.

He passed another doctor kneeling on the ground beside an officer who gulped and sobbed convulsively. The wounded officer's right trouser leg had been cut away, revealing a white thigh twitching in spasms and a bloody mass of bone, cartilage, and gore where there had been a knee. The doctor was trembling. From the wounded officer's mouth, he took a Minie ball the officer had flattened with his teeth. His gory work far from done, the surgeon forced a replacement between the man's jaws.

Next, Macneil came to two dozen medical orderlies from both the Heavy and Light Brigades who were setting up three large tents as dressing stations. Behind the tents, the Woronzow Road crossed the south end of the North Valley. Neil walked along it for a hundred yards, kicking spent cannon balls out of the stumbling horses' path. When they came to a stream at the foot of the slope leading up to the Sapoune heights, he stopped, unsaddled the mounts, and began to rub them down with handfuls of dry grass while they drank. He left them there grazing, knowing the farriers would find them. There was nothing more he could do for them.

Climbing the lower slope to a point where he could see the entire length of the North Valley again, Macneil sat down and looked out at the ghastly spectacle now revealing itself through the thinning smoke. Again, he wished for a pencil and sketch pad. Weary though he was, this scene should be preserved for the future. The day before he had heard that a photographer named Fenton had come to Balaklava to take pictures of the Crimea military actions, but Macneil had not seen him anywhere.

The acrid smell of saltpeter and of something else—was it death, or blood?—assaulted his nostrils as wisps of smoke floated past on their way south. From the floor of the valley, where most of the slaughter had taken place, came the piercing, prolonged screaming of the dying horses and the pistol shots of the farriers who ran among the animals, ending their suffering as fast as they could.

At the far end of the valley, the Russian scavengers retreated from the field, stopping occasionally to snatch some trophy or valuable from a fallen figure. With the smoke now mostly gone, a few of the British wounded fired their pistols at the fleeing scavengers. From the wounded on the field and those nearing the dressing stations below came a dreadful, blood-chilling chorus of cries for help. Macneil was close enough to the dressing station tents to hear the Light Brigade men inside them swearing in raucous voices, begging for whiskey, groaning, calling for their mothers, or God.

Beyond the dressing stations, the surviving officers of the 17th Lancers and the 13th Light Dragoons were lining their men up in formation for roll call. It was a heart-crushing but brave sight. Those two units had formed the first line of the charge. Fewer than fifty were left to answer roll call, but the men sat their horses with dazed heads held high.

Approaching the roll call formation from the rear came a single riderless horse, its entrails dragging on the ground from a hole in its stomach. Perhaps the well-trained animal had heard the commands and was trying to get to its accustomed place in the formation. The wounded horse caught the eye of an officer who pointed at it with his saber and said something to a nearby sergeant. Just then, the horse's rear hooves became entangled in its entrails, preventing it from moving any father. Cocking his pistol, a farrier ran toward the sad-eyed creature.

Macneil looked back over his shoulder at Lord Raglan's command post, less than fifty yards behind and above him. The women appeared to be weeping, while some of the officers were turning away from the scene below them.

At last, the valley floor was completely clear of smoke. The scavengers had returned to the protection of the Russian batteries. Hundreds of dead men and horses carpeted this vale of violent death. Some of the wounded occasionally lifted their hands or swords to show they were alive and needed help.

Their work far from done, the farriers ran hither and yon while the stretcher bearers plied back and forth transporting pieces of humanity to medical aid.

Macneil could do no more. Certainly, he had no stomach for buying any of the weapons that had caused this carnage. When he had rested, he would make his way back to Balaklava. Later, he would go to the military field hospital to find Palmer and George St. James.

Though he wanted to keep the Russian pistol, the ammunition pouch was too heavy for a weary man to carry. *At least,* Neil thought, *I can lighten it.*

Opening the pouch, he looked inside.

What he found there drove all thoughts of the battle from his mind.

CHAPTER 46

Just below the old Genoese fort overlooking the harbor of Balaklava, the British army had set up a field hospital, which consisted of three uneven rows of six large medical tents each. As many as fourteen of the wounded were crowded into each tent, except for the one used exclusively as an operating room.

Those wounded who could safely be moved were being carried aboard navy transports in the narrow port, to be taken to the larger hospital in Scutari, on the Turkish shore of the Black Sea.

The next day, Macneil walked down the rows of tents looking for Palmer and George St. James. He saw George's terrier Jemmy outside one of the tents and went in. George was there, and Palmer lay on a cot next to him. An Englishwoman in a white cap and long skirt barred Neil's path.

"You'll have to leave, sir, unless you are a doctor."

She was a woman in her thirties with an oval face. Her light brown hair was parted in the middle and braided, and the braids were tied over her head. She spoke in the accent of the English upper class.

"I'm no doctor," Macneil told her, "though I wish to God I were."

"What is your business here?"

Nodding at the St. James brothers, he said, "I'm a friend of theirs—the one who carried them off the field yesterday."

Her face brightened. "Ah, then, you must be Mr. MacNeven?"

"Macneil," he corrected.

"Yes, of course. Captain St. James has been asking about you."

"Who are you?"

"My name is Florence Nightingale."

"This is a terrible place for a woman to be, Miss Nightingale."

"I think every other man in the Crimea has told me that, sir, but I will say to you exactly what I have told the others. This is exactly where a woman *should* be. We nurses can help these poor suffering souls better than the heavy-handed medical orderlies can."

"Can't I see Captain St. James?"

"He's sleeping. Come back tomorrow, Mr. MacNelly."

"Macneil."

"Come back tomorrow, and we will see how he is then."

Palmer St. James was awake at three o'clock the next afternoon. George had been moved to a tent for the more critically wounded prior to being taken aboard a transport in the harbor. Palmer's voice was so weak Neil had to lean down to understand his words.

"Are you...all right, old boy?" St. James asked.

"I'm the one who should be asking you that question."

A ghost of his old devil-may-care grin flitted at the edges of his mouth. "I'm quite all right. Just a trifle weak from loss—of blood." He gripped Neil's wrist with one of his hands. "See about George, will you?"

Neil nodded that he would, then left after telling Miss Nightingale he would return soon.

For the following three days Macneil was kept busy buying weapons dropped by the Russians who had charged at the Highlanders and some that had been captured in earlier actions. The British army quartermasters were glad to dispose of them.

The money Macneil paid went into mess funds for the enlisted men of the military units that had been in action on the day of the ill-fated charge.

A small Greek sailing vessel was anchored in the harbor looking for a cargo so its master would not have to return to the Dardanelles with an empty hold. He agreed to carry the weapons—mostly muskets, pistols, ammunition, lances, and swords—as soon as Macneil could get them carted to the docks and stowed aboard the ship.

On the afternoon of the fourth day, Palmer was able to sit up on his cot with pillows at his back. He was cheerful about his own condition but despondent about George's chances.

"I'm to be sent home tomorrow, Neil," he said, "if I can escape the toils of that wicked witch over there." He nodded at Miss Nightingale, who listened with a forgiving smile.

"He is incorrigible, Mr. MacNelly," she said.

Neil started to tell her his name was Macneil but decided to let it go.

"I know I'll see you back in Hong Kong before long," he told Palmer.

"Of course, you will. Give Hut'ieh my love, won't you?"

Neil said he would, then added in a low voice, "Palmer, I

want you to take a look at this." He took out what he had found in the Russian soldier's ammunition pouch.

It was a jeweled crucifix, three inches wide by five inches long, attached to a massive gold chain. Embedded in the gold of the cross were two large glittering diamonds, six sizable rubies and many smaller precious stones.

" 'Pon my soul, Macneil! Where the deuce did you get this?"

Neil told him the story. "What I want to know, Palmer, is what I should do with it. Is it some kind of war trophy or spoils of war I should hand over to Lord Raglan?"

Folding his hands over the cross, St. James thought for a moment. "Frankly, old chap, I fail to see why you should. After all, you took it from a Russian soldier who was scavenging on the battlefield."

"But suppose he had stolen it from the body of an Englishman?"

"Most unlikely, I think. Just look at it." He uncovered the cross for a moment. "From its shape, I'd say it's a cross of the Russian Orthodox church. I doubt an Englishman would carry such a thing. The blighter probably lifted it from the body of one of his own officers."

"I really don't know what I should do with it."

"Don't you want it as a keepsake of the—what are they already calling it?—the 'Charge of the Light Brigade?' "

"All I want is to forget that charge as soon as I can."

"Tell you what, old fellow. Let me take it home with me, why don't you? I'll see if I can get a good price for it and send you the money."

The proposal appealed to Macneil.

"When you sell it, Palmer," he said, "give half of whatever you get to Ai. I know you're taking care of her now, but sooner or later, you'll be coming back to the Far East, and I'd like for her to have something in the bank to rely on when you're not there."

The Englishman looked surprised but agreed to do as he was asked.

"One last thing, Neil," he said as Neil stood up to leave. "Jemmy, the terrier."

"She's waiting outside."

"Bring her in and tie her to my cot, won't you? I'll take her back to England with me."

"But she's George's dog," Neil protested. "She won't want to leave him."

"Georgie is in no condition to do anything about her. I rather doubt that he will...." Palmer could not finish the sentence.

"Goodbye, Palmer. God speed you. My—ah—my best to Ai."

"Thank you, old chap. You saved our lives, you know."

By chance, Macneil met Miss Nightingale on one of Balaklava's muddy streets late the next afternoon.

"Good day, Mr. Mac...ah, Macneil, isn't it?" she said.

"Yes."

"The captain took me to task for calling you Mr. MacNelly. I'm sorry."

"Has he been taken aboard ship?"

"Yes, he has. Just this morning."

"And the dog?"

"It was rather strange. The poor little thing broke loose last night just before midnight and ran off. I chased after her and at last found her outside Colonel St. James' hospital tent. She just stood there whimpering and shivering."

"I suppose you took her inside to see the colonel?"

"Yes, I did, but, you see, the colonel had just died."

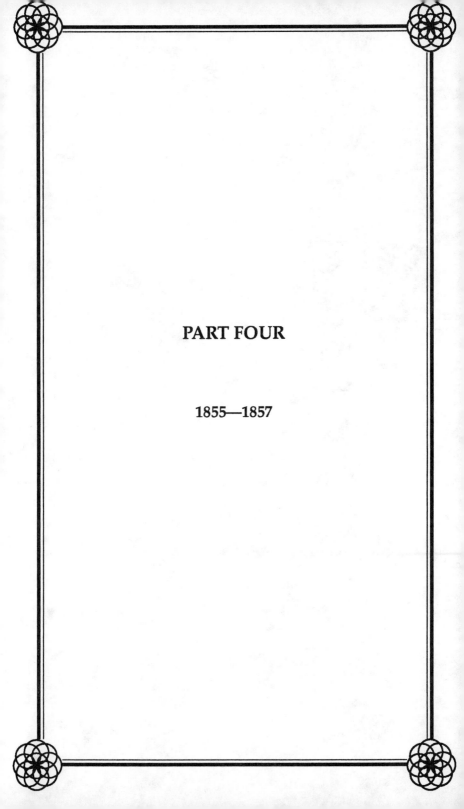

PART FOUR

1855—1857

CHAPTER 47

Hong Kong

As the Greek sailing ship entered Hong Kong harbor from the west, Macneil experienced the pleasant sensation of homecoming. It was, he knew, the thought of seeing his father and uncle as well as Hut'ieh Gonzaga and Tomi Uchida that created the sensation. It certainly could not have been the memory of a pleasant climate, which was as humid as ever.

He detected signs of much new construction around the docks and on the slopes of the hills. The harbor seemed more crowded than ever with ships of most maritime nations. Clearly, Hong Kong had not stood still during the thirteen months and eight days of Macneil's absence.

Telling the Greek master to anchor in midstream, he caught a walla-walla to the nearest dock on the island side and found a porter to carry his bags. Then he set out on foot for the office of Macneil Brothers, Ltd.

Little had changed there, except his father now occupied Uncle Neville's chair. When he caught sight of Neil, he sprang to his feet and hurried around the desk with open arms.

"Neil, laddie," he cried, "ye're back! It's been so long. Och, how aft ha'e I thought aboot ye." He enfolded his son in his arms and held him tightly for a moment.

"I can see you're as vigorous as ever, Father," Neil said, his voice husky. "And how is Uncle Neville?"

Releasing Neil, Nairn stepped back, a grimace of sorrow furrowing his face.

"Alas, m'boy, yere ooncle come doon wi' th' fever scarce five months after ye left."

"The fever? You mean cholera?"

"Aye, it was th' cholera a'right. An' he was gone, God bless 'im, within th' week, wi' th' meenister saying th' words o'er his body th' verra next day. Hardly seemed decent putting 'im in th' ground so quick lak that, but tis th' climate, they say, which is lak to making me wish we were all back in Oregoon."

That afternoon, Nairn took his son to Neville's grave. After placing a vase of red carnations on the still-raw earth over his uncle, Neil prayed for the repose of his soul. His heart went out to Anne, who was now fatherless but did not know it.

As they walked away from the cemetery, Neil berated himself for the thousandth time for being unable to find Anne and Margaret. He had been away on other business for thirteen months, and there was no telling what pain and indignity they might have suffered during that time.

When it seemed that the wells of their grief were dry, the two men repaired to Lap Tat's tavern, where Neil told Nairn about the charge of the Light Brigade, the death of George St. James, and the injury to Palmer.

"So yere friend Palmer is now heir to a fancy title, is he na'?" Nairn asked. "Joost as ye're heir to a fine oop and coming trading firm yerself."

"Only until I find Anne."

"An' then ye'll marry th' bonny lass, will ye na'? Ye're fair on yere way to being a *taipan*, laddie."

Back at the office, Neil told Nairn about the weapons he had bought in Balaklava.

"Did ye not deliver the weepons to Isaac Krakower in Coonstantinople?"

"That was my intention, Father, but the master of the Greek vessel persuaded me to let him bring them to the Far East. He also knew of a cargo of Portuguese sherry the owner of the vineyard wanted to sell in Macao, and I told him we could find him a cargo to carry back to the Mediterranean. He made me a fair offer, so I agreed."

"An' where be the weepons now?"

This was the news that pleased Neil most and he had saved till last. "I sold most of them to the Sultan of Johore at a wee profit."

"A wee profit, didna' ye say? An' joost how *wee* is tha?"

When Neil told his father the figure, Nairn blinked in surprise. "Tha' *mooch*? Yere ooncle would be right proud of ye, son. Profits like tha' joost might o'ercome my scruples aboot this dirty arms business."

Neil too was proud. This was his first major business transaction for Macneil Brothers, Ltd., and he had turned a respectable profit for the hong, although he had spent two months bargaining with the sultan.

Nairn wanted to give his son Neville's old office, but Neil wouldn't hear of it. "We'll put in a partition and make space for my desk in that corner," he said, pointing to the northeast corner. Even though he now had proxy for sixty percent of the stock of the hong, he had no intention of demoting his father to a subordinate role. Neil still had much to learn, and when he went back to Japan to look for Anne and Meg, his father would be in charge in Hong Kong.

"Och, I nearly forgot," Nairn exclaimed as Neil was leaving the hong. "Letters ha'e come for ye." He handed him two envelopes, one thick, the other thin, which Neil tucked away in the inside pocket of his coat.

In his rooms, he found Tomi down on her hands and knees scrubbing the floor. When she saw him come through the door, she dropped her cleaning rag, placed both hands on the floor just in front of her knees, and performed the deep *koto* bow in which the forehead touches the floor between the fingers of the hands.

"*O-kaerinasai-mase,*" she said softly. "Welcome home."

"*Kesa kaetta yo.*" Neil told her he had returned that morning. It was good to speak Japanese again.

He asked her to make tea so they could sit and talk. He watched as she set the tea kettle over the glowing coals in the brazier and put out fresh-baked bread with butter and English jam. She was dressed in a light blue cheong-sam dress, the kind European ladies in Hong Kong thought so scandalous because the skirt was slit up both sides nearly to the waist.

When she had served tea, Tomi brought out her household account book and began to go over each expenditure with Neil. Her records were meticulous.

"No need to go into such detail, Tomi," Neil said, struggling to find the words he wanted in Japanese. "Just show me the total for each month and whatever sums you drew from the hong counting room."

It pleased his Scottish nature to see how little she had spent on household supplies and food. She must have eaten like a sparrow.

He did, however, find one mystifying expense—"singing lessons."

"What's this?" Neil asked, pointing to that ledger entry.

Hanging her head, Tomi blushed. "Forgive me, honorable master. I'll repay you from my contract wages."

"Never mind, Tomi," he said, "but what is it? What kind of singing?"

"Madame Keogh says I have a good voice for opera."

"Are you joking?" Neil asked. "You want to be an opera singer?"

"Does the honorable master object?" she asked, her head still lowered and her voice a bare whisper.

"No, as long as you don't practice while I am at home. But why do you want to do this?"

"If I ever return to Japan, I want to be a geisha. I know I'm not pretty, and that men may not desire my body, but beauty is not so important for geishas."

"No? Well, what is?" Neil asked.

Tomi looked directly at Neil for the first time. "Their ability to entertain guests in the private rooms of restaurants. They play musical instruments, sing, tell amusing stories, and pour the sake."

"But they also sell spring, do they not?" Neil asked, using the Japanese euphemism for the sale of sexual services.

Tomi looked faintly offended. "Many geishas have patrons with whom they sleep. A geisha may change patrons now and then, or she may have the same patron from the beginning until she retires of old age or until he buys her out of her contract and gives her a tea house or flower shop. Only a *daruma-geisha* takes on any customer who has the price."

"So you want to be a geisha."

"When I return to Japan, I don't want to be a poor fisherman's wife in Amakusa." Her eyes flashed with a spirit of independence she had suppressed until now. She looked carefully at Neil to see whether he had taken offense. "The top geishas have daimyos or high shogunate officials as their patrons. They have great influence."

"Is that why you want to learn opera singing?"

"I know I could never become a famous prima donna like Madame Keogh, but it's not necessary to go that far. Probably, it's only a foolish thought on my part." She lowered her eyes. "But a geisha who could sing a few arias from Italian operas would be unique in Japan and would attract much attention and many customers."

"I see."

"May I continue with the lessons?"

"Very well," Neil answered, "but just remember: no practicing while I'm at home."

"Doesn't the master like music?"

"I love music. That's why I don't want to hear anyone shouting their lungs out in Italian. How would I know someone was not maiming a dog?"

Tomi looked at Neil with suspicion, as if she couldn't believe he had made an attempt at humor.

"I still intend to return you to Japan as soon as I can, Tomi, but in the meantime, you may continue to study opera. Is there anything else you would like to study while you are here—like dancing or calligraphy?"

She got down off her chair, knelt, and touched the floor with her forehead. "*Domo osoreirimasu,*" she said in thanks. "If it is not presumptuous of me to ask, I would also like to study English, master."

"Well, I would like to learn more Japanese, so we should set up our own private school. One night, I will help you with your English. The next, you teach me Japanese."

"To hear is to obey. But, if I may say so, the master is already fluent in Japanese."

"Nonsense. Besides, I must start learning more of the written language."

They chatted on about language studies over a second cup

of tea. Finally, Neil asked, "What else have you been doing in your spare time? Have you found a sweetheart?"

"A sweetheart? You mean a lover? No, I have kept myself a virgin in case the master should want to use my body upon his return. I realize that breaking my maidenhead may not be a task the master will relish, it being a messy chore, but then I didn't think the master would want to have second-hand goods in his bed, either."

"Tomi!" Neil exploded. "I told you before, and I'll tell you again. You are *not* my bed wench. I have no intentions of that sort. You told me you may...hmm, have difficulty restraining your natural...ah, appetites. Well, go ahead and release them. Find yourself a boy friend. Be with him when you have free time. It's perfectly all right with me."

"I know I'm not worthy of the master's caresses."

"It is *not* that, Tomi," Neil cried. "Damnit, you *are* worthy! I mean, you *are* desirable."

"It gladdens my humble heart to hear the honorable master say those words." She wiped a tear from one eye.

"But that doesn't mean I will—"

"But I can always hope," she said.

"*Bonno no inu wa oedomo sarazu.*" Neil had heard Ai Koga use this proverb in the formal literary language. It meant, "No matter how often the hounds of passion are chased away, they always return."

He knew it would be difficult to escape from those hounds tonight.

CHAPTER 48

When he reached out to extinguish the lamp, Macneil remembered the letters Nairn had handed him earlier that day.

The thicker of the two posts came from Palmer St. James and reported that he was recovering from his Balaklava wound. His father, the First Lord of the Admiralty, had urged his son to remain on half-pay status and manage the family estates and investments in England, as present heir to the earldom.

Stunned by the death of his son George St. James, the earl no longer seemed to have the energy to manage both the affairs at the admiralty and the family's vast country estates and business interests. Palmer felt he had no choice but to comply. He did not expect to be free of these obligations until the First Lord stepped down from the wheel at the admiralty, which might not happen for some time yet.

Ai Koga, Palmer wrote, was in "tip-top physical shape" and "quite the rage" in London and was "knocking their eyes out" with the dresses he had bought her from Paris and Berlin. In fact, Palmer had a great deal to relate about Ai. He seemed to be on such intimate terms with her that Neil wondered if Ai might not be taking Hut'ieh's place in the captain's affections.

So much did this trouble him that Neil had to face the plain fact that what he felt was jealousy, although as Anne's fiance, he had absolutely no right to such a selfish reaction.

Palmer's letter went on:

Be pleased to know that I was able to sell your Russian crucifix for not less than *seven* thousand pounds. (Count them: seven!) It appears to have been a rather well-known piece of jewelry with the upper of the two diamonds weighing eleven carats and the lower slightly more than seven. One former Moscow resident now here in London identified it as having belonged to Prince Menshikov. We believe the prince must have given it to his son, who was killed at Balaklava. My theory then would seem to be most likely correct, that the Russian you shot had scavanged it from the body of one of his own officers.

I sold it to Lady Jane Vandiver, an extremely wealthy widow who roams the globe on a perpetual shopping expedition, buying exotica by the case lot and filling her several country houses with these purchases. She can hardly wait for Japan to be opened to foreign traffic so she can get an early shot at what she calls "untouched hoards of Japanesque trinkets and antiques." The governor had it in his mind, I might add, that my brother should marry Lady Jane, since the amalgamation of the Vandiver fortune with the holdings of the St. James family would doubtless result in the empire's largest accumulation of private wealth. With poor Georgie gone, the governor is now tirelessly promoting her to me and urging that I sue for her hand. For my taste, however, Jane is too horsey a woman and, in any event, marriage for me would be like tying a horny goat with piece of thread.

Beside that, I still have a craving for Hut'ieh, with whom right now I should like nothing more than to be playing her favorite game of "four times shallow, two times deep."

How I do run on, but frankly, old fellow, I am bored with business affairs and discussing crops and weary of hobbling off to parties and clubs on my crutches. Be that as it may, as per your instructions, I gave half of the seven thousand pounds to Ai, who asked me to invest it for her. We chanced just then to be building a rather small but highly mechanized textile mill in Lancashire, so I assigned twenty-two percent of the shares to Ai. I have sent the remainder of the money to you in care of the Hong Kong and Macao Banking Corporation.

Ah, yes, Ai wrote you a few lines in Japanese, which I enclose.

Having been on the field at Balaklava, I am being lionized and placed on an undeserved pedestal by London society, to say nothing of the papers, although no one seems to be able to comprehend what a sailor like me was doing there that day. Ai and I are often invited to the same dinners, so I escort her. She captivates everyone with her beauty and her wit which,

with her progress in English, are growing like a butterfly emerging from its chrysalis. You are a lucky scamp,
Macneil, and if it were not for the fact that you have my
Hut'ieh in your power, I would surely lay lustful
hands on this toothsome young woman. By the way, I
have given Georgie's terrier Jemmy to Ai. It was a case
of love at first sight for both of them. Ai even sleeps
with the little beast and spoils it rotten.

Lords Cardigan and Lucan have both returned to
England and are trying to defend themselves against
charges of incompetence for the debacle at Balaklava.
The entire nation is terribly upset about the stupidity
of such officers. Cardigan in particular is one of those
natural fools for whom the English upper classes seem
to be ever ready to make a comfortable, if undeserved,
space. So far, I have kept my mouth closed tight,
although I think that both you and I could come closer
to putting the blame for the idiotic charge where it
belongs than anyone who has spoken up until now.
The system is a poor one, no doubt. As long as the
upper classes can buy army and navy commissions,
even at birth, and also regimental commands, we will
continue to be saddled with charlatans and rogues of
breathtaking deficiencies. About all that can be said in
their favor is that most of them, like Lord Cardigan, do
show extraordinary courage in the face of the enemy.
In this respect, they remind me of what you said about
the samurais of Japan.

I will keep you informed of this rake's progress
through English society.

Fraternally yours,
Palmer St. James

P.S. Oh yes, I almost forgot. The next time a tea
clipper sails for London put Hut'ieh aboard and send
her to me, will you? There's a good chap. And let me
know when you want Ai sent back to you. Lady Jane is
mad about Ai and wants to take the little charmer
along on Jane's next voyage to the Far East. She could
drop her off in Hong Kong, if you like.

P.P.S. Any word of Anne or Margaret?

Those eight pages from England contained a great deal of
news, so Macneil digested the contents slowly, sitting in the
rocker next to his lamp. He thought, *How does Palmer know that*

Ai sleeps with the terrier Jemmy? He didn't like that part at all.

Next, he opened Palmer's single-page enclosure on which were penned four lines of Japanese poetry. Although he could read the *kana* portion, that written in *kanji* was largely a mystery to him. He set the poem aside to show to Tomi, then turned his attention to the second letter.

It was addressed to Neil in care of "Macneil's" in Hong Kong and had been penned with a *fude,* a Japanese writing brush. The writer began in English—"Dear Teacher"—and followed that with, "How are you? I believe the Hong Kong weather and your esteemed health to be fine."

After that effort, the writer had given up correspondence in English and had reverted to Japanese. Again, Neil would need Tomi's help to understand that part.

This letter had made remarkable time in reaching Hong Kong, for it had been written only four weeks before. Neil's father had not said how long he had held it, but probably it had just arrived. On the back of the envelope, Neil found a short line of characters. He recognized two as the *kanji* for "upper" and "field". They would be read as "Ueda," the name of the Naze agent. The letter writer—Neil thought it must be Thomas Sakamoto—had followed his instructions as to how to find him.

The letter was written on thin sheets of rice-paper. At four places, Neil found the name "Anne" written in English and standing out incongruously among a welter of Japanese *kanji* and *kana.*

He could not wait until morning to learn what the letter said, so putting on shirt and trousers, Neil went into the next room to awaken Tomi, who was already asleep on her pallet in one corner.

CHAPTER 49

Coming quickly awake at Neil's nudge, Tomi Uchida rose to her knees and pulled her sleeping *yukata* together. She asked, "Has the honorable master changed his mind?"

"Changed my mind about what?"

"Shall I join the master in his bed?"

"Of course not. What on earth gave you that idea, Tomi?"

"I thought perhaps lustful thoughts would not let the master sleep."

"It's something else entirely. Now get up and light a lamp."

When the lamp was burning, Neil sat down at the small dining table and told Tomi to fetch his four-volume set of Japanese-Dutch-English dictionaries and to make more tea. He feared this task would occupy much of the night.

Although Macneil was eager to plunge right away into Thomas' message, the one from Ai was so short, only four lines, that he decided to read it first. It took half an hour to work it all out.

First, Tomi read the poem to Neil in Japanese: *"Tachi wakare Inaba no yama no mine ni oru matsu to shi kikaba ima kaeri-komu."*

Next, he looked up the words he was not familiar with and asked Tomi for further explanation of several of them. At length, Neil produced the following translation:

If breezes on the top of Inaba
Sigh through the ancient pine tree,
Saying softly in my lonely ears
That you pine for me,
Quickly will I speed to thee.

Ai

Sending a love poem to a man seemed out of character for the Ai he knew. He asked Tomi, "Do you think Ai wrote the poem?"

"Oh, no. It's a famous verse written long ago by a man named Ariwara. Even a stupid country girl like me knows it."

Neil wondered what vagrant romantic impulse had inspired Ai to pen such a poem, then resolutely turned his thoughts to Anne. "Please go through this other letter carefully, Tomi."

Briefly, he explained to her that Thomas ("*Tomasu*") Sakamoto had been one of the American's samurai pupils of English in the Nagasaki temple-prison and knew much about his search for Anne and Margaret.

"Read it through once to yourself, and then we can have a go at it together, line by line," he told the *karayuki-san*.

Plainly, Tomi was puzzled. "Who are Anne and Margaret, master? Shouldn't I know that much to understand this letter better?"

When he had satisfied her curiosity, Neil let Tomi go ahead with her perusal of the pages from Thomas, while he gnawed his lips with impatience.

At last, Tomi laid down the *kanji*-covered pages. "This is written in the literary style, master, but I can tell you what it says in everyday words."

"All right, but speak slowly, Tomi. I may have to look up some of what you call 'everyday' words in the dictionary."

This is the story that unfolded:

Thomas Sakamoto continued at his job in the Tosa agency in Nagasaki and was looking forward to Neil Macneil's return to Japan. Commodore Perry and his fleet had visited Edo again in February of the previous year and had signed the Treaty of Friendship and Commerce with the shogun. The date of the actual opening of the ports, however, had still not been announced.

Thomas had received a message from Edo, from Katsuko Ito, the high-born woman Neil had mistaken for the *yuna*—a prostitute from a public bath house. For strategic and political reasons, Katsuko's father had arranged for her to wed the young shogun. Soon she would journey to Kyoto to be presented to the emperor. She had urgent reasons to talk to Thomas, reasons she dared not put down on paper. If Thomas could arrange to be in Kyoto during the week she was to be there for the imperial audience, she would send a message to him through the Tosa representative to the imperial court so they could meet secretly.

It had not been easy for Thomas to obtain permission to make the journey, but at last he was successful. He was able to spend an hour with Katsuko in a private room in a nunnery on Mt. Hiei, outside Kyoto.

What Katsuko told Thomas when they met was what he wanted to relay to Neil.

First of all, Katsuko had been packed off as expected to the isolated island of Sado, a favorite exile place in Japan, to have her baby. This had been arranged by her brother Osamu. Their father had insisted on Osamu's appointment as *o-metsuke-yaku* in Edo as part of the wedding agreement between his daughter and the shogun. As superintendent of the shogun's police and spy force, Osamu Ito had enormous powers to work behind the scenes to carry out the shogun's and his own confidential schemes. That power enabled Osamu to keep secret his sister's pregnancy and the birth of her half-foreign child. The upbringing of Neil's son by Katsuko had been entrusted to a minor samurai's family in an inaccessible mountain valley on Sado.

Katsuko cried while telling Thomas of her son's fate, but she swore she would someday regain possession of the child. In her mind, there had been no doubt from the beginning of her pregnancy that Neil Macneil was the child's father, a belief confirmed when she first saw her son's foreign features and light brown hair. She did not appear to bear Neil any enmity, Thomas wrote. On the contrary, she held the young American in warm regard and seemed to have magnified their Nagasaki liaison into the great romance of her life.

(Although Neil did not recall any particular difficulty at the time of physical entry, he wondered if his really could have been the only intimate male intrusion into her cloistered life up to that time. After all, he had taken her to bed—or, at least, to bath—with considerable ease.)

Knowing that her pending marriage to the shogun effectively blocked the chance of any but the most casual relation with Neil in the future, Thomas wrote, Katsuko had determined to do what she could to help him in his quest for Anne and Margaret. In return, she wanted him to retrieve their son when the boy was older and raise him properly. At least, until Katsuko could assert her rights as the boy's mother.

Tearfully, Katsuko told Thomas that, without intending harm, she had told her brother Osamu about Neil's search for Anne and Margaret when she had confessed her affair with him. Since she was now living in Edo to prepare for her forthcoming marriage, she visited her brother often. While in his home, she had been able to collect odds and ends of information that convinced her that Osamu Ito was trying to find Anne and Margaret himself, no doubt for his own devious purposes. Further, her brother apparently had learned through his network of confidential agents that the Macneil women were being held in the castle of a certain daimyo.

Later, much to Katsuko's surprise, she heard that a blonde foreign woman had been brought to Osamu Ito's residence in Edo. Immediately, Katsuko visited her brother but was given no chance to see the woman. She had, however, heard two serving girls refer to the unseen visitor in whispers as "Anne-*san*."

After a month in Edo, "Anne-*san*" was sent on to yet another daimyo, but despite untiring efforts to learn Anne's destination, Katsuko was unable to do so. Whenever she made any reference, however oblique, to Neil Macneil or Anne, her brother Osamu would fly into an instant and prolonged rage.

Katsuko did, however, hear that Anne had left a book behind in Edo. It had been found by a serving girl and given to Osamu Ito. This serving girl told another, who told Katsuko, that Anne had been seen writing in the book. (Neil assumed it was her diary.)

If she learned more about Anne or Margaret, she would inform Thomas, Katsuko said, though once she was wed to the shogun, it would be even more difficult for her to have any semblance of a private life.

At the end of their hour together, Katsuko begged Thomas to relay to Neil that she would help him in his search in fond memory of their all-too-brief time together and for the sake of their son. The baby had been entered in the Sado village rolls as Ichiro—for "first son"—Ito.

It was well past midnight when Neil and Tomi finished the arduous translation. Now, Tomi seemed to regard Neil with even deeper respect than before, and Neil guessed it was because of his intimate involvement with the future wife of the actual ruler of her country. The words she used in addressing Neil became so polite that their complexity lost him more often than not. He had to insist she speak to him informally, as she would to a friend. Though Tomi could not bring herself to go that far, gradually Neil was able to get her to speak so he could understand her.

"Take away these tea cups, Tomi, and bring me some Scotch whiskey."

She sprang to her feet to obey.

"Join me in a glass," he told her when she had fetched the bottle of Old Parr.

"I propose a toast," Neil said, using the Japanese word *shukuhai* for toast.

"To whom, master?"

"To my first son, Ichiro, God bless him!" To this Neil added the silent prayer, *May God speed the day when I can look on his face!*

Next day, when Hut'ieh heard that Palmer wanted her to come to London, she danced about her room. What a lovely girl, Neil thought, but of such volatile passions. Dark-natured and morose at times, she was almost hysterically gay and ebullient at others.

"So you really want to go to London?" Neil asked.

"Of course, I want to go, Neil. Did you doubt it for a minute?"

"I thought you would be heart-broken at leaving me."

"Umm," she said, as if reflecting. "We haven't really got to know each other very well, have we?"

"Oh, I think I know more than a little about you, young lady."

"Oh, you do, do you?" she asked with a saucy swirl of her skirt. "And just what might that be, sir?"

"That will have to wait till later," Neil said, edging toward the door, "but somehow your eyelashes put me in mind of butterfly wings."

"Oh, that *horrid* Palmer St. James!" she screamed. "He *did* tell you after all, didn't he! I'll run him through the instant I next lay eyes on him. Just wait! And you, sir, you come back here! We must settle this once and for all. I'll not allow—"

By then, Neil had retreated, closing the door behind him.

When the tea clipper *Ariel* sailed one week later with Hut'ieh aboard, Neil and Tomi settled down to a workaday existence in Hong Kong. He had dinner with his father once or twice a week, but spent most other evenings studying languages with Tomi. Little by little, they became more familiar and comfortable with each other. The reserve between them broke down, and, except for separate beds, they were becoming more like a married couple.

One night, Macneil found Tomi had dragged her pallet into his bedroom. She offered no explanation, and he demanded none. If she wanted to sleep closer to him, Neil did not mind. He did not intend, however, to go beyond that point of intimacy.

As the weeks passed, he waited with growing impatience and frustration for further word from Japan, perhaps news that Katsuko or Thomas had learned the present whereabouts and condition of Anne and Margaret.

At last, news of the greatest importance *did* come, but it was of a different kind and from a different source.

The captain of a Dutch trading ship, en route from Nagasaki to Batavia, unloaded part of his cargo in Hong Kong. While in port, he told an English sea captain of his acquaintance that three Japanese ports would open to trade with the outside world the following year.

Then, he added—and this was the part that overjoyed Macneil—the Nagasaki magistrate had informed the head of the Dutch factory on Dejima that his government would tacitly permit merchants of the treaty nations, including the United States and Great Britain, to enter Japan even before the official opening date to find offices and houses and otherwise make preparations for the formal opening of the ports.

Neil whooped with joy. Everyone in the hong office stopped working and looked at him in amazement. The comprador jumped to his feet and hurried over to see what had happened.

Nairn too rushed out of his office. "Good news, is it, lad?"

"Wonderful news, Father! Captain Livingstone here..." Neil introduced Nairn to the man who had dropped by to give him the message. "...says the Japan ports will open next year."

"Well, it's aboot time, is it nae?"

"But wait till you hear the rest of it! Nagasaki will let us go there any time to prepare for the port openings."

"E'en now?" he asked.

"Even *now!*" Neil cried.

He felt like doing a Highland fling.

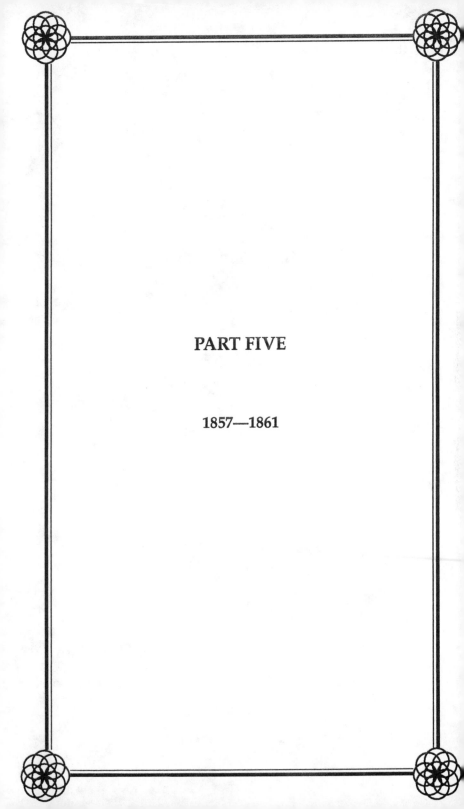

PART FIVE

1857—1861

CHAPTER 50

Nagasaki

From the garden, the view of Nagasaki harbor was magnificent.

Falling dusk washed the scene with several shades of blue. Lanterns were being lit by the thousands. The evening meal finished, the city was readying itself for its customary nocturnal activities—theaters, brothels, and strolls through the streets of shops, which stayed open until late.

Standing at the edge of the spacious garden, Macneil looked up at the star-spotted heavens and said a prayer of thanks for the fine weather and for the commercial progress he had made over the previous ten months since his arrival.

Shifting his gaze to the harbor below, Neil Macneil could make out in the roadstead the outline of *Rainbow*, which had brought his father Nairn to Nagasaki yesterday from Hong Kong. There too rode *Philadelphia*, a splendid U.S. ship of the line that had all Nagasaki agog with excitement and admiration. The warship, a Goliath of the oceans, measured 247 feet in length and 85 feet in beam. She carried 140 guns—some, the 64-pounders made by Paixhans—in three tiers. No one had any doubt that a few broadsides from *Philadelphia* could wipe Nagasaki off the map, though, needless to say, hostility was not the object of her visit. Still, it was a thought always high on the list of Japanese concerns.

The Americans in Nagasaki, including Macneil, had persuaded Timothy Cates, U.S. consul, to request that the ship pay them a visit to celebrate the formal opening to trade of the three ports of Nagasaki, Kanagawa and Shimoda.

Macneil Brothers, Ltd., was celebrating the port opening first, since Neil had been the first trader to reach Nagasaki, except, of course, for the Dutch and the Chinese, who had been there for more than 250 years. By prearrangement, so none would interfere with the other, the remaining merchants, the consulates and Nagasaki officialdom would follow suit with their own celebrations over the next several weeks.

Turning back to the garden, Macneil decided to assure himself that all was ready for his guests. He expected they would soon come climbing up the steep path to this rambling old house, the former Nagasaki residence of the Hizen daimyo, which Macneil rented for eighty-four Mexican trade dollars a month. He would live here till he was ready to buy land and build his own home. Though spacious enough, this old mansion was now too rickety to serve as the permanent Nagasaki domicile of the Clan Macneil.

Seeing her master looking around, Chizu Motoyama, Neil's amah from the temple-prison, came hurrying over. She walked in that mincing gait forced on Japanese women by their kimonos, which were wrapped tightly around their hips and upper legs.

Chizu had come to work for Macneil within a week of his arrival. She had taken charge of his household with energy and good cheer, while Thomas Sakamoto supervised everything not connected with the interior of the house.

Her cheeks stretched wide in her habitual smile, Chizu asked, "Do you have something for me to do, master?"

"The guests will arrive soon, Chizu. Is everything ready?"

"Those shiftless scullery maids are so excited about seeing such famous people that they neglect their cooking, but I am sure we will have the food ready in time."

They had laid out low tables in the forty-eight-mat room opening onto the veranda and the garden. Thomas had supervised the construction of eight temporary stalls outside, each of which served several different dishes, including pheasant meat preserved in rice paste, chestnut meal cakes topped with pickled radish, sweet fish, black beans, chicken en brochettes, shrimp, lobster, duck, two kinds of noodles, and blow-fish *sashimi*. The guests could sit inside or walk through the two-acre garden sampling dishes from the stalls they passed. This was a kind of European garden party unknown, except for the food, to the Japanese. He hoped it would not be marred by any inconvenience or confusion.

"Remember, Chizu, our foreign guests will not drink the water, so be sure to keep the drink stalls well supplied with the imported Bass and Allsops beer and St. Julien claret."

When she started to turn away, Macneil remembered the insects. "Did you dust the *tatami* mats with that flea powder we just imported from Persia?"

"Yes, master."

Neil's father Nairn stepped down from the veranda and walked along the gravel garden path toward his son. Dressed in a kilt and wearing a glengarry on his head, he was sure to be a center of attention among those attending the reception. Neil folded him in his arms.

"Will nae ye wear th' tartan of Barra, laddie?"

"I was going to, Father, but the kilt was torn and Chizu hasn't had time to mend it, what with all this going on." Neil gestured around him at the house and the garden. He saw Thomas, who was busy stationing the servants at the food and drink stalls and giving them last-minute instructions. "Maybe we should make ourselves a new tartan for Clan Macneil of Nagasaki.

"Will you play the pipe for us this evening?" Neil asked.

"Ye could nae stop me," Nairn said, "but ye'll hav' tae play th' second pipe."

"Aye, that I will."

"It canna help but be a braw evening wi' all th' nabobs sure tae coom."

"Did the shorthand dictionary come?"

"Nae yet, but I left strict word for it to be sent oop here by th' first clipper. Canna ye mak' heads nor tails oot o' the diary?"

"Nary a word," Neil said. "I'll show it to you later, if you want."

Anne's diary—he was certain that was what the book was—had reached Neil, through Katsuko Ito and Thomas, six months ago. When he saw it was beyond his power to decipher, Neil had written immediately to Nairn in Hong Kong to ask him if any of the British or American ladies living there had studied the new shorthand. If there were none, he asked his father to send off as soon as possible to England or Scotland for a shorthand dictionary and textbook.

Even so, Neil had sat in his living room for many long evening hours staring at the diary, savoring the fact that this was his darling Anne's handwriting. Doubtless, it revealed her innermost thoughts and probably even her recent whereabouts. It was frustrating to be so close to the secret, yet so far from it.

On more than a few nights Neil had gone to sleep slumped over in a living room chair. His last conscious sight was of one or another of the three hundred hand-written pages of the leather-bound book. If he stared at the mysterious curls, dashes, whorls, and slashes long enough, he thought their meaning might little by little become plain.

For the fact that the diary had come into his hands at all, Neil was devoutly thankful. When the serving girl had turned it over to Osamu Ito, he—being curious about its contents—had shown it to foreign language scholars in the shogun's employ. They had no idea what the marks meant and could only certify it was not Dutch, Chinese, Russian, Korean, French, English, Portuguese, or Spanish.

Thereupon, Osamu Ito lost interest in it. After that, it was purloined by Katsuko Ito, now the shogun's wife, during one of her regular visits to her brother's Edo house. She had sent it through devious Tosa channels to Thomas Sakamoto in Nagasaki.

Neil had spent as much time as he could with his father

Nairn since *Rainbow* had anchored on the far side of the bay last evening. Dozens of matters needed talking about, so their conversation jumped from one to another like a frog on a hot rock.

"We're quit o' th' opium trade now," Nairn had said, "but I'm trying tae fill th' gap wi' more tea, porcelain, and silver services—the finest and cheapest in the world anywhere. How aboot business oop here?"

"Arms are doing fine. I'm not supposed to sell ships or weapons to any but the daimyos loyal to the shogun or to the Tokugawa agents. Osamu Ito's spies have been very watchful lately to see that no shipments reach any rebellious clans like Choshu. I get around that by consigning the shipments to Satsuma, where they are transferred to smaller Choshu coastal boats. The shogun may control the highways, but not the seas."

"Wha' aboot th' ither merchandise?"

"The usual—vegetable wax, coal, camphor, gold, gall nuts, and—oh yes, by all means, silkworm eggs."

"Aye, there might be enormous profits in th' eggs, laddie, wha' wi' th' blight on th' cocoons in Europe."

"Any mail from Palmer or Ai?"

"None."

Thomas nudged Neil and pointed to their first guest of the evening. It was the six-foot, six-inch Dr. Jason Willits, the only American doctor in Nagasaki. Willits was only a little taller than Neil Macneil, but he must have weighed twice as much. Clinging to his right arm, like a pigeon perched beside a rhino, was a petite Japanese woman dressed in stylish European clothes. She was one of that growing class of Japanese women called *rashamen*—foreigners' mistresses.

The naval officers off the warships in the roadstead and most of the merchants except those who had brought wives with them had lost little time in seeking out such companions. The introductions and the arrangements leading to such contractual cohabitation were conducted by laundrymen throughout the city. Willits had been in Nagasaki five months but had signed the contract for his *rashamen* Yoko-*san* within a few days of his arrival. Neil dined with the couple often and knew that Yoko was genuinely fond of this gigantic man, as he was of her.

Willits crossed the garden in enormous strides, Yoko half running to keep up with him. Despite his bulk, he moved with the power and assurance of USS *Philadelphia*, whose masts could now barely be seen in the gathering dusk behind him.

"Neil! My felicitations!" The doctor's voice was high-pitched for such bulk. He smoothed down his sideburns, a recent affectation copied from General Burnside of the Union forces in the recent Civil War.

Neil greeted him, said words of welcome to Yoko, and introduced both to Nairn. After a few minutes, his father had to leave to instruct the drink waiters to begin loading their trays with glasses and open bottles.

"What shall I do with this, Neil?" Jason Willits asked, holding out the lighted lantern hanging from the bamboo branch in his hand.

Neil took the branch from him and handed it to one of the temporary helpers Thomas had hired for the evening. At the bottom of the foot path leading up to this old daimyo mansion, Neil had stationed two men whose task it was to light the candle in a lantern and hand one, on its bamboo branch, to each guest. Though a white ribbon showed the guests which path to take, it would be too dark for them to see their way when full night had enveloped the hillside.

Willits told Neil about two smallpox cases he had found in Nagasaki that week. He said he hoped the new vaccine recently developed in Europe would soon arrive in sufficient quantities to curtail the spread of the dread disease.

Felix Beato was the next guest to approach. Beato was the first photographer to arrive in Nagasaki. Neil had joined him at local restaurants for a few *tokkuri* of sake on three boisterous occasions.

"Hello, Neil."

"Felix, how I wish that camera of yours could take pictures in this dim light."

"It will be able to one of these days, I believe. How's the arms business?"

"Matter of fact, I sold a stand of 1,100 Model 1851 Sharps carbines only today."

"Who made them?"

"Robbins and Lawrence of Windsor, Vermont."

"Any ships? That's where the real money is, eh?"

"I sold *Lightning* to the Saga clan three days ago. She's over fourteen hundred tons. Built by Mackay Shipyards in Boston."

After Beato came John Black, a round-faced Australian journalist who had been talking about starting an English-language newspaper in Nagasaki, though Neil had advised him to wait until there were more readers of English.

Next came Henry Donker Curtius from Dejima in Nagasaki harbor. The cadaverous, bald man was a Dutchman who had lived in Nagasaki longer than Macneil had lived anywhere. Behind him walked Mrs. Kei Oura, an older Japanese woman who had taken her invalid husband's place in the family tea business. Her teeth were painted black, a warning that she was married and flirting was out of order. Even if she had had pearly white teeth, Neil doubted that any man would have the stomach for her.

After Curtius and Kei Oura, the upper end of the path began to produce one new guest every twenty seconds or so. The three leading British merchants—Frederick Alt, Robert Winger and W.J. Walker—came in a group. On their heels appeared one of the two Nagasaki magistrates, Kawazu Izu no Kami, then representatives of the Hizen and Chikuzen clans who held joint autonomy over the surrounding area. They climbed the last few steps of the path with weary sighs, as did those who followed.

Thomas was there to point out the sword racks where it was customary for all samurais to leave their long swords, their *tachi*, before final entry into the grounds of their host.

Now, in groups of twos and threes, came representatives— the *kiki-yaku*—from the thirteen other clans that maintained offices in Nagasaki for trading purposes. Neil had long since learned that all of them, whether *fudai* or *tozama* by persuasion, were angry with the Tokugawa shogun for trying to monopolize foreign trade, which now showed every promise of being extremely profitable. That alone, Neil thought, could be ample cause for rebellion against the *bakufu* of the Tokugawas.

Mingled with the clan *kiki-yaku* were German, French and Russian merchants and naval officers, several of whose warships had sailed to Nagasaki to help celebrate the opening of the port. Some officers escorted their *rashamen*, looking mightily pleased with their temporary consorts.

Neil stood behind Nairn as his father—with his lean, gentle face—greeted the Japanese officials and clansmen who approached with occasional pauses to bow. Neil was learning to identify them by their clan crests—the *mon*—embroidered on the front shoulders of their *kami-shimo* garments. He whispered each to Nairn as they neared: the six asarum leaves in hexagonal form of the Matsudaira family, the buttterfly with unfolded wings of the Ikedas, the three triangles of the Hojos, and the Dutch hat and two pipes of the Kurodas. Of course, the sixteen-petaled chrysanthemum of the imperial family was too sacrosanct to be seen at a mundane affair such as this.

As the officials and clansmen set aside their long swords, they took out from the deep pockets in their jacket sleeves elaborate fans, which were apparently as *de rigueur* for samurais as for ladies. To Neil, the sword and the fan seemed to be at opposite ends of the spectrum—one the embodiment of violent masculinity and the other the epitome of delicate femininity— but the Japanese were not troubled by such a contradiction. A Japanese samurai always appeared to have in his hand one or the other, if not a silver tobacco pipe.

The Macneils had expected 200 guests, but more than that number had already entered the garden when the last group, the missionaries, began to show up. These men of God and their prim-lipped wives looked around at the rising revelry with evident distaste. Cocking his eye at them, Neil wondered why they had bothered to come.

Guido Verbeck appeared first, then his shapeless wife Maria. He was Dutch-born but American-raised and represented the Reformed (Dutch) Church in America. His confrere but rival, the Reverend J. Liggins, lagged not half a minute behind. Liggins had just published his little booklet on the Nagasaki dialect, a remarkably fast effort, Neil thought, and one that warmed him toward Liggins. When he was not staring in frustration at Anne's diary, Neil was trying to learn more of the local dialect from the missionary's text.

Both Verbeck and Liggins taught English in Nagasaki. Christianity was still outlawed by the shogunal authorities, so the Christian missionaries had entered Japan under the guise of English teachers. They did not teach religion, they said, but could they be blamed if—in their English language classes—they made occasional references to God, Christ and the tenets of Christianity, merely as examples of English sentences?

As Neil strolled through the crowded garden of his home he listened to the polyglot words wafting by his ears in the mild evening breeze. There was, of course, English—good, bad, and worse; Dutch, in which even the British consular officials were still conducting all their official business; Japanese, in two or three dialects; German, both high and low; French, so womanly and emotional; and Russian, which Neil identified only because he knew it was not one of the other tongues.

The new representative from Shaw, Maxton, and Co. of London and his sharp-nosed wife came by to wish Neil and Macneil's well. Though he was six or seven years older than Neil he treated the American—somewhat to Neil's surprise—as his senior.

Captain Van Pabst of *Gesina Antoinette*, a gruff man with a sea-wrinkled face, toasted Neil in champagne.

As the evening wore on, the din of his party heightened, making Neil thankful he had no next-door neighbors on this plot of land with its sharp drop-off to the bay. In their cups, some of the Western guests waxed sentimental, throwing their arms around the shoulders of their samurai friends to the latters' obvious disgust.

Three of the topknotted warriors—from the Iwami, Fukui and Satsuma fiefs—cornered Neil to discuss the purchase of arms. Since these clans were among those most likely to rebel against the Tokugawas, Neil whispered to them that they should see him privately in the hong office. The Tokugawa clan still governed Japan with an iron fist and its representatives were attending the reception in force.

As the hour of ten approached, Nairn insisted they regale their guests with bagpipe music. They played "Hector MacLean's Warning" and "Black Donald's March to the Isles" for the boisterous crowd.

The puzzled stares of the Japanese guests suggested that they were far from certain that the "skirl of the pipes" was music at all, though the applause from the foreign guests spurred Neil to offer "Scotland, the Brave" as a finale.

Just as the dying wind sighed out from the bags through the drones, Neil's chronometer showed one minute before ten. He nodded to his father and they herded the guests over to the side of the garden overlooking the harbor. By prearrangement, *Rainbow*, *Philadelphia* and five other foreign vessels in the roadstead began their fireworks show at ten sharp.

As toastmaster, Nairn raised his glass in succession to the shogun, the emperor of Japan, the opening of Nagasaki port, Queen Victoria, the two magistrates of Nagasaki, the United States, France, Germany, and Russia. The magistrate of the north, coached by the Reverend Mr. Verbeck, offered a final toast to Macneil Brothers, Ltd. The hong was at last officially on its way.

After bidding the guests goodnight at the head of the path, Neil Macneil wandered back to the edge of the garden and looked down at the gentle harbor waves lapping at the boulders directly below. He wondered where Anne was tonight. At last, he was in Japan legally, although he and the other foreigners still labored under certain restrictions. They could not, for example, travel more than twenty-five miles from the port without special authorization, which was hard to obtain.

Despite the restrictions, Neil was determined to intensify his efforts to find Anne and Margaret. Love, duty and the Macneil stubbornness would not permit him to falter. He had Anne's diary. One way or the other, he would solve its mysteries. Katsuko Ito, who had married the shogun in an elaborate ritual in Kyoto, might make efforts on his behalf, though it was uncertain how much she could do. Doubtless, her actions were always scrutinized in the court of the *bakufu* by her brother's agents.

Tomi Uchida—the *karayuki-san*—held forth more hope. She had returned to Japan as a member of Neil's household and had lived under the same roof with him for two and a half months while she completed her geisha training. With money Neil had lent her, she opened her own *okiya* or geisha restaurant. This entitled her to membership in the League of Geishas, which had branches in all the major towns. For the last two months, she had been confidentially alerting her fellow geishas—or *geiko* as they called themselves—to listen for any mention of one or two blonde women being kept anywhere in Japan.

At least, Neil was now in the same country—if an archipelago of 265 secretive, jealous and recalcitrant fiefdoms could be called a country—with Anne and Margaret. With friends and the financial power of a rising merchant house behind him he would find the Macneil women sooner or later.

CHAPTER 51

In the months following the official opening of the ports, the people of Japan came to embrace one or the other of two widely different views regarding the opening of their country to the West.

One view, spread by masterless samurais and certain anti-Tokugawa clans, held that the presence of the hairy barbarians polluted the sacred soil of Japan. The smell of the "red-hairs" in itself offered an insufferable insult to His Majesty, the cloistered emperor in Kyoto, to whose imperial presence and wishes few of them had paid the slightest heed in the past.

While not necessarily differing in their dislike for the Western barbarians, holders of the other view foresaw little chance of resisting encroachments by the West. Accordingly, they found the prospect of having a few foreigners in Nippon somewhat less intolerable than Japan becoming an out-and-out colony of an imperialistic Western power.

At the same time, a much smaller number of Japanese, like Thomas Sakamoto and Ai Koga—with minds broad enough to cast off past prejudices—were willing to associate with the arrivals from America and Europe on a basis of equality.

That this schism would lead to civil strife and warfare became obvious to those who understood domestic politics, given the heated passions on either side.

Though it would be hard to judge which side despised the barbarian intruders more, the *Joi*—the exclusion of foreigners— party rallied around the emperor, for lack of a better magnet to unity. The shogun's faction, however, pushed toward accommodation with the U.S. and the European powers as its only reasonable recourse.

Neil Macneil found himself favoring the clans wanting to restore the emperor to full power, overthrow the shogun and drive out the Westerners. He told Thomas Sakamoto his reason for supporting the group that wanted to expel foreigners from Japan.

"I'm sure, Tom, that one or another daimyo supporting the Tokugawa clan holds Anne and Margaret. When the shogun is overthrown, those *fudai* daimyos will fall, too."

Macneil further justified his support of the anti-Tokugawa clans by saying he thought their xenophobia was a weapon designed to embarrass and harass the shogun rather than the undying hatred of foreigners it seemed at times to be. In his debates with other Americans and Europeans, Neil pointed to the *volte-face* of the Choshu clan as an example.

Earlier, that clan—at the southern tip of Honshu—had been among the most rabid of those affecting to despise the West. After their recent defeat at the hands of a foreign naval squadron, however, they turned about completely and became quite friendly with the Western powers. This proved again to Macneil that the Japanese were an intensely practical race. Once shown the error of their ways, they saw no benefit in stubborn, costly adherence to a lost cause.

So convinced was Macneil that most clans would follow the lead of Choshu once the Tokugawas were overthrown that he had recently smuggled eleven anti-Tokugawa samurais—including some of his former English pupils—out of Japan on *Rainbow*. He sent them to the United States and Europe for one or two years of study, partly at Macneil expense. It was an investment he was gambling would pay handsome rewards later.

"I hope it does," Dr. Jason Willits said, when Macneil told him what he had done, "for your sake."

The huge American doctor was drinking sake with Neil Macneil and Thomas Sakamoto in a small *izakaya*, a neighborhood bar with six stools.

"We should also be doing something about these attacks on foreigners," the doctor said. "They're getting out of hand. What do you think, Tom?"

"I think you Westerners are in more danger now than ever. In fact, I'm in danger, too, just for being with you."

Many resentful samurais and *ronin* were roaming Japan's streets and congregating in out-of-the-way teahouses, watching for chances to cut down hapless Westerners and any Japanese consorting with them.

At first, only two isolated killings occurred. While shocking, these did not greatly alarm the growing Western communities in Nagasaki and Kanagawa. But because of them, the latter group was being moved to the nearby village of Yokohama, where the shogun's government said it would be better able to protect them.

Then the number of attacks increased. Richardson was slain in Namamugi and seven French sailors in Sakai. Heusken, U.S. Consul Townsend Harris' interpreter in Edo, was cut down. Next, a Japanese popinjay and hanger-on at the British consulate, who had taken on arrogant Western airs, fell to the swords of his fellow Japanese.

In Nagasaki, two Russian sailors out on a spree tread thoughtlessly on samurai sensitivities and were dispatched by the topknotted warriors.

Macneil did not allow this danger to interfere with his evening walks through the streets of Nagasaki, in which he took great delight.

If the evening hour was early, many Nagasaki residents would either be in the public baths or in large wooden tubs placed in the streets outside their homes. If an acquaintance chanced to walk by, the bathers—male or female—thought nothing of standing up in their stark nudity to bow and greet that friend. Though many female bathers were of voluptuous form, Macneil was put off by their numerous insect bites, shaven eyebrows, and blackened teeth. When one opened her mouth, it was like looking down into a dark-red sepulcher.

Soon after the bathing hour, the streets filled with throngs on their way to the theaters, brothels or tea houses. Many congregated around street performers.

Each night, Macneil would pause to listen and watch these marvelous entertainers. One, for example, would gather neighborhood gossip all day, then relate it in shocked confidential tones to any who paid him the few coins he asked.

Another would dress one side of his person in the garments of, say, a samurai—the other side, those of a merchant. In his one-act play, he would perform the roles of both samurai and merchant, turning one way or the other to indicate who was speaking just then.

It was a colorful, shifting, kaleidoscopic scene with a noisy background of the constant clatter of wooden clogs. Sellers of lamp oil, halting beggars with gongs, idol sculptors, acrobats, jugglers, and masked shrine dancers jostled each other for the crowd's attention.

On both sides of the street, indifferent to the circus-like activities going on behind them, squatted dozens of children, many marked for life by smallpox scars, fishing for frogs in the deep gutters.

Bantams and fat albino ponies seemed as much at home wandering freely among these evening throngs as did human beings. There were also people whose occupation Macneil could not at first identify. He eventually learned they were wandering *eta,* herb-hawkers, tobacco leaf cutters, jelly men, sword sharpeners, and *mogi-yaki,* men who formed a sweet paste into the shapes of animals, birds and written characters.

Among the throngs strode the haughty, swashbuckling samurais, ready to berate or punish any foolhardy enough not to spring out of their lordly way or to brush against their swords.

The streets of Nagasaki were lighted by mineral oil lamps

hanging inside and outside the shops and, to a lesser extent, by the lanterns carried by pedestrians. These lanterns often had one, two or sometimes three *kanji* painted on them. As Macneil gradually became more adept at reading the *kanji*, he realized they were family names. In fact, the *Ometsuke* office of the shogun had decreed that people walking the streets at night should carry this easy form of identification. As yet, however, the authorities had not got around to requiring this of foreigners.

One languorous evening, Macneil was beset by restlessness, troubled even more than usual by worries about Anne and Margaret. Lost in thought, he walked farther than was his wont. At length, he found himself striding along a residential street, which had only an occasional shop. The darkness grew thicker the longer he proceeded.

As he was on the point of turning back, Macneil came upon an isolated bamboo shack with a counter and eight stools where customers drank sake and ate noodle dishes. Two samurais wearing the crest of the Fukui clan came out. They were walking on *chidori-ashi* or plover feet, as the Japanese called the erratic gait of a tipsy person. When they sighted Macneil, one muttered "*Chikusho-me!*" meaning "Beast!" or "Animal!"

It was too fine a night to provoke a deadly encounter with these malcontents, for Macneil had at that moment been listening to a nightingale warbling plaintively in the darkness above a house off to his right.

He determined to walk on for a way, hoping his path would diverge from that of the bellicose swashbucklers. Unfortunately, their direction seemed to coincide with his. He heard them clacking along behind him on their *geta*, coming steadily closer.

Their wine-fostered bravado and overweening pride were evident in their loud curses and predictions of how Japan would soon drive the *keto*, the despised hairy foreigners, back into the seas over which they had come.

"I would like nothing more than to open air holes in a barbarian's stomach tonight," said one in a voice he obviously meant for Macneil to hear.

"I'm of the same mind. I had my sword sharpened two days ago, so I'm ready."

Just then, a large brown cur slunk out into the street near Macneil, its ribs showing and its tail tucked between its legs. The dog cringed along, evidently hoping someone would throw it a scrap of food, but ready to scamper off at the first sign of hostility.

"Look, Tamura-kun!" crowed one of the Fukui samurais, "a chance to test our blades!"

Dreading what was about to happen, Macneil turned back, but not in time to interfere. Drawing their long swords, the pair were upon the creature before it could flee. Both swords flashed simultaneously in the dim light from the sake shop. One lopped off the dog's tail, the other its right ear. Blood flowed. Yelping in pain and fear, the beast spun round and round trying to bite its bleeding stump of a tail.

As an arms merchant, Macneil had in his godown a broad selection of arms, not only cannon and rifles but also pistols and blades, and the cane he carried on his walks was a sword cane, while in his vest pocket he carried a watch fob pistol, a Wesson Baby .22.

"Leave the dog be!" he shouted.

Both samurais twisted around to face the American. One said, "Fortune has truly blessed us tonight, Tamura-kun," and kicked the quivering, bleeding dog out of his path.

Drawing the sword from his cane, Macneil thought that if he could dispatch one samurai with his sword, he might drop the other with the .22 pistol.

Holding their swords above their heads with two-handed grips, the two samurais charged at Macneil in their slithering run. No sword fighter, the American took what he hoped was a good defensive stance. Probably through sheer luck, he was able to pink the one called Tamura in his left shoulder.

That enraged the attacker, but did not seriously deter him.

CHAPTER 52

"Cowards!" came a voice from the shadows behind Macneil's attackers. "You are nothing but *shomben* samurais with no testicles." *Shomben* meant piss.

"*Nan dai!*" yelled one of the samurais, twisting around. "What's this?"

"Fight like men or run home to suckle your bitch mother's milk, you sniveling weaklings," the voice goaded.

"*Kuso kurae!*" shouted the second samurai. "Eat my shit!"

"No, you eat mine," said the figure emerging from the shadows. "You'll eat it and like it or I'll send you home in four pieces."

It was Thomas Sakamoto. Looming large and straight in the semi-darkness, he came walking toward the Fukui men. Passing the injured dog on the way, he bent over to rub its head. "Neither of you insects is worth even the vomit of this creature," he said.

Ignoring Macneil, both samurais had turned to face Thomas, who still had not drawn his sword.

When he did, it was with a swiftness that took Macneil's breath away. Stepping closer to the samurai pair, Thomas slashed first left, then down.

His first cut removed Tamura's sword arm above the elbow, his second opened the other samurai down the middle, from throat to pelvis.

Screaming in pain and clutching what was left of his arm, Tamura staggered off down the street toward the harbor, trailing a blood stream. Sheathing his sword, Thomas said to Macneil, "Quick, help me! We'll drag this other fool into those temple grounds and leave his body there."

Back at the scene of the sword fight, Macneil wrapped his handkerchief around the stump of the dog's tail, which it was trying to wag. Thomas lifted the whimpering animal to carry him to Macneil's house.

His usual broad smile back on his face, Thomas said, "Let's call him '*O-nashi*,' Neil-*san*." *O-nashi* meant "No-tail."

"By the love of God, Thomas, I can't tell you how grateful I am," Neil said. "But how did you happen to be here?" A thought occurred to him. "Have you been following me on my walks?"

The Tosa samurai's smile broadened. "To tell the truth, I have. There have been so many of these attacks on foreigners lately." He looked around constantly, and Macneil supposed he was on guard against the arrival of the *yoriki* from the magistrates' office. On their lanterns would be written "*Goyo*" for "Official Business." They would be armed with long trident-like *jitte* with which they subdued those who dared to disturb the shogun's peace.

With the mongrel whimpering in Thomas's arms, they managed to reach the foot path leading up to Macneil's home without being pursued.

When the dog had been fed and doctored and introduced to Chizu as a new member of Neil's household, Thomas and Neil settled themselves at a low table in a *tatami* room to drink sake.

Thomas had fetched a bag containing camellia oil, honing stone, and pieces of soft paper with which to clean, sharpen and oil his precious blade. The shining graceful weapon had been made 700 years before by Tomonari, one of the most famous swordsmiths.

"I should teach you how to use a sword," Thomas said, intent on his sharpening. "Your sword-cane is not much good against one of these."

"Perhaps we should begin tomorrow." Neil said. "I could do that here in the garden early."

"Without years of practice, you could never defeat a really good swordsman, but you're strong and quick. Within a few months, you could give a good account of yourself."

"Thomas, there's something else we need to talk about."

Thomas filled Neil's cup for him, and Neil returned the courtesy.

"Because the daimyo of Satsuma seems determined not to pay the indemnity ordered by the shogun for the murder of Richardson in Namamugi," Neil said, "a British naval squadron will sail for Kagoshima Bay to demand full payment."

"What if Satsuma still refuses?"

"The squadron will raze Kagoshima," Neil said.

"Can we join the squadron? It would be a good chance to buy the salvage rights to any ships that are sunk."

"Just what I was thinking, so I'm going along. Captain Leckie of *HMS Leopard*, that paddle-sloop in port now, has agreed to take me."

"Do I go with you?"

"No, but I've got an even more important job for you. I want you to go aboard *Rainbow* and sail down to the Amakusa Islands. I remember seeing at least one flat uninhabited island among them. There may be more than one for all I know. Find one and buy it or take a long lease on it."

"I suppose you want a place where we can teach our customers how to fire the heavy weapons?"

Thomas was like that. Quick as a whip. Too often for the welfare of Neil's ego, he seemed to be a step or two ahead in his thinking.

"The island itself should be cheap," Thomas said, "but there may be problems in getting control of it. They don't like outsiders down there."

"Then try to find Ai Koga's father. Tell him everything I have told you about her and how she is doing in England. I'll send along several cases of modern rifles for his people, but even without any gifts, I'm sure he would help us get the island."

After the two had discussed the purchase of the island in enough detail, Thomas, whose words were beginning to slur, said, "Neil-*san*, there's something else I must tell you, but first, I have to apologize for not mentioning it before." He set aside his cup and bowed deeply, his forehead almost touching the table top.

Looking off toward one corner of the room as if ashamed to face Neil, Thomas said, "It's about my meeting with Katsuko Ito near Kyoto."

"Yes, you wrote me all about that."

"Not quite all. Since then, a day has not passed that I haven't wanted to tell you, but each time I started to, I thought better of it."

He cleared his throat, then looked Neil in the eyes. "I knew there was nothing you could do about it and that what I wanted to tell you would only torment you more."

CHAPTER 53

"Katsuko Ito told me," Thomas said, "that she thought both your sister and fiancee had been tortured."

Dear God, Neil thought.

"Katsuko overheard one of her brother's agents talking to Osamu. It was about two foreign women who had been whipped and beaten and even burned with live charcoal. Then, the agent lowered his voice and moved closer to Osamu so that Katsuko couldn't hear anything more. Whatever he said, however, must have pleased her brother mightily, for Osamu kept smiling and chuckling and pressing the agent for more details. Knowing her brother as well as she does, Katsuko said he would never gloat like that unless he was being told about some cruelty or misfortune."

Choking with distress, Macneil pounded his fist on the table, overturning the sake jug. "Great God in heaven, Thomas! We must find them! I'll lose my mind just sitting here in Nagasaki."

"We have a lead to where they may be," Thomas said. "Tomi Uchida came up today, while you were out. She said a geisha in the town of Otsu had heard from a *bikuni* nun about a blonde woman in a castle somewhere near Otsu. Tomi sent back word to Otsu by a *hikyaku* runner to find the *bikuni* and offer her a reward for more details." A *bikuni*, Neil remembered, was a wandering nun who begged alms for her temple with her body, the guise Ai had adopted when he wore the *komuso* outfit.

"You said 'a blonde,' Thomas. Just one?"

"Just one."

"Suppose we do learn that a blonde is being held in a castle near Otsu. What can we do?"

"Obviously, we cannot make a frontal attack on a castle, so a few of us will have to creep in unseen at night."

Remembering Ai Koga and the capabilities of her *funakainin* clan, Neil told Thomas, "When you're in Amakusa, talk to

Ai's father about this. Offer him more weapons or gold. Tell him I may need some of his *funa-kainin* to help release a prisoner from a castle."

Since the "flying feet" runner sent by Tomi to Otsu could not possibly make the round trip in less than two weeks, there was time enough for Macneil to go with Captain Leckie aboard his paddle-sloop *HMS Leopard* (18 guns) to Kagoshima. If fighting took place, Macneil might be able to buy captured or damaged vessels he could repair and resell at a good profit.

Along the way to Kagoshima, Macneil spent most of his time leaning over the rail of *Leopard*, wondering if the blonde reported to be living in a castle near Otsu was one of the Macneil women. If the rumor turned out to be false, he would have to try harder to find a clue to their whereabouts in Anne's diary.

Having found no one in Hong Kong with the slightest knowledge of the new shorthand art, Nairn Macneil had ordered from Scotland the shorthand textbook his son had requested. Long before it arrived, however, Neil had decided it would be foolish for him to try to learn shorthand himself in order to decipher Anne's diary. Logic told him it would be faster to have a teacher of shorthand in Glasgow—perhaps even the one who had taught Anne the skill—decode the diary and send Neil ten or so pages at a time immediately upon completion, so that he would not have to wait for the entire diary to be finished before he could read even the first page. Neil had, therefore, long since mailed the diary itself, through Nairn, to Glasgow.

From Tomi's news, it seemed Anne and Margaret had been separated, so the blonde reported to be in the Otsu castle might be either of the two women. When Anne arrived at Osamu Ito's residence in Edo, she obviously carried the diary with her. The question was, did she know then where she was being taken, and if she knew, did she note the destination in her diary? It was possible that Anne may have been returned to Otsu and Margaret given to some other daimyo.

The British naval squadron rendezvoused at the mouth of Kagoshima Bay, formed a six-ship line behind the flagship *Euryalus* (35 guns) and sailed north up the thirty-mile-long deep-water inlet. Anchoring off Kagoshima, the capital of the fief of Satsuma, the British sent ashore a demand for the indemnity payment ordered by the shogun for the murder of the British subject Richardson in Namamugi. Lord Nariakira Shimazu, daimyo of Satsuma, replied that if the shogun was so eager to have an indemnity paid to Great Britain, let him pay it himself.

The admiral ordered his warships to bombard Kagoshima with round shot, hot grape and rockets. Fires were set. Rising winds from an approaching typhoon spread the flames until they destroyed eighty percent of the city.

In the northern end of the long, narrow bay, the fleet came

upon the same three steamers that Macneil Brothers, Ltd., had sold to Satsuma. After the British had sunk one, the other two surrendered. Macneil submitted a bid for them, which was accepted, and prize crews were put aboard to sail them back to Nagasaki, where Macneil planned to refurbish and resell them.

The British admiral had planned to drop anchor and wait in the bay for word of surrender from Lord Shimazu, but the falling glass warned him of the approaching typhoon. The admiral wanted sea room for his squadron. Macneil remembered that Commodore Perry had refused to tarry at the mouth of Nagasaki Bay for the same reason. The squadron left the bay in single file to sail before the wind, away from the storm, up the west Kyushu coast for Nagasaki.

Thomas and Neil returned to Nagasaki within a few hours of each other. Before talking with the Tosa samurai, Neil asked if there had been a message from Tomi Uchida. Chizu replied that the geisha had sent a messenger up to the house two days before to ask if the young master had returned. He told Chizu to send someone to inform Tomi he was once again at home and was waiting for word from her. Next, he called for Thomas.

"I bought the island," Thomas said, then described it in detail. "I had to buy it in my name, but I have deeded it to you, if anything happens to me. I'll hire a crew of workers to go there. They'll build a pier and the targets and measure off the ranges."

"Do it quickly, Thomas. Tomi was looking for me, so she may have word from Otsu. Did you find Ai's father?"

"I did."

"How?"

"I saw a midget on the street in Ushibuka one day and followed him when he took a path back into the hills. He led me to a building hidden in a bamboo grove in the center of the island."

Macneil did not understand. "A midget? Why did you follow a midget?"

"The *funa-kainin* always have midgets with them. The midgets can get in and out of places we cannot."

Macneil recalled seeing midgets in the *funa-kainin* training camp in the mountains north of Edo.

Thomas said he had met Heihachiro Koga, Ai's father, arranged to deliver the rifles Macneil had sent as gifts, and passed on to the venerable *funa-kainin* leader the latest information about his daughter in London. The old man had treated Thomas with the greatest respect, bowing innumerable times and insisting Thomas remain with them for two days so that he could be regaled with feasts of sake and *sankai no chimmi* or the "delicacies of sea and mountain."

When he was told that Thomas wanted to buy, on Macneil's behalf, an uninhabited island belonging to a certain merchant in the town of Ushibuka, Koga-*san* sent word he would be beholden if that merchant would sell it, and at a fair price. The transaction was completed in two days. Macneil guessed that the merchant was only too happy to be of service to the leader of the *funa-kainin*.

"Did you tell him I might need some of his people to raid a castle near Otsu?"

"Koga-san said that, because of what you have done for his daughter, he and his clan are forever in your debt. He will gladly lend you his very best men."

"I should hear from Tomi sometime today, Thomas. If she has verified that rumor and knows what castle the blonde is in, we may have to leave at any time. You had better clear up other odds and ends of business and be ready."

"I'm scheduled to sail to Shanghai on *Rainbow* tomorrow," Thomas said. "Should I cancel that?"

"Let Captain Loubet handle the conversion of the gold bars into silver." Armand Loubet was the new captain of *Rainbow*.

"Maybe we should wait till we return to Nagasaki. It's a tremendous sum of money."

"No, this is not the time to worry about such matters, Thomas. You go ahead and do whatever else you have to."

After Thomas had gone, Macneil sat at his desk in contemplation. The gold transaction concerned the currency exchange rate that was rapidly making him a very rich man. Shortly after arriving in Nagasaki, he had found that the Japanese standard for the exchange of gold and silver was one to three: that is, one pound of gold was equal in value to three silver pounds.

In China the standard was one gold to fifteen silver. Having brought with him the money from the sale of the jeweled Russian crucifix in the form of ten-pound gold bars, he decided to experiment with currency manipulation. On the next vessel destined for Shanghai, he sent along with the supercargo one of the ten-pound gold ingots. This was exchanged in the Chinese port for 150 pounds of *sycee*, the walnut-size balls of silver used by the Chinese instead of ingots. Back in Nagasaki, Macneil traded that silver for fifty pounds of gold.

Business in Hong Kong required that Macneil go there on the next voyage of *Rainbow*, so he turned over the fifty pounds of Japanese gold to a Chinese money-changer on the Kowloon side. In return, Macneil received 750 pounds of silver, which it took the Chinese four days to accumulate. What had started as ten pounds of gold was now 250 pounds.

In the eleven months Macneil had been playing at this game of international currency exchange, he had arranged thirteen such round-trip transactions. The amount earned had grown so large he did not trust it to any one bank, but had opened accounts in two banks in Hong Kong, one in Macao, two in Nagasaki, one in Shanghai, and one in Yokohama.

In Yokohama, Macneil had bought a large tract of land on the Bluff overlooking the sea, thinking he might build a second home if Macneil Brothers opened an office in that town, which was nearer to the capital at Edo.

More of the profits had been lent to Macneil Brothers, at one percent less than the going commercial rate, with Nairn Macneil's knowledge and approval. Neil had even sent along ten thousand British crowns to Ai in London for her to invest or spend, as she liked.

That evening, just as Macneil was about to leave for his evening stroll through Nagasaki, Tomi Uchida, still panting from her climb up the hill, was led into his study by Chizu.

Chizu retired, whereupon Tomi performed the deep *koto* bow, with her forehead touching the floor. When she looked up and smiled, Macneil was unpleasantly surprised to see that she had blackened her teeth.

Seeing the distress on his face, she covered her mouth with one hand and tittered.

"Don't you like my appearance, master?" she asked, still kneeling on the floor.

"Get up, Tomi, and sit in one of these chairs," Macneil said. "What's happened? Why are your teeth black? Are you married?"

"No, master," she said sitting down and delicately arranging the skirt of her light-green and silver kimono. She was dressed for the evening of geisha parties still ahead of her.

"Then why?"

"Some of our customers—they want to be my patron. I had to blacken my teeth to show them I was not available."

"Then you *are* engaged! I'm very happy for you."

"No, but I'm still under contract to you, master."

Macneil was amazed. "But I told you to tear up that contract. You owe me nothing."

Tears welled up in her eyes. "Then, you no longer wish to be my patron? Please, I beg of you, don't cast me aside like this. You must know how I feel."

"Am *I* your patron, Tomi? I didn't realize that."

"You gave me the money to start my *okiya* and gain control of the League of Geishas, didn't you? So you really *are* my patron. Don't you agree?"

He saw her reasoning and decided not to argue. "Tomi, do you have a message for me?"

"Oh yes. I heard from my friend in Otsu. The blonde woman is being kept in the castle of the Lord of Kuwana, on the Bay of Ise."

At last!

He would summon Thomas. They would lay their plans tonight. Macneil's thoughts raced ahead: *A ship can take us to the Bay of Ise and lay off the coast while Thomas and I—with a team of picked* funa-kainin —*land, slip into the castle and spirit out the woman.*

Macneil knew it had to be one of his loved ones. Even with three Japan ports now open to trade, only a handful of foreign women lived in Japan and none of them had been reported missing as far as he knew.

So exhilarated was he that he lifted Tomi to her feet and kissed her on one cheek, avoiding her tomb-like mouth. She clung to him for a tender moment, then left in a dither of excitement.

For the rest of the evening, Thomas and Macneil talked, pored over maps and decided what actions they would take next morning.

CHAPTER 54

The arrival in port of a ship carrying mail was a grand event to the growing colony of Europeans and Americans in Nagasaki. Until recently, the United States, England, Germany, and France each had its own post office and mail service in that port.

Now, Japan's newly established Ministry of Posts received all letters and packets and delivered those addressed to the consulates and businesses by runner. Letters addressed to residences were given out to the addressees who lined up at the windows of the new Nagasaki Post Office on the Bund facing the harbor.

Macneil had been down at the harbor inspecting vessels to find one he might lease for the raid on Kuwana Castle. Having found a *Kitamae-bune* junk that had sufficient cargo space and appeared seaworthy, at least in coastal waters, he had just reached an agreement with the captain and owner. Leaving the junk, Macneil sighted two clippers flying mail pennants, which were being towed to anchorages in the harbor. Since he was expecting the first translated installment of Anne's shorthand diary, it was with difficulty that he restrained himself from rowing out and demanding to examine the mail even before the sacks were lightered off.

Next morning at the Macneil office, he was disappointed that the diary translation was not in the stack of communications the postal runner brought in. There was, however, a letter from Ai. It was written in reasonably good English and thanked Neil for the ten thousand crowns he had sent. She had invested them in a Belfast shipyard and linen mill.

She chatted on and on about spending the past week at Lord and Lady so-and-so's country place in the Chiltern Hills and the masked costume ball to which Palmer had taken both her and Hut'ieh Gonzaga. With some asperity, she said Palmer had spirited both of them away before the unmasking hour. She wondered at his reason for leaving so early.

In the late spring, she had traveled to Paris and to the south of France with a small group of titled Englishmen and women and had a "perfectly marvelous time," beginning to sound more and more like Palmer St. James in her speech. With a chuckle, Macneil wondered what those fine ladies and gentlemen would have thought of Ai if they had seen her as he had, slitting a man's throat with no more compunction than he would have had stepping on a termite.

She ended the letter with one of her poignant *haiku* in Japanese. This one Macneil kept to himself. If he had shown it to Tomi—whose teeth were now white again—she might well have asked questions Neil did not wish even to try and answer.

A letter from the Macneil agent in New York contained a newspaper clipping Neil showed to Thomas Sakamoto at once. The article was taken from the *New York Sun*. Thomas read it sitting in the chair in front of Neil's desk, then handed it back.

"A Gatling gun?"

"Exactly. Six barrels revolving around a central axis. Crank operated. It fires a copper-cased rimfire cartridge of .58 caliber. Two hundred rounds a minute. Just think of it, Thomas. *Two hundred!* Like a machine."

"That might be a good name for it. A *machine* gun."

"The inventor—a Chicago dentist named Richard Jordan Gatling—hasn't gone into production yet, but we must have some of those guns, Thomas. As soon as we get back from Kuwana, I want you to take a clipper to San Francisco, then go overland to Chicago. Find Dr. Gatling. Offer him anything within reason. A gun like that could decide the outcome of battles when the *tozama* daimyo try to overthrow the Tokugawas."

"Which is sure to happen soon," Thomas said.

Sitting at his desk after Thomas had gone, Macneil reviewed the preparations he had made for their departure for Kuwana the next morning. Thomas had gone to oversee the loading of a stand of 115 Starr percussion breech-loading carbines Macneil thought could be sold to the Lord of Takasu in Mino province, near Kuwana. Takasu's agent had come to Macneil about the purchase of weapons and Neil had shown him the Starrs, in which he was most interested. Even though no agreement had been reached, Macneil thought Takasu would buy the carbines if they showed up at the moat of his castle, ready for on-the-spot delivery.

To be sure, the peasants of Takasu harvested only 150,000 bushels of rice yearly, so their lord might not be financially able to buy all the carbines, but the attempt to sell them would give Macneil's leased junk legitimate reason to dally along that part of the coast of Ise Bay and anchor off Takasu, only a short distance from Kuwana.

Five men sent by Heihachiro Koga of Amakusa were billeted in Macneil's residence, including one midget. Ai's father had not come, saying he was getting too old for this sort of adventure. He had dispatched a lone agent directly to the

Kuwana area by faster boat than the junk to make contact with the Iga clan of *shinobi-mono* who lived in the mountains behind Kuwana. The Igas were to stealthy land operations what the *funa-kainin* had originally been to sea ventures. Although the two clans were competitors in a sense, both were passionately anti-Tokugawa and would surely assist each other in any effort aimed at harassing or bringing down the shogun.

The Igas, Ai's father had explained to Thomas, were almost certain to have spies in every castle in the several provinces surrounding them, to enable them to learn quickly of any plans to raid the Iga mountain stronghold. Macneil hoped the Igas would give them details about the interior of the Kuwana castle—its strengths and weaknesses, its guards, the room where the "blonde" was kept, and other information that might help get Anne or Margaret out of the castle unharmed.

All that remained now for Macneil to do was to visit the arms warehouse of the hong to pick up three small Marston superposed three-barrel pistols of .32 caliber.

Each of the barrels measured only four inches, so Macneil could carry them tucked into the broad sash he would wear over his dark blue jacket. These pistols were accurate up to twenty feet and he had fired them often enough to be expert in their use. He was still far from proficient in the use of the *tachi* or long sword, but intended to carry one anyway.

That night, Tomi came to him. "Thomas just told me about tomorrow. I want to go with you."

"It's too dangerous, Tomi."

"That's why I want to be with you."

"Absolutely no."

"Listen, master," she said. "A geisha in Otsu is the one who sent me the report from the *bikuni* nun. Suppose you wanted to find that *bikuni* to get more information. How would you do it?"

Macneil was silent.

"Without me, you couldn't find the geisha. Even if you did, she wouldn't talk to you. You might be able to go ashore at Takasu because the daimyo there wants to buy arms, but how would you go overland to Otsu? You foreigners still are not permitted to travel freely on land."

"Tomi, I just do not think your going is a good idea."

"Master, let me speak openly to you. I know what's in your heart. If it is your fiancee being held in the Kuwana castle and if you rescue her, that means she and I will be aboard the junk together returning to Nagasaki. You think there will be jealousy between Anne and me."

"You're right, I must admit. That's what I am worried about. And your safety, of course."

"Master, I want to tell you something important about us Japanese. Even as my patron, you have never talked about love, and I don't expect you to do so now. You're like Japanese men. They never talk about love. They don't even like for us women to talk about love, but sometimes we can't help ourselves, and it slips out. For example, I love you deeply, but seldom have I said so. Isn't that true?"

He didn't answer.

She took a sip of water from a glass on the table. "Anyway, I owe you my love and loyalty because you're my patron."

"You could exist and even prosper without me, Tomi."

"Yes, but were it not for you, I would probably now be a half-slave, half-concubine in the home of an old Chinese man in Indo-China."

Macneil could think of nothing to say in reply to that.

"But what I wanted to tell you is this: We Japanese women can accept a man having two or more women. One must be his formal wife. He may not love or desire her, but he must have this Number One wife to carry on his family line. And she must come from the same level of society as his. Farmers marry farmers. Merchants marry merchants' daughters, or sometimes those of penniless samurais. But prosperous merchants like yourself do *not* marry geishas. You become our patrons, but you don't marry us. You can be my patron as long as you like. I'll be content with that. When you tire of me, you can cast me aside. I may mourn and weep for weeks or even months. I may even throw myself off the cliff from your front garden, but I'll have no choice but to accept your decision."

"So what you are saying, Tomi, is that—"

"That I would quietly accept your marriage to this blonde Scots woman you love so much and I would never let her become aware of my existence."

Macneil's heart went out to Tomi for the sorrow he knew lay ahead. And as a salve to his conscience he told her she could go with him and the others to Kuwana.

CHAPTER 55

From Nagasaki to Kuwana Castle

With sails filling, the junk *Isahaya-maru* cleared Nagasaki
harbor in mid-morning. Just before it weighed anchor, the
runner from Macneil's office came out to the leased vessel,
madly pushing the stern oar of his skiff back and forth. He was
almost skimming over the waves. Without climbing aboard the
junk, he threw up to Macneil a small sack of mail just received
from the Nagasaki Post Office.

Macneil had someone carry the sack down to the cabin he
and Tomi Uchida had taken over from the captain of the junk.
The Starr carbines, even in their cases and with ammunition, did
not take up much space in the cargo hold, the remainder of which
was assigned to the five *funa-kainin* sent by Heihachiro Koga of
Amakusa. The captain and Thomas found enough room there for
themselves as well.

Standing in the high prow of the junk under warm blue
skies and a brilliant sun, Neil and Thomas reminisced briefly
about Neil's release from the temple-prison in Nagasaki and the
time they spent on Kami-no-Shima at the mouth of the bay
waiting for the British survey vessel.

Passing the island to starboard, the junk turned to begin its
slow voyage up the northwest coast of Kyushu. Then Macneil
had time to turn his attention to the mail.

One packet contained a translation of the first ten pages of
his Anne's diary. With a whoop of delight, he ran up on deck to
share the news with Thomas.

Settling himself on a coil of rope on the poop deck, he took
a firm grip on the pages, for the wind was strong out of the south,
and began to read.

The first three pages were written by the shorthand teacher
in Glasgow, a Miss Dunleavy, who addressed herself to Neil's
father. In part, her letter read

> Your niece Miss Anne Macneil studied Pitman's
> shorthand under the tutelage of a colleague of mine.

Please understand that shorthand teachers are rather like telegraph operators, in that each has his or her own "fist," meaning idiosyncrasies. I had to visit your niece's former teacher Mr. Blake to get help with the first few pages, but I caught on to her style quickly after that. There was, however, still another problem in that we have found that almost everyone who learns shorthand sooner or later devises his or her own symbols, for reasons of convenience or secrecy. I have taken a guess at some of Anne's unique symbols, although a few continue to puzzle me and will have to be marked "illegible." In any event, I will press on with this work as fast as possible, for I understand from your letter the terrible urgency of your son's situation. My deepest sympathies to you and your son. I could not but be struck with the most profound admiration for his perseverance in what must surely be a most difficult and heart-rending search.

Having raced through that letter, Macneil's eyes had slowed to devour the first part of the diary itself. He wanted to imprint every word on his consciousness and to analyze every line for clues to where Anne was and how she was being treated.

But the form of the diary, as Miss Dunleavy had written elsewhere in her letter to Nairn, was unusual, even "quite odd," to use the teacher's phrase.

For one thing, there were no dates, not even days of the week. This, Neil reflected, could have been because Anne had lost track of dates and because the Japanese calendar was different from the Western, as were their clocks.

Another unusual aspect of the diary was the lack of paragraphs and divisions between the entries. It seemed that if Anne stopped writing in the middle of a sentence one day, she merely continued on with that same sentence the next chance she had to make an entry.

Sometimes Anne would, for no evident reason, insert a *tanka*, a short poem, in what she was writing. Since Miss Dunleavy could not read the script or even transcribe it she merely noted the presence of five or six lines of Japanese writing.

Anne plunged into her situation on the very first page:

Dear Diary: How long has it been? Six months? Eight? So much has happened since that day Margaret and I abandoned the sinking *Eliza Grayson.* How we have suffered and how we have been mistreated! What cruelties and (illegible)! Although I am revolted by some of the things done to us, I have learned to accept them without outward protest—for to protest only means more punishment—whereas poor Margaret hasn't. Not in the least. She cries herself to sleep every night. The dear thing has been like a mother to me, and I love her for it. The diary I kept on *Eliza Grayson* went down with the ship, I suppose, and it is only now that I have obtained something to write with and a book of sorts to write in, given to me by the older of the two women—maids, I guess I should call them—who care for us. Even with this book, which has Dutch printing on the leather cover but lined blank pages within and is probably a Hollander's accounting journal of sorts, and the *fude* and ink-slab, I was not sure I wanted to bare my soul to you, my diary, as I had done in the past, for fear of the dreadful punishment that would surely be inflicted on me if I wrote the (illegible) truth about what our daimyo had done to us and if he were somehow to have the diary read to him—perhaps by those Dutch people in Nagasaki. After all, their trading vessels come to Nagasaki from Europe, I am told, and they might have shorthand dictionaries or even people who take and read shorthand. But, at last, I could stand it no longer. I had to have someone to confide in. Margaret cries so much of the time and keeps saying she wishes she were dead that I cannot burden her with my troubles and (illegible), besides which I do have private thoughts, as you well know, dear diary, that I would not want even precious Margaret to be privy to. How much I long for N!

(Six lines of Japanese writing)

Just thinking about our one time together makes me warm and wet. Even now, every time I have to provide sexual services to the daimyo or one of his honored guests, I close my eyes and grit my teeth and dream that it is N instead of the daimyo or one of his bestial cronies gnawing at my breasts or forcing his organ into one or the other of my openings. Sometimes, I also have fantasies about Captain Turner of the ship that took me to San Francisco, and who gave me such unforgettable delight so often. Sadly, few of the samurais have performed as well, although I recall one who had a splendid piece of equipment, but regrettably, he achieved his climax just as I was beginning to savor the sheer size of it. Though I tried valiantly to arouse him for a second go at it, he was, with typical Japanese male indifference to a woman's needs, not in the least interested. When he left, I was almost crying in frustration and had to use my fingers...you know what I mean.

By this page, Macneil felt nauseated. Anne had confirmed his worst fears. Standing up unsteadily from the coil of rope on deck, he had every intention of flinging the offending pages into the sea, but slowly his anger cooled. He had to go on reading the diary, no matter how much it hurt, to find clues to Anne's whereabouts, if it turned out she was not the blonde now held in the castle at Kuwana.

It would take another book of this size to describe all that happened to Margaret and me from the time we were picked up half dead from cuts and broken bones on the beach up north and carried in palanquins—what these people call *norimono* or *kago*—to the south, where we are now. If ever we are rescued, I may write about those many hardships and gross violations of our persons for you alone, my diary, but now it is all I can do to record some of what happens to us day by day where we now are. We are kept in an airy room on what seems to be the third level of the castle keep. We can see a bay from our east window, which has heavy wood bars over it. We are fed well enough, and I'm even getting to like some of the Japanese food. During the day, we have nothing at all to do except rest from whatever labors and (illegible) were forced on us between the *futon* the night before. Sometimes a teacher comes and we study Japanese and try to learn these squiggly marks they call the *kanji*. Or we may play a game they call the One Hundred Poems, which our teacher says will improve our Japanese. Late in the afternoon, the maids take us down to the bath, which is the finest experience of the day, except when the daimyo joins us, for he insists that Margaret and I soap our pubic hairs and use them as wash cloths to scrub him all over. What a depraved and perverted creature he is! Then we are served dinner—always fish, seaweed, pickled vegetables, and rice, with bitter tea—after which we dress in the kimonos that have been made to fit us and let the maids tie our *obi* and do our hair with all those tortoise-shell ornaments. Then we sit around waiting for the daimyo to summon us, if he is in the castle. (His rooms are next to ours.) I give fervent thanks to God that often he is not here, for he is an ugly, pock-marked, cruel man who likes to ravish Margaret and me at the same time—what the Japanese call *uguisu no tani-watari* or a nightingale flitting back and forth across a narrow valley. He is never tender or kind or loving. He always has the most ferocious scowl on his face even when he is reaching his climax and should be ecstatic. In the beginning, my greatest fear was that I would become pregnant by this monster. While I long for children of my own to nurse and raise, my hatred for our daimyo is so great that I might drown any baby of his shortly after birth. Luckily, our maids provide us with large quantities of a soft absorbent paper called *sakura-gami* or cherry paper, which we insert into our vaginas before intercourse. So far, this paper has prevented either of us from becoming pregnant. Knock on wood! By now, of course, if I did become pregnant, it is most unlikely that I would know who the father was and would therefore be unable to hate the infant in the way I would if I were certain it had been sired by this horrid little man. So hateful do I find him that, disgusting though it is in one sense, I actually welcome those times when he sends me to another room to spend the night with an important guest whose favor he seeks to curry. Though these men are often complete strangers to me, I would rather do what I have to do with one of them than with this repulsive brute. Though my sexual pleasure is not a matter of the slightest concern to any of them, I think they like the exotic idea of getting wedged in between the legs of a blonde foreign woman. Some take me twice. This gives me—I blush to write it—a better chance to achieve some pleasure for myself. May God forgive me for writing this, but were it not for these forced sexual experiences with strangers, which I hated at first, I would have absolutely nothing to live for. I have little hope—no, let me be honest at least with you, my diary—I no longer have any hope at all of ever being found and rescued. With *Eliza Grayson* at the bottom of the Pacific and the occupants of the second life boat either drowned or captives of the Japanese like us, N cannot know where to look for us and may even think that our ship sank off Okinawa or Taiwan or even somewhere in the mid-Pacific. I pray to God nightly that somehow we will be rescued, but I know the odds are very long against its happening. When I think of all the plans and expectations I entertained for my life, I could scream in anguish and anger and grief. Those dreamed-of nights by the Taj Mahal! The temple-dancers of Bali! Those gold-topped pagodas in Bangkok! Those whippet-like tea clippers racing over the Indian Ocean! Oh, dear God, will I miss them all? Am I destined to die prematurely in this horrible castle in the middle of this cruel backward country giving myself to whatever daimyo or samurai chances to please our master, who, for all I know, may be demanding payment as rent on our bodies? Are my only pleasures in life to be the evening bath and the occasional release I achieve from those few of my violators who are slower in reaching their sexual spasm than most? (More Japanese writing) When this happens, I am so delirious with pleasure that I almost faint and have no idea what I do or what I cry out. What if N should ever learn of this? God forbid, for I would die of shame if he did, but it is, I think, a needless fear. I love him, but I'm sure I'll never see him again.

This was the end of the next to the last page of the diary "translation." Between it and the final page was a folded sheet of stationery addressed on the outside to "Mr. Neil Macneil."

Before opening and reading it, Macneil closed his tired eyes and rubbed his temples. Already, his head ached from the intensity of his concentration on the contents of the diary. Yet, he had still learned nothing about the location of Anne and Margaret, except that they were, at the time of writing, then in a castle overlooking a bay. Probably that much could be said of a hundred castles. All that he had got from the diary so far were things he wished he hadn't read.

The enclosed folded sheet was a short letter from the translator, Miss Dunleavy.

> I can imagine with what distress you have read this much of your fiancee's diary. I had no choice but to make a complete translation, for those were your father's precise instructions. For the rest of the diary, however, if you should wish me to omit certain delicate and embarrassing parts, please let me know and I will certainly do so.
>
> Faithfully yours,
>
> *Nancy Dunleavy*
> Glasgow, Scotland

The last page of the shorthand translation contained only a few lines:

Must stop. One of the maids just came in to say I am to be stripped and taken to his rooms. Anyway, must...

What was going to be done to her? Dear God, would he have to wait weeks for the next installment of the diary? Even though that might have been the end of the specified ten pages of the diary, surely Nancy Dunleavy should know better than to leave him hanging in suspense like this. Once back in Nagasaki, Macneil would write her a sharp note of protest.

His only consolation was the fifty-fifty chance that Anne was the blonde in the castle at Kuwana.

CHAPTER 56

It was late afternoon when the junk *Isahaya-maru* sailed slowly past Kuwana Castle. The setting sun behind the gold-leafed roof, watch towers and redoubts of the castle presented so breathtaking a sight Macneil ran below to fetch his sketchbook.

The castle was medium size, for the annual rice production of this fief did not exceed 500,000 bushels, an amount that did not leave much room for extravagance.

Around it was a moat so close to the shore on one side that sea water filled the ditch, according to Endo-*san*, the leader of the five Koga *funa-kainin* who had come with the rescue expedition.

"There's a short tunnel between the moat and the sea that lets the tide flow in and out," he said, pointing. "This keeps the moat water from becoming stagnant."

"Is the moat dry at low tide?"

"No. The water is always deeper than a man's head, no matter what the tide."

How he knew this, Macneil could not say. He supposed it was Endo's business to know the structural details of many castles.

From the *hon-maru* or center circle of this castle rose a white keep with curving eaves and fluted tiles. The base of stonework was surmounted by white plastered walls. The stonework itself consisted of massive granite blocks piled irregularly one atop another with no mortar or evident pattern. The shutters over the barred windows were pulled upward like awnings instead of being pushed to the side during the day. Numerous slits for archers were placed so that all angles of possible attack were covered.

Macneil noted one advantage. The many tiled roofs that gave the castle the appearance of a multi-winged bird were so arranged that if a man could get out of one of the top windows, he could easily slide down one roof after another until he reached the beginning of the stonework. From there, he would have a nearly straight drop into the moat.

In the growing dusk, they sailed on up the coast for three miles past the castle to their anchorage for the night. The Koga agent, Bamba-*san*, sent by Heihachiro Koga on a faster vessel, would board the junk there. His instructions had been to visit the Iga clan of *ninja* in the mountains behind Kuwana to obtain the floor plan of the castle and other details they needed. Tomorrow morning, Thomas Sakamoto would have the stand of Starr percussion carbines unloaded and hauled several miles inland to the Lord of Takasu.

"Sell the rifles at cost if you have to," Macneil told Thomas, although it pained his Scot's soul to say so. "In fact, you may even sell them at a loss, or agree to take payment later. We cannot bother with hauling the damned things back here at a time like this."

Macneil let Tomi Uchida leave the junk as soon as the captain had dropped anchor. She was to hire a palanquin and ride in it to Otsu, where she would meet the geisha who had sent her the *bikuni's* information. Perhaps she would even meet the temple prostitute herself, if the woman still chanced to be in the vicinity. Geishas and "sellers of spring" could travel on the shogun's roads with relative ease, for they always flirted with the barrier guards, who tended to let them pass without travel permits.

Tomi's mission was to see if the Otsu geisha had any new useful information before the rescue team tried to enter the Kuwana castle. They would wait at anchor near Takasu until she returned. In the meantime, Macneil and the rest would spend the time reviewing and perfecting their plans.

At last, they were ready. The Koga agent Bamba-*san* who had visited the Iga clan had come aboard the junk on schedule. More trips had been made ashore to obtain needed equipment. Thomas had returned, having sold the Starr carbines to Takasu at cost, half payment now and half within sixty days. Hours had been spent in the cargo hold going over the plan time and time again, looking with what the Japanese called "cormorant eyes" for flaws, because their lives depended on disguises, ruses and perfect timing. Macneil had the captain of the *Isahaya-maru* join them in this conference, since it was essential that he know what they planned to do. To the very last, Macneil fought against one part of the plan.

"No, no!" he yelled, slapping his palm on the low table. "I won't have Tomi exposed to such danger."

"There's no other way, Neil-*san*," said Thomas. "How else can we get Anne out of the castle if she is sick? She couldn't climb down those walls and swim the moat like the rest of us."

Thomas had said "Anne" with good reason. The Iga clan of *ninja* had told Bamba-*san*, the Koga *funa-kainin*, that the blonde woman being kept in a room on the same castle floor where the Lord of Kuwana lived had a scar on the right side of her neck, under her ear.

She had to be Anne.

The near ecstasy that flooded through Macneil when he heard that was shattered by the rest of the report.

"But the woman is very sick and seldom rises from her bed. There's no longer even a guard outside her room nor a lock on her door. She is too weak to escape."

Shocked and with heavy heart, Macneil forced himself to ask, "What's wrong with her?"

"Consumption."

That word chilled Neil to his marrow. People with consumption—or tuberculosis as he had heard Dr. Jason Willits call it in the new medical parlance—usually died.

Neil would have to take her aboard the junk and transport her to Dr. Willits in Nagasaki as fast as humanly possible. If the American doctor could not help her, Macneil would have *Rainbow* standing by to carry her to any place in the world where she might stand a chance of recovery.

Raging inwardly, he told the others, "I swear I will kill the Lord of Kuwana with my own hands."

"You take care of your woman," Endo said. "Koga-*san* has already given us clear orders about how we are to deal with the caterpillar who rules Kuwana." In Japan, a caterpillar or *kemushi* was regarded as a vile, loathsome insect.

Macneil knew Thomas was right. The only way they could get the dying Anne Macneil out of the castle was to carry her out in a palanquin, which meant they first had to get one of those sedan chairs with its curtained sides into the castle. And the only way to accomplish that feat was to have Tomi, dressed in her geisha finery, gain entrance in a rented palanquin by charming the guards at the gate into believing the Lord of Kuwana had summoned her to serve at a dinner.

The junk was drifting with the current slowly down the coast. It would not reach the Kuwana castle for another hour. By then full dark would have fallen, with less than two hours before moonrise.

Four of the men from the Koga clan were dressed as palanquin bearers. The plan was for them to shoulder the pole from which would hang the curtained sedan chair Tomi rode in. Bamba-*san*, the *funa-kainin* who had come alone via the Iga stronghold, would go with Macneil and Thomas through the sea tunnel into the moat.

The sixth *funa-kainin* was the midget, Kozo. His specialty was climbing perpendicular walls and squeezing through narrow openings. He too was to go through the sea tunnel.

When they had reviewed the plans, they all toasted each other in water, as was the custom before a mission in which it was possible, even likely, that some of them would die. As they stood to go on deck, Macneil told the captain, "Stay at anchor two hundred yards off shore. No matter what happens, don't raise anchor without all of us aboard. Remember you are dealing with the *funa-kainin* of Amakusa, and it wouldn't be wise to earn the wrath of Heihachiro Koga."

Dressed in extra outfits brought along by the *funa-kainin*, Thomas, Bamba-*san*, and Macneil, with Kozo leading the way, swam through the sea tunnel at low tide and quietly dog-paddled across the still moat in the darkness. At the base of the stone wall, the midget Kozo—using the same *nekode* or gloves with claw-like hooks on the finger ends Ai had used—climbed the perpendicular wall while Macneil watched in amazement. At the top of the stone embankment, where the white plaster walls began, he lowered a rope. The others followed the midget, though more slowly. He led them up one wing-like tile roof to another until they at last reached the windows of the room where Anne was said to be held.

Taking out a short saw blade, Kozo whispered, "Macneil-*san*, stay beside me while I saw through two of these bars. If your woman sees or hears me, you warn her not to raise an alarm."

It took eighteen minutes—about what they had calculated—for Kozo to remove the bars and make room for them to climb through the window into the *tatami* room. A dim night lamp burned in the far corner. Once inside, Kozo coiled the long rope and handed it to Thomas, who fitted it over one shoulder and under the opposite armpit.

Pulling Thomas down to his mouth level, Kozo whispered, "Make Macneil-*san* give me his sword. I have a use for it."

Since Macneil had three pistols, he relinquished his sword without protest. The blade was longer than Kozo was tall.

It was time to awaken Anne. Macneil had waited so long for this moment that he hesitated, trying to think of what to say, until Thomas pushed him from behind.

Quietly, Macneil stepped across the soft reed-matting to the sleeping woman's *futon*. In the dim light, he could see strands of golden hair on the bean-shell pillow. Lifting the mosquito netting, Macneil slowly knelt and crawled in beside her, his hand ready to stifle any outcry.

Gently, he pulled back the upper *futon* and placed a hand on the sleeping woman's shoulder. With a low groan, she turned toward him.

First, one eye opened, then the other. In the dim light, he could hardly make out her features, but he could see her mouth open to cry out. He clamped a hand over it.

"It's me, Neil. Be quiet, for God's sake!" he whispered in

English.

Even as he spoke those words, Thomas came up behind him with the night lamp in one hand.

Now Macneil could see the blonde woman more clearly.

CHAPTER 57

It was not Anne, but his sister Margaret.

Her eyes widened. "Neil? *Neil?* Oh, dear God! Is it really you?" She gasped for breath as if her lungs were too weak to do their work.

Choked with emotion and grief at her appearance, Neil clasped her frail body to his chest, as Thomas, Bamba-*san*, and Kozo gathered around. It was only with the greatest effort that Neil could speak.

"I've looked for you so long. Thank God, at last."

In the dim light, her eyes burned feverishly. Gripping his shoulders, she said, "Neil, listen to me. I'm very sick. I may not be long for this world. Can you take me away from here?"

"That's why we're here, my dear. We'll take you away from here, away from Japan. You'll get better soon. Believe me."

"You know what happened to us and *Eliza Grayson?*" Her voice was so weak he had to strain to understand her words.

"I know. And listen, I have good news. *Eliza Grayson* didn't sink. Nairn's alive, in Hong Kong."

"Oh, thank God for that! What about Anne?"

"I was hoping you could tell me."

"She was here with me for a while, but then they sent her to another daimyo."

"Meg, can you move about?" Neil asked. Thomas was already nudging him as a reminder they had to make ready.

"I can't walk very far. All I can do is stagger to the toilet."

Neil told the others in Japanese what Margaret had said.

Kozo said, "Ask her where the toilet is."

Margaret understood him and pointed to a door on one side of her room. Kozo stood up and went to it.

"Neil," she said, "we must be careful. The Lord of Kuwana is a terribly cruel man. He has a vicious temper. If he catches you here, you'll surely be beheaded. He has mistreated me and Anne in ways you could not believe." A spasm of coughing shook her thin body like a leaf in a gale.

Laying her back on the *futon*, Neil wondered why Kozo had gone to the toilet at a time like this. Perhaps there was another exit inside. Neil decided to look, but the toilet was only a small square room with a slit about nine by eighteen inches in the center of the floor. As Neil entered, Kozo was trying to lower his body through the opening. When he was satisfied that he could do so, he pushed himself up out of the slit with his powerful arms.

"What are you up to?" Neil asked.

"The Lord's rooms are next to this one. He probably has a toilet of the same size. I'm just checking to be sure I can get through the opening and lower myself into the tank."

Gagging from the stench, Neil peered down into the tank under the opening. It looked like a metal receptacle three feet by three feet square and four feet deep.

"What are you going to do?" he asked Kozo.

"You'll find out. Now, go take care of your woman."

They had to wait for Tomi to come. If she succeeded in getting through the gate in her sedan chair, she would have her bearers wait in the space reserved for that purpose, then make her way up the stairs to this floor. If challenged, she would say she was on her way to the daimyo's rooms, from which Neil could hear the sounds of revelry.

As they waited, Macneil spoke softly to Margaret. He saw the scar on the right side of her neck, similar to the one Anne had. Margaret said it was from a cut she had suffered when waves threw her up on the shore rocks, after they had left *Eliza Grayson* and her lifeboat had capsized in the surf.

"Thomas," Neil said, "I don't think Tomi is coming. Something must have happened."

Even as he said that, the door slid open and Tomi hurried in on silent feet.

"Be quick," she said. "We have very little time." With Bamba-*san* helping to untie her *obi* in the rear, she stripped herself down to her undergarments. "Take down that mosquito net and remove Anne's robe," she said.

"It's not Anne," Neil told her. "It's my sister Margaret."

"Strip her naked," Tomi said, taking off her own undergarments.

When Margaret's emaciated body was nude, her brother gasped at her scars.

"Did you get those wounds on the rocks coming ashore?"

"The daimyo here gave me most of them," she said with a shudder. "He hated me."

"But why?"

"When I caught this lung disease, I was no longer any good to him, so he wanted to get rid of me," Margaret said. "But someone in Edo—I think it was the head of the *metsuke* office—

told him to keep me here. This angered the daimyo, but he had to obey, so I think he took out his rage on me."

Closing his eyes, Macneil swore a solemn oath in his heart that when Meg was safe in Nagasaki, he would come back here and slowly inflict unthinkable pain on the Kuwana daimyo, and take great pleasure in watching him die.

It took ten minutes, but Tomi dressed Margaret completely in her own geisha outfit, putting a black wig on her head and heavy white powder over all her face and neck. Tomi slipped into Margaret's *yukata* robe.

"Now," Tomi said to Bamba-*san*, "guide her down to the palanquin. Your four men are waiting there to take it through the gate. If you have to carry her down the stairs, it's all right. Pretend she is drunk and the daimyo has sent her home because of that."

"I hope the gate guards believe that."

"They will," Tomi said. "I pretended to be very tipsy when I came through the gate and gave the guards two bottles of sake. They've probably emptied one already."

"When you get my sister into the palanquin," Neil told Bamba-*san*, "leave the others to carry it. You go to your next assignment. Are you sure you have everything you need?"

Nodding, Bamba-*san* left the room with an arm around Meg's waist.

Tomi, Thomas, Kozo, and Neil had to wait quietly in the dim room for the shattering noise they hoped to hear shortly.

CHAPTER 58

When Macneil had almost given up hope that it would happen, a mighty explosion rent the night air. It came from somewhere in the castle grounds.

The gun powder magazine had been blown up. Macneil felt the floor under him tremble.

The Iga clan of *ninja* had told Bamba-*san* about the existence and location of this powder magazine and had given him the fuses he would need to blow it up. His instructions from Macneil had been to place Margaret safely in the curtained sedan chair and send the four *funa-kainin* bearers on their way through the gate and toward the shore. Then he would break into the magazine and light a five-minute fuse, giving him time to escape over the wall on the far side of the castle.

Macneil calculated that the explosion would send the gate guards running to the site of the magazine. Hard on their heels would come everyone else in the castle, including the Lord of Kuwana and the samurais carousing with him in the rooms next to Meg's.

Macneil heard shouts from the men next door and the clamor as they ran down the stairs. He and his team climbed through Meg's window and down toward where the massive stone wall began its sheer drop into the moat. Neil went first, Tomi next, and then Thomas. When Neil looked back for Kozo, Thomas said, "He had business in the daimyo's rooms."

"But the room is empty now. What business can he possibly have there?"

Neil could see Thomas shrug in the light of the rising moon.

The risk of being seen as they swam across the moat was great, but there was no other way to escape. When the three of them were in the water, Tomi said, "Master, I can't swim."

"You go on, Thomas. I'll take care of Tomi."

Macneil removed his sash, feeling his small pistols sink into the moat water. He told Tomi to get on his back and hold on with her arms and legs. He tied the sash around both their waists so he wouldn't lose her, then started swimming across the moat. By now, the hunter's moon had cleared the top roof of a watchtower and bathed the scene with illumination.

Swimming with such a weight on his back was slow and tiring. Macneil stayed under the water as much as he could, and each time he came up for air, he heard Tomi gasp for breath. Once, when they had almost reached the mouth of the sea tunnel, Neil surfaced and heard her gasp again, then moan. Her arms around his neck tightened convulsively.

Treading water for a moment, Neil said, "Tomi, take a deep breath. We're going to swim through the tunnel. The tide has come in, so there's no air inside. Just hang on, and I'll get us through."

The length of the tunnel measured fifteen yards, but Macneil was sure he had swum at least fifteen miles by the time he burst up into the night air at the far end. The air he gulped was more delicious than anything he had ever tasted. Thomas was waiting there to pull them up onto the sand beach. As Neil untied the knot in the sash, Thomas walked around behind to give Tomi a hand. She had been silent since Neil had surfaced.

Macneil could feel Tomi's weight being lifted from his back. He looked up the beach toward Takasu and saw in the now bright moonlight an empty palanquin standing at the edge of the gently lapping bay water. *Isahaya-maru* was anchored offshore right where it should be. Meg and the four *funa-kainin* should be safely aboard. Now, the skiff was coming for Macneil and Thomas, stern-oared by a crew member.

"Neil-*san*," Thomas said, a peculiar note in his voice. "Look here."

Neil turned.

Tomi Uchida lay face down on the beach in her sodden *yukata*. Thomas was pointing to her back, but there was no need for him to do so.

Macneil could see what Thomas wanted to show him only too well.

CHAPTER 59

From Kuwana to Nagasaki

Something had warned Macneil not to take Tomi along. Because he ignored that warning, she was now only a wet lump of lifeless flesh lying on a moonlit beach, an arrow protruding from her back.

The arrow had struck Tomi to the right of her spine and must have penetrated her liver. Whether she died from this wound or from drowning in the tunnel, Neil had no way of knowing.

A guard on a watch tower had probably spotted the pair swimming across the moat in the moonlight and shot the fatal arrow shortly before Macneil reached the mouth of the sea tunnel. That would account for the moan he heard. If the arrow hadn't killed her but had only rendered her unconscious, Tomi's lungs would have filled with water during the long swim through the tunnel.

Kneeling, Macneil pounded his forehead on the sand, then cried out his anguish to the moon rising over Ise Bay.

Breaking off the arrow in Tomi's back, Thomas draped her dripping body over his shoulder.

"We must be on our way, Neil-*san*," he said softly, "else we will join Tomi on her journey to Takamagahara." By "Takamagahara," he meant the paradise of the Japanese gods. Though a Christian, Thomas sometimes said things like that.

Back in Nagasaki, Margaret was given a large room on the second floor of her brother's house where the breezes and the view were best. At Neil's insistence, Dr. Jason Willits came by every day but had little encouragement to offer.

"Isn't there anything else we can be doing?" Macneil asked him repeatedly.

"Nothing I know of. The climates of Hong Kong and Shanghai are far worse, and she might not survive a sea voyage."

"How about here in Japan? Nagasaki is so damned humid."

"She might do better in the Japan Alps."

Macneil thought of the *funa-kainin* training camp in the mountains Ai had taken him to. But getting her there would surely drain what little strength she had left.

Immediately upon their return to Nagasaki, Macneil had sent *Rainbow* for Nairn, so both of them could be with Margaret during whatever time remained to her. Though he prayed daily for her recovery, Macneil could tell she was growing steadily weaker. He sat by her *futon* for an hour or so every morning and evening, talking about their Fort George home and about all he had seen and done since they parted there.

His mind teemed with questions he wanted to ask about what had befallen her and Anne since the storm had struck *Eliza Grayson*, but talking tired Margaret and she quickly drifted off into incoherent semi-consciousness. The most Neil could do was to ask a question now and then in the hope something in her brief, almost inaudible answers would give him a clue to where Anne was.

That Margaret had been cruelly mistreated in Kuwana was obvious. He learned not to question her about such matters, because when he did, her eyes closed and a weak shudder passed through her as she turned her head away.

One morning, Neil told her about Anne's diary.

A spark of interest shone in her half-closed eyes. "I saw...Anne writing in it...many times. She took it with her when she was sent away."

"And you have no idea where she was sent?"

"None at all, Neil. Two samurais came for her early one morning. I thought...I thought maybe the daimyo wanted her to come to his room."

"In the morning?"

"Sometimes, he wanted to...you know...in the morning, too. I was only thankful he hadn't called for both of us. Then...then a maid came in and collected Anne's belongings. I saw her put the diary in the bundle. After that, I never...never saw Anne again. When I asked the daimyo about her, he beat me."

One evening, when Macneil was sitting with Margaret, Thomas came in to tell him Bamba-*san* was downstairs with news.

After escaping over the Kuwana castle wall, Bamba-*san* was to flee to the mountain camp of the Iga *ninja*, where he would wait for Kozo, the midget. After that, Kozo and Bamba were to go north across the Ibuki Mountains to Tsuruga on the Japan Sea coast and take a coastal vessel south to Nagasaki. They were to stay in the mountain stronghold behind Kuwana until the Iga spy in the Kuwana castle could send back a report about what had happened there.

Macneil was eager to know such details, for he had every intention of returning and subjecting the Lord of Kuwana to a painful death in revenge for what he had done to Margaret and Anne.

Tomi's account also had to be settled. The geisha's body had been buried at sea and Macneil was thinking how to get word to her Amakusa family. They were now, he supposed, the legal owners of Tomi's geisha restaurant and quarters. Neil had asked Koume or Little Plum, one of Tomi's top geishas whom he knew well and trusted, to manage the establishment temporarily. Since Tomi's League of Geishas had found Margaret, they might also lead him to Anne, so he wanted to keep close ties with them.

Bamba-*san* and Thomas were seated at the low table in a guest room downstairs drinking sake when Macneil joined them. Though they had protested against taking the money, Macneil had already paid off the four *funa-kainin* who had carried the palanquin in and out of the Kuwana castle. He had not yet paid Bamba or Kozo.

"Bamba-*san*," Neil said, after the usual lengthy amenities had been exchanged, "money cannot really compensate you for what you have done, but come by my office tomorrow, anyway. I have something for you and Kozo."

A sadness crossed Bamba's face, with its high cheek bones and strong jaw. "Kozo never reached the Iga camp, Macneil-*san*. I waited a week; then the Iga spy in the castle sent back word about what had happened.

"Our chief Koga-*san* knew how you would feel about the Lord of Kuwana. In order to repay part of his debt to you, he ordered Kozo to stay behind and assassinate the daimyo."

"Was that why Kozo wanted my sword? But how could he kill the daimyo, especially if the daimyo was surrounded by guards?"

Bamba emptied his own cup of sake and offered to fill Macneil's. "After the daimyo and his samurais ran down the stairs toward the powder magazine explosion, Kozo entered the daimyo's room and lowered himself into the metal waste tank in the toilet. He waited there until the Lord came in to squat over the opening. Kozo was fortunate in not having to wait long in such a place."

"You mean he took my sword and—?"

Bamba nodded. "Kozo thrust your sword straight upward."

"What happened to Kozo?" Thomas asked.

"By that hour of the night, the lord was alone in his rooms, so his dying groans were not heard. Kozo crept out of the castle through the window in Margaret's room. He dropped into the moat and got as far as the beach, where he was caught."

"We'll have to go back to get him," Macneil said. "Right away!"

Bamba shook his head. "It's too late, Macneil-*san*. Kozo

knew he would be tortured to reveal what he knew about the
funa-kainin, so he committed suicide."

"How?" Thomas asked.

"He bit deeply enough into his tongue that he bled to
death."

CHAPTER 60

Next month was feverishly busy at Macneil's house and at the hong. Nairn Macneil arrived from Hong Kong to be with Margaret. Thomas Sakamoto left for Yokohama to board ship for San Francisco. He would go by stagecoach to St. Louis and by train to Chicago to buy the new Gatling guns.

Unexpectedly, Palmer St. James and Hut'ieh Gonzaga arrived in Nagasaki three days after Nairn. At Neil's insistence, they took up residence in his house.

When Macneil saw how crowded his house had become, he called in a newly arrived American architect and commissioned him to build a fine, roomy dwelling in front of the present structure. Neil specified a place whose veranda would look out over the harbor and down on the beach and rocks far below.

The rebellion of the *tozama* daimyos against the shogun was spreading and growing more violent and explosive daily. The shogun had sent an army to subdue the recalcitrant Choshu clan in the fief around Shimonoseki, but the battle had ended in a draw, giving other *tozama* daimyos the courage they needed to defy the Tokugawas themselves.

Macneil's arms business boomed. Though he hated to leave Margaret's side, he had to make trips to the island Thomas Sakamoto had bought in Amakusa to supervise the training of the *tozama* rebels in the arms they were buying from Macneil Brothers. Even the cloistered emperor in Kyoto must have known what Neil was doing, for the Court sent an imperial messenger to express His Majesty's confidential appreciation of the American's efforts.

"Tell the emperor I am deeply grateful for his message," Macneil told the messenger. "Then say that my fiancee is being held against her will somewhere in Japan, most probably by one of the daimyos supporting the Tokugawa cause, and that I would appreciate his help in finding her."

The messenger appeared taken aback. The effrontery of a

mere foreigner in submitting such a petition to the throne! But Macneil could not resist taking advantage of the opportunity. Now that he had seen what had been done to Margaret, every moment that Anne remained in captivity was torture to him.

Completely recovered from his wounds, Palmer St. James had changed little in the years since Macneil had first seen him. Hut'ieh, however, seemed somehow to have soured. Though still pretty, her previous girlish pertness had changed to a kind of grouchy, constant moodiness.

In the garden one morning, watching the construction of the new house, Palmer spoke to Neil about her. "You see, old bean, she insists we get married, and the trouble is, I don't really want to."

Hut'ieh walked out of the house in a red and yellow Chinese robe of sheer flowing silk and joined the two men in a morning stroll. No more was said about the matter until two days later when Palmer and Macneil were aboard *Highflyer*, a shallow-draft schooner of 120 tons used to transport arms to and from the training grounds on Takarajima, the Macneil island in the Amakusas. In the hold were stored 500 of the first model of the Enfield percussion rifle made in the Enfield Royal Manufactory. This .577 caliber rifle weighed nine pounds and three ounces. Satsuma had bought the entire first shipment. Palmer, who was beginning to suffer from boredom, had agreed to supervise the training of the Satsuma troops on the island in the use of these Enfields.

Standing at the taffrail of *Highflyer*, the Englishman and Macneil watched the lovely islands drift by the port side while digesting their noon meal. Palmer was wearing his uniform as a British navy captain—he was now on half pay—since he thought that would make a better impression on the Satsuma troops.

Pointing to the largest of the Amakusa chain, Macneil said, "That's Ai's home island. Her father lives there, somewhere back in those hills."

"I saw Ai a week before leaving London, old boy. I suppose she told you everything in the letter I brought. She's in good health and fine spirits. Sends her love and all that to you, though for the life of me I can't imagine how a rotter and knave like you deserves such affection. If the shogun ever rescinds the order for her arrest, she'll come back here instantly, she says. Her investments are making her rich, you know. Marrying her would be a sound financial move."

"Doesn't she have proposals of marriage?"

"Lots of young men from absolutely top-drawer families squire her around, but I'm not aware of any who have tried to marry her."

"Why?"

"I hate to say it, my dear fellow, but in England today, it's one thing to take women like Ai and Hut'ieh to the theater and dinner, but for a member of the upper classes to marry an Oriental is quite another matter."

"Is that why you don't want to marry Hut'ieh?"

"Putting it bluntly, chum, yes. My father has retired as First Lord of the Admiralty, you know, for he was getting on. He absolutely insists I marry an Englishwoman of good family, preferably one with money, to carry on the family name and all that poppycock."

"I thought your father doted on Ai."

"He does, he does. He told me once that if he were younger, he would carry Ai off to the South Seas and spend the rest of his days making love to her."

"Then why?"

"He knows, just as I do, that any half-Japanese or part-Chinese offspring of the Earl of Oxbridge would never, never be accepted in England. English society is a pack of mad buggers, I grant you, but I'm afraid I can't change that."

"So what are you going to do?"

"My father keeps pushing Lady Jane Vandiver at me. She's really not a bad sort. Too fond of horses, of course, and other barnyard creatures, and I'd probably have to make an appointment if I ever wanted to exercise my conjugal rights, but the governor can't forget all that money she has. He sits at his desk on the estate and keeps adding her wealth to ours and drools over his prediction that we could buy the Bank of England if only she and I married."

From the overcast a few drops of rain began to spill. The two men stayed by the railing. Takarajima had come into sight, and Neil wanted to show Palmer the gunnery ranges as *Highflyer* neared the island.

"You could marry Lady Jane, set Hut'ieh up in a fancy house in London, and divide your time between the two, as the pukka sahibs in Hong Kong do, couldn't you?"

"I'm dazzled by the clarity of your reasoning. Those were my intentions exactly. Despite her occasionally bizarre sexual demands, Hut'ieh has a simply smashing arse, and after having once had her, I find it most difficult to get my blood heated up for a white woman—especially an equine type like Jane."

"But Hut'ieh spiked the whole idea with—"

"—her rum insistence on marriage. Precisely. Foolishly, I blurted out that before I would marry her, I would first get in bed with a puff adder, so she started wailing and calling out obscenities and running about as if demented. A quite preposterous scene, really, that brought a number of constables pounding at the door of my London rooms in response to complaints from the insolent varletry nearby."

"What happened then?"

"I invited the constabulary in, identified myself, and offered them whiskey, a bottle of which they quaffed in high good humor. They then asked if I wanted them to handcuff and muzzle that wretched Hut'ieh, who was still pounding on the walls and keening away back in a bedroom."

Now, the silky rain started to fall in earnest, so the two men sent below for rain capes.

"Does all this mean you've decided to live in sin out here in the Orient—with Hut'ieh?"

"Alas, I have to get back to England."

"And Hut'ieh?"

"I have given her a cheque drawn on the Midland Bank for a very large sum of money, and I have promised that I would help get her settled either in Hong Kong or here, where you could watch out for her."

This did not appeal to Macneil in the least, but he had no choice in view of what Palmer had done for Ai.

"And you?" Neil asked.

"I told Jane Vandiver that I would marry her," Palmer admitted, reluctantly. "She'll be leaving London soon for India, where she has some investments—I think she owns the better part of Calcutta—and then will come on to Nagasaki to pick me up. We may be married by the captain of her yacht at sea."

Cocking his left eyebrow, Neil asked, "Does Hut'ieh know about your marriage plans?"

"God's wounds, no! There's no telling what she might do if she found out. Run amok, most likely. Even now, she has the wildest tantrums at any mention of my returning to England. I truly suspect—surely, you've heard those plaintive coital screams of hers!—that her sexual fantasies have caused her to lose all touch with reality."

Palmer thought for a moment, then said, "As a matter of sober fact, she may be certifiable."

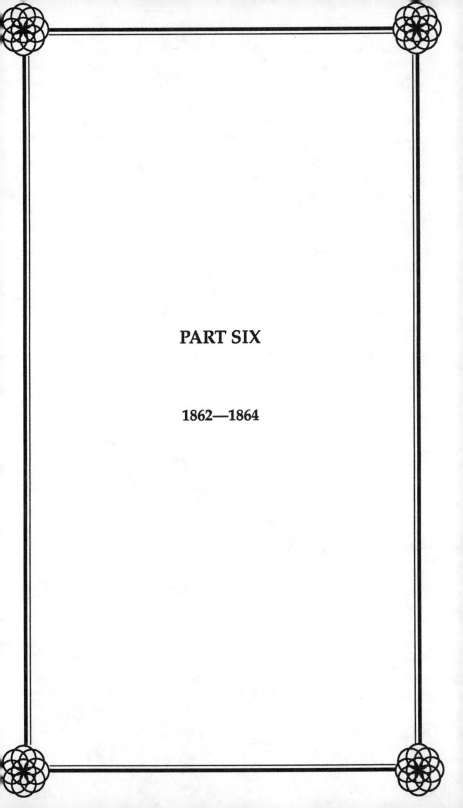

PART SIX

1862—1864

CHAPTER 61

Week after week, the new *Nagasaki Shipping List and Advertiser* devoted at least one of its four front-page columns to the mounting rebellion against the Tokugawa shogun. (The other columns took up topics such as Palmerston's foreign policy in England and speculation that Tom Sawyers might box John Heenan for the heavyweight championship of the world.) In fact, the foreign community in Nagasaki judged the seriousness of the revolt by the number of outbreaks and clashes reported in the local English language newspaper pages.

What made the situation especially explosive was that a dozen or more of the larger clans maintained troops in both Edo and Kyoto. The duty of guarding the palaces of the shogun in Edo and the emperor in Kyoto rotated among certain of these clans, so that forces from both the *tozama* and the *fudai* fiefs were quartered in the same city and free to swagger through the streets at night, high flown with wine and insolence. Minor tiffs quickly grew into pitched battles, such as those recently reported at Fushimi and Toba.

Macneil's business in warships and arms doubled then tripled as the prospects for all-out rebellion magnified. He longed for Thomas to return with the Gatling guns, but Thomas wrote that the Civil War in the United States gave President Lincoln's government priority on orders for those magnificent new weapons.

During his stay in Chicago, where the inventor of the gun lived, Thomas had become emotionally involved with Miss Louise Gatling, daughter of Dr. Gatling himself.

Reading between the lines of Thomas' letter, Macneil gathered that the young lady was so smitten with the big, handsome samurai from Tosa that she had prevailed on her father to work the men in his factory all night for two successive nights to turn out a "special order" of one gun just for Thomas.

This new gun had to be shipped by rail to New York and

then by ship around Cape Horn to Japan—a very long voyage. To hasten his own return, Thomas had decided he would not ride with the rapid-fire weapon around the Horn but would return by the shorter way he had come. When he reached St. Louis, however, he discovered Louise Gatling had followed him in another car of the same train, and he had felt obliged to escort the young girl back to her father in Chicago, causing still more delay.

Palmer St. James was now spending most of his time on Takarajima, doing an excellent job of training troops in field maneuvers and marksmanship, and crews in handling warships. Whenever he could, Palmer returned to Nagasaki to be with Hut'ieh, though their meetings often ended with her screaming insults and threats at him. The showdown between Hut'ieh and Palmer came one night after Lady Jane changed her mind about where and how she wanted to be wed.

She decided she did not wish to be married at sea by the captain of her yacht, so, from India, she wrote to Her British Majesty's consul in Nagasaki, asking him to talk to the bishop of the Anglican church in Nagasaki and arrange that she and Palmer be married on the date she specified. Either Lady Jane knew nothing of existence of Hut'ieh Gonzaga or she did not allow that knowledge to affect in the least her plans for a grand wedding on shore.

Like a forest fire, the news spread through the Nagasaki foreign colony, and small wonder it did. The future Earl of Oxbridge and Lady Jane Vandiver were to wed in this tiny outpost of European civilization. The European wives—one of whom fainted dead away when she heard the tidings—called urgent meetings to discuss the reported wedding, and their tongues wagged so fast they smoked when it became known that Palmer St. James was living in sin with one Hut'ieh Gonzaga— a Eurasian, no less—in the local residence of prominent arms merchant Neil Macneil.

Macneil's new house was nearly completed. He had moved Margaret in so she would not be disturbed by the wrangling between Palmer and Hut'ieh during his brief visits from Takarajima.

Macneil still lived in the old house, and Japanese-style house interiors being of flimsy construction, he could hear the words that flew between Hut'ieh and Palmer in their entirety.

After dinner one night, Neil and Palmer had played a game of chess in Neil's study, then retired to their rooms on the second floor.

Through the paper-covered *fusuma*, Macneil heard Hut'ieh say, "Are you enjoying your games down in Amakusa?"

"Jolly good sport, it is," Palmer said. "And how about you, Hut'ieh Fujen?"

"Oh, I've been busy with one thing and another."

"I see."

"Mostly, I've been waiting for my invitation to your wedding."

"Wedding?"

"Yes, your wedding to Lady Jane Vandiver. The Anglican bishop here has arranged to celebrate your nuptials in the British consulate, hasn't he?"

"Anglican bishop? Who on earth are you talking about?"

"Why, Mr. Morris, of course. Who else?"

"The only Morris I know," Palmer said in a placating tone, "is one of the local English teachers."

Hut'ieh's voice sharpened. "Don't play games with me, you evil bastard. You know very well Mr. Morris actually represents the Anglican church, though he has to pretend to be an English teacher in order to remain here."

"Very well, Hut'ieh," Palmer said, his voice heavy with resignation.

"Then the story *is* true?"

"Quite true. I plan to marry Lady Jane Vandiver and return to England. I regret doing this to you, my love, but you may recall that I never promised you marriage. You might also bear in mind that—"

"You wicked son of a bitch!" Hut'ieh cried out.

"—that I gave you a draft on the Midland Bank that should keep you in luxury for the rest of your life."

In great choking gasps, Hut'ieh began to sob. "Then you love her, don't you? And hate me."

"I have neither the time nor the inclination to explain to you my innermost feelings, Hut'ieh Fujen. Suffice to say that love and hate are not the primary factors governing my decision."

"You hate me. I know that," she said. "Be man enough to admit it."

"I don't hate you at all, Hut'ieh Fujen. In fact...but let's not go into it. Don't you think it would be better to part in a civilized manner?"

"Would you marry me if I weren't half-Chinese?"

"Possibly."

"Oh, Palmer, Palmer!" she wailed.

Macneil could imagine that the nun-educated woman had thrown herself into Palmer's arms. "I love you so much. I adore you! Don't you know I can't possibly live without you? Let's take ship for America and spend the rest of our lives in each other's arms. I love you so much. I know you love me. Please, Palmer, please, *please!*"

Nothing else was said. Macneil heard more sobbing and then the sound of a door sliding open and shut. In a moment, Palmer knocked at Macneil's door to tell him he was going down to the dock to spend the night aboard *Highflyer* and would sail for Takarajima the next morning.

"I believe," he said in a whisper, "that Hut'ieh Gonzaga is tottering on the verge of losing her reason."

In response to Neil's letter, Nairn Macneil came back to Nagasaki after a protracted stay in Hong Kong. The letter said Margaret had grown weaker and might leave them at any time.

When Nairn disembarked from *Rainbow* at Pier Number Three, his appearance shocked Neil almost as much as Margaret's had. Time had not dealt kindly with his father. The hot, muggy climate of the Crown Colony took its toll of white men foolhardy or greedy enough to live there, what with one fever after another sweeping over the island like a scourge.

To be sure, Westerners in Nagasaki did not fare well either, for though the climate was more benign, that port was a hotbed of venereal diseases. Only recently, an American warship had brought with it the dread cholera, which had kept Dr. Jason Willits so busy he had not called on Margaret nearly as often as Neil would have liked, but at this terminal stage of her consumption, there was little the doctor could do.

By then, Macneil had moved into the new house on the edge of the cliff to be near Margaret and away from Palmer and Hut'ieh and their bickering.

With Nairn Macneil from Hong Kong had come another installment of Anne's diary. That evening when Neil retired to his study in the new house, he was of two minds as he settled himself beside an oil lamp in an easy chair and poured half a glass of The Glenlivet.

He knew he had to plow ahead through repellent soil looking for clues to Anne's whereabouts. A year had passed since the rescue of Margaret, with no word about Anne from Koume's League of Geishas or the *funa-kainin* of Amakusa or the British consul in Edo, to whom Macneil sent a monthly reminder of Anne's plight. He had drawn heavily on his accounts in several Far Eastern banks to pay bribes to every clandestine group that appeared to have entree into the castles of any of the *fudai* fiefs, all to no avail.

Anne's diary alone held forth some hope, so he knew he had to continue to digest it with care even though his heart quaked with fear of what unwelcome or heart-shredding revelations he might find there. This installment, though only ten pages like the others, appeared to cover a longer period of time. It seemed Anne had not made daily and sometimes not even weekly entries.

Phrases such as "Dear Diary, it's been eight days since I last talked to you," or "Forgive me, my friend, for not coming to visit with you for two weeks," or "I wonder if you will believe what has happened to me during the past month," were frequent.

The way of life of Anne and Margaret—written before Anne was sent away from Kuwana—continued much as before. Idle days, evening baths, the same food, study of the One Hundred Poems, nights spent with the Lord of Kuwana or an important guest. Anne did, in two places, note Margaret's frequent coughing and pale countenance, making Macneil think his sister's consumption had already begun to take its terrible toll.

Thinking back to his receipt of the second diary installment, Macneil recalled how, with trembling fingers, he had torn open the envelope to find out what had happened to Anne when she had been on the point of being stripped and taken to the Lord of Kuwana's rooms.

He found on the first page of the second installment the reason for the summons. The daimyo wanted to exhibit her naked to a visitor to settle an argument about the color of a blonde woman's pubic hairs. Winning the argument had put him in a good humor, so the daimyo sent Anne back to her room unharmed.

In the third installment, Anne again wrote explicitly about her sexual activities. At a dinner with a group of his guests, the daimyo had announced to all that Anne, who was pouring sake for the party, had three vaginas, but that the one he liked best was the one in her face. Embarrassed, she had fled the room, only to be soundly beaten later.

Still, she confessed in the last installment of her diary:

> I actually prefer for him to use what he calls my second vagina or even the third one, since they afford no danger of my being impregnated by this loathsome creature's seed. Of course, both Margaret and I continue to use the cherry-paper, though I have never trusted it completely. In fact, we stuff ourselves so full of it that now and then one of our *futon* partners will protest he can't get his (illegible) in there and will demand that we remove some or all of it. Not all the samurais and daimyos are so repulsive, however. I suppose that in comparison to our Lord of Kuwana, even a rutting, leprous boar would look handsome and lovable. In fact, there is one samurai from the province of Omi, not far from us. He is quite young—and handsome, I might add. I was given to him one night. Once between the *futon* with him, I learned that he was a male virgin, so I got astride and rode him to our simultaneous climax. Oh, diary, my friend, if only I could tell you how marvelous it was to be with a clean, gentle, innocent youth who responded meekly but willingly to my lead! How good it was not to be beaten or cursed or coldly kicked away! With shame I admit I became a complete wanton.

With a snarl, Macneil threw the pages from him, quaffed

the rest of The Glenlivet in his glass, and began to pace the study floor in angry strides.

Macneil believed a truer love never existed than theirs. In their hearts—in his heart, certainly—they still loved each other, but her debauchers had changed her, made her somehow coarser.

But no, that wasn't fair, either. Anne had been forced to submit, and she was only doing what she had to in order to survive.

Outside the house, the chorus of cicadas joined voices in shrill whirring melodies, making the hillside below vibrate like crystal. There was no moon and most of the lights in the town had been snuffed out for the night. An evening breeze tinkled the wind chimes on the veranda. From the floor above, Macneil could hear Margaret weakly coughing.

Calmer now, Neil picked up the diary to read on, but the first line to meet his eyes contained more of the same debauchery. After that, he could read no more that night.

Nairn Macneil found he could no longer postpone his return to Hong Kong. The comprador at the Macneil hong there faced too many pressing decisions that he did not wish to make alone. As Neil helped Nairn limp up the gangplank of *Rainbow*, his heart went out to the stooped, faltering figure, old before his time. He kissed his father's whiskery cheek, and they clung to each other for a long moment on the white-wood deck of the spic-and-span clipper ship. Neither could give voice to what was in his heart. The Macneils of Nagasaki were disintegrating as a clan. Even as their wealth grew, their numbers decreased.

How Margaret held on to life after Nairn's departure, Neil could not imagine. Dr. Willits, whose twenty-hour-a-day rounds during the cholera epidemic had trimmed eighty pounds from his huge frame, could not say what kept Margaret alive.

Margaret had read the rest of the diary installment that Neil could not bring himself to read and confirmed that all of it had been written while Anne was still with Margaret in Kuwana.

Neil said, "I hated to ask you to read that part of the diary, Meg, but I couldn't take any more of it. Yet I had to know if there were any clues as to where she might have been taken later. Were you terribly upset?"

"My dear brother," Margaret said, all the world's pain reflected in her dimming eyes, "you forget that I was subjected to the same outrages, often together with Anne."

"But Meg," Neil cried, "there were times when Anne *liked* it—or, so she said—whereas I know you didn't. I know you too well, darling Meg, to think that of you."

"Do you really know me so well, Neil?" she asked, her lips showing the only hint of a smile her brother had seen in weeks.

Shock ran through him.

She took one of his hands in hers. "I'm only teasing you,

Neil. You're right. I hated it. But don't think harshly of Anne, please. Some of us Macneil women have stronger passions than others. And remember that Anne and I really believed we would have to spend the remainder of our lives in the Kuwana castle. Put yourself in her place."

Two days later, Chizu came running to say Margaret was bleeding copiously from the mouth.

Macneil sent Chizu for Dr. Willits, then took the stairs to the second floor two at a time. The late afternoon sun over the harbor made her blood on the *tatami* even redder.

Neil lifted her in his arms, oblivious of the blood soaking his shirt.

"Neil," she gasped.

"Yes, Meg?"

"Forgive Anne."

"I will."

"Promise?"

"I promise."

She coughed. Neil wondered how one body so small and thin could hold so much blood.

"And...find her...soon."

"I will, Meg. I will."

With her thin arms, she pulled his face closer to hers. "Neil," she said, her voice finding one last hidden reserve of strength, "do this much for me, if you do nothing else. Find her...and forgive her."

She died then, in the late afternoon sunlight.

From a house on the hillside below came the joyous laughter of two little girls, playing some game in their garden.

It was dark before Neil would let the others take his sister's body away.

CHAPTER 62

Yokohama and Edo

Thomas Sakamoto wrote to Macneil that he was back in Yokohama waiting for the vessel that carried the Gatling gun to arrive. Given fair weather en route, it should enter the port of Yokohama soon, he said.

Macneil took a coastal packet to Yokohama. The rebellion of the *tozama* clans against the Tokugawa shogun had entered its final stage. Most of the fighting was either in the capital city of Edo or to the north and west of there. It was in the northwest that the *fudai* daimyos—the pre-Sekigahara vassals of the Tokugawas—were now strongest. Those clans included Aizu, Mito, Echigo, Iwaki, Kozuke, Echizen, Makino, Murakami, Kurokawa, Mikkaichi, Shibata, Muramatsu, and Kishu.

Virtually all resistance to the imperial restoration in southwestern Japan, beyond Nagoya and including Kuwana, had sputtered out. Doubtless, some clans would be quick to proclaim their steadfastness in support of the Tokugawas should the shogun's forces win the battles in the north.

After gathering in the Bay of Sendai, all the Tokugawa warships had sailed north for the island of Yezo under the command of Admiral Enomoto. At the same time, they had proclaimed their intent to make that northern island a separate kingdom for the Tokugawa shogun should his forces be defeated in the land battles near Edo.

In Edo itself, a full-scale battle was being fought in the Ueno district even as Macneil's packet reached Yokohama.

Neil found Thomas at the Tosa agency in Kanagawa. The agency had not yet moved to the new port of Yokohama. The big Tosa samurai appeared very impressive in one of the suits Louise Gatling had persuaded him to have tailored in Chicago. Macneil took him along as they made their way to Edo on horseback up the Tokaido highway, clogged with refugees from the heavy fighting. They entered a city Macneil had not visited since the night he and Ai Koga had skirted it in their race to catch

Commodore Perry's *Susquehanna.*

On a hill atop a slope called Kurayami-zaka, the Tosa clan maintained a mansion in the Shiba district of Edo. As a Tosa samurai who had always been loyal to his clan, Thomas was made welcome. He and Macneil were given quarters and food. They ate in a 30-mat room with a dozen other Tosa men, most of whom had never met a Westerner who could speak Japanese. They all seemed friendly to the Western powers, except for France, whose consul had decided to side with the shogun.

This consul had provided the services of a battalion of French troops who were even now marching north to the defense of the fiefdom of Aizu. It was at the mighty Aizu fortress in the town of Wakamatsu that some thought the Tokugawas would make their last stand if they lost the battle of Ueno now in progress.

One of the Tosa samurais said, "We heard today that Saigo himself is acting as intermediary between the shogun and the emperor."

Takamori Saigo, a famous Satsuma warrior, commanded the imperial forces.

"Is there any chance for a negotiated peace?" Macneil asked.

"They say the shogun would rather abdicate than see the streets run red with blood."

"I had heard that the shogun was a cruel, war-loving ruler."

"That was true of the present shogun's father, but this one, Keiki, is different, it seems."

"If the shogun abdicates, what will become of him?"

Several Tosa men laughed. "Nothing very drastic," one said. "We Japanese always leave our enemy a door through which to escape."

"If Keiki withdraws," Thomas said, "will the fighting stop everywhere?"

This question brought forth mixed opinions, but the consensus was that the diehards around Keiki who were urging him not to abdicate would flee north to Aizu with all the forces they could muster. There, in the castle of the daimyo of Aizu, whose family name was Matsudaira, they would make their stand. The men of Aizu, long known for their fierce loyalty to the Tokugawa house, were reputed to be, along with the samurais of Satsuma and Tosa, the most ferocious fighters in Japan.

"When is General Saigo to meet the shogun?" Macneil asked.

"Today or tomorrow."

Later, as Neil and Thomas were bathing in the large communal bath, Neil thought of all the implications of the shogun's abdication.

"If Keiki quits," he said to Thomas, "won't that mean Ai Koga will be able to return to Japan?"

"I'm sure it will."

"I wish you would have someone in our office send word to her."

"I've heard a rumor that Keiki and his wife may leave Edo soon to retire in the fief of Sumpu."

That news gave Macneil something to chew on. "Can you arrange for me to meet Katsuko?" he asked.

Half-hidden in the steam from the hot water, Thomas replied, "Neil-*san*, for the shogun's wife to meet a Westerner in times like these—"

"I could disguise myself as a begging priest, a *komuso*, the way I used to."

"Perhaps then I could arrange a brief meeting. You could be near at hand in your disguise," Thomas said. "If the circumstances seem safe, I might try to take her to you. I hear she goes to the Zojoji temple almost daily to pray for the safety of her family."

"Please try," Neil said. "And something else I've wondered about for a long time. Although Keiki may not ever have learned Katsuko gave birth to my son on Sado, he must have become aware she wasn't a virgin on their wedding night. Why wasn't he wild with rage? Why didn't he throw her out of the palace?"

Thomas chuckled. "I'm sorry to say your understanding of Japan is still imperfect, Neil-*san*. Virginity is important in some clans like that of Ai Koga's *funa-kainin*. But in most of the noble houses, it's the appearance of morality that counts more."

"What do you mean?"

"I mean that much will be forgiven if it doesn't become a public embarrassment."

"Even for a woman in Katsuko's position?" Macneil asked.

"Especially for such a woman. You should remember that allying the shogun even more closely with the Ito clan of Kii was the main purpose behind the marriage. If Keiki had rejected Katsuko after the nuptials, he would have insulted her clan and angered her father. How much better to have the Ito clan friendly to him than to have an unbroken maidenhead in his wife when they married. Remember, Neil-*san*, marriages in Japan are not made for love."

A *sansuke* entered the steamy room to wash their backs, so Neil and Thomas switched to English.

"What about the Gatling gun?" Neil asked.

"What a magnificent weapon it is! I fired it many times, Neil-*san*, but it has one flaw. I will tell you about it when I demonstrate it."

"If it doesn't get here soon, this war will have ended, and we'll have wasted our money."

"There'll be other wars. There always are."

"How about this American girl who fell in love with you?" Neil asked, cocking his eyebrow.

Thomas reddened. "It was just a case of *osana-koi*. How do you say that in English?"

"Puppy love. How old was she?"

"Nineteen."

"But she followed you to St. Louis. Couldn't Dr. Gatling do anything with her?"

"Not much. She inherited a lot of money from her grandmother in California, where her grandfather had been one of the gold rush people. The Forty-Niners, I believe you call them."

"Well, anyway, that's behind you.

From the look on Thomas's face, Macneil couldn't tell whether he was pleased or saddened.

The Tokugawa forces were soundly beaten at the Battle of Ueno, in the northern sector of Edo, and Shogun Keiki Tokugawa was compelled to turn his control of the nation over to the imperial court, as the rebels demanded. Keiki would have three weeks in which to vacate Edo castle and retire with his family to his new fiefdom of Sumpu, on the Tokaido highway south of the Izu Peninsula. Many reportedly urged Keiki to commit *hara-kiri*, but Macneil thought the shogun did not seem to have any such inclination.

Many of Keiki's followers would not give up the struggle that easily. Withdrawing from Edo with the remnants of their vanquished army, they set out for the stronghold of Aizu in the mountains north of Edo. At the same time, they sent runners to all the Tokugawa adherents in northern Honshu, calling on these loyal clans to gather every warrior capable of wielding a weapon and make haste for the Tsurugajo or White Crane Castle. This massive fortress dominated the town of Wakamatsu on the shores of Lake Inawashiro. From there, Lord Katamori Matsudaira reigned over the seventy-two villages in his fief of Aizu.

General Takamori Saigo of the imperial forces had 38,000 troops at his command, but no cannon with which to batter down the granite walls of the White Crane Castle. On the day Thomas was to take Macneil to the Zojoji Temple for a clandestine meeting with the shogun's wife Katsuko, General Saigo sent word to the Tosa clan mansion that he wanted to see the American arms merchant.

Saigo had his temporary headquarters in the Edo mansion of the Satsuma—his own—clan. This was on the far side of Edo castle, in the Koishikawa district. As soon as Macneil arrived, Saigo received him privately, and offered him cold sake and dried chestnuts.

The Satsuma warrior as a large man, almost as tall as Macneil but far heftier. He looked like a sumo wrestler, which, in fact, he had been in his younger days. Saigo had huge black eyes without the Mongolian fold in their corners, eyes that were said to pierce men's souls. What he had to say to the American over tea was brief and to the point.

"We are aware of your efforts on behalf of His Imperial Majesty."

"I have dedicated myself to the overthrow of the Tokugawas," Macneil said.

"Because you believe your fiancee is held captive by one of the Tokugawa supporters?"

Macneil was surprised Saigo knew this until he recalled his earlier plea to the emperor's messenger in Nagasaki. He nodded.

"Her name, I believe, is Anne Macneil. Is that correct?" Saigo had spoken, for the first time, in English. He was one of those Satsuma samurais who had looked far into the future and decided to study English. Two years earlier a British engineer hired to construct a textile mill in Kagoshima had become his teacher.

Macneil nodded again, gazing in wonder at this gigantic man. "I know where she is," Saigo said.

Unable to take his next breath, the American waited.

"She's being kept in the White Crane Castle in Aizu, as the concubine of Lord Matsudaira."

Macneil closed his eyes. He must have swayed.

Saigo started to stand. "Are you all right?"

Straightening, Macneil looked the large general straight in the eye and said, "I'm now better, General Saigo, than I have been for a very long time."

"We need cannon to crush Aizu. Have you any?"

"I have ten twelve-pounder Wiard rifled field guns in Nagasaki. They're muzzle-loading."

"We would like to buy them," Saigo said.

"They are yours at no cost if you will let me fight with your army against Aizu."

"Agreed." Saigo smiled for the first time in the interview. "The emperor knows of your generous aid to his cause. Is there naught we can do for you?"

Returning his smile, Macneil said. "There's a Japanese woman in England who is wanted by the shogun's *Ometsuke-yaku;* I want that order rescinded."

"Give the details to my adjutant."

"And I might have another request later," Neil said. "It will concern a boy named Ichiro Ito on Sado Island."

"We will listen, whatever it is." Saigo stood up. The interview was over.

"I will leave today for Nagasaki to get the Wiard field pieces. Where shall I deliver them?" Macneil asked.

The general called an aide for a map, which he consulted briefly. "Bring them to the port of Nakoso. It's closest to Aizu."

In English, he said, "Goodbye, Mr. Macneil," and shook the American's hand.

The streets of Koishikawa were clogged with people returning to their homes, now that the Tokugawa forces defeated at the Battle of Ueno had left Edo. Macneil sighted a vacant *jinrikisha*—now being called a "rickshaw" by the foreigners—and hailed it. This two-wheeled vehicle drawn by a coolie had been invented the year before by an American living in Yokohama. It was beginning to appear in the major towns in increasing numbers. Everyone agreed these new vehicles were faster and more comfortable than the palanquins or sedan-chairs.

At the Tosa mansion, Thomas waited. The hour was still early, for the noon cannon had just been fired from atop Atago Hill. "Hurry, Neil-*san*," he urged. "We can still make it."

He jumped up into the rickshaw with Macneil. The coolie started off down Kurayami-zaka at a dead-run, then turned right at Juban Street. He covered the three miles from there to the Zojoji Temple at what may have been a record speed for the new rickshaws.

The faded red and black gate-house of the temple precincts had stood since the early 1600's, when the temple was built as the principal worshiping place of the Tokugawa family. Its many gardens and buildings covered fifty acres. In its deep woods, small children had been known to become lost, and wild badgers had been sighted.

Thomas had brought a *komuso* outfit for Macneil wrapped in a *furoshiki,* and Neil put it on in a secluded corner between the gate-house and the original stone-and-mortar wall, which stood ten feet high. Thomas left him there and went alone to the small temple where the shogun's immediate family prayed.

Twenty minutes later, Thomas returned at a half-run and when he was still some distance away, signaled for Macneil to follow him. Walking behind the samurai at a smart pace, Neil entered a patch of woods near the north wall. "There," Thomas whispered, pointing to a Buddhist nun dressed in black. She wore a cloth hood over her head.

"I'll wait for you here," he said. "If I whistle, leave her quickly and follow me over the wall."

As Macneil walked over to the nun standing in the deep shade of the trees, his memory went back to the Katsuko Ito he had met years before, a woman he would have recognized more quickly had she been unclothed. The woman he had known intimately was fairly tall and willowy, with an oval face, large eyes, and an aquiline nose.

When he was within four feet of this nun, Macneil removed his basket hat and tossed it aside. She lowered the hood from her head and started toward him. The years had added maturity to her face, but Katsuko Ito, now Tokugawa, was still a fairly young, attractive woman.

Before he could say her name, she came into Neil's arms

with a rush. "Neil-*san*, oh, Neil-*san*!" she cried. "How often have I thought of you!" She lifted her lips to his. "And about the times we washed each other's backs in Nagasaki." She was smiling as he kissed her. It seemed the least he could do. After all, she was the mother of his son.

"So much has happened," Macneil started to say, but she stopped his words with another kiss.

"There's so little time," she whispered. "The shogun and I must leave Edo for Sumpu very soon. Now that he has decided to abdicate, Japan will be turned upside down. This means you will be able to retrieve our son. Oh, Neil, you *will* do that, won't you?"

"Of course, Katsuko."

"I'll send word to your retainer Sakamoto-*san* and give him our little Ichiro's exact whereabouts. When the House of Tokugawa falls, the samurai family raising our boy will be more than willing to give him up. I'll send along a letter identifying you as the boy's true father. Promise me, Neil, that you will go for him soon."

"I swear it."

From behind him came a soft whistle. It was Thomas. Neil looked back. The Tosa samurai signaled that someone was coming.

"Neil," Katsuko said, clinging to him, "promise you will bring him to see me in Sumpu?"

"Do you think I should?"

"It will be all right," she said. "Keiki and I will just be a retired country squire and his wife."

"But won't your husband mind?"

"Keiki is really a decent person, Neil. Not an evil man like his father, or my brother Osamu. He will understand."

Thomas whistled again. Macneil disengaged himself from Katsuko and ran for the wall. Thomas already straddled the top of it and leaned down to give Neil a hand up.

Neil looked back at Katsuko. She picked up his basket hat and came running over to the wall.

"I don't need the basket hat now, Katsuko," he told her.

"It's not the hat," she said, tossing it aside. "I wanted to tell you something about your fiancee."

"What?" Thomas had already dropped to the ground outside the wall and was making urgent motions for Neil to follow.

"My brother Osamu," she said, "brought your Anne to Edo from Kuwana and kept her in his residence here for at least a month."

"Yes, I've heard that."

"Then he sent her north."

"Do you know where?"

"To Aizu—to the castle there," she said, looking back over her shoulder.

"Where is Osamu?" he asked, preparing to jump down.

"He's leaving Edo today for Aizu. He swears he will fight to the death for the Tokugawa cause."

"Do you believe him?"

"Yes, I do. My brother has always been a bloodthirsty fool."

CHAPTER 63

Nagasaki

Thomas stayed in Yokohama, awaiting the arrival of the Gatling gun. Neil took the fastest coastal packet back to Nagasaki. Tying up to the Macneil wharf in front of the hong arms warehouse, he went inside and gave orders for loading the ten twelve-pounder Wiard field guns aboard *Highflyer*, which was also tied up to the wharf. If Palmer St. James had come up from Takarajima on one of his periodic visits, Macneil would ask him to go along to Nakoso, then overland to Aizu to join in the battle.

A young Swiss named Graf, whom Macneil had recently engaged as assistant manager of the arms warehouse, ran up to him as he was telling the Japanese manager to start loading the Wiard field pieces.

To Graf, Macneil said, "Put all the shells for the Wiards aboard *Highflyer*, too. Every last one of them, as well as 100 of those new land mines."

"Mr. Macneil," Graf said, his voice shaking. "You had better go up to your home straight away. Something terrible has happened."

Macneil took the Swiss by the shoulders. "What is it, man? Speak up!"

"I'm not sure, sir, but your female servant Chizu-*san* came running in here earlier, asking us to help her find Dr. Willits and send him up there."

Not stopping to look for a palanquin or rickshaw, Neil ran for the footpath that led up the hill to his residence.

At the top of the path, Macneil paused to catch his breath. He was not sure whether to go to the new house or the old, but Chizu chanced to see him from the second floor of the old house and pointed urgently toward the new one. Macneil could see she was crying.

At a run, he entered the new building through the kitchen door. Two scullery maids stood by the large coal cooking stove Macneil had imported from a factory in Pennsylvania. Both were blubbering and incoherent.

He went into the large Western-style living room looking out over the harbor. Through its bay windows, Neil could see Hut'ieh Gonzaga standing on the veranda, gazing toward the west.

He started to go out to her, but Jason Willits came in, stooping to avoid hitting his forehead on the door frame. He carried his medical bag.

"I stanched the flow of blood," he said, "but by the time I got here this morning, he had already lost a great deal." He placed a huge hand on Macneil's shoulder. "I doubt he'll make it through the night."

"Who?" Macneil cried. "My God, Jason, who are you talking about?"

"You haven't heard? It's your friend Captain St. James. He's been injured. I've done all I can. I'll be back in a couple of hours. He may not last that long."

Palmer? Injured? Neil raced up to the second floor and into the room where Palmer and Hut'ieh slept.

Palmer St. James lay between *futon* in the middle of the room, a bean-shell pillow under his head. Everything seemed normal, except for some bandages and two basins of reddish water beside him. He appeared to be asleep. Beneath his black hair, his face was chalk white.

"Palmer?" Neil said gently, kneeling beside him. "It's me. What's happened here?"

A grimace of pain, then a weak smile crossed Palmer's handsome, aristocratic features. "Neil?" His voice quavered, and his eyes seemed to have trouble focusing. "So glad you got here in time for us to bid each other a proper farewell."

"In God's name, Palmer! What's wrong? Don't talk about farewells. Jason Willits will pull you through."

"Really, old chap, I'd rather he didn't."

"But *what* happened?"

"Hut'ieh Fujen did me in, old boy."

"Hut'ieh did you in? What on earth do you mean?"

"This morning, while I was still asleep. The little bitch took me unawares. Give Jane Vandiver my apologies, won't you, and tell her how sorry I'll be to have missed our wedding."

"*What* did Hut'ieh do to you?"

Palmer managed a sardonic smile. Macneil had a fleeting memory of this naval officer on the deck of *HMS Mariner* receiving heavy fire from *Wolodimir* with the same smile.

"She did what she knew would be the worst punishment of all—castration."

Dear God! A red film of anger clouded Macneil's eyes. He swore to turn the vicious creature over to the Chinese consul and have her beheaded.

"Try to send her out of Japan, old fellow. Otherwise,

they're certain to execute her. Send her to a distant port and let her disappear. I forgive her, and I now forgive all my enemies, as Christ is my witness. You'll do that much for me?" His lips were barely moving now.

"Palmer," Neil protested. "Surely you don't want her to go free, do you?"

He waved one hand feebly, as if shooing away a fly. "Do what you think best, there's a good chap. Now, one last thing. Fetch paper and something to write with. I must dictate a letter to my father."

It was a long letter, and Neil could sense Palmer sinking with each paragraph.

"Now hand it to me, so I can sign it."

Neil did so.

"Something else, old boy. Look over there among Hut'ieh's things. Find that cheque on the Midland Bank."

Macneil found it and gave it to him. Palmer tore it up.

"Add a postscript to the letter to my father. Tell him I have torn up one cheque for fifty thousand pounds. I want him to issue another in the same amount to...."

Palmer's eyes closed. His mouth went slack. Bubbles formed at one corner. He spoke again with his eyes closed. "Tell him to make the other cheque for fifty thousand pounds payable to Miss...to Miss..." His voice faded, so Macneil brought an ear down closer to his lips.

Behind them, Dr. Willits entered the room.

"Payable to Miss...Ai Koga."

"You'd better leave, Neil," Jason Willits said, kneeling by the *futon*.

"Wait!" Palmer commanded. "I must sign that postscript.

"You and Ai...you'll name your first son after me, won't you?"

Macneil didn't know what to say. He dipped the quill in ink and handed it and the last page to Palmer. Palmer's signature was an illegible scrawl. He must have realized this, for he told Jason Willits, "You sign it, doctor, as a witness to my signature."

"Of course, Captain," Willits said, and signaled for Macneil to leave the room.

Downstairs, Hut'ieh Gonzaga was still standing on the veranda in her flowing red and yellow Chinese robe. Neil walked out to her.

She was flying a small Japanese kite made to resemble a rooster. A strong breeze from the east kept the kite aloft. A ten-foot tail swayed back and forth under it.

Hut'ieh turned to look at Neil. "Is he dead?" she asked.

"Not yet."

She looked down from the railing to the rocks far below. Neil followed her gaze but could see nothing down there other than the gentle harbor waves lapping against the boulders.

"Why are you flying that kite, Hut'ieh?"

"Why? You ask me why?" She looked at Macneil and he saw the insanity in her eyes, under the long lashes. "Do you see that little white bundle at the end of the kite's tail?" she asked.

He narrowed his eyes. Something wrapped in white paper or cloth dangled from the end of the tail.

"That was mine. I won't let it be buried with him. Maybe the kite will take it all the way to Hong Kong. We were happy there."

Hut'ieh released her hold on the string. The kite soared higher and higher—off to the west, over the China Sea.

"Neil?" It was Jason Willits.

Macneil turned to face him.

"He's gone," the doctor said.

While Macneil's back was turned, Hut'ieh climbed atop the railing of the veranda.

"Grab her!" Willits yelled, shoving Macneil aside.

CHAPTER 64

Willits was too late. The red and yellow silk robe billowed around Hut'ieh's falling form. She looked like a colorful bird—or butterfly—fluttering to the rocks below.

The next morning at his office, Neil posted Palmer St. James's last letter to the earl and wrote one to be held for Lady Jane Vandiver, who was scheduled to reach Nagasaki the next day. He left up to her the decision about where to bury Palmer, but told her there was a private burial plot on Macneil property. His sister Margaret was buried there, and one day he would lie beside her. Palmer was welcome to join them, he wrote.

Dr. Willits hurried through the formalities of informing the authorities of the two deaths. He was eager to sail north with Macneil on *Highflyer*, to treat the wounded in the battle sure to be fought at Aizu. Chizu sent down a small trunk containing Neil's kilt, glengarry, and bagpipe as well as his sword and sketch pad and even a *komuso* outfit. He could depend on Chizu to think of such things. He added a selection of pistols and a trident-like *jitte* from the hong's stock of weapons.

Just before leaving the office to board *Highflyer*, Macneil called in the Chinese money counter. The Chinese were the best money counters in the Far East, and every commercial house had one. It was believed they could heft a gold or silver coin and tell if it had been mixed with base metal.

This one bowed before his employer.

Speaking in Japanese, Macneil said to him, "I know that in Chinese 'Hut'ieh' means Butterfly, but tell me the meaning of the expression 'Hut'ieh Fujen.' "

"*Cho-cho Fujin*," the money-counter said. "Or Madame Butterfly."

CHAPTER 65

Yokohama to Aizu

Looking as pleased with himself as a butcher's dog, Thomas Sakamoto was waiting for Macneil in the new branch office of the hong on the Yokohama Bund. The Tosa samurai still wore a Western outfit, including a bowler hat he had adopted during his recent trip to the United States.

"Judging from the look on your face," Macneil said in Japanese, "the Gatling has arrived."

"*Two* Gatlings have come," Thomas corrected him.

"Excellent! Get both of them loaded on *Highflyer* while I ride up to Edo to see General Saigo."

"I'll load one of them on *Highflyer*, but the other has to stay here in Yokohama."

"My God, Thomas," Macneil said. "Why? We'll need both of them at Aizu."

The samurai's smile threatened to split his face. "The Gatling that stays here is *Louise* Gatling."

"Well, she must be a determined young woman to make it to the Orient on her own, I'll say that much for her. What are you going to do with her?"

"Put her up in that new hotel—the Oriental. She can stay there until we return from Aizu."

"I want to meet her when I get back from Edo," Macneil said. "But now I must be on my way."

"There's no need to ride to Edo, Neil-*san*. General Saigo has already left for Aizu, but he assigned a company of militia to sail with us on *Highflyer*. He wants us to train them in the use of the Wiards on the voyage to Nakoso. Then they can help haul the guns overland to Aizu. He said he would have teams of bullocks waiting for us at the port."

Next morning, sailing north along the Boso Peninsula for Nakoso, they uncrated the Gatling gun, cleaned the packing grease from it, and assembled it for firing from the stern.

"This isn't the gun I read about," Macneil told Thomas.

"It's a later model. With ten barrels revolving around the axis, this gun can fire up to 450 rounds a minute. And it has an all-metal Broadwell carriage."

"How much does it weigh without the carriage?"

"Just over a thousand pounds."

"The bore looks larger."

"It is—100 caliber, inside-primed centerfire, and fires both solid lead and eighteen-ball canister cartridges, with a charge of three-quarters of an ounce of mortar powder in each."

Macneil whistled. Eighteen balls in each canister cartridge and 450 rounds per minute? "Why, that's...what, about 8,000 pieces of metal spewing forth every sixty seconds! What's the range?'

"Excellent accuracy at four to six hundred yards, on a flat trajectory."

"Maximum?"

"Elevate it to ten degrees and forty seconds, and you can hit targets at 2,800 yards. Over a mile and a half."

"You said it had one flaw. Tell me about it."

Checking to assure himself the weapon was not loaded, Thomas stepped behind it and began to turn the crank, causing the ten rifled barrels to revolve around the axis.

"It jams easily," the samurai said, "but the reason it jams is that the gunner turns the crank too fast. In the excitement of battle, when the enemy is charging your battery, it's devilishly hard not to turn the crank faster and faster. The gunner is tempted to fire eight or nine hundred rounds a minute instead of only 450."

"And that's the flaw? Human error?"

Thomas nodded.

"Well, load it up and fire it for me. Then let me try my hand."

By the time *Highflyer* reached the tiny port of Nakoso that evening, Macneil was fairly adept with the Gatling, and Saigo's militia had mastered the Wiard field guns, having practiced all day from the stern, firing at empty barrels thrown overboard in the wake of the ship.

Transporting the Gatling, the Wiards, and their ammunition to Aizu from the port of Nakoso turned into a nightmare. An early fall rain drenched them most of the way. Time after time, the guns mired in the soft earth of the road, on which the shogun had seldom permitted improvements, until the column reached the foothills. There, the composition of the road changed to more rock and less dirt, and the steeper slopes had steps dug into them for human feet. Few wheeled vehicles traveled this way.

More and more peasants came to the side of the road. Many volunteered to help carry and push the guns and ammunition.

Saigo's reinforcements now marched through the territory of the clan of Itakura, whose taxes on the peasantry had been confiscatory. The farmers welcomed any change in administration as a change for the better.

Whenever the column passed through a village, the volunteer porters briefly detoured to burn down the office of the *nanushi* or village headman. One explained to Macneil that this would destroy his tax rolls so that a new administration could not use the old tax assessments as the basis for new ones. Most caught up with the column again and continued to push and pull, until replaced by other peasants farther along the road.

Jason Willits, who had come puffing up the *Highflyer* gangplank at the last moment, kept the peasants in high spirits with ribald jokes in his peculiar Japanese. He had a fair vocabulary, 80 percent of it being words for parts of the body, medicines, and physical ills recognized by the Japanese medical profession. For ailments and treatments recognized only by Western medical science, he contrived his own special terms, which sometimes, but not always, got his idea across.

Once when the peasants suggested half in jest that this huge man replace a team of tired bullocks pulling one of the field guns, he laughed and strapped himself into a harness between the wooden shafts. To the vast amusement and cheers of the column, by himself he hauled the heavy gun limber fifty yards along the muddy road.

Descending from the hills, the column traveled along the Keisando, one of three principal highways leading into the town of Wakamatsu, the capital of Aizu and the site of Lord Matsudaira's White Crane Castle. This narrow fertile valley, known for its production of linen, embraced the Yugawa River, which protected the south side of the castle. High, steep mountains, including the twin peaks of Mount Bandai and the abrupt precipices of Mount Itoya, protected the valley from the chill winter winds that blew out of Siberia across the Sea of Japan.

As the soaring keep of the White Crane Castle loomed in the middle distance, a body of horsemen came charging at the column from the direction of Wakamatsu. General Saigo himself rode in the lead, dwarfing the horse he sat astride. Leaping off the exhausted beast, he threw his arms around Macneil like a hungry bear and roared, "By the Imperial grace, you made it!"

Turning from the American, he lumbered down the column patting the field guns in joyful anticipation of the help they would give him. When at last he reached the Gatling, he turned back to Macneil.

"What in the name of the seven gods is this?" he asked in Japanese.

"That's my personal weapon, General. Remember you said Sakamoto and I could fight with you? Well, this is what we will fight with."

"But *what* is it?"

Macneil knew that if he told Saigo the actual wonders of the Gatling, the general might confiscate it out of hand, so he merely said, "It is a gun with ten barrels. We fire the barrels one after another."

"Well, we must hurry on," Saigo said. "We have the castle surrounded. I have 40,000 men now, and my *suppa* tell me Lord Matsudaira of Aizu and General Kakekigo have only 18,000. But remember they are behind the immensely thick walls of one of the best-constructed castles in Japan. And they have deep wells within the castle for water, and plenty of rice in their godowns."

"Winter comes early up here," Thomas said.

"That it does, Sakamoto-*kun*, that it does," Saigo said, "And they will be *in*side and warm, while we'll be outside and cold."

"We'll have to reduce the castle gates before hard winter hits," Macneil said, his voice grim and his thoughts with Anne Macneil.

"I like your spirit, Macneil-*san*. You would make a good samurai," Saigo said, bellowing with laughter.

"Even a Satsuma samurai?"

"Even a Satsuma or," the general said with a sly grin at Thomas, "a Tosa samurai. We both know how to die for our daimyo, and for the emperor, don't we?"

Macneil grinned with them, but he had not the least intention of dying here in Aizu for anyone, neither emperor nor daimyo. He was here to find Anne Macneil. Hers was the only cause he would die for.

The walls of the White Crane Castle were pierced with slits for archers, rounded embrasures for riflemen, and by sixteen gates. This meant the besiegers had to position the ten twelve-pounder Wiard field guns behind breastworks with an open field of fire toward one gate at least, but preferably two. Macneil told Saigo they couldn't hope to batter down the walls themselves with only two hundred shells for each of the Wiards. It would take two thousand or more. And with the strong possibility that Anne Macneil was being kept in a room in the castle keep, he did not want to direct any fire in that direction. Their best chance, Macneil told Saigo, was to demolish several of the massive wood gates with the field guns and charge through them into the castle grounds. Saigo agreed and left the placement of the field guns and their protective parapets to Macneil.

For the Gatling, Macneil had other plans.

When the column reached Wakamatsu, the siege of the castle had been in progress for a week. It took Macneil two days to complete his preparations for the opening bombardment. Thomas became his chief gunnery officer, going from gun crew to gun crew, drilling them toward perfection in the loading, aiming, firing, and cleaning of these sturdy French field cannon.

The 40,000 imperial troops under Saigo had formed a solid line around the White Crane Castle, either digging shallow trenches or piling up rocks for protection. For the moment, both sides fired arrows and bullets at each other in desultory fashion, neither inflicting much damage.

"Before we bombard their gates," Macneil told Saigo, "the Aizu forces may decide to attack us. But if we break through into the castle grounds and corner them inside, they would have little room to maneuver."

"My thoughts exactly," Saigo said. His dog Taki stood beside him barking for attention. *Taki* meant waterfall in Japanese. The general had chosen the name because of the little animal's habit of incessant urination.

"I want to get the Gatling gun up there," Macneil told Thomas, pointing to a cave in the face of a cliff behind them. The mouth of the cave was at least two hundred feet above where they stood and would give the Gatling a clean field of fire across the open ground on the northwest side of the castle. If the pro-Tokugawa forces were to sally forth to attack the imperial lines, it would probably be through one or more of the six gates on that side. The Yugawa River flowed on the southwest and south. To the east, the terrain was either rough and broken or spotted with the homes of the townspeople, most of whom had been ousted and replaced by Saigo's soldiers.

During the hours of darkness the second night after their arrival, Macneil had sent 100 Tosa and Satsuma *nohei* or peasant soldiers crawling out into the field on the northwest side of the castle. Their mission was to bury the land mines Macneil had brought along. These weapons were new to him, having been received from the Langley Arms Manufactory of Boston only days before *Highflyer* sailed from Nagasaki. Each mine was a dish-shaped metal container holding 2-1/2 pounds of gunpowder that exploded when ten pounds or more of weight triggered the ignition plug on top.

Knowing General Kakekigo of the Tokugawa forces in Aizu had the reputation of being crafty and competent, Saigo and his army were ready for imaginative ruses and stratagems. Macneil was certain Kakekigo could not come across the river to the south or through the houses and over the ravines to the northeast, but would have to charge the besiegers through the northwestern gates. There Macneil's land mines and his Gatling gun would give the Aizu men a hot welcome, provided Macneil could get the Gatling to the mouth of that cave, where it would be high enough to sweep the field effectively.

The danger they faced was that the cliff stood only about 200 yards from the castle wall on that side, within easy range of the seven-shot Spencer rifles the Tokugawa forces got from a Swiss named Edward Schnell in the port of Niigata. Since the cliff was almost vertical at that point, men had to climb long ropes on moonless nights, then pull up the ammunition and disassembled pieces of the gun carriage.

The main piece of the Gatling gun itself weighed just over a thousand pounds. A tremendous effort would be required to haul it up to the cave. The Tokugawa forces had started shooting off fireworks at intervals throughout the night to illuminate the ground outside the castle walls, a precaution against night attacks with scaling ladders. When the "flower flames" or *hanabi* as the Japanese called fireworks, bloomed, the face of the cliff was as visible as at high noon in summer.

One night, Macneil and his men tied a number of stout ropes to the ten barrels and axis of the Gatling and the men in the cave began to pull it—inch by arduous inch—up the cliff without the benefit of pulleys. If the ropes held, they hoped to have the gun into the cave and out of sight by first light. Their worry was that the Aizu forces would light up this side of the castle with *hanabi* before then.

Thirty minutes before dawn, when the eastern sky was already tinged with streaks of silver and yellow, the Gatling perversely caught on a projecting root. The imperial samurais strained to break it loose, but to no avail.

Macneil stood waiting at the foot of the cliff, not yet knowing the reason for the delay. A Tosa samurai came sliding down a rope off to one side and ran over to him. "The gun is caught on a root, and we cannot budge it. Sakamoto-*san* is going to slide down the rope to see if he can set it free."

Macneil looked east. It was growing lighter by the minute. If the enemy caught sight of Thomas on that rope struggling to free the Gatling, they would open fire on him.

Backing away from the base of the cliff, Macneil looked up. Sure enough, the Gatling was caught on a tree root about twenty feet below the ledge of the cave. Thomas was going over the edge, holding onto one of the ropes.

Hardly daring to breathe, Macneil watched him slide down the rope to the Gatling where he began working to free the weapon. But if Macneil could see him clearly, so could the guards on the castle walls, if they looked in his direction.

Remembering advice given him long ago by William Amanuma aboard the whaler *Phoenician*, Macneil summoned a Satsuma militiaman and ordered him to go at a dead run and fetch the small trunk from Macneil's tent.

He had stripped down to his undergarments when the trunk came. He stepped into his kilt, put on his leggings, donned his glengarry, and picked up the bagpipe. Inflating the bag with its blowstick, he ran toward a spot a hundred yards off to one side of the cliff and the same distance from the guards along the castle wall.

CHAPTER 66

White Crane Castle in Aizu

With head high and chest out, Neil Macneil of Barra and Nagasaki marched forward playing "Scotland, the Brave" on his bagpipe. From nearby trees, ravens took wing.

Once Ai Koga had said Macneil's bagpipe music sounded like someone torturing a cat. He had resented her insult then, but now he hoped she was right, for the sake of the attention it would attract. Already Macneil could see more heads appearing over the parapets on the castle walls and fingers pointing toward him.

In the clear mountain air, the skirl of the pipes must have penetrated every recess, however remote, of the White Crane Castle. If Anne heard the familiar screech, what would she think?

At the end of fifty paces, Macneil did a sharp about-face and marched back to his point of departure, kilt swaying above his white leggings. Movements atop the castle walls had multiplied. The Macneil tartan made up the bold design of the kilt that was Neil's battle flag that morning.

Looking up out of the corner of an eye, Macneil saw that the heavy Gatling gun had at last swung free. Thomas scrambled back up one of the ropes. When he was over the ledge and safe, the gun crew began hauling the Gatling up behind him. Then it too disappeared into the cave.

A true Scot never tires of entertaining an audience, even a heathen one, with the soul-stirring sounds of his bagpipe. While marching steadily farther away from the marksman on the castle wall, Macneil went through his repertoire of "Macrae's March," "MacIntosh's Lament" and the "Battle of Waternish" with only two false notes, which the castle defenders appeared not to notice.

But not all the shogun's soldiers appreciated fine classical music. Some had the insolence to open fire at Macneil—or at his bagpipe—bringing an end to his alfresco concert.

Behind the walls of the White Crane Castle, in comparative comfort and safety, waited the 18,000 troops of what was being called the *Ou Reppan Domei*, the Alliance of Aligned Clans of Ou. Ou was an old name for most of northern Honshu. The battle flag of the alliance had been a vertical banner displaying the holly-hock crest of the main branch of the Tokugawa family, but when Keiki Tokugawa abdicated and retired to the rural ease of his new holdings in Sumpu, with its annual production of 3,500,000 bushels of rice, the northern clans of Ou adopted a five-pointed gold star on a black background as their new standard.

At the head of the Aizu defenders stood Lord Katamori Matsudaira, long known as one of the three most loyal support-ers of the shogun, the lords of Mito and Kuwana being the other two. But Kuwana was dead and Mito was under house arrest, replaced by a younger relative. The emperor had ordered both Mito and Kuwana to send samurais and *nohei*, peasant militia, to join General Takamori Saigo, forcing the most ardent of the shogun's supporters to make war against their previous friends and allies.

With Lord Katamori Matsudaira in the castle were his younger brother Nobuyoshi; General Kakekigo, in field com-mand of the *Ou Reppan Domei* troops; Keinosuke Kawai, the *karo* or senior councillor of the House of Aizu; and Osamu Ito, head of the office of *Ometsuke*, the shogun's intelligence bureau.

Although they had enough water, food and ammunition to withstand a long siege, it was certain that Aizu's situation would not improve. Not only were the supply lines to their castle cut off, but also the fiefs who had sent fighting men to support the Alliance of Ou Clans were now having second thoughts. They wished they could call their men home, for day by day it became apparent that the imperial power was being strengthened and would win in the end. Those who had straddled the fence were vying to see who could declare his support of the restored emperor first and most loudly.

Of the foreign consuls, only M. Roches of France had sided with Shogun Keiki Tokugawa. Roche sent a battalion of French soldiers and their officers to fight with the shogun and to train his soldiers in the techniques of modern European warfare. France had also begun the construction in Yokosuka of a ship-yard to compete with the Macneil yards in Nagasaki harbor.

M. Roches, however, had recently tested the wind and, after sober reflection, had decided to return to France, pleading ill health. He could not, unfortunately, take his French soldiers with him, for they were trapped behind the walls of the White Crane Castle.

Takamori Saigo, the field marshal in command of the second major force in Wakamatsu, had told Macneil, "Aizu can only grow weaker, whereas our army is reaching the point where I have more men than I need. With winter coming on, I want to end enemy resistance quickly. Then we can proclaim to the world that the emperor rules an undivided Japan, which should discourage those imperialistic nations who might want to make my country a colony. After that, I can let these men get back to their farms and other work."

The third force present in Wakamatsu was Neil Macneil. His influence on the events taking place came from his contribution of ten Wiard field guns capable of battering down the gates of the castle. He and Thomas had trained the gun crews and were on the scene to supervise their performance in battle.

Macneil was confident the Aizu forces would sally forth from one or more of the castle gates to charge through the siege lines. Equally confident was he that Saigo's imperial troops would try to break into the castle where their superior numbers would crush the enemy in hand-to-hand fighting. He wanted not only to be witness but also participant in the combat, striving for an early imperial victory. The sooner they won, the sooner he could find Anne Macneil.

Macneil's Gatling gun had been installed in the mouth of the cave, covered with concealing brush. The rapid-fire weapon commanded a splendid field of fire from its 200 feet of elevation, not only the open spaces on the northwest side of the White Crane Castle, but also a considerable distance along the Yugawa River that flowed from east to west on the south side.

Standing back in the cave with his telescope, Macneil spent hours studying the troops of the Alliance of Ou Clans as they sat or stood on the castle walls. Each of the fourteen fiefs that had sent soldiers, both samurais and *nohei*, to Aizu in response to Lord Matsudaira's call had been assigned a section of the castle wall to defend. It was important to Macneil as well as to General Saigo to know what fief guarded which section of the wall and with what weapons they were armed.

In Japan, only those few forces under the direct command of the shogun had standardized their uniforms, and this standardization was a recent development, encouraged by the French training officers. Those without standardized uniforms were identified by the *sashimono,* an individual vertical banner tied to a short slender stick attached to the back of a fighting man. The color and design of the miniature banner showed which fief the man came from. The Satake clan, for example, had an open fan for its emblem, the House of Kuroda had a black circle on a white background, and one branch of the Ii clan had the *kanji* for tree inside a white circle against a red background.

By identifying the clan, Macneil could often tell what firearms they were equipped with. Some of the weapons came from his hong, and his several salesmen kept him well informed about what firearms the fiefs were equipped with, their range, accuracy, rate of fire, and effectiveness in battle.

Arms merchants like Macneil had reams of figures on the

performance of various firearms in battle, many of which would surprise the layman. For years it had been accepted as the basic rule of thumb in warfare that one million rounds of musketry produced 2,000 casualties: that is, one man would be hit for every 500 rounds expended.

But other specialists in the study of firearm effectiveness, such as Pibert and Gassendi, had concluded it actually required 3,000 rounds to produce a single casualty.

Recent studies reaching Macneil reported that in one German-French battle, the Germans had used 80,000 needle-gun rounds to kill or wound 400 Frenchmen. But in one of General Crook's fights with Indians in the U.S., it took 25,000 rounds to cause ninety-nine Indian deaths or wounds. In a battle with the Zulus in South Africa, one British battalion shot more than 20,000 rounds from their Martini-Henrys at very close range to kill 470 of the natives who had attacked a British square.

One of the strangest reports Macneil read concerned the battle at Gettysburg in the American Civil War. After Lee's withdrawal, some 37,000 rifles and muskets had been picked up on the battlefield. Of those, 24,000 were still loaded and had not recently been fired. Had that many men in blue and gray thrown aside their weapons to flee in terror? Had they been killed before firing even one shot? There was evidence that 6,000 of these men did not know how to use their weapons, since 6,000 of the unfired guns had between three and ten charges loaded in them, one on top of the other.

Macneil was particularly eager to know what section of the wall the French battalion defended because they were armed with the Chassepot rifles that in previous battles had caused one casualty for every 119 rounds fired. If the French were within range of Macneil's Gatling, he would have to sweep them from the castle wall before General Saigo sent any men charging at a bristling array of Chassepot rifles in the hands of veteran sharpshooters.

Macneil was looking at the wall with his telescope when he heard a samurai assigned to Thomas say, "Here comes Udo."

In Japanese *udo* or *udo no taiboku* meant a big gawky fellow. General Takamori Saigo's troops called him that affectionately, although not to his face. Others called him *Omedama* or the Big Eyeball.

"There you are, Macneil-*san*," the general said. "Care to inspect our lines with me?"

"I'd like nothing better," Macneil said.

With four Satsuma samurais in attendance, the two men started out behind the entrenchments and breastworks surrounding the castle. It would be a five or six-mile hike.

"Any particular reason for the inspection, General?" Macneil asked.

Saigo lowered his voice. "I can't help feeling that something will happen tonight," he said. "If it doesn't, I want your field guns to start blasting away at the gates tomorrow. The nights are getting colder, and we're not equipped for a long winter siege."

The tour of inspection around the White Crane Castle taught Macneil a great deal about Japanese fighting men and methods. What caught his eye first was the number of flags and banners carried by the imperial forces. Besides the small *sashimono* banners on the backs of most soldiers, he saw tall poles stuck into the earth, with both vertical and horizontal banners of diverse designs and colors—emerald, scarlet, orange, royal-blue, brown, black, and gold.

Some had characters painted on them. One had the *kanji* for *makoto* or sincerity. That and nothing more. Another had a long line of characters that Macneil stopped to decipher under General Saigo's amused gaze: "He who advances is sure of heaven, but he who retreats will suffer eternal damnation."

Some of the samurais wore elaborate heavy helmets, many of which were decorated with horns and long tufts of horse hair. Under the helmets were masks and visors so demonic and hideous Macneil caught himself recoiling from them in shock.

The peasant-soldiers protected their heads with a hat called a *jingasa*, made of heavy rope or lacquered wood or, in a few cases, metal.

Some more fortunate samurais were encased in ribbed armor of leather and iron—pieces of armor so expensive they were the first items of booty to be seized by the *Eta* or *Hinin* scavengers who filtered through the fallen dead after a battle.

As Saigo and Macneil walked along to the cheers and bows of the soldiers, the general pointed out to Macneil what fiefs they came from. "Those," he would say, "they're from Hizen, and those from Hyuga, and those over there from Igo."

It seemed no two military outfits were alike. Every man, whether peasant or samurai, dressed much as he pleased. Many had foreign blankets—some surely imported by Macneil's—draped over their shoulders like cloaks. Most wore tunics with sashes and their skirts tucked up under the sashes to permit easy leg movement.

None but the samurais carried two swords. Macneil saw three of the warriors with the famous *nodachi*, huge swords longer than the men carrying them. Mixed in with the samurais were a lower-ranked class of fighting men called the *ashigaru* or light-foots, who were permitted to wear one sword.

Many of the samurais and *ashigaru* carried bows and arrows. To extract an arrow from a quiver, the warrior removed a cap from the bottom and pulled the arrow out from below. The enclosed quiver protected the feathers from rain.

A samurai from Noto was writing on a piece of paper with *fude* and *sumi* ink.

"What's he doing?" Macneil asked.

"He has just written a *haiku*."

They stopped to watch.

Wrapping the poem around an arrow shaft, the samurai tied it in place with string, then shot it over the castle wall.

"He sent the enemy a poem?"

"A common practice," Saigo said. "Probably he wrote an original poem about children at play or about the moon rising over the mountains at home or the cries of geese flying south in the fall. Or he may have borrowed something from the *One Hundred Poems*."

"To what purpose?"

"To arouse *kyoshu*," Saigo said.

Macneil looked up the word in his small dictionary. It meant homesickness.

A glance at the sky showed rain clouds forming in the east. "I should have brought an umbrella or a cape," Macneil said.

"Never mind. I'll get an umbrella for you," Saigo said, snapping an order to a samurai following them.

"I notice, General, that you always carry an umbrella, even on sunny days."

"I use it in place of a *saihai*."

A *saihai* was a tasseled baton that Japanese commanders carried during battles as their symbols of authority. Sometimes these tassels, topped with feathers, were tied to the end of twenty-foot poles and stuck in the ground to show the location of a command post.

Occasionally, they passed a samurai dressed in especially elaborate armor. Pieces of metal and leather would be woven together with stout cords in vivid and dazzling colors and designs.

Chuckling, the general said, "He's just showing off. Armor like that protects the wearer no better than a suit like that one over there." With his umbrella he pointed to a grizzled campaigner encased in a rusty, colorless suit of ancient *yoroi*.

The two men walked along for another ten minutes, Saigo stopping now and then to pass out words of encouragement to his men.

Neil had been wondering about something.

"Isn't Lord Katamori Matsudaira married?" he asked Saigo. "What would his wife say about her husband having Anne as a concubine?"

"His *honsai*—what we call his legal wife—has always been in Edo. Another of the shogun's edicts. The wives and children of all the daimyos live in Edo the year around."

"Then the families are hostages?"

"Yes, they were, but as soon as Shogun Keiki Tokugawa abdicated, most of the wives and children of the daimyos left Edo for their native fiefs. Matsudaira's wife got here just before we completed the encirclement of the castle."

"So now she may know that her husband keeps a concubine?"

"She knows all right, but it would not be proper for a Japanese wife of any rank to ask questions about such matters."

That night an eerie chanting from within the castle walls kept Macneil awake. A chilly wind had risen from out of the west, giving a kind of instrumental accompaniment to the choral sounds inside the castle. Wrapped in a blanket, Macneil had been sleeping inside the cave beside the Gatling.

Feeling his way through the dark to the mouth of the cave, he asked the samurai on guard what the chanting meant.

Spitting in disgust, the man said, "It's the Buddhist service for the dead. They're trying to plant fear in our hearts."

As Macneil had just turned back into the cave, he heard a conch-shell trumpet being sounded on the castle wall. Although he couldn't see anything, he could hear a creaking sound.

Galvanized into movement, the samurai cried, "They're opening a gate!"

"*Okiro! Kogeki da zo!*" ("Get up! It's an attack!")

CHAPTER 67

Shouts of alarm, cursing, and the clatter of arms came from below. Macneil threw off the branches camouflaging the Gatling, and, with the samurai's aid, rolled the gun to the front of the cave.

In a moment, Saigo's men began to throw lighted torches far out into the open space in front of their breastworks. The flames provided just enough light for Macneil to make out dim figures rushing out from one of the gates. There were fifty or sixty of them, and they carried halberds—curved blades on poles about seven feet long—and the short swords called *kaiken*. When they realized they had been seen, they cried, "Take Saigo's head!" and "May the House of Tokugawa last ten thousand years!"

Their voices were oddly shrill and high-pitched.

Snatching up two magazines of canister shot for the Gatling, Macneil fitted them into the feeding mechanism and put rocks under the trail of the gun to lower the muzzle elevation. In the darkness he knew he would barely be able to see the front sight on the Gatling, but with eighteen pieces of round ball in each of the 3.75-inch-long cartridges, all Macneil had to do was point his weapon in the general direction of the raiders' sounds. He would leave the rest up to General Gatling.

Before Macneil could turn the crank to fire the first round, he remembered the location of the mines.

Judging from the direction of the sounds of charging enemy, he realized they would either run directly over the mine field or skirt dangerously close to it.

With that realization came another even more chilling. Suddenly, he knew why their battle cries were so high-pitched and why they were armed with *kaiken* and halberds—traditionally, female weapons in Japan.

The attackers were women.

Running to the front of the cave, Macneil shouted down at

the men below, "*Josei-gun da! Josei-gun da!*" ("It's a band of women!") "*Utsu na yo!*" ("Hold your fire!")

But before the words had left his mouth, Saigo's men were shooting at the attackers, who reached the mine field just as the first volley found the mark.

In the flashes of light from the exploding mines Macneil saw that the women wore white headbands and had their sleeves tied up for freedom of movement. With their long-bladed *naginata* or halberds held straight out in front of them, they came rushing forward with swiftness and magnificent determination.

Those among Saigo's men who could now see that the attackers were women stopped firing, though some farther off kept up an uneven crackle of rifle or musket fire. The volleys felled many of the women, but it was the land mines that did the greatest harm.

The mines had been laid out in rows parallel to the castle wall. Since the Aizu women were attacking in lines on the same parallel, twenty or more mines detonated almost simultaneously. The noise was deafening, the light flashes blinding. Macneil saw women—or pieces of women—catapulted high into the air, their halberds and *kaiken* and even their clothes being torn from them by the force of the exploding mines.

Catching fire from the flames of the explosions, some of their garments floated back to earth ablaze, illuminating the gory carnage even more. Macneil could see six women—two limping—retreating to the castle gate.

Miraculously untouched, four others came running on through the mine field shouting, "*Totsugeki!*" or "Charge!" When they reached the imperial entrenchments, the flashing swords of Saigo's samurais neatly severed the bladed heads of the *naginata* just below where the metal joined the wood, or knocked the short *kaiken* blades out of frailer hands.

A samurai who received a flesh wound was being treated by Dr. Jason Willits by the time Macneil got there. One of the attacking women had crumpled to the ground in a heap, sobbing convulsively. The other three sat in a circle, their arms on their knees, staring silently and stoically at the ground.

Wiping sleep from his large black eyes, General Saigo joined the soldiers standing around the four surviving women. It was two hours before dawn.

Sickened by what had happened, Macneil spoke to Saigo. "Why not send one of these women back inside to ask for a truce? Have her tell Lord Matsudaira we will remove the remaining mines so that his people can come out and collect the bodies."

"If we do that, Macneil-*san*," Saigo said, "it will only encourage Lord Matsudaira and General Kakekigo to use tricks like this time and time again. What would we do if they armed all the women in the castle and sent the whole lot of them charging out at the same time? If their officers gave the women better training in the use of the halberds, they might even overrun our lines."

Macneil knew that he could not afford to make Saigo lose face before his lieutenants. He bowed to the general, then took him off to one side. "I am sorry, Saigo-san, but the mines belong to me," he said. "I brought them here from Nagasaki and I supervised their placement. I'll find a better use for them elsewhere."

That apparently being satisfactory to the general, they returned to the captured women. One of them, dressed in a blue robe with her skirt tucked up under her sash, stood up and listened to Saigo's offer of a truce. When she spoke, her voice was bitter. "I will go back with your message. I know Lord Matsudaira will accept the truce, for he will want to come out with the burial party to collect the remains. Do we have General Saigo's word that the truce will be strictly observed until noon tomorrow?"

"I swear it," Saigo said.

"Why are you so sure that Matsudaira himself will come out to help collect the bodies?" Macneil asked her.

"It was his wife," she used the word honsai for legal wife, "who led our charge. She was the first to step on one of your explosives."

CHAPTER 68

Shortly after first light, Macneil and Thomas Sakamoto walked cautiously over to the mine field, carrying a white flag of truce, which they stuck upright at the edge of a plot littered with human parts. On the wall above the castle gate stood four Aizu officials waving their own white flag slowly back and forth to signal the beginning of the truce that was to last until noon.

Setting to work to dig up the remaining mines, Macneil and Sakamoto placed them in woven baskets for removal to the ammunition stockpile. Because of the danger, Macneil had not assigned the job to others.

"How many so far?" Neil asked.

Thomas counted. "Thirty-seven," he said.

"How many to go?"

"Six, I think."

"We'd better be damned sure."

"I'm sure."

Macneil's experience on the battlefield at Balaklava had showed him what artillery could do to human and animal bodies, but there the Russian shells seldom struck the British cavalry directly. Most of the injuries were inflicted by shrapnel from shells exploding ten or twenty or even thirty feet away from the horses and their riders.

Here the fighting women of Aizu had trod on the mines with their 2-1/2 pounds of gunpowder each. Instead of bodies tossed hither and yon with a shrapnel hole in the stomach or a foot blown half off or a face torn beyond recognition, these bodies had been blown into at least five or six parts. Pieces of unrecognizable flesh and bones covered an area about seventy by forty yards. Many were charred. Some had clinging to them scraps of fabric, and all were drained of blood and gray. Only the heads seemed to retain their integrity as parts of the human form, though the hair was often burned off and the facial features mutilated.

Macneil and Thomas walked back to their lines with the baskets of mines and signaled all clear to the Aizu officials waiting on the castle wall.

The massive gate creaked open and two Buddhist priests in black came out, with their heads lowered and their fingers entwined in their *juzu* beads.

Behind the priests marched a soldier carrying a white flag. Next in line came two dozen menials with woven baskets similar to those Macneil and Thomas had placed the unexploded mines in. Finally came Matsudaira himself, surrounded by a body-guard of samurais.

It was Macneil's first sight of the Lord of Aizu—the man he believed had kept Anne as his concubine for years.

Macneil started forward, but Thomas grabbed him from behind.

"Neil-*san*," Thomas grated in his ear. "The truce! Remember the truce. Saigo's men would cut you down before you could get near him."

The sight of Matsudaira nauseated him, but Macneil had to get a closer look at him.

Matsudaira was a man in his middle thirties, thin and short. His skin was dark for a Japanese, and his nose was hooked. He wore a blue and black *jimba-ori* tunic with the gold stars of the Ou clans emblazoned on it. On his head perched that ridiculous paper hat, shaped like a small loaf of black bread, that only a daimyo can wear. A string running under his chin held this odd contraption on the shaved top of his head.

When Matsudaira saw the tall American studying him, he stopped and stared back, perhaps because Macneil was a Westerner—or because he had learned from Osamu Ito that Anne's American fiance was hunting for her. Then he turned back to the task at hand, finding the remains of his legal wife.

Having already surveyed the mine field, Macneil knew the daimyo's task was hopeless. Unless she had had a large scar or a particularly noticeable birthmark on her body, her head was the only part of her that he might be able to recognize—and even that was far from certain.

At first, Matsudaira's pace was rapid, so that his attendants panted keeping up with him. He may have expected to find his wife's body in one or two easily recognizable parts, but the longer he strode about the field of gory carnage, the slower and more hesitant his steps became. Picking up a broken halberd, he used it to turn over this or that piece of bone or flesh, hoping, Macneil supposed, for a skin blemish he would know at sight.

When he had walked over half of the field of death, the daimyo stopped.

He must have ordered his attendants to pick up all the human debris, for that is what they began to do. Lord Matsudaira stood there for a long while, staring off toward Mount Bandai and Mount Itoya.

At length, he turned toward his enemies and looked directly at Macneil, across the thirty yards that separated the two. His dark face was devoid of expression. If he knew that Macneil was the fiance of his concubine as well as a Nagasaki arms merchant, he may well have reached the conclusion that the tall American was the man responsible for these new explosive devices. If so—and if he was a vengeful man of great cruelty like his dead ally, the Lord of Kuwana—it did not bode well for Anne that night.

Later, Macneil lay awake as his feverish imagination painted visions of Anne being beaten by merciless fiends in a dark chamber of the castle.

CHAPTER 69

The bombardment of the White Crane Castle began early the next day, with Macneil pulling the lanyard on a cannon to fire the first explosive shell.

It was a calm, clear morning. The early sun was eroding the mists on the slopes of the mountains around the town of Wakamatsu. The reds of the maples and the light greens of the bamboo were becoming brighter with each passing moment. The top of the castle keep had emerged into plain sight.

Higher overhead a flight of southbound geese broke apart at the roar of the cannon, but quickly came together again. Their honking was a faint echo of the Wiards that had opened fire at four castle gates on Macneil's signal.

The plan Macneil had worked out with General Saigo was straightforward. They had ten twelve-pounder Wiard field guns with 2,000 rounds of ammunition, half canister and half explosive. The canister would be used to ward off onslaughts by the Aizu forces; the explosive shells would be directed at the gates.

With sixteen gates to the castle and a thousand explosive rounds, they could, if they chose, fire a little over sixty rounds at each gate. Judging from the effect of the first round, Macneil figured sixty more would demolish a gate, even though it was constructed of massive planks of wood and reinforced by iron bars. How quickly the Aizu forces within the castle could repair a gate would depend on how much wood and iron and how many sandbags they had stockpiled nearby.

One of Saigo's lieutenants said, "We should bring up more field guns and concentrate on just one or two gates. That way, we can knock them down and be inside the castle in short order."

"If we do that," Saigo answered, "the defenders can charge out of the gates we have taken the Wiards away from."

"And if we concentrate our fire on only one or two," Macneil said, "General Kakekigo will know where our attack will come. He will then gather most of his 18,000 men to defend only those gates."

They compromised on four gates, and positioned the cannon so three gates would be bombarded by two Wiards simultaneously and one gate would be bombarded by three guns. One Wiard would be held in reserve.

Saigo had given Macneil the privilege of firing the first round. After that, the American climbed the rope ladder to the cave and made the Gatling ready.

Counter-charges might sally forth from the northwestern gates at any time. By the time he reached the cave and loaded the Gatling with canister magazines, the Wiard crews had already fired a dozen rounds each. Macneil could make out Thomas and Saigo hurrying from gun to gun, calling for greater speed in loading.

Deadly yellow tongues shot forth from the guns, with the crews dancing and spinning around the cannon like lust-maddened savages. Each shell knocked a hole in a gate. The weapons were so close to the gates that there were no misses after the first two or three rounds, but the stout portals had been built to withstand more than just one or two dozen shells.

The officers in charge of the gun crews did not stand behind their commands with the coolness Macneil remembered of Palmer St. James on the deck of *Mariner* in the *Wolodimir* fight or of Lord Cardigan as he led the Light Brigade toward the Russian guns at Balaklava. Instead, they bobbed about like whirling dervishes or storm-whipped banshees, roaring directions so loud Macneil could hear them from his considerable distance.

It was thirsty work. The water carriers, with one bucket at each end of a pole balanced on the shoulders, sped back and forth between the guns and the Yugawa River.

Over and over again came the commands of the officers in charge of the gun crews: "Stop your vents!—Sponge!—Load with explosive shell!—Ram!—Lock!—Ready?—Fire!"

In response, the field guns spewed forth their flashes of lightning. In the still morning air, the seething pall of smoke thickened over the field guns and moved away but slowly, partially concealing the gun crews from the Aizu defenders firing from the top of the walls and through the embrasures.

When each gun had fired fifty rounds, Saigo halted the barrage to give the crews a rest and to let the smoke clear away so he could assess the damage to the gates. The four gates had disintegrated into scattered rubble.

"Now!" Macneil shouted down to Saigo. "Attack! Attack!"

He ran to the rope ladder to descend the cliff and join the attacking force when through two of the gates came galloping the Aizu cavalry, followed by cheering foot soldiers: samurais, *goshi, ashigaru,* lance men, *nohei,* and grooms for the samurais' horses.

By the time Saigo's gun crew commanders got their weary

men back on their feet and started them loading their pieces with canister, it was too late to impede the attack. The mounted samurais came charging into the imperial lines with slashing swords and stabbing lances. Macneil saw Saigo sending runners to the rear, probably to call up his own cavalry reserves.

Then Saigo appeared to be trapped by the Aizu cavalry. Only a few of his personal bodyguards were left alive to defend him. From the neighboring gun crew, Thomas, seeing the danger to the field marshal, came running to help with lifted sword.

He and two Satsuma samurais reached Saigo's side at the same time and formed a ring of steel around him. The Aizu cavalry turned aside to seek easier targets.

By then, Macneil was behind his Gatling and sighting it at the hundreds of foot soldiers pouring through the castle gates.

CHAPTER 70

Aizu soldiers continued to stream from the two northwest gates.

Having already swept across the open field between Saigo's breastworks and the castle walls, the Aizu cavalry ranged back and forth behind the imperial lines slaughtering everything in its path.

Macneil turned the crank on the Gatling, testing the range. The showers of lead fell short of target.

"Raise the elevation screw," he ordered one of the Tosa men. Two others stood by the wheels to move the weapon laterally. A third crouched on the right by the canister magazines, with a fourth on the left ready to spring forward with magazines of solid shot when needed. The last man stationed himself near the mouth of the cave, but away from the ten rotating muzzles. His job was to fend off an attack if anyone from Aizu should climb to the ledge.

Macneil gave a crank a half-turn. This time he was right on target, the bullets striking in the very middle of the massed foot soldiers streaming across the field, cheering and shouting, toward the imperial lines.

"Here we go," Macneil said to himself. He turned the Gatling crank at the steady, not-too-fast rate that would produce the maximum output with the least chance of jamming. The solid blast of sound all but deafened the crew within the confines of the cave and left their ears ringing. The men at the wheels strained to move the Gatling a few inches back and forth following Macneil's signals. Those crouched to his right raised and lowered the elevation screw so the canister shots struck all over an area two hundred yards square.

The Aizu men fell with screams and groans, their bodies tossed about like bloodied toys.

At last from the north galloped General Saigo's reserve cavalry to grapple with the Aizu horsemen, relieving the pressure on the lines of imperial riflemen and permitting them to open a rapid, uneven crackle of musket and rifle fire on the Aizu infantry. This sudden volley drove the enemy back toward the gates.

The crews of the Wiard field guns had reformed and were adding their canister barrages to those of the Gatling.

Thomas appeared at Macneil's side. "Shall I relieve you?"

"Just for a minute or two."

Macneil leaned against the wall of the cave and tried to catch his breath. The battlefield between Saigo's lines and the castle was concealed by a thick pearly curtain of smoke, into which the imperial forces continued to pour volley after volley, whether they could detect living targets or not.

Behind them, Saigo's cavalry was pushing the horse-borne samurais of the enemy back to the north and away from the castle. It looked as if the emperor's forces would soon control the field.

To conserve precious ammunition, Macneil told Thomas to stop cranking the Gatling, and General Saigo ordered his riflemen to cease fire. They waited for the powder smoke to drift away. Like a stage curtain opening to the west, the haze of mist and smoke was drawn aside to reveal a ghastly spectacle.

As far as Macneil and Thomas could see, up and down the entrenchments below them, Saigo's soldiers stood or sat or staggered about in search of water. They were in shock and stunned by the field of unspeakable suffering and death before their eyes. The steady harsh rattle of the Gatling gun and the continuous rumble of the Wiards had been replaced by the prolonged, piercing shrieks of horses and the cries, moans, pleas and curses from the hundreds of Aizu wounded. It was a sea of anguish.

"Dear God in heaven," Macneil said to Thomas, who stood on the other side of the ten-barreled weapon. "Did we do that?"

"We did a lot of it," Thomas said in a low voice that might have been a prayer for forgiveness.

"General, I beg of you. Charge the castle now. Four gates are down. Judging from reports from around the perimeter, Aizu has lost forty percent of its forces in casualties. Their cavalry are being pushed back to the north."

Saigo stood in deep contemplative thought, his eyes fixed on distant Mount Myojindake with its early fall mantle of snow. He nodded to show he was listening.

Macneil pressed his case. "They're stunned by my Gatling and by the canister from the Wiards. There'll never be a better time. I'll lead the charge myself, if you will let me."

Saigo turned. "As I said before, Macneil-*san*, you would have made a good samurai." The field marshal used the tip of his umbrella to scratch Taki's back. The little dog wriggled in delight. "But," he said, turning his large black eyes full on the American, "there's a difference. You are a samurai of the European style, what we call a *kishi*. As a *kishi* or knight, you are ready to lay down your life for your loved one, the lady of your heart."

Macneil stared at Saigo. Thomas, who stood beside Neil, explained, "A Japanese samurai would seldom die for his sweetheart, Neil-*san*. For the sake of his sister or mother, yes, he might risk his life, but not for a sweetheart. That kind of romance weakens the samurai soul."

"The Japanese samurai," Saigo said, "thinks first of his lord and master, his daimyo, his emperor, his teacher, his *onjin*—one who has done significant favors for him. Do you see what I'm driving at?"

"I'm not sure."

"You are the European warrior who thinks only of love and devotion to your fiancée. I'm a Japanese samurai who must think first and always of his emperor. You want to attack quickly to save your sweetheart. I want to save the lives of as many of those men whom the emperor has entrusted to my care as I possibly can. I believe we can capture the castle with less loss of life if we wait a few days and wear them down."

"They'll reconstruct the gates, General," Macneil warned him.

"So let us not use any more of the explosive shells until the final assault. We will use only the canister rounds when Aizu charges us again—and I assure you they will. Hold your Gatling and its ammunition in reserve, too, for the final assault."

"And when will that be?" Macneil asked, "If the Lord of Aizu has connected me with Anne Macneil, he might be taking revenge on her even now."

"Soon," Saigo said. "The final assault will come sooner than you think."

He dismissed Macneil with a wave of his umbrella.

Macneil did insist that they offer Aizu another truce so the enemy could cart away their pitiable wounded from the field of battle. This was not an entirely unselfish act. The cries of the wounded throughout the first night after the battle, the beating of the drums to drive away evil spirits, and the chanting of Buddhist sutras for the dead unnerved Saigo's newly recruited peasant-soldiers. To worsen matters, Aizu continued its practice of fireworks displays off and on throughout the night, illuminating the contortions of the dying.

Saigo's veteran samurais occupied themselves with writing letters or drinking sake or burning incense in their helmets so that if they were decapitated on the morrow, the "stench of death" would not cling to their heads—heads that might be mounted somewhere on boards.

That night the temperature dropped far below normal for that time of year, adding greatly to the suffering of the hundreds of wounded. Early the next morning, as Macneil was choosing two Satsuma samurais to walk with him across the field to the castle with the second truce offer, he saw imperial soldiers urinating on their own hands. They did this, they said, to make their fingers warm and flexible. A few saved some of their urine to cauterize their wounds, though Dr. Jason Willits scoffed at the idea.

One samurai led the way with the white flag tied to a lance tip. Macneil was second in line, another samurai following him. They had to pick their way carefully. There was little open space among the wounded, some of whom still had the strength to thresh about in their agony or to raise an arm to show they still lived. Other wild-eyed wounded sobbed and gulped convulsively, opening and shutting their mouths like fish out of water.

Some of the dead were sawed in half at the waist, probably the work of the Gatling.

As the three truce bearers approached, General Kakekigo appeared on the walls. One of the Satsuma samurais spoke to him, offering a truce until noon so that he could collect his wounded.

In armor and wearing a helmet on which stood a single golden horn, like that of a unicorn, Kakekigo called down, "We don't have the facilities to care for them. If you wish to treat them, we will withhold our fire until noon to give you time to do so."

Macneil hurried back across the field, trying to ignore the hands outstretched for help. General Saigo was not pleased at the prospect of extending mercy to enemy wounded, but, at the American's insistence, finally agreed to let Dr. Willits go onto the field of battle with stretcher bearers and take those who might be saved to the row of hospital tents he had set up behind the imperial lines.

"But remember," Saigo warned Willits, "you are not to treat even one of the enemy until all my men have been cared for. Do you understand that, *kusushi*?" *Kusushi* was a older, slightly contemptuous word for doctor. Slowly it was being replaced by the more modern *isha*.

When Willits had collected seventy-eight of the Aizu wounded, he went back to his work among the imperial injured. With an hour of the truce remaining, Macneil walked along the row of tents, peering into each one.

In one of the tents, he came upon Jason Willits working with two assistants at a low table covered with an old *futon* so soaked with blood its original color could not be discerned. Beside him in a tray were his tools of amputation—knives, saws, tenacula, needles, waxed hemp ligatures, and artery forceps. On another stool were arrayed quinine, dressings, sutures, licorice powder, soap, castor oil, brandy, and three empty chloroform bottles.

Nearby, on a stool, a lacquerware bowl was filled with clear liquid. It held a dozen or so misshapen bits of lead. These were the bullets certain samurais had bitten down on when the doctors started to amputate. They refused anaesthesia, perhaps wanting to demonstrate their stoicism in the face of pain.

Eleven men, in various stages of consciousness, lay on the ground inside the tent, waiting for the doctor's services. Two of them seemed alert and kept calling to Dr. Willits and holding out their hands to him, urging him to accept whatever it was they held.

"They're offering me money," Willits explained. "It's the custom here. If you're wounded in battle, you have to pay for medical services. Otherwise, you don't get any."

"My God!"

"Saigo's against the system. He's trying to change it, but a lot of the Japanese military doctors still treat only those who can pay."

Macneil returned to the lines to wait for the attack Saigo had promised would come from the castle. The general was right. In the early afternoon, gates on all sides of the castle were pushed open, and out poured the Aizu infantry with renewed energy and hostility. Above their heads fluttered a multitude of flags like colorful birds.

This time Saigo's Wiard gun crews were ready for them. They poured volley after volley of canister—like murderous hornets—into the streams of Aizu warriors. As each gun belched forth its tongues of flame and reared back on its trail, the gun crew, working with berserk speed, sponged, loaded, rammed, locked, and fired again and again and again.

With each new blast of sound, clouds of cannon smoke materialized, and the gun crews became phantoms that whirled and danced in the haze.

Macneil worked with one of the crews, sighting the Wiard himself, for he had more experience with the weapon than any of the others. Above and behind him, inside the cave in the cliff, the Gatling stood silent, as he intended it should. He would use the rapid-fire weapon and what ammunition was left on the day of the final assault on the White Crane Castle, a day, Saigo had assured him, that would come "soon, very soon."

For the rest of that day and all during the next, the assaults on the imperial lines by the dwindling Aizu infantry continued. By counting the dead and wounded on the fields around the castle, Saigo's staff could calculate how weak the enemy had become.

They knew that Aizu was striving desperately to break through the imperial lines to open an escape avenue for their people, but the numerical superiority of Saigo's forces and the judicious placement of the field guns prevented that. The supply of canister shells for the Wiards, however, had been exhausted. The explosive shells left would barely be sufficient to knock aside the sand bags and other debris piled in the four gates the Wiards had opened up before.

At the end of the second day Takamori Saigo called his commanders together.

"Their force of effectives cannot number more than a few hundred now," he said. "Tomorrow we go in."

Macneil promised himself to be among the first through those gates.

"I'll give the field guns thirty minutes to clear away the obstructions in those four gates," Saigo said. He named the clans and their order of attack. Looking at Macneil, Thomas, and the other field gun commanders, he said, "Try to open up the gates with as few shells as possible. The enemy is certain to retreat to the castle keep, so we may have to batter part of it down to get at them."

Shock filled Macneil, for Saigo had said he would fire the cannon only at the walls and gates. It was the castle keep where Anne was most likely to be.

CHAPTER 71

Next morning, before the Wiards could begin clearing the four gates, another gate on the northwest side of the perimeter was pushed open. The band of soldiers that came charging out was so small in stature Macneil at first took them to be midgets, and wondered if Aizu used those small men as the *funa-kainin* of Amakusa did.

But when he studied them more closely through his telescope, he saw they were boys. Some may have been as young as ten. Certainly none was older than fifteen or sixteen. They wore the jackets and wide-legged trousers of samurai with white cloth headbands. Each held a *tachi* or long sword above or in front of him, and carried a short sword under his sash on the left. They came charging at the imperial lines, over the bodies of the Aizu dead and wounded, crying in shrill, immature voices, *"Kubo sama banzai!"* (May the daimyo live ten thousand years!)

Many among Saigo's troops burst out laughing until it occurred to them that if the nineteen boys whose leader waved a banner with the *kanji* for *Byakko-tai* or White Tiger Unit written on it reached the imperial lines, the slashes from their swords could be just as painful and deadly as those wielded by grown men.

When the youthful band had run to within twenty or so yards of the besiegers' entrenchments, Saigo's men began throwing rocks at them.

That slowed but did not stop the youngsters. Next, those imperial troops armed with lances turned their weapons around so the blunt ends faced outward. When the boys came within ten feet, the reversed lances stopped them and prevented them from pressing forward.

While holding the White Tigers at bay with their lances, Saigo's veterans began to chide them good-naturedly. "Your mother is calling you, sonny." "Time to change your diapers." "What kind of White Tigers are you? *Tora no hariko?"* (A toy tiger made of papier mache.) "Better hie yourselves home, boys. It looks like a storm is coming, and the thunder'll make you wet your pants."

Sure enough, it did begin to rain and thunder within a few minutes, further dampening the spirits of the young warriors. Their leader—the one with the flag—signaled them to follow him and led them to an open spot among the battlefield corpses, fifty yards from Saigo's lines. After a brief conference and much head nodding, all nineteen boys bared their torsos. Nine of them knelt on the ground and drew out their short swords.

When Saigo saw that, he jumped up in full view of the enemy and called out, "Stop that, you little fools! Think of your parents! Come over here, and you'll be well treated."

"What are they going to do?" Macneil asked Saigo.

"They're about to commit ritual *seppuku*."

"We ridiculed them, so they've lost face," Thomas explained to Macneil in a hushed voice.

Two of Saigo's men, both samurais from Hizen, leapt to their feet. "We'll stop them," they cried, but before they had taken ten paces, one suddenly grunted as if he had been struck in the stomach with a club. The other clutched his throat with a gurgling sound. Both fell mortally wounded by enemy rifle fire.

The ritual of *seppuku*—the two *kanji* for *hara-kiri* were read *seppuku* when reversed—proceeded, the boys paying not the least attention to their foes' pleas to desist.

Through his glass Macneil could see that the nine White Tigers now kneeling on the ground were saying something to their comrades, perhaps words of farewell. Each had his short sword in this right hand, poised over the left side of his bared abdomen. Behind each stood one of the other boys with a long sword raised over his head.

"Those with the long swords," Thomas said, "are the *kaishaku*, the ones who assist at *seppuku*. The stomach cut does not actually kill the man committing *seppuku*. Sometimes it's a mere scratch along the skin of the stomach. When the man about to die has brought the tip of the blade all the way across from left to right, whether the cut be deep or shallow, he will nod his head or lift a finger or somehow signal his *kaishaku* that he is ready. Then the *kaishaku* makes the fatal slash on the back of the neck with his long sword."

"Can't we stop them?" Macneil asked.

"Do you want to go out there and try?"

Macneil wanted to shut his eyes, but the ritual held a hypnotic fascination.

Four of the nine *kaishaku-nin* took two strokes each to sever the heads for which they were responsible. One had to make the downward slash three times. As before in Hong Kong, Macneil was amazed that blood spurted so far out from a headless torso.

Now ten were left. Five of these knelt, made the ritual cut

from left to right, and had their heads severed. Then two of the five knelt—and died.

At last, only one remained alive. He would have to make the stomach cut deep enough to drain away his own life, for he had no one to perform the rite of *kaishaku* for him.

From the walls of the castle rose wild cheers for this brave but tragic band.

Just then Saigo's little dog Taki—inspired by what, they could not figure out—jumped over the breastworks and ran to the side of the sole surviving member of the White Tiger Band, a boy of about thirteen. Standing on hind legs, with paws on the kneeling boy's shoulders, Taki began to lick his face.

CHAPTER 72

The boy was crying. Taki licked away his tears.

The cynical among Saigo's forces said the dog liked the taste of salt, while others said the general's pet was begging the youngster not to throw away his life.

Whatever the reason, the young White Tiger tossed aside his short sword, patted Taki on the head, and ran back to the castle gate.

Tail wagging, Taki watched him for a moment, then turned and trotted back to the imperial lines. He ran up to Saigo, and the general gave him a bite of something from within the deep sleeve of his jacket.

No sooner had the ritual suicides of the White Tiger unit ended than the castle gate closest to the river swung open. Through it came running, in a column of fours, the battalion of French officers and enlisted men. In blue uniforms and white kepis, they numbered about 120. Since the field gun crews had exhausted the canister and were under orders to reserve the explosive shells for clearing the gates, they had no choice but to fire at the fleeing French with rifles and muskets.

The French appearance had been so sudden and their flight so precipitous that they broke through Saigo's lines and reached the bank of the river before the general's attention had been called to them.

Tossing aside the pencil and sketching pad with which he had been drawing the *seppuku* rites of the White Tiger unit, Macneil ran around to the side of the cliff and scaled the rope ladder to where the Gatling stood waiting to deal out death. By the time he had the Gatling loaded, the Frenchmen had jumped into two of the large flat-bottomed river scows the emperor's army had been using to transport its supplies.

Under duress, the boatmen poled the scows out into midstream where they were caught in the current and began to make rapid progress downriver to the west and away from the castle.

Through his glass, Macneil had watched the soldiers shoulder each other aside in their desperation to board the scows. They all wore French uniforms, so there was no reason to believe that any Japanese were among them. Saigo was now aware of what was happening, so Macneil called down to ask what he wanted done.

Had the decision been his to make, Macneil would probably have let them go on their way unharmed, despite the fact that they had contributed to the training and formation of the shogun's army, and the French minister, M. Roches, had tried to frustrate American and British policies and interests, to say nothing of Russian and German, at every turn over the past few years.

"Shall we let them escape?' Macneil called down to Saigo.

"No, no!" the commander shouted back. "Open fire! Open fire! Use canister on the bastards!" He didn't actually say "bastards," which Macneil knew was a word—*shiseiji*—without pejorative meaning in Japanese. Instead, Saigo said *"kon-chikusho,"* meaning something like the worst kind of beast.

Macneil had already loaded the Gatling with solid shot, knowing these larger pellets would sink the scows. His Tosa crew, however, had also heard Saigo's orders and were replacing the solid shot magazines with canister by the time the American took up his position behind the gun.

The Yugawa River current being swift, the scows were nearing extreme range. Macneil had the muzzles elevated to ten degrees and fired a round from each barrel, then grabbed his telescope to see the effect. The canister pellets fell fifty yards short, spattering the surface of the river behind the scows like a sudden downpour of fat rain drops.

Panting, Thomas Sakamoto came running into the cave. "Let me crank it," he cried. "You watch and tell me when I'm on target."

The harsh, rattling reports of the Gatling filled the cave as the crew shifted the weapon about in accordance with Macneil's instructions. Calmly, Thomas kept up his slow, steady cranking of the gun.

The extreme range of the Gatling was 2,800 yards. In a minute or perhaps two, the scows would be out of range. For the moment, however, the canister shells were hitting dead on target, sloshing both scows from bow to stern. Already the men in the white neck-kepis were jumping overboard.

"Enough, Thomas," Macneil said at last. "We must save some of the canister."

By the time the American returned to Saigo's command post, the general had ordered the Wiards to open fire on the four gates through which his forces would enter the castle grounds. Ten rounds from each field gun cleared away the sand bags and other temporary obstructions.

The conch-shell trumpets sounded the charge. With wild

cheers, Saigo's clansmen climbed over their breastworks and sprinted, banners flying, toward those four gates. Macneil thought, *How I would love to hear the skirl of the pipes and see the Ladies from Hell among them!*

"Stay here with the Gatling," he told Thomas, "and watch for targets of opportunity." He ran to climb down the rope ladder and join the charge of the hundreds of imperial infantry into the castle. When he reached an open gate, he found Thomas running at his side. "I won't let you go in there alone," the Tosa samurai panted reproachfully.

Inside the castle walls, they could see none of the Aizu adherents. Only the imperial infantry, yelping like a pack of hounds, were running this way and that searching for foes to cut down or shoot.

The doors to the castle keep were only slightly less formidable than the castle gates themselves. Saigo had to order two of the Wiards pulled through the gates by ten panting men each and positioned to knock down the doors that were barred from within.

This took only a few minutes, and then the besiegers were on the bottom floor of the huge castle keep. Even as they shoved their way in, Macneil looked over his shoulder and saw that the muzzles of the two Wiard field guns had been elevated. They opened fire at the upper levels of the keep.

"Damn Saigo to hell!" he yelled at Thomas. "Anne may be up there!"

The bottom floor of the keep, with its spiral staircase in the center, was thronged with a milling mass of imperial soldiers and samurais. Some darted into rooms in search of the enemy. Neil and Thomas dashed for the stairs. The higher they climbed, the closer they came to where the shells from the Wiard field guns were exploding.

On the third level, Thomas warned, "We had better not go any higher yet."

"You search for Anne on this floor, Thomas," Macneil said, "I'll take the next one up."

Some of the rooms he shouldered his way into were empty. Other were filled with kneeling Aizu retainers, their heads bowed in resignation and their swords set aside in surrender. Macneil had no time for them.

On up to the fifth level he ran. He found fewer rooms bordering on the stairwell here, since each level shrank in size as it neared the top of the keep. The smoke and dust were heavy, indicating that some of the Wiard shells must have struck the outside walls, although he could see no interior damage.

As he rounded one corner at a dead run, he saw a samurai step cautiously from a room on the west side.

"*Kora!*" Macneil yelled at him. "Hey!"

Turning, the man saw Macneil and drew his sword. It was

Osamu Ito.

"You heathen fiend!" Macneil shouted. "You arrogant, ugly vermin!"

"So, it's the barbarian dog who seduced my sister."

"I know what you did to Anne Macneil," Macneil said. "I only wish I could kill you the way we killed the Lord of Kuwana."

Ito's face reflected shock for an instant, then became confident and arrogant again.

"You'd better forget about the Macneil slut. She's not worth the trouble."

"Then why did you keep her in your home in Edo for a month?"

"I kept her there long enough to get her pregnant, the way you got my sister pregnant in Nagasaki. She was very good on the *futon*."

"Where is she now?" Macneil spat at him, drawing his sword and *jitte*, a miniature pitchfork with a short handle.

"In there," Ito said, nodding toward the room he had just left. "One of your artillery shells scored a direct hit. Lord Matsudaira will be most unhappy to hear that she was killed by your cannon fire. He had a strange fondness for the wench that I could never understand."

"You bastard!" Macneil yelled in English, charging at Ito.

But Ito was the better swordsmen. With a fluting whistle of his long blade, he knocked the sword from Macneil's hand, then raised his sword again and came at him.

Macneil caught the sword between two of the tines of the *jitte* and twisted it out of Ito's hand.

Ito leapt back, turned, and ran up the next flight of stairs. In a rage, Macneil reached for the pistol in his holster and followed him.

On the top level Ito threw open a door, ran through the empty room and out a window onto the tiled roof. Macneil followed a few steps behind.

The angle of the roof was so steep Ito's upward progress was slowed. Shifting the pistol to his left hand, Macneil drew his short sword and slashed at his enemy's heel. The strained tendon made a faint popping sound when cut.

Dragging the foot behind him, Osamu Ito reached the ridge of the roof, straddled it and glared down at Macneil. The artillery barrage had started fires on the upper levels of the keep. The flames would soon reach them. Ito must have seen escape was impossible. Resignation was plain on his face as he watched the swift approach of the fire.

Macneil drew his .50 caliber Beaumont-Adams pistol, determined to exact revenge in full measure on his old enemy. Before he could take aim and fire, however, Ito pulled his short sword from his sash, placed its point in his mouth, and from a kneeling position fell forward into the flames. The hilt of the sword struck the roof first, driving the blade into the back of his throat. If the thrust of the weapon did not kill him, the fire did.

Watching, Neil nodded in grim satisfaction. He would have stayed longer, but smoke and flame belched from the upper windows of the keep. He ran back down to where he had first seen Ito and burst into the room the shogun's spymaster had vacated.

The room had been hit by an explosive shell and the outer wall knocked away. Broken masonry covered the floor. The air was filled with dust. Panting in fear and exhaustion, Macneil pulled aside some of the larger chunks of broken masonry.

Maybe Ito lied. Maybe Anne isn't here at all, Macneil thought. *I'll find Thomas, and we will search all the other rooms.*

But wait. A human hand was visible under the debris in one corner of the room. A white delicate hand. Was it Anne?

"Anne? Anne?" Macneil cried, throwing himself on the *tatami* beside the pile of debris. In fifteen seconds he had it pulled off her body. He turned her over.

It was Anne!

"Thank you, dear God," Macneil breathed as he gently brushed the dirt from her face.

But Anne was bleeding from a head wound and Macneil could detect no sign of breathing.

Her face was as pale as death.

CHAPTER 73

Anne's heart beat faintly but steadily. Neil chafed her wrists and bathed her cheeks and forehead with water, but she did not respond.

Carefully, he felt for broken bones and found none. He opened her blue and white *yukata* robe, too light a garment for the early autumn chill in this mountain valley, to look for wounds. He found no cuts, contusions, or blood, though he saw plentiful evidence of past injuries. The gash in Anne's head appeared to be the cause of her unconsciousness, but the explosion of the shell might have caused internal harm as well. With her robe open, she was naked, revealing the beautiful body Neil had seen so often in his dreams.

Lifting her over his shoulder, Macneil started down the stairs of the keep, looking for Thomas. Some Aizu retainers had surrendered and were walking docilely down the stairs. Others resisted in groups of twos and threes. Thomas confronted two of these on the third level. They had him backed up against a wall and were attacking from two directions.

With Anne unconscious and perhaps more seriously injured than Macneil thought, this was no time for demands for surrender. Wrenching the .50-caliber Beaumont-Adams pistol from its holster, he shot the pair in the back.

"Thomas," Neil cried, "lead the way! Get us to Jason Willits fast!"

Using his sword where necessary, Thomas shoved aside ally and foe alike as he made a path for the two Macneils down the stairs and out into the castle yard. The imperial soldiers caught sight of Macneil and Sakamoto, and knowing the role played by the Gatling gun and the Wiards, they set up a cheer as Thomas led the way through the castle gate.

Jason Willits and the other surgeons were hard at work in the medical tents, though Saigo's losses had not been so heavy that day.

"Jason," Macneil cried. "I've found her! Here she is. This is Anne Macneil. She's hurt."

Willits took Anne's pulse, looked under her eyelids, listened to her heart, and examined the gash on her head, which was behind an ear and not far from the scar like the one Magaret had.

"Maybe a mild concussion," the doctor said. "She needs rest and cold compresses on her wound. I see the bleeding has almost stopped. Handle her gently, but get her out of here. Now you'll have to excuse me, my friend. I've got men dying here."

"Thomas," Macneil said, "send one of your Tosa men into Wakamatsu and hire two palanquins. The kind with curtains, you know the ones I mean. Put Anne in one, you ride in the other. Take four of your samurais from Tosa as guards and get away from here. Fast!"

"There are hot springs in Yumoto," Thomas said, "maybe two or three hours by palanquin from here if I hire four bearers instead of two for each *norimono*. It's quiet there, and the mineral waters are recuperative."

"Where would you stay in Yumoto?"

"We can stay in the *honjin*, now that the Tokugawas have been overthrown. It will be an ordinary inn now."

"Go, then. If there is a doctor in Yumoto, have him stay with Anne. Hire him for full-time duty. I want someone next to her day and night."

"When will you come?"

"Tomorrow. I can't leave here until Saigo tells me he doesn't need me any more. And I want to see what Saigo does to Lord Matsudaira."

General Takamori Saigo used the castle keep as a prisoner pen for the 912 Aizu retainers, all that survived of the 18,000 stationed within those walls when the imperial army laid siege to the castle. The others were dead or wounded, or had escaped.

Next morning, Saigo and Macneil walked through the castle yard. Some prisoners sucked in their breath and bowed as they passed; others glared at them with hostility. Most of the officers in their surcoats of bright colors and helmets with waist-long wisps of black or white hair ignored the passing victors.

At mid-morning Saigo convened a court martial to decide what to do with the captured Aizu leaders. The emperor had given him *carte blanche* to punish them however he saw fit, with the exception of Lord Matsudaira himself.

Saigo and his lieutenants sat crosslegged in a semicircle on rice-straw mats, in the open behind the unmanned entrenchments. The morning was chilly but sunny. Macneil composed himself well behind the general and off to his left. He would have no part in these proceedings, except as an observer.

Saigo did not bother with the Aizu enlisted soldiers or the

lower-ranking officers. Someone had prepared a list for him of those men, military and civilian, who had been the most active in their opposition to the restoration of the emperor. The rolled list was long. Half the names on it were even now in the prisoner pens.

As each prisoner was brought forth, hands bound behind him, the general referred to his list and conferred briefly with one or another of his lieutenants, some of whom were daimyos, others high-ranking samurais from the fiefs supporting the imperial cause.

He asked few questions of the prisoners, and his sentences were brief and delivered without emotion.

While waiting to hear what would happen to Lord Katamori Matsudaira, Macneil listened aghast to the punishments handed down by General Takamori Saigo of Satsuma, but harsh though they were, he knew most of the men who bowed before Saigo's black, brilliant eyes had practiced inhumanity on an even larger scale.

Almost all the officers of the League of the United Clans of Ou army were condemned to death, the only variation being the manner in which they were to die. Most were sentenced to be beheaded and have their heads salted, their hair oiled, and their cheeks rouged, then their heads displayed on stakes or boards for sixty days. About ten percent were crucified upside down, so that the escaping body wastes would flow down over their chest and faces. A few were sentenced to five or ten years imprisonment, after which they were to be decapitated.

Lord Katamori Matsudaira's younger brother was sent into exile on Sado island, where Macneil's young son Ichiro Ito was said to be hidden.

Macneil hoped Katamori himself would now appear, but next on the court martial list was General Kakekigo, the commander-in-chief of all the forces of the Ou League of United Clans. Macneil had heard him called an intelligent and brave soldier.

General Kakekigo was kneeling on a tatami mat with two Aizu samurai behind him. He wore full armor but without a helmet. His hands were encased in heavy gloves with pointed steel talons on the fingertips.

Saigo knelt, then bowed.

Kakekigo returned the bow.

"Saigo-*kun*," Kakekigo said in greeting. With the -*kun* suggesting much familiarity, Macneil sensed that, since the two generals did not come from the same clan, they must have served together in Kyoto or Edo at an earlier time. "It's been a long time."

"I would much rather be drinking sake with you in a Kyoto *izakaya* than doing what I'm about to do, Kakekigo-*kun*."

"I'm certain you will do your duty. You always have."

"Your men fought well," Saigo said. "Except the French."

"I would like to ask you to spare Lord Matsudaira."

"I have just sent his younger brother into exile, on Sado."

"I know.

"Where is Katamori Matsudaira himself?"

"You don't know?"

"No."

"Neither do I."

"Are you sure?"

"Would I lie to you?"

"No."

"What can I do to get you to spare his life?"

"Does his life mean that much to you?"

"He's a good man." Kakekigo looked off at the mountain in the west. "He was on the wrong side in this war, that's all."

"The emperor may want him beheaded."

General Kakekigo bowed again. "What can I do to save him from that?"

"Are you offering me a gift, a bribe? That doesn't sound like you."

"I'm not offering you money or women. I know they mean nothing to a man like you, but I would accept any punishment you mete out to me."

"You'll have to do that anyway."

"Isn't there something I can do to make such a strong impression that you will be more lenient in dealing with my lord and master?"

"Is he such a fine man?" Saigo asked.

"He has many virtues."

"He must have, if you revere him so much."

"He is my master, Saigo-kun. You know the code better than I. Even if he thinks nothing of my existence, I must live for him. I must die for him. His knowledge or appreciation of what I do for him means nothing. All that matters is that I live and die for him. Each minute he continues to exist, I take delight in knowing of that existence. That is bushido, Saigo-kun. You know our samurai code. You—of all men—know it."

"In your case and the others, I'm the one who decides the sentences," Saigo said. "But in the case of your daimyo it's the emperor who will decide."

"Your voice will carry much weight."

"It will carry some weight. Maybe."

"Then tell the emperor what I do to convince you of my sincerity," the enemy general said. "Say I beg of him to...."

"Just what is it you will do?"

"This."

Kakekigo thrust the steel fingertips of his gloves into the inner corners of his eyes and with an effort plucked out both his eyeballs. He dropped the bloody orbs in the dirt in front of Saigo.

For a moment Saigo contemplated the brilliant fall colors in the surrounding hills. Then he said, "I will report to the emperor what you have done."

Kakekigo bowed in silent appreciation.

"As for your punishment," Saigo said, "I sentence you to be blinded."

CHAPTER 74

From Aizu to the Yumoto Hot Springs

Since no one knew the whereabouts of Lord Katamori Matsudaira, Macneil got General Saigo's permission to leave Aizu. He rode to the Yumoto hot springs on a borrowed cavalry horse.

Above Yumoto, on the hillsides of its valley, the dark blue-green of the pines served as backdrop to the delicious tints of autumn. On the lower hills, a dozen massive cryptomeria, so like the redwoods of Macneil's Oregon, stood guard around a Shinto shrine where the ardent believer must prove the depth of his devotion by climbing hundreds of stone stairs to reach the place of worship.

Macneil found the Yumoto *honjin* or inn on the main road going through the small town. Macneil went to Thomas Sakamoto's room and found him having dinner alone.

"How is Anne?" Macneil asked.

"She's up and about," Thomas said, putting aside his chopsticks and rice bowl. "Probably taking her evening bath."

"Is the doctor with her?"

"I sent him away. He said there's nothing wrong with her now, except a slight headache."

"Thank God for that. Does she know what has happened?"

"She knows nothing. She was shut up in that castle room for several days before our final attack."

"Does she know where Lord Matsudaira is?"

"No," Thomas said, resuming his meal.

"Who did you say you were?"

"I told her my name and where I come from. I said I had gone to Aizu to help free her from captivity."

"How did she react to that?"

"She shed tears."

"Was my name mentioned?"

"No. I said only that someone would come here today or tomorrow to explain everything to her."

"What kind of mood is she in?"

"She seems in good spirits and healthy enough, except for the gash on her head. It's not deep. The doctor said he would come back tomorrow and again the day after to change the bandage."

"Did you speak to her in Japanese?"

"Yes. She speaks Japanese very well. She doesn't know as many technical words or business terms as you do, but her pronunciation is better than yours, and she knows a lot of literary or poetic Japanese. Since she parted from your sister in Kuwana, she has had no one with whom to speak her native tongue."

The two men sat looking at each other for a moment.

"Well, aren't you going up to see Anne?" the samurai asked.

"I'm nervous, Thomas. I've searched so long for her that I can't just walk into her room and say something like, 'Well, here I am.' Maybe you should go up and prepare her."

Rising, the big samurai walked around the table and yanked Macneil to his feet. "Stop acting like a child," he said, "and get yourself up there."

At the foot of the stairs, Thomas nodded to the armed guard looking down from above. The guard led Macneil down the corridor to a room where he bowed and slid open the door. The inner door opened quietly, revealing a kneeling maid.

"This man can enter," the guard said to the young woman. "You may go downstairs now."

Removing his corridor slippers, Macneil stepped up into the inner room and closed the door behind him. He removed his sword, pistol and jacket. The room was empty.

On his left were the entrances to the bath and the toilet. The door of the bath was ajar, and Macneil knew from the darkness within that Anne had finished her bath. In the center of the room where he stood was a low table with three cushions surrounding it on the reed matting. An *andon* burned dimly on the right. Beyond it another sliding door suggested one more room.

Crossing the *tatami*, Macneil stood for a moment in front of that door, knowing that when he opened it, he would find Anne Macneil. His legs grew weak. The blood pulsed in his temples. His breath quickened. His heart beat like thunderclaps.

Touching the door, he started to push it open. It stuck. The woman within must have heard the faint sound.

"*Tsuchie-san? Ocha wo moraitai wa.*" She was telling her maid Tsuchie she wanted a cup of tea. Thomas was right. Her Japanese had a native quality to it. Macneil knew the woman inside had to be Anne, but he could not have sworn that he recognized her voice.

He pushed the door open.

CHAPTER 75

Yumoto Hot Springs

A woman was sitting on a *futon* with her back to the door, brushing her thick, deep-gold hair. A bean-shell pillow lay at the head of the *futon*. Just beyond it were a night lamp and a tobacco tray. The upper *futon* lay rumpled at the foot.

She was dressed in a short, light-blue *nemaki* or sleeping gown with a pink sash. Charcoal glowing in a brazier at one side took the chill from the autumn evening air.

"*Shibaraku desu,*" Macneil said. "It's been a long time."

In fright, she twisted toward him. Her loosely worn *nemaki* pulled open, partly revealing her breasts and thighs. The hand holding her hairbrush remained suspended halfway between her head and shoulder. Her brown-green eyes were wide open in surprise.

Closing the door behind him, Macneil knelt on the *tatami* to show he had not come to harm her.

Her beauty amazed him.

Her eyes narrowed and she leaned forward and peered at him. "*Anata...dare desho?*" She asked who he was.

On his knees, Macneil bowed low in the proper Japanese fashion and said formally, "*Macneil to mosu mono de gozaimasu.*" Literally, "I am he who is called Macneil."

Then she knew. In her eyes, recognition dawned, more joyous than birdsong in spring.

"Neil? Neil? *My* Neil?" Her English words were like the sudden frightened cries of a bird in the forest. "But no, you can't be. Neil Macneil? Are you? Oh God, are you really? No, I don't believe it."

Rolling off the *futon*, she crawled to him on her hands and knees.

"Let me see your face! Neil? Here? But how? Oh, Neil, Neil!"

Pulling her into his arms, Neil said softly in her ear, "Anne, dearest. Calm yourself. I've been looking for you all this time."

His voice choked with emotion. "Darling, I've found you. I've come to take you away."

CHAPTER 76

When Neil Macneil joined his cousin Anne at the hot springs of Yumoto, he was not without carnal experience, despite the vow he had made to her so long ago in Fort George.

Even so, Neil quickly realized Anne was the master of this game with a variety and scope of experience far exceeding his own. Once their initial bewilderment, and something akin to embarrassment on his part, had worn thin, they plunged into what is best described as an orgy.

For the first three days they simply dissolved into each other. They tolerated few interruptions. The *honjin* maids, led by Tsuchie, brought trays of food which were left on the table in the outer of the two rooms and as often as not taken away untouched. The local doctor came twice, but the amorous couple let him in only once. Changing the bandage on Anne's head, he declared his satisfaction with the progress of the healing of her wound but warned her, with a sharp glance at Neil, against "extreme exertions."

With the autumn days becoming colder, Neil and Anne found the hot springs bath attached to their room to be the most comfortable place in the *honjin*. They passed two or three hours in it every day, but in no way did this prevent them from continuing what they had been doing with considerable enthusiasm between the *futon*.

For much of the first half of the week there, they talked little, except for murmurs of elation and incoherent cries.

Exhausted though he was, Neil often could not sleep for congratulating himself on his good fortune. With Anne nestled in his arms, he would lie awake thanking God that his Macneil stubbornness had made him persevere in the quest. He marveled at events leading to her discovery and shuddered when he thought how close to death she had come at the siege of the White Crane Castle. He smiled when he thought of the good years ahead, with Anne as mistress of his new residence in

Nagasaki and with the Macneil Brothers' business interests prospering and spreading throughout the world.

At such times, Neil would kiss Anne gently on the cheek, then fall asleep until one of them awakened with renewed desire for the other.

The years had added maturity but had not aged Anne. There were as yet no wrinkles in the corners of her eyes, but in the eyes themselves Neil glimpsed at times the kind of mature understanding and resignation that come from sorrow, pain and humiliation. There was also—he could not deny it, though he wished he could—a modicum of calculating, determined toughness, which he took pains to remind himself should be expected, considering her tribulations.

One morning, while they were closely entwined, Neil chanced to glance at Anne's face through half-lidded eyes. It was just at the moment of the ultimate pleasure, and he could have taken an oath that her eyes, which had been fixed on the space above, crossed for a moment.

In the paroxysms of passion, her body became a wondrously active and even contortionistic instrument of heaving breasts, corrugating stomach muscles, and vaginal clutching, as her eyes grew darker and swam awry with desire.

When they at last fell apart, he would prop his head on the bean-husk pillow, turn toward her and study the clean, elegant structure of her face. With Anne's eyes closed, hair falling in disarray over her face and mouth slack with spent desire, her body would continue to shudder for so long Neil wondered if the long-held tradition about the lustiness of the Barra Macneils had not been perpetuated by its women rather than its men. Anne's appetite for coupling seemed never to be quite satisfied.

Neil found her in possession of a vast Japanese vocabulary of picturesque words describing the private parts and their functions, in which she instructed her cousin as if he were a kindergarten pupil. She called her own genitalia such names as the Roaring Furnace, Vale of Delight and Cradle of Eternity. What Palmer St. James had once referred to as his "John Thomas," she named the Pillar of Pleasure, Great Divider or Pulsing Charger. Neil could not help wondering which of her many samurai and daimyo lovers had taught her such terms.

She knew only too well the standard forty-eight positions of the love art in Japan and demonstrated most of them to Neil. Her favorite was one in which, with Neil standing, she climbed him with the natural fluid grace of a healthy animal and circled his waist with her legs and his neck with her arms. This position, she explained, was called the Wailing Monkey Clasping a Tree.

During their days together, he told Anne he loved her many times. But Anne never said she loved him. Finally, miffed by those one-sided professions of love, Neil asked her, "Do you love me, Anne?"

"Do I love you?" she repeated slowly.

Then she came to life and answered with conviction. "Of course, Neil. Of course, I do."

"You haven't told me so."

"I suppose it's because men and women don't talk about being in love in my...in this country."

Had she started to say "*my* country?"

Another matter that puzzled Macneil was why Anne used the *sakura-gami* or cherry-paper as a contraceptive. He regarded their stay in Yumoto as a honeymoon of sorts, one they were taking before completing the legal niceties of wedlock. He certainly wanted Anne to bear his children.

"Aren't we going to have children, Anne?"

"Children, Neil?" she asked as if a totally strange concept had been offered for her inspection.

Then her eyes cleared, and she took both his hands in hers. "Listen, Neil. I must tell you this. I have children already. Two children."

Neil remembered what Osamu Ito had said before he died.

"Who are the fathers?" he asked.

"Fathers? Why do you assume one man did not sire them both?"

"I don't know. Who is the father?"

"Lord Katamori Matsudaira of Aizu, my master, is the father of both, one boy and one girl," she said. "Oh, Neil! They're such adorable children. I love them so much."

"You called Matsudaira your master. You're free of him now."

"A slip of the tongue, since he's dead."

"How do you know that?"

This startled her. "You mean he may not be dead?"

"We don't know. We haven't found his body."

"I was so sure he would be killed. He often swore he would seek death rather than surrender."

"The odds are against his being alive," Neil said, "But we do know his wife is dead."

"The Lady Matsudaira?"

"Yes."

"Are you sure?"

"She led a band of women warriors against our lines early in the siege. She was blown to pieces by a land mine."

Anne said nothing for a long time but sat sipping sake from the tiny cup Neil kept filled for her. She looked off at the hills behind Yumoto, where the first snow—the *hatsu-yuki*—would soon fall, as it already had around Aizu.

At last, she turned her sake cup upside down, indicating she wanted no more.

"Anne, darling, I know how he must have mistreated you," Neil said. "The scars on your body are proof enough. If

Matsudaira isn't dead, I'll find him and cause him as much pain as he caused you."

In sudden anger, she turned on him. "No, Neil, I couldn't permit you to do that. He was the father of my children."

"Where are the children?"

"Lord Matsudaira sent them to stay with relatives in Aizu."

"Don't you want more children?"

"Yes, I do. I've been using the *sakura-gami* mostly from force of habit, I suppose."

CHAPTER 77

Though Anne was at times almost insatiable, the couple had to take time out to eat, sleep, bathe and talk.

At first, the conversation was halting, as it sometimes is when one has hundreds of things to say and doesn't know in which order to arrange them. In relating to her what had happened to him over the years, Neil tried to speak first about what was most important—the rescue and death of Margaret, the death of Anne's father in Hong Kong, her ownership of sixty percent of Macneil Brothers' shares, and the grisly death of the Lord of Kuwana at the hands of the *funa-kainin* dwarf.

Later on, the words began to flow faster. Starting at the beginning, Neil told her the entire story in minute detail. He omitted only his cohabitation with Tomi and the fact that he had sired a son with the woman who became wife of the shogun.

Anne interspersed Neil's story with hers, starting with the storm and their coming ashore in Japan, then being captured by bandits and sold to the Lord of Kuwana. Having read that part of her diary, Neil knew much of what had happened to her and his sister in the castle of that daimyo, but he saw no reason to tell her he had invaded her privacy: at least, not yet. Anne told him about her mistreatment in detail but omitted any mention of having lovers other than the Lord of Kuwana himself.

When Kuwana could no longer keep her, she was sent to Edo, where she spent several weeks in the residence of a high official named Ito. After that, she was taken to Aizu where she passed the remaining years of her captivity as the concubine of Lord Katamori Matsudaira, whose wife was in Edo as a hostage of the shogun, even though Matsudaira was one of his most loyal supporters.

In the early afternoon of the sixth day, they received a visitor.

CHAPTER 78

Macneil knew it was the doctor Jason Willits who had come to see them. No one else could have caused the *honjin* stairs to groan and protest so loudly at the unaccustomed load.

Willits slid open the inner door and lumbered across the room to Anne, enfolded her in his arms, and kissed her on the forehead.

"I'm Jason Willits, my dear. I tended to your wound in Wakamatsu, though you won't remember it.

"Watch out, Anne," Neil said. "Jason Willits is known from here to Singapore as the Scourge of the Orient—thanks to his lascivious inclinations toward young maidens."

"Why don't you do something useful," Willits said to Neil, "and order up an *issho* of the innkeeper's best sake. I've been riding bent double in one of those accursed palanquins for hours, and I'm thirsty enough to drink ditch water."

"You came here in a sedan chair?" Neil asked. "Saigo only had 40,000 men at his disposal. Where did he find the rest of the porters needed to carry you?"

"Pay him no heed, my dear," Jason said to Anne. "He's merely jealous because I have my hands on you. Now, my dear girl, I want you to lower your robe."

"We all have our particular sins to struggle against," Neil said, "and I suspect yours, Jason, is lechery."

"If this will embarrass you, Macneil, you're free to step into the corridor for several hours. And you, young woman," he said to Anne, slapping her lightly on the rear, "get a move on. I must press on to Edo tonight."

Anne lowered her light-blue *nemaki* to her waist.

"By Old Nick, she does have perfectly splendid breasts, doesn't she?" Willits said. "Speaking strictly as a medical practitioner, of course."

Macneil thought Willits' examination took twice as long as necessary, but in a sense he was glad the doctor was examining her with such care.

"All these scars," the doctor said. "What caused them?"

"Whips and the flat sides of swords—as well as the wounds I got when I was thrown against boulders in the surf."

"They're all old."

"Yes, nothing like that has been done to me in a long while."

"Thank God for that," said Jason, lifting Anne's *nemaki*. "Whoever did all that should be given severe punishment."

"He was killed," Macneil said grimly.

"Obviously then, it was not Lord Katamori Matsudaira, since he is alive, though not exactly well."

Anne's eyes widened, and she turned her face toward the window.

CHAPTER 79

Jason and Neil sat crosslegged—a position that brought forth groans of discomfort from the doctor—at the low table and poured each other thimblefuls of hot sake from the heated *tokkuri* bottle Tsuchie had brought. The *tokkuri* was a porcelain bottle, containing something less than a pint, which was immersed in boiling water to heat the sake.

Anne did not join them but sat at a low table next to the window and looked silently at the mountains west of Yumoto.

After another *tokkuri*, Jason Willits asked, "Why so pensive, my dear? Aren't you feeling well?"

"I was thinking of a poem," Anne said.

"May I ask which one?"

"I was wondering which of several *tanka* best describes those hills in their autumn foliage."

"Ah, then you're a devotee of Japanese poetry."

"Yes, indeed. Are you?"

"I fear I don't know enough written Japanese to truly appreciate the form. Are you well versed?"

"For nearly two years of my captivity, the only book I was permitted to have was a collection of old poems—*tanka*."

"The trick here, old boy," Jason said to Neil, "is not to drink from these infernally small cups but from the *tokkuri* itself."

"Tell me about Matsudaira," Macneil said.

"It seems he donned a French uniform and escaped with the French battalion from the castle. The Frenchies formed a protective cordon around him."

"Go on."

"But their cordon did no good when your canister shells from the Gatling began to slosh down on the river scows. He was struck twice. The boatmen had been killed or had jumped overboard, so the scows drifted out of control down the Yugawa River to where it flows into the Agano and on to the town of Gosen.

"Luckily for Matsudaira, the French had their own doctor with them, and a good one at that. I know him by reputation. He kept the daimyo alive until the scows tied up down river at Gosen."

"How bad were his wounds?" Neil asked.

"Bad enough. He lost a hand and a leg. The wound that cost him his leg struck high on the thigh, quite near the groin."

"I wonder if he'll be executed," Macneil said.

"It's being rumored he won't be. Some say he may even be set free."

"Because of what General Kakekigo did?"

"That may have helped, but also the Matsudaira clan has many branches and members with close ties to the imperial house. Also, I suspect that if he were put to death, diehards in Aizu would flee north to Hokkaido to continue the struggle against the emperor. In exchange for amnesty, their emperor could demand allegiance from Matsudaira and the entire clan."

Anne arose and walked into the bath.

She remained there for an inordinately long time. When at last dinner was served, Neil had to call her to come out. By then, Neil and Jason were two sheets to the wind, and in that state they entertained Anne through dinner with tales of strange adventures and marvelous sights from the past. She listened and smiled and laughed at the right times, but was more subdued than before.

After the doctor had gone, Neil was ready for bed, but Anne poured Neil a cup of lukewarm sake.

"Do you have influence with the emperor, Neil?" she asked.

"Only through General Saigo. Why?"

"Nothing."

"If there's anything you need."

"No, nothing. Really."

"Anne, dear, I want to make plans. About you and me. I want us to take up residence in my new house in Nagasaki right away. We can be married when we get there. I don't know whether the Aizu clan would turn your children over to you, but I could ask. Saigo might help."

Anne looked at him in silence. She had a seeing, yet unseeing look in her eyes.

"Neil, why can't we live in Edo? It's the capital, isn't it? It's where everything will be happening."

"Not quite everything. For one thing, Macneil Brothers doesn't have an office there."

"Couldn't you establish one?" she asked.

"I was thinking of opening one in Yokohama next."

"I would prefer Edo," Anne said.

"Anne, listen," Neil began. "Maybe in ten years we could open—"

"You did say I now own sixty percent of the hong shares

and your father the rest, didn't you?"

"Yes, but—"

"Neil, I'm going to make myself taipan of the hong and set up our main office in Edo. I can do that, can't I?"

"My father is taipan."

"I'll give him an honorary position."

Neil changed to a sleeping gown and retired to his *futon*.

Anne stayed up until Tsuchie-*san* entered to close the shutters for the night.

CHAPTER 80

For the whole of the following day, neither Neil nor Anne made reference to their disagreement, but their lovemaking was a shade less ardent, a trifle less prolonged than before.

When resting from their labors, Anne interrogated Neil about the business of the hong, asking dozens of questions.

"How did the hong get into the business of selling weapons?"

Neil told her, and said, "I thought you would be dismayed. Most women are."

"Not at all. I find arms fascinating. You must show me how to fire some of them. How about opium?"

"We no longer handle it."

"Why not?"

"My father is opposed. He says it steals men's souls."

"It seems your father is another of those people who want to shoulder the burdens of mankind and be his brother's keeper."

Next morning, while Anne was still asleep, Neil heard the rising sounds of shouts and marching feet and hooves from the street in front of the *honjin*. He hurried down the stairs to the entranceway to investigate.

A hundred or more armed men, mostly samurais, were moving south past the inn. Macneil recognized Takamori Saigo's personal standard at the head of the column.

The general himself marched in the rear. Macneil had expected this. Japanese horses, like Hana, were scrawny little beasts, and Saigo had said he had an aversion to burdening one of them with his weight, especially over long distances.

When he saw Macneil, he walked over to him, letting his bodyguard go on ahead.

"I detoured through Yumoto to give you something," he said, withdrawing a folded piece of paper from the pocket in the sleeve of his tunic.

Macneil unfolded the paper. On it were written several lines of Japanese.

"We intercepted it just before I left Aizu," Saigo said. "We made the messenger confess he had been told to deliver it secretly to Lord Matsudaira."

"Where is the daimyo?"

"He's still in the town of Gosen. The messenger intended to deliver the message to the lord's family in Aizu and ask them to get it to Matsudaira somehow."

Puzzled, Macneil studied the Japanese characters on the paper. After a moment, he returned it to Saigo. "My written Japanese isn't good enough. What does it say?"

The general read, "*Ima wa tada omoi-taenamu tobakari wo hitozute nara de iu yoshi mo gana.*"

Macneil laughed. "I still understand only three or four words. It must be written in the old literary language."

Saigo nodded. "It's a poem written about 800 years ago."

"Anyway, why should it concern me?"

"This message was written by your woman."

"What? How can you tell?"

Saigo pulled Macneil over to a bench in front of the *honjin* and sat down with a sigh. "The characters are awkward, so it wasn't penned by an adult Japanese. Anyway, the messenger told us it came from her."

Macneil took back the unsigned piece of paper and studied it with more interest. "I wonder why Anne should send a poem to Lord Matsudaira? Maybe she sent her best wishes for his recovery?"

The general shifted his bulk on the bench to face Macneil squarely. "If that were so, I wouldn't have come this far out of my way to bring you this."

An alarm bell rang in Macneil's mind. "You'd better tell me whatever it is you suspect."

"Your cousin is a very clever woman, Macneil-*kun*. She has done something not many Japanese could do. Since she couldn't be certain her letter would not be read by others, she found a way to express her feelings so no one could prove duplicity or a change of heart against her."

"Duplicity? You'd better tell me exactly what the poem means."

"It has two meanings, and only people who have studied the old poetry would know this."

Saigo took back the poem and paraphrased it in simpler Japanese: "If you and I could meet in private, I would tell you these words, I will think no more of you."

"Well, that's about what I would have expected Anne to say to Matsudaira, but I don't see why she had to send the message secretly."

Looking down the road toward the tail of his disappearing

column, the general said, "The key word is *omoi-taenamu*."

Macneil nodded. "That means something like I will stop having thoughts of you, doesn't it?"

"Yes. That's what most Japanese would say, but its older, hidden meaning is, 'I am dying of love for you.' "

Stunned, Macneil could say nothing. He turned away from Saigo's look of sympathetic concern.

The general took a deep breath. "Speaking frankly, I see her as a calculating woman who wants to keep two gates open. Anyway, I thought I should tell you this." The general handed the message to Macneil, then got to his feet. "I must leave you. My army is about to desert its general."

Macneil watched the general with his umbrella and small dog Taki disappear down the road to the south. When his friend was out of sight, Macneil found he could visualize other people and other prospects that had been hidden from him until now. They were, in fact, becoming more distinct with each passing minute.

He knew what it was he had to do. He would gather his few belongings, leave most of his money for Anne, and head south for Edo.

And beyond Edo to Nagasaki.

CHAPTER 81

Nagasaki

Neil Macneil walked the half-mile from his hong office to the hotel where he would take his noon meal. He hoped the exercise in the mid-winter cold of Nagasaki would whet his appetite, something ten or more daily hours at his desk failed to do.

The Western-style hotel where he would dine was called the Shimabara and was the one nearest Macneil Brothers. It stood close to the docks so that most foreign visitors, seeing its three floors and modern architecture from the deck of their passenger vessel, chose to take rooms there, if they had not already made reservations elsewhere by cable or mail.

Walking through the crowded lobby toward the dining room, Macneil reflected on what a tedious routine of work and sleep his life had become since leaving the Aizu-Yumoto region two months before. Work had piled up in his office, some of which he was only now getting caught up on. With the restoration of peace, commerce was expanding and Macneil Brothers had to set itself a brisk pace to keep up with its growing number of competitors.

As yet he had received no demands from his cousin Anne to move the main hong office to Edo. In fact, he had heard nothing directly from her at all, although Thomas had reported she was still in Aizu nursing Lord Matsudaira and that the lord had legitimatized her children. Knowing Anne, he doubted this dormant period would last long.

With Margaret and Palmer dead and his father still running the business from Hong Kong, Macneil's life in post-restoration Nagasaki was a lonely one. He did not have the heart to spend an evening in Maruyama among the geishas, knowing that to do so would only bring back memories of Tomi and her friendship.

His pleasures each day were reading the list of arriving vessels and watching the mail bag being opened. The mail from each country was bundled separately and tied with twists of bamboo leaf. The hong mail clerk knew to hand Macneil those letters from England first. If there was nothing of particular interest to him in that bundle, his shoulders would slump and he would return to his desk in morose silence.

"Ah, Mr. Macneil. How are you today, sir?" asked the waiter. "Will you choose from the menu?"

"What do you suggest?" Neil had selected the Chinese dish called *shippoku* yesterday.

"The *champon* is good today."

Macneil nodded, then listened as he heard two women being seated at the table immediately behind his. He heard them order their meals in the slightly nasal drawls favored by the upper crust of English society.

Neil glanced over his shoulder at the pair. One, a tall brunette, sat facing him on the far side of their table. She was an attractive, beautifully dressed woman in her late twenties or thereabouts. When she looked at him mild interest flickered in her eyes and he wondered if he might offer himself as an escort around the city on the bay.

All he could see of the other lady was that she was small and slim, and that her dress—styled in the European fashion of the day—was pale blue with a long skirt and frilled sleeves. Her black hair was cut short.

The woman facing Neil said in a clear commanding voice, "As I told you aboard that perfectly dreadful ship, my dear, I'm far from certain your coming here was a good idea. You could have made such a good marriage in London."

"I'm sorry. I truly am, but I just wasn't interested," said the smaller lady in a low voice.

"Pity. Well, you'll have to get married one of these days, you know."

"So will you, Virginia, so don't preach to me."

"I know, I know," Virginia said, "but I'm always suspicious that they're more interested in the family fortune than in my," she paused with a wicked chuckle, "undeniable physical charms."

"Half the young men in London say they'd sell their mothers' souls for a night in your bed."

"And I'd rather give them a toss in the hay than let them wed me," Virginia said with a laugh.

"Anyway, it's your future I'm concerned about. Tell me the truth now. Is it that Macneil fellow you left behind here in Japan?"

"Oh, Virginia, really! He was just an unrefined Scot raised in the Oregon wilderness." She hesitated. "Besides, I won't know till I find him."

Macneil wrote rapidly on the back of a menu, "If I hide my rough exterior under a *komuso* outfit, would you permit me to take both of you to dinner tonight?"

Folding the menu, Macneil handed it, with a coin, to his waiter and told him in a low voice to deliver it to the lady in the pale blue dress.

He heard Virginia say, "A note from a masher? How uncivilized. Throw it away at once, my dear."

Macneil turned to watch Virginia's companion read what he had written. She spun around, located him with her eyes, and started toward him.

"Neil!" Ai cried.

"Neil Macneil?" Virginia said, rising. "The one who carried my brothers off the field at Balaklava?"

"Oh, Neil, I've missed you so!"

"So you thought you would spend a few days sightseeing and maybe then look me up?"

"You fool. We only arrived this morning."

CHAPTER 82

Amakusa

The old man was not at all the sinister figure Macneil had imagined. Quite the contrary. He was jovial, humorous and congenial.

Heihachiro Koga sat on the *tatami* matting at a low table in his ramshackle home, dispensing *jizake*—the rice-wine brewed locally—to his guest. His daughter Ai had to fill her own cup and then only under the faintly disapproving eyes of her sole surviving parent.

"Tell the American I welcome him to my home," the small, white-haired man with the clear skin said to Ai.

"Tell him yourself, father. He speaks fair Japanese, though his pronunciation needs working on."

Macneil, who had worn his kilt for the occasion, raised a questioning eyebrow at the woman who would soon be his wife, if this old man gave his permission.

"I will try," the father said dubiously. "I hear you want to," he paused as if to reassure himself that his guest really understood his Japanese words, "marry this worthless daughter of mine."

"*Sayo de gozaimasu.*" Bowing, Macneil said he did.

The head of the once feared but now largely docile clan of the *funa-kainin* beamed his approval of the American's use of extremely polite Japanese. "It's my duty to warn you she is far past the proper age for marriage."

"I know that," Macneil said, as Ai pinched him under the table.

"She is over thirty, you know," the clan chieftain went on.

"She still has all her teeth," Neil said, "but I'm worried she may soon begin to lose her hair."

"I see you're a man of understanding." Koga-*san* accepted a refill of his sake cup from Macneil. "I can't give you a large dowry. As you can see, we are poor. But I must give you something for taking her off my hands."

"A mere token would be all right," Macneil said.

"I wish you two would stop that nonsense," Ai interrupted. "Just tell him, father, you'll give him a barrel of that vile sake you brew out behind the house and have done with it."

"If that would be enough."

"I believe it will," Macneil said.

"And that you'll accept him as an honorary member of the Koga clan," Ai said.

Cautiously, the old chieftain agreed.

"Then that completes our business with you, father. We'll stay overnight to give you two a chance to get drunk together, and return to Nagasaki tomorrow."

"Why so soon? Can't you stay for a week or so?"

"You don't have enough sake left for that. Besides, our wedding will take place this coming Friday, and I have many things I must do."

"Then promise you'll come back after the wedding for a longer stay."

"Very well," Neil agreed. "We'll spend our honeymoon here."

"Excellent!" Koga-*san* said, lifting his cup. "Oh, yes. I nearly forgot. There's one more matter I must take up with you, daughter."

"Go ahead."

"In private."

Next morning three of the older *funa-kainin* escorted Neil and Ai down the goat path from the valley below Mount Hashira to where *Rainbow* was anchored in Urauchi Bay. The walk took an hour and a half with two stops along the way to catch their breath.

At one stop Macneil remembered what he had promised himself he would tell Ai. "I have something to confess and I might as well tell you now. Then, if you decide to call off the wedding, you won't have to return to Nagasaki with me."

Alarm showed in Ai's eyes.

"I might as well say it straight out. I killed Shigeo Iki and dumped his body over—"

Ai burst into laughter, startling their three guides.

"I've never heard of a woman laughing," he said peevishly, "when told one of her fiances killed the other."

"Oh, Neil, I've known that for years."

"And you don't mind?"

"Mind? Of course not. If Shigeo had harmed you in any way, I would have killed him myself."

"Well, now that I've got you in a forgiving mood, I might as well tell you also that I have a son on Sado Island."

"I only wonder that there aren't more around somewhere."

"The boy's mother is—"

"Katsuko Ito. Oh, Neil, darling, do you think I just went to England and forgot all about you? I always knew what you were doing."

Macneil got to his feet and helped Ai to hers. Their guides were ready to proceed.

"Then how about telling me what your private conversation with your father was all about? Or do you get to know everything about me and me nothing about you?"

Ai smiled. "I wonder if you really want to know."

"I want to know, all right. Too many things seem to be going on."

"Remember I told you that our clan has a tradition that all its daughters must be virgins on their wedding night?"

It was Neil's turn to laugh. "So your father wanted to know if you are still—"

Ai nodded.

What a preposterous idea, Neil thought. *Imagine a lovely woman over thirty still....*

"What did you tell him?" he asked.

"I didn't lie to him."

"But what did you tell him?"

"You'll find out Friday night, won't you, dear," Ai said, and ran ahead down the path.